A READER IN BIBLICAL GREEK

**EERDMANS
LANGUAGE
RESOURCES**

The Eerdmans Language Resources series is a collection of textbooks, readers, reference books, and monographs pertaining to languages commonly used in biblical and theological studies. In these volumes, students and scholars will find indispensable help in understanding and mastering Hebrew, Aramaic, Greek, and other languages.

Other ELR Titles

Jacob N. Cerone and Matthew C. Fischer, *Daily Scriptures: 365 Readings in Hebrew, Greek, and Latin*

N. Clayton Croy, *A Primer of Biblical Greek*

S. R. Driver, *A Treatise on the Use of the Tenses in Hebrew and Some Other Syntactical Questions*

Holger Gzella, *Aramaic: A History of the First World Language*

William L. Holladay, *A Concise Hebrew and Aramaic Lexicon of the Old Testament*

Mark Jeong, *A Greek Reader: Companion to "A Primer of Biblical Greek"*

Page H. Kelley and Timothy G. Crawford, *Biblical Hebrew: An Introductory Grammar*, 2nd ed.

Page H. Kelley, Terry L. Burden, and Timothy G. Crawford, *A Handbook to "Biblical Hebrew: An Introductory Grammar,"* 2nd ed.

William Sanford Lasor, *Handbook of Biblical Hebrew*

Rodney A. Whitacre, *A Grammar of New Testament Greek*

A READER
IN BIBLICAL GREEK

Richard A. Wright

Wm. B. Eerdmans Publishing Co.
4035 Park East Court SE, Grand Rapids, Michigan 49546
www.eerdmans.com

Book design by Jamie McKee

28 27 26 25 24 23 22   1 2 3 4 5 6 7

ISBN 978-0-8028-7924-0

Library of Congress Cataloging-in-Publication Data
Names: Wright, Richard A., 1961– editor, writer of added commentary.
Title: A reader in Biblical Greek / [edited and supplied with commentary by] Richard A.
    Wright.
Other titles: Eerdmans language resources.
Description: Grand Rapids, Michigan: Wm. B. Eerdmans Publishing Co., 2022. | Series:
    Eerdmans language resources | Includes bibliographical references and index. | Text
    in Biblical Greek, with introduction and notes in English. | Summary: "A graduated
    reader of biblical Koine for anyone who has completed at least one year of Greek, with
    selections from the New Testament, the Septuagint, and noncanonical early Christian
    writings"—Provided by publisher.
Identifiers: LCCN 2022004033 | ISBN 9780802879240 (paperback)
Subjects: LCSH: Greek language, Biblical—Readers. | Greek language, Hellenistic
    (300 B.C.-600 A.D.)—Readers. | LCGFT: Readers (Publications)
Classification: LCC PA695 .R43 2022 | DDC 487/.4—dc23/eng/20220204
LC record available at https://lccn.loc.gov/2022004033

Contents

Section III: Texts Exhibiting More Sophisticated Greek

Preface

I discovered the joys of teaching Greek comparatively late in my teaching career. But much of my teaching now revolves around helping students read texts in Hellenistic Greek. Much of that work has been focused on students in their second year of study, both undergraduate and graduate students. This volume has arisen out of that pedagogical context.

At Oberlin College, I had the privilege of working with three fine classical language teachers. Nathan A. Greenberg, James J. Helm, and Thomas Van Nortwick intertwined careful attention to syntactical details with concern for the ways in which those details might shape the understanding of an ancient text and combined these foci with an enthusiasm and humor that I can only hope make their way into my own classes.

I have incurred a number of debts in the production of this volume. Trevor Thompson has been a patient editor and has offered sage advice at crucial points in the writing process. Several friends and colleagues have given generously of their time and expertise. Ken Cukrowski, Chris Hutson, and Mark Hamilton, colleagues at Abilene Christian University, and Timothy Brookins at Houston Baptist University have read sections and provided meaningful feedback that saved me from numerous errors. Jeffrey Peterson at Lipscomb University, Austin Center, has been a friend and conversation partner for many years and has been a valuable sounding board throughout the process. My graduate assistants Dominique Rideout and Troy Wade provided significant feedback along the way. The errors that, no doubt, remain are my own responsibility.

I am grateful to my own students who have helped shape both my selection of texts and my approach to those texts. I am also grateful to Professor Hutson, who used sections of the book with students in his second-year Greek courses.

My wife, Claudia, as she has always done for my work, read the entire manuscript and improved the clarity of my writing. Without her support and encouragement, this volume could not have been completed.

Abbreviations

<	The word that follows this sign is the lexical form of the word
1	first person
2	second person
3	third person
acc.	accusative
act.	active
adv.	adverb
aor.	aorist
BDAG	Danker, Frederick W., Walter Bauer, William F. Arndt, and F. Wilbur Gingrich. *A Greek-English Lexicon of the New Testament and Other Early Christian Literature.* 3rd ed. Chicago: University of Chicago Press, 2000.
BDF	Blass, Friedrich, Albert Debrunner, and Robert W. Funk. *A Greek Grammar of the New Testament and Other Early Christian Literature.* Chicago: University of Chicago Press, 1961.
BHGNT	Baylor Handbook on the Greek New Testament
Conybeare & Stock	Conybeare, F. C., and St. George Stock. *Grammar of Septuagint Greek: With Selected Readings, Vocabularies, and Updated Indexes.* Peabody, MA: Hendrickson, 1995.
dat.	dative
ESV	English Standard Version (2011)
fem.	feminine
fut.	future
gen.	genitive

GELS	Muraoka, Takamitsu. *A Greek-English Lexicon of the Septuagint*. Leuven: Peeters, 2009.
GNTG	Whitacre, Rodney A. *A Grammar of New Testament Greek*. Grand Rapids: Eerdmans, 2021.
Heb.	Hebrew
Hist. eccl.	*Historia ecclesiastica*
impf.	imperfect
impv.	imperative
ind.	indicative
indecl.	indeclinable
inf.	infinitive
LXX	Septuagint, cited from Alfred Rahlfs and Robert Hanhart, *Septuaginta, editio altera* (Stuttgart: Deutsche Bibelgesellschaft, 2006).
LSJ	Liddell, Henry George, Robert Scott, and Henry Stuart Jones. *A Greek-English Lexicon*. 9th ed. with revised supplement. Oxford: Clarendon, 1996.
masc.	masculine
MT	Masoretic Text
MP	middle/passive
mid.	middle
NET	New English Translation
NETS	New English Translation of the Septuagint
NIV	New International Version (2011)
neut.	neuter
nom.	nominative
num.	number
NRSV	New Revised Standard Version (1989)
pass.	passive
ptc.	participle
pf.	perfect
pl.	plural
plpf.	pluperfect
prep.	preposition

pres.	present
SCS	Septuagint and Cognate Studies
sg.	singular
subjn.	subjunctive
voc.	vocative
v(v).	verse(s)
Wallace	Wallace, Daniel B. *Greek Grammar beyond the Basics: An Exegetical Syntax of the New Testament.* Grand Rapids: Zondervan, 1996.
WGRW	Writings from the Greco-Roman World

Introduction

This Greek reader has been put together to serve the needs of persons who have completed one year of Hellenistic or Koine Greek and are looking to improve their facility in reading that language. I have constructed the content of the volume with a classroom setting in mind, imagining that an instructor and peer readers will provide a stimulating context within which to explore the included texts. The number of texts and their length provide an instructor with enough material, from a variety of authors and styles of Greek, to construct a fascinating third and/or fourth semester for students who have successfully completed two semesters of Greek. There is sufficient material to build out a full academic year's reading. The instructor can choose to use fewer authors or shorter segments of readings if she or he will only be working with a single semester.

But a classroom context is not required to benefit from this volume. Any person who has successfully completed one year of Hellenistic Greek should be able to pick up this volume and improve their reading skills. The only assumption I have made is that one year of Greek has been completed.

Content

How does one assemble a reader for students of the Greek New Testament seeking to solidify their reading skills? The texts contained in this volume include authors we are confident that at least some Christians in the fourth century of the Common Era were reading. Many (though not all) of the New Testament authors are represented. Texts are also included from the early Christian Bible, the Greek translation of TANAK (the Septuagint). Finally, a few texts from early Christian authors are included. The authors included were widely read by Christians, and their texts were bound together with so-called canonical texts: the Epistle of Barnabas and the Shepherd of Hermas were included in Codex Sinaiticus (a fourth-century manuscript); 1 Clement was bound in Codex Alexandrinus (a fifth-century manuscript).

The primary consideration for inclusion in this volume was the content of the selection, not its grammar. I wanted to create a reader that would not only help students improve their ability to read Greek but also provide content that would introduce them to some of the ideas that were important to the early church. I decided that I would let grammatical considerations arise out of the thematic content of a given selection. The New Testament texts included represent different genres found in the New Testament: narrative, letters, and apocalyptic visions. In addition, the selection(s) from each author are illustrative of that author. The student who reads the selections from the Gospel of Matthew will not only have a sense of Matthew's writing style but also some of the ideas that are important to this author; the same is true for the other samples of New Testament authors.

Similar values were used in the selection of texts from the Septuagint. In these texts, students will gain experience reading both narrative and poetry; they can read selections from each division of TANAK: Law, Prophets, and Writings. Furthermore, each of the texts included from the Septuagint is demonstrably important to early Christian writers; students are engaging with texts that were important to the early church. Some of that importance is demonstrated within the volume itself. For example, Genesis 17, one of the Septuagint texts included, is an important retelling of Israel's understanding of its growing relationship with its god. This fact is illustrated by the selection from Deuteronomy 6, which makes reference to the promises described in Genesis 17. But three of the Christian texts in this reader also make reference to that text: Paul (Rom 4), James (ch. 2), and the selection from the Epistle of Barnabas. The benefit of this strategy is that the student will have the opportunity to read, in Greek, some of the intertextual connections present in the literature the early church was reading and writing. The cost of the strategy is that the student will only encounter translation Greek from TANAK; additions to TANAK that were composed in Greek (e.g., the additions to Daniel or Judith) are not included. This means that, occasionally, the Greek that one reads from the Septuagint introduces challenges that arise from the fact that these texts attempt to translate Hebrew texts into Greek. Many of these peculiarities are pointed out in the notes.

Finally, the early Christian texts included, as I mentioned, were chosen because they were widely used by Christians into at least the fourth century (and in some cases much later). Again, the content selected introduces the student to material that is distinctive to these authors. And, as with the Septuagint material, in some cases intertextual connections with other literature in the volume are present: Barnabas makes reference to Genesis 17; the Didache is clearly influenced by the Gospel of Matthew; 1 Clement points to the historical figures of Peter and Paul.

Other kinds of intertextual relationships are present in the volume. Both Matthew's and Luke's birth narratives are included, providing an opportunity to discuss the Synoptic problem on the basis of the Greek texts. There is the possibility of reading both Paul's and James's use of Abraham and the significance of that figure for thinking about faith. Jesus's prediction in Luke 12 about the disciples being brought before rulers is fulfilled in the reading from Acts 4. The volume offers the possibility to foster discussion (in a class setting) or to investigate in Greek (for students reading on their own) not only of the Greek language in a more nuanced way than occurred during the first year's study, but also to engage theological and christological ideas that the early church was exploring.

The selections are organized loosely into three sections. The first section includes texts that, for the most part, use simple sentence structures and do not draw from a large vocabulary set. The second set of texts includes more complex sentence structures and exhibits more frequent use of ellipsis (the leaving out of words that the reader was expected to supply). The third set of texts illustrate some of the more complicated Greek that one can find among early Christian authors. These texts include longer sentences and more frequent use of participial or infinitival phrases. Such organizational strategies are always artificial. Any given text might exhibit aspects of more simple or more complex syntax. Some selections clearly belong in the section into which they have been sorted; other texts might be moved according to the values of the one assigning the readings. Within each section, no attempt has been made to place the texts in order according to degree of difficulty: Septuagint texts are listed first, then the New Testament texts, and then the early Christian writers.

Texts Used

The New Testament texts included in this reader are based on the editorial decisions of the Nestle Aland 28th edition.[1] The textual apparatus has been stripped out and the paragraph structures have been reformatted for this volume. For the most part, text critical concerns have been set aside to focus on the goal of increasing facility in reading Greek. In a few instances, however, an awareness of textual variants is crucial to understanding the interpretive issues of a given verse. In these cases, a limited discussion is included in the notes. The text of the Septuagint included is the edition of Rahlfs revised by Robert Hanhart.[2] There are a couple of places where emendations to that text have been made on the basis of suggestions from the scholarly literature. These emendations are identified in the notes. The texts for the Apostolic Fathers are those found in Michael W. Holmes's edition.[3] Any variance from Holmes's text is identified in the notes.

Vocabulary and Notes

I have included in a vocabulary list any term that occurs fifty times or fewer in the New Testament. I have not attempted to build in a system to gradually increase the student's vocabulary as they work progressively through the reader. The downside to this is, of course, that words a student no longer needs will still be provided in each vocabulary list. The upside, though, is that the instructor (or independent student) is not obligated to work through the reader in a particular order; the student will still have the vocabulary needed, assuming the student has mastered the vocabulary they were introduced to in their first year of Greek. These vocabulary lists occur at the end of the chapter reading.

The notes include a variety of translation helps. Notes that refer to a phrase in the Greek occur after the last word in that phrase. I include

1. *Novum Testamentum Graece*, ed. Barbara Aland, Kurt Aland, Johannes Karavidopoulos, Carlo M. Martini, and Bruce Metzger, based on the work of Eberhard and Erwin Nestle, 28th ed. (Stuttgart: Deutsche Bibelgesellschaft, 2012).

2. *Septuaginta: Id est Vetus Testamentum Graece iuxta LXX interpretes*, ed. Alfred Rahlfs, rev. Robert Hanhart (Stuttgart: Deutsche Bibelgesellschaft, 2006).

3. *The Apostolic Fathers: Greek Texts and English Translations*, ed. and trans. Michael W. Holmes (Grand Rapids: Baker Academic, 2007).

translation suggestions for a term used in a peculiar way or for idiomatic expressions. These are frequently drawn from BDAG (and sometimes from *GELS*) if available. When one of these lexica explicitly refers to the text in the reader, I mark the reference with an asterisk (*). The point of doing this is to remind students that BDAG attempts to aid the reader in translating the texts of the New Testament in particular. Students should not think, though, that BDAG settles the issue. The student should take the suggestion of BDAG into consideration but should rely on the process of exegesis to determine which gloss or translation best conveys the nuances of the Greek in English.

For the most part, I do not provide parsings of nouns and verbs. I expect the student to use the skills learned in first-year Greek to handle most of the parsing work. When a word form is peculiar or is more difficult to discern, I do provide an identification.

I focus attention in the notes primarily on the nuances of participles and infinitives and on recognizing and filling in ellipses. These are areas that present challenges for the student attempting to move beyond the first year's learning where the discussion of these phenomena is either minimal or more rigid. The goal is to begin to appreciate the subtlety of these constructions. I illustrate the likely range of options for a given construction but do not attempt to identify which of those options best fits that particular context. It is only through a more thorough exegetical process that a final decision can be made with respect to the nuance of a given participle or infinitive.

For certain syntactical elements that frequently are introduced toward the end of the first year's study, I provide some help by way of reminder in the notes of the first section: for example, first-class conditions are noted in section 1 but not in subsequent sections; substantival participles receive translation assistance in section 1 but not in subsequent sections—unless there is something peculiar that prompts the inclusion of a translation. Many of the readings include allusions or quotations from other ancient texts. In those cases when allusion is recognized or a quotation is evident, I provide the Greek in the note.

Finally, in an attempt to cultivate in the student a habit of turning to more advanced grammatical tools as they attempt to understand complex Greek texts, I regularly include references to three reference grammars: Daniel Wallace's intermediate grammar includes a wealth of illustrations for any grammatical construct that one might encounter in the New Testament; Robert Funk's revision of Blass and Debrunner's grammar has been the standard reference grammar for students of the New Testament; and Rodney Whitacre's grammar, clearly written and up to date.[4] If one of these grammars explicitly refers to one of the texts included in this reader, that citation is marked with an asterisk (*).

One's facility with a language increases with one's use of that language. A person gets better at reading Greek by reading more Greek in a variety of different genres. The student who works through this reader will gain experience with representative texts from a variety of authors written in a variety of genres. It is my hope that the student who works through these texts and gives diligent attention to the help provided in the notes will gain confidence and skill in the reading of the Greek language used by the church.

---

4. Daniel B. Wallace, *Greek Grammar beyond the Basics: An Exegetical Syntax of the New Testament* (Grand Rapids: Zondervan, 1997); Friedrich Blass and Albert Debrunner, *A Greek Grammar of the New Testament and Other Early Christian Literature*, trans. and rev. Robert W. Funk (Chicago: University of Chicago Press, 1961). Rodney A. Whitacre, *A Grammar of New Testament Greek* (Grand Rapids: Eerdmans, 2021).

Texts Exhibiting More Elementary Greek Syntax

1.1. GENESIS 17:1–22

Covenant, Circumcision, and Abram

The first five books of Torah were the first to be translated into Greek. According to the fictional Letter of Aristeas, this occurred in Alexandria in the middle of the third century BCE. Although the events, as described in that text, are no doubt fictional, the timing and location for the translation are plausible.[1]

Much of the book of Genesis concerns the struggles of four generations of the family of Abraham and Sarah (chapters 12–50). Chapter 17 describes, for the third time in the book, God's plans for Abraham (see also chapters 12 and 15). In this chapter, God establishes a covenant with Abraham, promising numerous offspring that will come through a son given to Sarah, that many nations will come from these offspring, and land. In addition, God requires that the males of this lineage be circumcised. It is in this section of the narrative that God changes the names of the man and woman to Abraham and Sarah.

Barnabas 9 (§2.9), Romans 4 (§3.3), and James 2 (§3.6) are all connected to the content of this chapter.

1 Ἐγένετο[2] δὲ Αβραμ ἐτῶν ἐνενήκοντα ἐννέα, καὶ ὤφθη κύριος τῷ Αβραμ καὶ εἶπεν αὐτῷ Ἐγώ εἰμι ὁ θεός σου· εὐαρέστει[3] ἐναντίον ἐμοῦ καὶ γίνου ἄμεμπτος, 2 καὶ θήσομαι τὴν διαθήκην μου[4] ἀνὰ μέσον ἐμοῦ

---

1. For a discussion of the letter, including the Greek text and translation, see L. Michael White and G. Anthony Keddie, *Jewish Fictional Letters from Hellenistic Egypt: The Epistle of Aristeas and Related Literature*, WGRW 37 (Atlanta: SBL Press, 2018).

2. γίνεσθαι plus ἐτῶν with a number indicates age (*GELS* 297.c*; BDAG 401): "Abram was 99 years old."

3. εὐαρέστει: pres.-impv.-act.-2-sg. < εὐαρεστέω.

4. θήσομαι τὴν διαθήκην μου: "I will establish my covenant" (BDAG 1004.4.b).

καὶ ἀνὰ μέσον σοῦ[5] καὶ πληθυνῶ σε σφόδρα. 3 καὶ ἔπεσεν Αβραμ ἐπὶ πρόσωπον αὐτοῦ, καὶ ἐλάλησεν αὐτῷ ὁ θεὸς λέγων[6] 4 Καὶ ἐγώ[7] ἰδοὺ ἡ διαθήκη[8] μου μετὰ σοῦ, καὶ ἔσῃ πατὴρ πλήθους ἐθνῶν. 5 καὶ οὐ κληθήσεται ἔτι τὸ ὄνομά σου Αβραμ,[9] ἀλλ᾿ ἔσται τὸ ὄνομά σου Αβρααμ, ὅτι πατέρα[10] πολλῶν ἐθνῶν τέθεικά σε. 6 καὶ αὐξανῶ σε σφόδρα σφόδρα[11] καὶ θήσω σε εἰς ἔθνη,[12] καὶ βασιλεῖς ἐκ σοῦ ἐξελεύσονται. 7 καὶ στήσω τὴν διαθήκην μου ἀνὰ μέσον ἐμοῦ καὶ ἀνὰ μέσον[13] σοῦ καὶ ἀνὰ μέσον τοῦ σπέρματός σου μετὰ σὲ εἰς[14] γενεὰς αὐτῶν εἰς διαθήκην αἰώνιον[15]

5. ἀνὰ μέσον ἐμοῦ καὶ ἀνὰ μέσον σοῦ: "between me and between you" (BDAG 57.1.b).
6. λέγων: verbs of speaking (ἐλάλησεν) will sometimes be supplemented with an adverbial participle. This participle is called "redundant" or "pleonastic"; it is a kind of participle of means (Wallace 649–50; BDF §420; *GNTG* §5.199). When the redundant participle introduces direct discourse, translators sometimes leave the participle untranslated; the presence of the participle in Greek is reflected in English by the use of quotation marks.
7. ἐγώ is a pendent nominative. This nominative appears at the beginning of a sentence, but in the sentence that follows, this subject is replaced with a pronoun in the case required by the syntax: μου (Wallace 51–53; BDF §466.2; *GNTG* §5.29.b): "and as for me."
8. ἡ διαθήκη is the predicate nominative of an implied ἐστίν (Wallace 39–40; BDF §§127–28): "This is my covenant."
9. κληθήσεται ἔτι τὸ ὄνομά σου Αβραμ: Αβραμ, although indeclinable, is likely to be read as nominative here. Verbs that can take a double accusative of object and complement in the active (καλέω) can end up with two nominatives when used as a passive. The word that would have been the accusative of object in the active becomes the subject in the passive (τὸ ὄνομά), and the accusative complement becomes a nominative complement (Αβραμ) (*GNTG* §5.30; Wallace suggests that καλέω can take a predicate nominative [40]). BDAG indicates that in the passive, καλέω comes close to meaning "to be" (503.1.d) and so would take a predicate nominative.
10. πατέρα: some verbs (τέθεικά) can take two accusatives. πατέρα is the complement in an object-complement double accusative construction with σε as the object (Wallace 181–89 [183 n. 24]; BDF §157; *GNTG* §5.77): "I have made you the father."
11. The reduplication of σφόδρα translates the reduplication of the Hebrew syntax for emphasis (John William Wevers, *Notes on the Greek Text of Genesis*, SCS 35 [Atlanta: Scholars Press, 1993], 229): "I will increase you very much" (*GELS* 665.h*).
12. θήσω σε εἰς ἔθνη: "I will make you into nations" (BDAG 1004.5.a.α).
13. The repetition of ἀνὰ μέσον in this clause translates a repetition found in the MT syntax.
14. εἰς with the accusative indicating duration of time (BDAG 289.2.b): "throughout their generations."
15. εἰς διαθήκην αἰώνιον: A second prepositional phrase indicating the duration of time (BDAG 289.2.b): "for an eternal covenant."

εἶναί¹⁶ σου θεὸς καὶ τοῦ σπέρματός σου μετὰ σέ. 8 καὶ δώσω σοι καὶ τῷ σπέρματί σου μετὰ σὲ τὴν γῆν, ἣν παροικεῖς, πᾶσαν τὴν γῆν Χανααν, εἰς¹⁷ κατάσχεσιν αἰώνιον καὶ ἔσομαι αὐτοῖς¹⁸ θεός.

9 καὶ εἶπεν ὁ θεὸς πρὸς¹⁹ Αβρααμ Σὺ δὲ τὴν διαθήκην μου διατηρή-σεις,²⁰ σὺ καὶ τὸ σπέρμα σου μετὰ σὲ εἰς τὰς γενεὰς αὐτῶν. 10 καὶ αὕτη²¹ ἡ διαθήκη, ἣν διατηρήσεις, ἀνὰ μέσον ἐμοῦ καὶ ὑμῶν καὶ ἀνὰ μέσον τοῦ σπέρματός σου μετὰ σὲ εἰς τὰς γενεὰς αὐτῶν· περιτμηθήσεται²² ὑμῶν πᾶν ἀρσενικόν, 11 καὶ περιτμηθήσεσθε τὴν σάρκα τῆς ἀκροβυστίας²³ ὑμῶν, καὶ ἔσται ἐν σημείῳ²⁴ διαθήκης ἀνὰ μέσον ἐμοῦ καὶ ὑμῶν. 12 καὶ παιδίον ὀκτὼ ἡμερῶν²⁵ περιτμηθήσεται ὑμῖν πᾶν ἀρσενικὸν²⁶ εἰς τὰς γενεὰς ὑμῶν, ὁ οἰκογενὴς τῆς οἰκίας σου καὶ ὁ ἀργυρώνητος²⁷ ἀπὸ παντὸς υἱοῦ ἀλλο-τρίου, ὃς οὐκ ἔστιν ἐκ τοῦ σπέρματός σου. 13 περιτομῇ περιτμηθήσεται²⁸

---

16. εἶναί is an epexegetical infinitive, explaining διαθήκην (Wallace 607; BDF §394; *GNTG* §5.167): "to be your God and your seed's [God] after you."

17. εἰς with the accusative indicates the duration of time (BDAG 289.2.b): "for an eternal possession."

18. αὐτοῖς is a dative of possession (Wallace 149–51; BDF §189; *GNTG* §5.61): "their God."

19. πρὸς here is used with a verb of speaking to indicate the addressee (BDAG 874.3.a.ε).

20. διατηρήσεις is an imperatival future indicating a command (Wallace 452, 569; BDF §362; *GNTG* §5.108): "you will keep."

21. αὕτη is the nominative subject of an implied ἐστίν (Wallace 39–40; BDF §§127–28): "this is the covenant."

22. περιτμηθήσεται is an imperatival future (see n. 20).

23. περιτμηθήσεσθε τὴν σάρκα τῆς ἀκροβυστίας: περιτμηθήσεσθε is an imperatival future (see n. 20): "you shall have the flesh of your foreskin excised around" (*GELS* 23*); or more smoothly in English: "you will be circumcised in the flesh of your foreskin."

24. ἔσται ἐν σημείῳ: "It will be a sign"; ἐν is explained variously: as similar to εἰς, showing movement or transformation (*GELS* 233.17*); as expressing a state or position (Wevers, *Genesis*, 234).

25. ὀκτὼ ἡμερῶν is an attributive genitive modifying παιδίον (Wallace 86–88; BDF §167; *GNTG* §5.44.a): "a child of eight days."

26. πᾶν ἀρσενικὸν is a parenthetic nominative (Wallace 53–54; *GNTG* §5.29.c) generaliz-ing παιδίον ὀκτὼ ἡμερῶν: "a child of eight days shall be circumcised among you—every male—throughout your generations."

27. ὁ οἰκογενὴς . . . ὁ ἀργυρώνητος are parenthetical nominatives explaining πᾶν ἀρσενικὸν (see Wevers, *Genesis*, 234–35): "the home-born . . . the slave bought."

28. περιτομῇ περιτμηθήσεται: περιτμηθήσεται is an imperatival future (see n. 20). περιτομῇ is a cognate dative; the force of this dative is to emphasize the action of the verb (Wallace 168–69; BDF §198.6; found frequently in LXX, Conybeare & Stock §61): "will be circum-cised with a circumcision." The verb is singular because the number of the first subject of the compound subject is singular (Wallace 401–2; BDF §135; *GNTG* §5.26.b).

ὁ οἰκογενὴς τῆς οἰκίας σου καὶ ὁ ἀργυρώνητος, καὶ ἔσται ἡ διαθήκη μου ἐπὶ τῆς σαρκὸς ὑμῶν εἰς διαθήκην αἰώνιον. 14 καὶ ἀπερίτμητος ἄρσην,[29] ὃς οὐ περιτμηθήσεται τὴν σάρκα τῆς ἀκροβυστίας[30] αὐτοῦ τῇ ἡμέρᾳ τῇ ὀγδόῃ, ἐξολεθρευθήσεται[31] ἡ ψυχὴ ἐκείνη ἐκ τοῦ γένους αὐτῆς, ὅτι τὴν διαθήκην μου διεσκέδασεν.

15 Εἶπεν δὲ ὁ θεὸς τῷ Αβρααμ Σαρα ἡ γυνή σου,[32] οὐ κληθήσεται τὸ ὄνομα αὐτῆς Σαρα,[33] ἀλλὰ Σαρρα[34] ἔσται τὸ ὄνομα αὐτῆς. 16 εὐλογήσω δὲ αὐτὴν καὶ δώσω σοι ἐξ αὐτῆς τέκνον· καὶ εὐλογήσω αὐτόν,[35] καὶ ἔσται εἰς[36] ἔθνη, καὶ βασιλεῖς ἐθνῶν ἐξ αὐτοῦ ἔσονται. 17 καὶ ἔπεσεν Αβρααμ ἐπὶ πρόσωπον καὶ ἐγέλασεν καὶ εἶπεν ἐν τῇ διανοίᾳ αὐτοῦ[37] λέγων[38] Εἰ[39] τῷ ἑκατονταετεῖ γενήσεται,[40] καὶ εἰ Σαρρα ἐνενήκοντα ἐτῶν[41] οὖσα[42] τέξεται; 18 εἶπεν δὲ Αβρααμ πρὸς τὸν θεόν Ισμαηλ[43] οὗτος ζήτω[44] ἐναντίον σου. 19 εἶπεν δὲ ὁ θεὸς τῷ Αβρααμ Ναί·[45] ἰδοὺ Σαρρα ἡ γυνή σου τέξεταί σοι υἱόν, καὶ καλέσεις τὸ ὄνομα αὐτοῦ Ισαακ, καὶ στήσω τὴν δια-

---

29. ἀπερίτμητος ἄρσην is a pendent nominative (see n. 7): "and as for an uncircumcised male."

30. περιτμηθήσεται τὴν σάρκα τῆς ἀκροβυστίας: see n. 23.

31. ἐξολεθρευθήσεται is an imperatival future (see n. 20).

32. Σαρα ἡ γυνή σου is a pendent nominative (see n. 7): "as for Sara, your wife."

33. Σαρα: regarding the nominative case, see n. 9.

34. Σαρρα: The LXX translator duplicates the letter rho to indicate the change in name. This is a similar strategy to duplicating the letter alpha to indicate Abram's name change in v. 5.

35. αὐτόν is in the manuscript, but it is puzzling. There is no masculine antecedent; τέκνον is neuter (though, of course, the child will be male). The Hebrew has a feminine pronoun, indicating that God will bless Sarah (see Wevers, *Genesis*, 237; and Susan A. Brayford, *Genesis*, Septuagint Commentary Series [Leiden: Brill, 2007], 308–9).

36. ἔσται εἰς has the sense of "become" (*GELS* 193.3; BDAG 285.6).

37. εἶπεν ἐν τῇ διανοίᾳ αὐτοῦ: "he said to himself" (BDAG 287.6).

38. λέγων is a "redundant" or "pleonastic" participle (see n. 6 above). It is introducing direct discourse.

39. Εἰ is the marker of a direct question (BDAG 278.5*). It is not translated into English.

40. γενήσεται: the subject must be supplied from the context: "Will a son be born?"

41. ἐτῶν is in the genitive case, with a number, to indicate the number of years old (BDAG 401).

42. οὖσα is an attributive participle (Wallace 617–18; BDF §412; *GNTG* §5.181), modifying Σαρρα: "who is 90 years old."

43. Ισμαηλ is a pendent nominative (see n. 7): "as for Ishmael." οὗτος is then the subject of the imperative verb (see Wevers, *Genesis*, 238).

44. ζήτω: pres.-impv.-act.-3-sg. < ζάω.

45. Ναί: "yes," "indeed."

θήκην μου πρὸς αὐτὸν εἰς διαθήκην αἰώνιον καὶ τῷ σπέρματι αὐτοῦ μετ᾽ αὐτόν. 20 περὶ δὲ Ισμαηλ ἰδοὺ ἐπήκουσά σου·[46] ἰδοὺ εὐλόγησα αὐτὸν καὶ αὐξανῶ αὐτὸν καὶ πληθυνῶ αὐτὸν σφόδρα· δώδεκα ἔθνη γεννήσει, καὶ δώσω αὐτὸν εἰς ἔθνος μέγα.[47] 21 τὴν δὲ διαθήκην μου στήσω πρὸς Ισαακ, ὃν τέξεταί σοι Σαρρα εἰς τὸν καιρὸν τοῦτον[48] ἐν τῷ ἐνιαυτῷ τῷ ἑτέρῳ. 22 συνετέλεσεν δὲ λαλῶν[49] πρὸς[50] αὐτὸν καὶ ἀνέβη ὁ θεὸς ἀπὸ Αβρααμ.

Vocabulary

ἀκροβυστία, ας, ἡ	foreskin, uncircumcision
ἀλλότριος, ία, ον	foreigner, stranger; foreign
ἄμεμπτος, ον	blameless
ἀπερίτμητος, ον	uncircumcised
ἀργυρώνητος, ον	purchased with silver
ἄρσην, ενος	male
ἀρσενικός, ή, όν	male
αὐξάνω	to grow; to cause to grow
γελάω	to laugh
διάνοια, ας, ἡ	understanding, intelligence, mind
διασκεδάζω	to scatter, break
διατηρέω	to keep, maintain
ἑκατονταετής, ές	hundred years old
ἐναντίον	(+ gen.) in the sight of, before
ἐνενήκοντα, indecl.	ninety
ἐνιαυτός, οῦ, ὁ	year
ἐννέα, indecl.	nine
ἐξολεθρεύω	to utterly destroy
ἐπακούω	to hear, listen; to heed, obey
εὐαρεστέω	to please, be pleasing
Ισμαηλ	Ishmael
κατάσχεσις, εως, ἡ	possession; holding back, restraining

46. σου is the genitive complement of ἐπήκουσά (Wallace 131–34; BDF §173; *GNTG* §5.36).
47. δώσω αὐτὸν εἰς ἔθνος μέγα: "I will appoint him to be a great nation" (BDAG 242.7); or "I will make him into . . ." (Wevers, *Genesis*, 240).
48. εἰς τὸν καιρὸν τοῦτον: "at this time" (BDAG 289.2.a.γ).
49. συνετέλεσεν δὲ λαλῶν: λαλῶν is a complementary participle, completing the idea introduced by συνετέλεσεν (Wallace 646; BDF §414.2; *GNTG* §5.183): "he finished speaking."
50. πρὸς here is used with a verb of speaking to indicate the addressee (BDAG 874.3.a.ε).

ὄγδοος, η, ον	eighth
οἰκογενής, ές	born in a household; member of a household; home-bred referring to slaves
παροικέω	to live nearby, dwell beside; to live as a resident alien, live as a foreigner
περιτέμνω	to circumcise; in the passive, to be circumcised or allow oneself to be circumcised
περιτομή, ῆς, ἡ	circumcision
πλῆθος, ους, τό	multitude; crowd
πληθύνω	to increase, multiply; to grow
Σαρα, ας, ἡ	Sarai
Σαρρα, ας, ἡ	Sarah
Χανάαν, ἡ, indecl.	Canaan

Keeping the Commandments of God

The first five books of Torah were the first to be translated into Greek. According to the fictional Letter of Aristeas, this occurred in Alexandria in the middle of the third century BCE. Although the events, as described in that text, are no doubt fictional, the timing and location for the translation are plausible.[1]

The book of Deuteronomy, as the name suggests, describes a second giving of the law. The book is loosely organized into a series of three discourses (1:1–4:43; 4:44–28:68; 29:1–30:20) and concludes with a narration of the death of Moses. In these sections, Moses reflects on the laws given by God at Horeb to the previous generation. In chapter 6, Moses exhorts the people to keep God's commandments and to teach the commandments to their children, and he warns them of the consequences of idolatry. Moses reminds the people that they are "inheriting" a land already cultivated and that they had nothing to do with this. This chapter also contains the "Shema," a confession that will become important for Second Temple Judaism. In the New Testament, references to the Shema appear in Mark 12:28–34 and parallels. The warning against tempting God (v. 16) appears in Matt 4:7 and Luke 4:12.

This text makes reference to God's promise of land found in Genesis 17 (§1.1).

---

1. For a discussion of the letter, including the Greek text and translation, see L. Michael White and G. Anthony Keddie, *Jewish Fictional Letters from Hellenistic Egypt: The Epistle of Aristeas and Related Literature*, WGRW 37 (Atlanta: SBL Press, 2018).

1 Καὶ αὗται² αἱ ἐντολαὶ καὶ τὰ δικαιώματα καὶ τὰ κρίματα, ὅσα ἐνε-τείλατο κύριος ὁ θεὸς ἡμῶν διδάξαι ὑμᾶς ποιεῖν³ οὕτως ἐν τῇ γῇ, εἰς ἣν ὑμεῖς εἰσπορεύεσθε ἐκεῖ κληρονομῆσαι⁴ αὐτήν, 2 ἵνα φοβῆσθε κύριον τὸν θεὸν ὑμῶν φυλάσσεσθαι⁵ πάντα τὰ δικαιώματα αὐτοῦ καὶ τὰς ἐντολὰς αὐτοῦ, ὅσας ἐγὼ ἐντέλλομαί σοι σήμερον, σὺ καὶ οἱ υἱοί σου καὶ οἱ υἱοὶ τῶν υἱῶν σου πάσας τὰς ἡμέρας⁶ τῆς ζωῆς σου, ἵνα μακροημερεύσητε. 3 καὶ ἄκουσον, Ισραηλ, καὶ φύλαξαι ποιεῖν,⁷ ὅπως⁸ εὖ σοι ᾖ καὶ ἵνα πληθυνθῆτε σφόδρα, καθάπερ ἐλάλησεν κύριος ὁ θεὸς τῶν πατέρων σου δοῦναί⁹ σοι γῆν ῥέουσαν¹⁰ γάλα καὶ μέλι.

4 Καὶ¹¹ ταῦτα¹² τὰ δικαιώματα καὶ τὰ κρίματα, ὅσα ἐνετείλατο κύριος τοῖς υἱοῖς Ισραηλ ἐν τῇ ἐρήμῳ ἐξελθόντων αὐτῶν¹³ ἐκ γῆς Αἰγύπτου

2. αὗται is the nominative subject of an implied εἰσίν (Wallace 39–40; BDF §127–28): "These are."

3. διδάξαι ὑμᾶς ποιεῖν: διδάξαι is a complementary infinitive following a verb of command (BDF §392.1.d; Wallace treats this kind of infinitive as indirect discourse [Wallace 603–4]; *GNTG* §5.163). Here it takes the accusative of person (ὑμᾶς) and a complementary infinitive (BDAG 241.2.f): "to teach you to do."

4. κληρονομῆσαι is an infinitive indicating purpose (Wallace 590–92; BDF §390; *GNTG* §5.161): "to inherit."

5. φυλάσσεσθαι is an infinitive that might be indicating result (Wallace 592–94; BDF §391; *GNTG* §162; John William Wevers, *Notes on the Greek Text of Deuteronomy*, SCS 39 [Atlanta: Scholars Press, 1995], 112–13); or it might be epexegetical (Wallace 607; BDF §394; *GNTG* §167) explaining φοβῆσθε.

6. πάσας τὰς ἡμέρας is an accusative of time (Wallace 201–3; BDF §161; *GNTG* §5.82): "all the days."

7. φύλαξαι ποιεῖν: φύλαξαι is aor.-impv.-mid.-2-sg. < φυλάσσω. In LXX, ποιεῖν frequently is used with φυλάσσω to indicate that the directives that follow should be carried out precisely. It is a Hebraism and a structure common to Deuteronomy (*GELS* 723.4.b–c; Wevers, *Deuteronomy*, 97, commenting on 5:1): "take care to do."

8. ὅπως with the subjective (ᾖ) indicates purpose (BDAG 718.2): "in order that it may be."

9. δοῦναί: the infinitive indicates indirect discourse (Wallace 603–5; BDF §397.3; *GNTG* §5.166).

10. ῥέουσαν is an attributive participle (Wallace 617–18; BDF §412; *GNTG* §5.181), modifying γῆν: "a land, flowing with."

11. Καὶ . . . Αἰγύπτου: this opening clause is not in the MT. Wevers calls it a "superscription" (Wevers, *Deuteronomy*, 114).

12. ταῦτα is the nominative subject of an implied form of εἰμί (Wallace 39–40; BDF §127–28): "These are."

13. ἐξελθόντων αὐτῶν is a genitive absolute; the aorist tense indicates time before that of the main verb (Wallace 654–55; BDF §423; *GNTG* §5.197): "when they came out."

Ἄκουε, Ισραηλ· κύριος ὁ θεὸς ἡμῶν κύριος[14] εἷς ἐστιν·[15] 5 καὶ ἀγαπήσεις[16] κύριον τὸν θεόν σου ἐξ[17] ὅλης τῆς καρδίας σου καὶ ἐξ ὅλης τῆς ψυχῆς σου καὶ ἐξ ὅλης τῆς δυνάμεώς σου. 6 καὶ ἔσται τὰ ῥήματα ταῦτα, ὅσα ἐγὼ ἐντέλλομαί σοι σήμερον, ἐν τῇ καρδίᾳ σου καὶ ἐν τῇ ψυχῇ σου· 7 καὶ προβιβάσεις αὐτὰ τοὺς υἱούς[18] σου καὶ λαλήσεις ἐν[19] αὐτοῖς καθήμενος ἐν οἴκῳ καὶ πορευόμενος ἐν ὁδῷ καὶ κοιταζόμενος καὶ διανιστάμενος·[20] 8 καὶ ἀφάψεις αὐτὰ εἰς σημεῖον[21] ἐπὶ τῆς χειρός σου, καὶ ἔσται ἀσάλευτον[22] πρὸ ὀφθαλμῶν σου· 9 καὶ γράψετε αὐτὰ ἐπὶ τὰς φλιὰς τῶν οἰκιῶν ὑμῶν καὶ τῶν πυλῶν ὑμῶν.

14. κύριος ὁ θεὸς ἡμῶν κύριος is a word-for-word translation from the Hebrew. Wevers suggests analyzing κύριος ὁ θεὸς as a pendent nominative used to identify the second κύριος as the covenant God of Israel (*Deuteronomy*, 114): "as for the Lord our God, the Lord."

15. ἐστιν is added by the LXX translator; the clause is verbless in the MT.

16. ἀγαπήσεις is an imperatival future indicating a command (Wallace 452, 569; BDF §362; *GNTG* §5.108): "you will love." Similar syntax occurs with: ἔσται (v. 6), προβιβάσεις (v. 7), λαλήσεις (v. 7), ἀφάψεις (v. 8), ἔσται (v. 8), and γράψετε (v. 9).

17. ἐξ indicates the source from which something comes (BDAG 297.g.γ*): "with your whole heart."

18. αὐτὰ τοὺς υἱούς: certain verbs (προβιβάσεις) can take two accusatives. αὐτὰ τοὺς υἱούς is a double accusative of a person (τοὺς υἱούς) and thing (αὐτὰ; Wallace 181–89; BDF §155.1; *GNTG* §5.76): "you will teach your sons, these things"; or, more smoothly in English, "you will teach these things to your sons."

19. ἐν indicates the object of discourse (*GELS* 232.15*); the antecedent of αὐτοῖς is αὐτὰ: "you will speak about them."

20. καθήμενος . . . πορευόμενος . . . κοιταζόμενος . . . διανιστάμενος: these participles are all likely adverbial participles indicating time; the present tense indicates time contemporaneous with the action of the main verb (Wallace 623–25; BDF §418; *GNTG* §5.188): "while sitting. . . ." Wevers identifies them as attributive (Wallace 617–18; BDF §412; *GNTG* §5.181), modifying the implied subject of λαλήσεις (*Deuteronomy*, 116 n.10).

21. εἰς σημεῖον: "as a sign" (BDAG 290.4.d).

22. ἀσάλευτον: "unmovable." The Hebrew word the translator appears to be struggling with is *ṭôṭāpōt* ("bands" or "frontlets"). This word was not likely familiar to the LXX translator; it only occurs three times in the Hebrew Bible (see the discussion in Wevers, *Deuteronomy*, 117).

10 Καὶ ἔσται²³ ὅταν εἰσαγάγῃ σε κύριος ὁ θεός σου εἰς τὴν γῆν, ἣν ὤμοσεν τοῖς πατράσιν σου τῷ Αβρααμ καὶ Ισαακ καὶ Ιακωβ δοῦναί²⁴ σοι, πόλεις²⁵ μεγάλας καὶ καλάς, ἃς οὐκ ᾠκοδόμησας, 11 οἰκίας πλήρεις πάντων ἀγαθῶν, ἃς οὐκ ἐνέπλησας, λάκκους λελατομημένους,²⁶ οὓς οὐκ ἐξελατόμησας, ἀμπελῶνας καὶ ἐλαιῶνας, οὓς οὐ κατεφύτευσας, καὶ φαγὼν καὶ ἐμπλησθεὶς²⁷ 12 πρόσεχε σεαυτῷ,²⁸ μὴ ἐπιλάθῃ κυρίου²⁹ τοῦ θεοῦ σου τοῦ ἐξαγαγόντος³⁰ σε ἐκ γῆς Αἰγύπτου ἐξ οἴκου δουλείας. 13 κύριον τὸν θεόν σου φοβηθήσῃ³¹ καὶ αὐτῷ λατρεύσεις καὶ πρὸς αὐτὸν κολληθήσῃ³² καὶ τῷ ὀνόματι αὐτοῦ ὀμῇ.³³ 14 οὐ πορεύσεσθε ὀπίσω θεῶν ἑτέρων ἀπὸ τῶν θεῶν τῶν ἐθνῶν τῶν περικύκλῳ ὑμῶν,³⁴ 15 ὅτι θεὸς ζηλωτὴς κύριος ὁ θεός³⁵ σου ἐν σοί, μὴ ὀργισθεὶς θυμωθῇ³⁶ κύριος ὁ θεός σου ἐν σοὶ καὶ ἐξολεθρεύσῃ σε ἀπὸ προσώπου τῆς γῆς.

23. At the beginning of a sentence, Καὶ ἔσται introduces a statement indicating what might or ought to happen, with a temporal (or conditional) clause, followed by a finite verb (*GELS* 193.12). It does not need to be translated; begin with ὅταν: "When the Lord your God."
24. δοῦναί is a complementary infinitive with ὤμοσεν (Wallace 603–5; BDF §397.3; *GNTG* §5.163).
25. πόλεις is the first in a series of five accusative objects of δοῦναί: οἰκίας, λάκκους, ἀμπελῶνας, and ἐλαιῶνας (all in v. 11).
26. λελατομημένους is an attributive participle (Wallace 617–18; BDF §412; *GNTG* §5.181), modifying λάκκους: "cisterns having been dug."
27. φαγὼν καὶ ἐμπλησθεὶς are likely adverbial participles indicating time; the aorist tense indicates time before that of the main verb (Wallace 623–25; BDF §418; *GNTG* §5.188): "when you have eaten and become satisfied."
28. πρόσεχε σεαυτῷ: "be careful"; "be on guard" (BDAG 879.1*).
29. κυρίου is the genitive complement of ἐπιλάθῃ (Wallace 131–34; BDF §175; *GNTG* §5.36).
30. τοῦ ἐξαγαγόντος is an attributive participle (Wallace 617–18; BDF §412; *GNTG* §5.181), modifying κυρίου: "who led you out."
31. φοβηθήσῃ is an imperatival future indicating a command (see n. 16): "you will fear." Similar syntax occurs with: λατρεύσεις, κολληθήσῃ, ὀμῇ (in v. 13), and πορεύσεσθε (v. 14).
32. κολληθήσῃ: in the passive, κολλάω means "to attach oneself to" or "cleave to" (*GELS* 405.b*).
33. ὀμῇ: with the instrumental dative τῷ ὀνόματι αὐτοῦ (*GELS* 495.1): "you will swear by his name."
34. περικύκλῳ ὑμῶν with the genitive means "round about" (*GELS* 550.II*). The article (τῶν) changes the prepositional phrase into an attributive modifier of ἐθνῶν (Wallace 231–38 [especially 236]; BDF §266; *GNTG* §5.15–16): "the nations that are round about you."
35. ὁ θεός is the nominative subject of an implied ἐστίν (Wallace 39–40; BDF §§127–28): "The Lord your God is."
36. ὀργισθεὶς θυμωθῇ: ὀργισθεὶς is an attributive participle (Wallace 617–18; BDF §412; *GNTG* §5.181) modifying ὁ θεός; in the LXX, it is frequently combined with θυμόω (*GELS* 334, 504): "Lest the Lord your God, growing angry, become furious with you."

16 Οὐκ ἐκπειράσεις³⁷ κύριον τὸν θεόν σου, ὃν τρόπον³⁸ ἐξεπειράσα-
σθε ἐν τῷ Πειρασμῷ.³⁹ 17 φυλάσσων⁴⁰ φυλάξῃ τὰς ἐντολὰς κυρίου τοῦ
θεοῦ σου, τὰ μαρτύρια καὶ τὰ δικαιώματα, ὅσα ἐνετείλατό σοι· 18 καὶ
ποιήσεις τὸ ἀρεστὸν καὶ τὸ καλὸν ἐναντίον κυρίου τοῦ θεοῦ ὑμῶν, ἵνα
εὖ σοι γένηται καὶ εἰσέλθῃς καὶ κληρονομήσῃς⁴¹ τὴν γῆν τὴν ἀγαθήν, ἣν
ὤμοσεν κύριος τοῖς πατράσιν ὑμῶν 19 ἐκδιῶξαι⁴² πάντας τοὺς ἐχθρούς
σου πρὸ προσώπου σου,⁴³ καθὰ ἐλάλησεν.

20 Καὶ ἔσται⁴⁴ ὅταν ἐρωτήσῃ σε ὁ υἱός σου αὔριον λέγων⁴⁵ Τί ἐστιν
τὰ μαρτύρια καὶ τὰ δικαιώματα καὶ τὰ κρίματα, ὅσα ἐνετείλατο κύριος ὁ
θεὸς ἡμῶν ἡμῖν; 21 καὶ ἐρεῖς⁴⁶ τῷ υἱῷ σου Οἰκέται ἦμεν τῷ Φαραω⁴⁷ ἐν
γῇ Αἰγύπτῳ, καὶ ἐξήγαγεν ἡμᾶς κύριος ἐκεῖθεν ἐν χειρὶ κραταιᾷ καὶ ἐν
βραχίονι ὑψηλῷ. 22 καὶ ἔδωκεν κύριος σημεῖα καὶ τέρατα μεγάλα καὶ
πονηρὰ⁴⁸ ἐν Αἰγύπτῳ ἐν Φαραω⁴⁹ καὶ ἐν τῷ οἴκῳ αὐτοῦ ἐνώπιον ἡμῶν·⁵⁰
23 καὶ ἡμᾶς ἐξήγαγεν ἐκεῖθεν, ἵνα εἰσαγάγῃ ἡμᾶς δοῦναι⁵¹ ἡμῖν τὴν γῆν

37. ἐκπειράσεις is an imperatival future indicating a command (see n. 16): "you will not tempt." Also: φυλάξῃ (v. 17) and ποιήσεις (v. 18).

38. ὃν τρόπον: "in the manner in which" or "just as" (BDAG 1017.1).

39. The reference is to events that are described in Exod 17:1–7. The location where Israel tested God is named Massah (*massâ*) in Hebrew; translated here as τῷ Πειρασμῷ.

40. φυλάσσων is an intensive participle found frequently in the LXX where a translator will use a participle with a finite verb of the same verb (Conybeare & Stock §81): "you will diligently keep," "you will carefully keep."

41. εἰσέλθῃς καὶ κληρονομήσῃς are both aorist subjunctives going with ἵνα.

42. ἐκδιῶξαι is a complementary infinitive going with ὤμοσεν (Wallace 598–99; BDF §397; *GNTG* §5.163).

43. πρὸ προσώπου σου: "from before you" (BDAG 888.1.b.β.ɔ*).

44. Καὶ ἔσται: see n. 23.

45. λέγων: verbs of speaking (ἐρωτήσῃ) will sometimes be supplemented with an adverbial participle. This participle is called "redundant" or "pleonastic"; it is a kind of participle of means (Wallace 649–50; BDF §420; *GNTG* §5.199). When the redundant participle introduces direct discourse, translators sometimes leave the participle untranslated; the presence of the participle in Greek is reflected in English by the use of quotation marks.

46. ἐρεῖς is an imperatival future indicating a command (see n. 16): "you will say."

47. τῷ Φαραω is a dative of possession (Wallace 149–51; BDF §189; *GNTG* §5.61): "Pharaoh's."

48. πονηρὰ: in this context, rather than "evil," perhaps: "disastrous" (*GELS* 576.2).

49. ἐν Φαραω καὶ ἐν τῷ οἴκῳ αὐτοῦ: "against Pharaoh and against his house."

50. ἔδωκεν . . . ἐνώπιον ἡμῶν means "he set before us" (Wevers, *Deuteronomy*, 124–25).

51. δοῦναι is an infinitive of purpose (Wallace 590–92; BDF §390; *GNTG* §5.161).

ταύτην, ἣν ὤμοσεν δοῦναι⁵² τοῖς πατράσιν ἡμῶν. 24 καὶ ἐνετείλατο ἡμῖν κύριος ποιεῖν πάντα τὰ δικαιώματα ταῦτα φοβεῖσθαι⁵³ κύριον τὸν θεὸν ἡμῶν, ἵνα εὖ ᾖ ἡμῖν πάσας τὰς ἡμέρας,⁵⁴ ἵνα ζῶμεν ὥσπερ καὶ σήμερον. 25 καὶ ἐλεημοσύνη ἔσται ἡμῖν,⁵⁵ ἐὰν⁵⁶ φυλασσώμεθα ποιεῖν⁵⁷ πάσας τὰς ἐντολὰς ταύτας ἐναντίον κυρίου τοῦ θεοῦ ἡμῶν, καθὰ ἐνετείλατο ἡμῖν κύριος.

Vocabulary

ἀμπελών, ῶνος, ὁ	vineyard
ἀρεστός, ή, όν	pleasing
ἀσάλευτος, ον	unmovable
αὔριον	the next day; soon
ἀφάπτω	to tie, fasten; to hang upon, append
βραχίων, ονος, ὁ	arm
γάλα, γάλακτος, τό	milk
διανίστημι	to rise up
δικαίωμα, ατος, τό	regulation, requirement, commandment
δουλεία, ας, ἡ	slavery; service
εἰσάγω	to bring or lead in/into
εἰσπορεύομαι	to enter

52. δοῦναι is a complementary infinitive going with ὤμοσεν (Wallace 598–99; BDF §397; *GNTG* §5.163).

53. ποιεῖν . . . φοβεῖσθαι: ποιεῖν is a complementary infinitive following a verb of command (see n. 3). The infinitive φοβεῖσθαι might be indicating purpose (Wallace 590–92; BDF §390; *GNTG* §5.161); or be epexegetical (Wallace 607; BDF §394; *GNTG* §5.167) explaining ποιεῖν. Wevers (*Deuteronomy*, 125) offers both possibilities but leans toward epexegetical suggesting that it fits the theology of the book.

54. πάσας τὰς ἡμέρας is an accusative of time (Wallace 201–3; BDF §161; *GNTG* §5.82): "all the time," "always" (BDAG 438.4b).

55. ἐλεημοσύνη ἔσται ἡμῖν: the apodosis of the condition has been shifted to the beginning of the sentence.

56. ἐὰν with the subjunctive introduces the protasis of a third-class condition. The third-class condition can indicate something likely to occur in the future, something that might occur, or something that will not occur but hypothetically could (Wallace 469–71, 663, 696–99; BDF §§371, 373; *GNTG* §5.237).

57. φυλασσώμεθα ποιεῖν: In the LXX, ποιεῖν frequently is used with φυλάσσω to indicate that the directives that follow should be carried out precisely (see n. 7): "take care to do."

ἐκδιώκω	to drive out, attack; to persecute
ἐκεῖθεν, adv.	from there
ἐκλατομέω	to cut in stone
ἐκπειράζω	to tempt, test
ἐλαιών, ῶνος, ὁ	olive grove
ἐλεημοσύνη, ης, ἡ	favorably disposed, kindly, compassion; alms
ἐμπίπλημι	to fill; to satisfy; to enjoy
ἐντέλλομαι	to give instruction, command, order
ἐξάγω	to lead out, bring out; to free
ἐξολεθρεύω	to utterly destroy
ἐπιλανθάνομαι	to forget; to neglect
ζηλωτής, οῦ, ὁ	jealous; enthusiast, loyalist, zealot
θυμόω	to make angry; pass. to become angry
καθά	just as
καταφυτεύω	to plant
κληρονομέω	to inherit; to come into possession of
κοιτάζω	to lie down, cause to lie down
κολλάω	to cling to, join to; to glue
κραταιός, ά, όν	powerful, mighty
κρίμα, ατος, τό	decision, decree; judgment; lawsuit; verdict
λάκκος, ου, ὁ	cistern; pit
λατομέω	to cut, hew
λατρεύω	to serve
μακροημερεύω	to live long, lengthen one's days
μαρτύριον, ου, τό	testimony, proof
οἰκέτης, ου, ὁ	household slave, domestic slave, slave
οἰκοδομέω	to build
ὀμνύω	to swear, take an oath
ὀργίζω	to be angry
πειρασμός, οῦ, ὁ	test, temptation
πληθύνω	to increase, multiply
πλήρης, ες	filled, full
προβιβάζω	to teach, persuade
πύλη, ης, ἡ	gate, door
ῥέω	to flow with
σήμερον	today

σφόδρα	extremely, greatly
τέρας, ατος, τό	wonder, marvel; omen, monster
ὑψηλός, ή, όν	uplifted; tall, high; proud, exalted; noble
φλιά, ή	(mostly in the pl.) doorpost, lintel
φυλάσσω	to watch, guard; to protect; to keep

The Coronation of the King

The book of Psalms contains several collections of poetic prayers composed throughout the history of Israel. Many of the psalms are attributed to David, but other authors are represented as well; some, like this psalm, are anonymous. Psalm 2 is frequently identified as a royal psalm. It depicts the transition to a new king in Israel. The specific king is unknown. The nations take this opportunity to conspire against God and God's "anointed." The coronation of this king is described using the metaphor of childbirth; the king is God's son.

In the New Testament, the language of sonship in v. 7 appears in Heb 1:5 and Acts 13:33. Verse 9 appears in Rev 2:27; 12:5; and 19:15. In many manuscripts of the Gospel of Mark, the title "son of God" appears in 1:1 (§1.4).

1   Ἵνα τί[1] ἐφρύαξαν ἔθνη
καὶ λαοὶ ἐμελέτησαν κενά;[2]

2   παρέστησαν[3] οἱ βασιλεῖς τῆς γῆς,
καὶ οἱ ἄρχοντες συνήχθησαν[4] ἐπὶ τὸ αὐτὸ[5]
κατὰ[6] τοῦ κυρίου καὶ κατὰ τοῦ χριστοῦ αὐτοῦ
διάψαλμα[7]

1. Ἵνα τί = ἱνατί: "Why." In the LXX, this word is regularly written as two separate words: Ἵνα τί (*GELS* 341.3; BDAG 477).
2. ἐμελέτησαν κενά: "imagine vain things" (BDAG 539.3*).
3. παρέστησαν: "approach with hostile intent" (BDAG 778.2.a.β*).
4. συνήχθησαν: Even though passive in form, it can have an active force (BDAG 962.1.b*).
5. ἐπὶ τὸ αὐτὸ: "At the same place," "together" (BDAG 363.1.c.β).
6. κατὰ plus the genitive, in this context, likely means "against" (BDAG 511.2.b).
7. διάψαλμα refers to a musical interlude that occurs between two passages in a poem (*GELS* 164*). It is used in the LXX, in the Psalms, for the Hebrew term *selâ* (LSJ 421). Here, the LXX translator inserts the term; the Hebrew term does not occur in this psalm.

3   Διαρρήξωμεν⁸ τοὺς δεσμοὺς αὐτῶν
           καὶ ἀπορρίψωμεν ἀφ᾽ ἡμῶν τὸν ζυγὸν αὐτῶν.
4   ὁ κατοικῶν⁹ ἐν οὐρανοῖς ἐκγελάσεται¹⁰ αὐτούς,
           καὶ ὁ κύριος ἐκμυκτηριεῖ αὐτούς.
5   τότε λαλήσει πρὸς¹¹ αὐτοὺς ἐν ὀργῇ αὐτοῦ
           καὶ ἐν τῷ θυμῷ αὐτοῦ ταράξει αὐτούς
6   Ἐγὼ δὲ κατεστάθην βασιλεὺς¹² ὑπ᾽ αὐτοῦ
           ἐπὶ Σιων ὄρος τὸ ἅγιον αὐτοῦ
7   διαγγέλλων¹³ τὸ πρόσταγμα κυρίου
           Κύριος εἶπεν πρός με¹⁴ Υἱός μου εἶ σύ, ἐγὼ σήμε-
           ρον γεγέννηκά σε·
8   αἴτησαι¹⁵ παρ᾽ ἐμοῦ, καὶ δώσω σοι ἔθνη¹⁶ τὴν κληρονο-
     μίαν σου

8. Διαρρήξωμεν . . . ἀπορρίψωμεν: Διαρρήξωμεν and ἀπορρίψωμεν are hortatory sub-junctives (Wallace 464–65; BDF §364; *GNTG* §5.137): "let us burst . . . let us throw out."
9. ὁ κατοικῶν is a substantival participle (Wallace 619–21; BDF §413; *GNTG* §5.182): "The one who dwells."
10. ἐκγελάσεται: ἐκγελάω is middle in form in the future tense (*GELS* 204).
11. πρὸς here is used with a verb of speaking to indicate the addressee (BDAG 874.3.a.ε).
12. Ἐγὼ δὲ κατεστάθην βασιλεὺς: the LXX syntax for v. 6 differs from the Hebrew. In Hebrew, God speaks about installing the king; the king then begins to speak in v. 7. In the Greek, the king speaks in both verses. Verbs that can take a double accusative of object and complement in the active (καθίστημι) can end up with two nominatives when used as a passive. The word that would have been the accusative of object in the active becomes the subject in the passive (Ἐγὼ), and the accusative complement becomes a nominative complement (βασιλεὺς; *GNTG* §5.30; *GELS* 350.4): "I was appointed as king."
13. In the Hebrew, the king indicates that he will report the content of the decree (what the Lord said to him). The LXX translator has used a participle to connect the reporting of the decree to the king's enthronement. The participle might be attributive (Wallace 617–18; BDF §413; *GNTG* §5.181), modifying Ἐγὼ: "I, who proclaim"; it might be an adverbial participle indicating time; the present tense indicates time contemporaneous with that of the main verb (Wallace 623–26; BDF §418; *GNTG* §5.188): "while proclaiming"; or it might be indicating means (Wallace 628–30; BDF §418; *GNTG* §5.192; this is how NETS translates the participle): "by proclaiming."
14. πρός με: see n. 11.
15. αἴτησαι is aor.-impv.-mid.-2-sg. < αἰτέω: "ask [from] me" (BDAG 30*).
16. ἔθνη: some verbs (δώσω) can take two accusatives. ἔθνη is the object in an object-complement double accusative construction with τὴν κληρονομίαν as the complement (Wallace 181–89 [183 n. 24]; BDF §157; *GNTG* §5.77): "the nations as your inheritance."

καὶ τὴν κατάσχεσίν[17] σου τὰ πέρατα τῆς γῆς·
9 ποιμανεῖς αὐτοὺς ἐν ῥάβδῳ σιδηρᾷ,
   ὡς σκεῦος κεραμέως συντρίψεις αὐτούς.
10 καὶ νῦν, βασιλεῖς, σύνετε·
   παιδεύθητε,[18] πάντες οἱ κρίνοντες[19] τὴν γῆν.
11 δουλεύσατε τῷ κυρίῳ ἐν φόβῳ
   καὶ ἀγαλλιᾶσθε αὐτῷ ἐν τρόμῳ.
12 δράξασθε παιδείας,[20] μήποτε ὀργισθῇ κύριος[21]
   καὶ ἀπολεῖσθε ἐξ ὁδοῦ δικαίας.[22]
   ὅταν ἐκκαυθῇ ἐν τάχει[23] ὁ θυμὸς αὐτοῦ,
   μακάριοι πάντες οἱ πεποιθότες[24] ἐπ᾽ αὐτῷ.

Vocabulary

ἀγαλλιάομαι	to be glad, rejoice
ἀπορίπτω	to throw out; to jump out
ἄρχων, οντος, ὁ	ruler, lord, prince; leader, official
δεσμός, οῦ, ὁ	bond, chain, imprisonment; bundle
διαγγέλλω	to announce through a messenger; to preach
διαρρήγνυμι	to tear, break, shatter
δουλεύω	to be a slave; to serve

17. τὴν κατάσχεσίν is the complement in an object-complement double accusative construction with τὰ πέρατα as the object (Wallace 181–89 [183 n. 24]; BDF §157; *GNTG* §5.77): "the ends of the earth as your possession."
18. παιδεύθητε is aor.-impv.-pass.-2-pl. < παιδεύω. Only the accent differentiates the aor.-impv. from the aor.-subjn.: παιδευθῆτε.
19. οἱ κρίνοντες is an attributive participle (Wallace 617–18; BDF §413; *GNTG* §5.181), modifying the implied subject of παιδεύθητε: "all of you who judge."
20. παιδείας is the genitive complement of δράξασθε (*GELS* 178.2). The Hebrew text is uncertain. The MT has *naššəqû-bar* ("kiss the son?"). See the discussion in the standard commentaries for more information.
21. κύριος: The LXX translator has inserted κύριος. In the MT, the subject is "son."
22. δικαίας is an attributive genitive (Wallace 86–88; BDF §165; *GNTG* §5.44): "righteous way."
23. ἐν τάχει: "quickly," "soon" (BDAG 992.2).
24. οἱ πεποιθότες is a substantival participle (Wallace 619–21; BDF §413; *GNTG* §5.182); it is the nominative subject of an implied εἰσίν (Wallace 39–40; BDF §§127–28). πείθω in the perfect tense with ἐπί has the meaning: "trust in" (BDAG 791.2.a): "Those who trust in him."

δράσσομαι	to take hold of, grasp
ἐκγελάω	to laugh at
ἐκκαίω	to kindle, start; to be inflamed (passive with an active sense; BDAG 303.2)
ἐκμυκτηρίζω	to deride, mock
ζυγός, οῦ, ὁ	yoke; scale
θυμός, οῦ, ὁ	passion; anger, rage, indignation
καθίστημι	to bring, take; to appoint, put in charge; to make, cause
κατάσχεσις, εως, ἡ	possession
κατοικέω	to live, dwell, reside, settle (down)
κενός, ή, όν	empty, vain
κεραμεύς, έως, ὁ	potter
κληρονομία, ας, ἡ	inheritance; possession
μελετάω	to think about; to care for, study, practice
μήποτε	never; negated purpose: that . . . not, lest
ὀργίζω	to be angry
ὀργή, ῆς, ἡ	anger; wrath
πέρας, ατος, τό	end, finish; at length, at last
ποιμαίνω	to shepherd, herd, tend, protect
παιδεία, ας, ἡ	instruction, training, discipline, correction
παιδεύω	to educate; to discipline
πρόσταγμα, ατος, τό	order, command(ment), injunction
ῥάβδος, ου, ἡ	rod, staff, stick
σήμερον	today
σιδηροῦς, ᾶ, οῦν	made of iron
Σιών, ἡ, indecl.	Mt. Zion
σκεῦος, ους, τό	thing, object; vessel
συνίημι	to understand, comprehend
συντρίβω	to shatter, smash, crush; to mistreat, beat severely
ταράσσω	to unsettle, disturb, throw into confusion
τάχος, ους, τό	quickness; haste
τρόμος, ου, ὁ	trembling
φρυάσσω	to be arrogant, haughty, insolent

1.4. MARK 1:1–20

The Beginning of Mark's Good News

Most scholars believe that Mark was the first of the canonical gospels to be written. The Gospel was written anonymously but was attributed to Mark in the early second century CE. According to Papias, Mark was the interpreter of Peter (Eusebius, *Hist. eccl.* 3.39.15). The place where the gospel was written is unknown. Its date of writing is also unknown, but most contemporary scholars place it either just before or just after the first Jewish war with Rome, sometime between 66 and 72 CE.

The following selection is the very beginning of Mark's Gospel. Unlike Matthew and Luke, Mark does not narrate the birth of Jesus but rather begins with the ministry of John the Baptist. In this section, Mark introduces the reader to John and describes the baptism of Jesus, briefly narrates Jesus's time in the desert, and then tells of Jesus's preaching in Galilee and the call of the first disciples.

1 Ἀρχὴ[1] τοῦ εὐαγγελίου Ἰησοῦ Χριστοῦ υἱοῦ θεοῦ.
  2 Καθὼς γέγραπται[2] ἐν τῷ Ἡσαΐᾳ τῷ προφήτῃ·
  ἰδοὺ ἀποστέλλω τὸν ἄγγελόν μου πρὸ προσώπου σου,[3]

---

1. Ἀρχὴ is a nominative absolute; it is not the subject of a verb and is grammatically independent from the rest of the sentence. These constructions are used for introductory material (such as titles or salutations) that are not parts of sentences (Wallace 49–51; *GNTG* §5.29a): "The beginning."
2. Καθὼς γέγραπται is a Scripture citation formula (BDAG 493.1*): "as it is written."
3. πρὸ προσώπου σου: "before you" (BDAG 864.1*). The opening quotation is not actually from Isaiah. Mark likely is influenced by Exod 23:20 (compare also Mal 3:1): Καὶ ἰδοὺ ἐγὼ ἀποστέλλω τὸν ἄγγελόν μου **πρὸ προσώπου σου**, ἵνα φυλάξῃ σε ἐν τῇ ὁδῷ, ὅπως εἰσαγάγῃ σε εἰς τὴν γῆν, ἣν ἡτοίμασά σοι. Mal 3:1: ἰδοὺ ἐγὼ ἐξαποστέλλω τὸν ἄγγελόν μου, καὶ ἐπιβλέψεται ὁδὸν **πρὸ προσώπου μου**, καὶ ἐξαίφνης ἥξει εἰς τὸν ναὸν ἑαυτοῦ κύριος, ὃν ὑμεῖς ζητεῖτε, καὶ ὁ ἄγγελος τῆς διαθήκης, ὃν ὑμεῖς θέλετε· ἰδοὺ ἔρχεται, λέγει κύριος παντοκράτωρ.

ὃς κατασκευάσει[4] τὴν ὁδόν σου·
3 φωνὴ[5] βοῶντος[6] ἐν τῇ ἐρήμῳ·
ἑτοιμάσατε τὴν ὁδὸν κυρίου,
εὐθείας[7] ποιεῖτε τὰς τρίβους αὐτοῦ,[8]
4 ἐγένετο Ἰωάννης ὁ βαπτίζων[9] ἐν τῇ ἐρήμῳ καὶ κηρύσσων[10] βάπτι-
σμα μετανοίας εἰς[11] ἄφεσιν ἁμαρτιῶν. 5 καὶ[12] ἐξεπορεύετο[13] πρὸς αὐτὸν
πᾶσα ἡ Ἰουδαία χώρα καὶ οἱ Ἱεροσολυμῖται πάντες, καὶ ἐβαπτίζοντο ὑπ᾽
αὐτοῦ ἐν τῷ Ἰορδάνῃ ποταμῷ ἐξομολογούμενοι[14] τὰς ἁμαρτίας αὐτῶν.

4. ὃς κατασκευάσει: a relative pronoun with a future indicative verb can indicate purpose (Wallace 571; BDF §378; see also Rodney Decker, *Mark 1–8: A Handbook on the Greek Text*, BHGNT [Waco, TX: Baylor University Press, 2014], 4). Here it explains the purpose of God sending the messenger.

5. φωνὴ is a predicate nominative of an implied form of εἰμί (Wallace 39–40; BDF §§127–28; *GNTG* §5.5). BDAG suggests "it is" (1072.2.e*); Decker suggests: "he will be" (*Mark 1–8*, 4).

6. βοῶντος is a substantival participle even though it lacks the article (Wallace 619–21; BDF §413*; *GNTG* §5.182). It cannot modify φωνὴ because φωνὴ is nominative but βοῶντος is genitive: "of one crying."

7. εὐθείας: some verbs (ποιεῖτε) can take two accusatives. εὐθείας is the complement in an object-complement double accusative; the object is τὰς τρίβους (Wallace 181–89 [especially 2d]; BDF §157; *GNTG* §5.77): "make straight his paths."

8. Mark is quoting Isa 40:3: φωνὴ βοῶντος ἐν τῇ ἐρήμῳ / Ἑτοιμάσατε τὴν ὁδὸν κυρίου, / εὐθείας ποιεῖτε τὰς τρίβους τοῦ θεοῦ ἡμῶν. See §2.2 in this volume.

9. ὁ βαπτίζων is an attributive participle (Wallace 617–18; BDF §413; *GNTG* §5.181), mod-ifying Ἰωάννης: "the baptizer." Some manuscripts omit the article. Without the article, the participle might be a periphrastic construction going with ἐγένετο (Wallace 647–50; BDF §354; *GNTG* §§5.184–85; see the discussion in Decker, *Mark 1–8*, 6). Contrast Mark's use of the participle here with his use of the noun ὁ βαπτιστής ("the Baptist"), in 6:25 and 8:28. Only Mark uses the participle to refer to John.

10. κηρύσσων is either an adverbial participle indicating manner (Wallace 627–28; BDF §418.5; *GNTG* §5.193): "preaching"; or an attendant circumstance participle, referring to an action that is parallel to the main verb (Wallace 640–45; *GNTG* §5.198; see discussion in Decker, *Mark 1–8*, 6): "and preached."

11. εἰς plus the accusative (ἄφεσιν) can indicate purpose: "for the forgiveness" (BDAG 290.4.f).

12. καὶ: because in Greek, authors tend to connect sentences with conjunctions, in English, translators frequently leave the word out of their translations (see the discussion in Decker, *Mark 1–8*, 7).

13. ἐξεπορεύετο: a compound subject (πᾶσα ἡ Ἰουδαία χώρα καὶ οἱ Ἱεροσολυμῖται πάντες) can take a singular verb (Wallace 399–400; BDF §135; *GNTG* §5.26.b).

14. ἐξομολογούμενοι is either an adverbial participle indicating manner (Wallace 627–28; BDF §418.5; *GNTG* §5.193): "confessing"; or an attendant circumstance participle,

6 καὶ ἦν ὁ Ἰωάννης ἐνδεδυμένος[15] τρίχας καμήλου καὶ ζώνην δερματίνην περὶ τὴν ὀσφὺν αὐτοῦ καὶ ἐσθίων[16] ἀκρίδας καὶ μέλι ἄγριον.

7 Καὶ ἐκήρυσσεν λέγων·[17] ἔρχεται ὁ ἰσχυρότερός μου ὀπίσω μου, οὗ[18] οὐκ εἰμὶ ἱκανὸς κύψας λῦσαι[19] τὸν ἱμάντα τῶν ὑποδημάτων αὐτοῦ. 8 ἐγὼ ἐβάπτισα ὑμᾶς ὕδατι, αὐτὸς δὲ βαπτίσει ὑμᾶς ἐν πνεύματι ἁγίῳ.[20]

---

referring to an action that is parallel to the main verb (Wallace 640–45; *GNTG* §5.198): "and confessed."

15. ἐνδεδυμένος: pf.-ptc.-MP-nom.-masc.-sg. < ἐνδύω. It is part of a pluperfect periphrastic construction (the imperfect form of εἰμί plus the perfect participle); equivalent in function to the pluperfect tense of the finite verb (Wallace 647–49; BDF §§352–53; *GNTG* §§5.184–85): "was clothed."

16. ἐσθίων is an imperfect periphrastic construction (the imperfect form of εἰμί plus the present participle); equivalent in function to the imperfect tense of the finite verb (Wallace 647–49; BDF §§352–53; *GNTG* §§5.184–85): "was eating."

17. λέγων: verbs of speaking (ἐκήρυσσεν) will sometimes be supplemented with an adverbial participle of speaking (λέγων). This participle is called "redundant" or "pleonastic"; it is a kind of participle of means (Wallace 649–50; BDF §420; *GNTG* §5.199). When the redundant participle introduces direct discourse, translators sometimes leave the participle untranslated; the presence of the participle in Greek is reflected in English by the use of quotation marks (see the NRSV on this verse; contrast that version with the ESV, which translates the participle: "saying").

18. οὗ is redundant with αὐτοῦ at the end of the sentence; they both modify τὸν ἱμάντα (BDF §297*; Decker, *Mark 1–8*, 10).

19. κύψας λῦσαι: This clause is awkward to get into English. κύψας is likely an attendant circumstance participle, referring to an action that is parallel to the main verb (Wallace 640–45; *GNTG* §5.198). BDF suggests the participle is adverbial, indicating manner; describing how the untying of the sandal will happen (BDF §418.5*). λῦσαι is likely an epexegetical infinitive, explaining ἱκανὸς (Wallace 607; BDF §394; *GNTG* §5.167*). Decker suggests that when an attendant circumstance participle is used with an infinitive, and both are related to the same finite verb, it is often best to translate in English as an infinitive: "to bend down and to loose" (Decker, *Mark 1–8*, 10).

20. ὕδατι . . . ἐν πνεύματι ἁγίῳ: the dative cases here can either indicate the means by which the baptisms take place or the location ("by means of water" or "in water"). The ἐν in the second phrase does not appear to provide different nuance from the expression without the preposition in the first phase.

9 Καὶ ἐγένετο²¹ ἐν ἐκείναις ταῖς ἡμέραις ἦλθεν Ἰησοῦς ἀπὸ Ναζαρὲτ²²
τῆς Γαλιλαίας καὶ ἐβαπτίσθη εἰς τὸν Ἰορδάνην ὑπὸ Ἰωάννου. 10 καὶ εὐθὺς
ἀναβαίνων²³ ἐκ τοῦ ὕδατος εἶδεν σχιζομένους²⁴ τοὺς οὐρανοὺς καὶ τὸ
πνεῦμα ὡς περιστερὰν καταβαῖνον²⁵ εἰς αὐτόν· 11 καὶ φωνὴ ἐγένετο ἐκ
τῶν οὐρανῶν· σὺ²⁶ εἶ ὁ υἱός μου ὁ ἀγαπητός, ἐν σοὶ εὐδόκησα.²⁷ 12 Καὶ
εὐθὺς τὸ πνεῦμα αὐτὸν ἐκβάλλει εἰς τὴν ἔρημον. 13 καὶ ἦν ἐν τῇ ἐρήμῳ
τεσσεράκοντα²⁸ ἡμέρας πειραζόμενος²⁹ ὑπὸ τοῦ σατανᾶ, καὶ ἦν μετὰ τῶν
θηρίων, καὶ οἱ ἄγγελοι διηκόνουν αὐτῷ.

21. Καὶ ἐγένετο: the phrase occurs at the beginning of sentences to introduce a time frame within which an event took place in the past (*GELS* 131.6; BDAG 198.4.f*; BDF §§442.5, 472.2*; *GNTG* §5.92.c.1). Older translations translated the phrase something like, "and it came to pass" (cf. KJV); more recent translations leave the phrase untranslated, only translating the temporal expression that follows; in this case: "in those days" (cf. NRSV).

22. ἀπὸ Ναζαρὲτ: this prepositional phrase could either function adjectivally, modifying Ἰησοῦς: "Jesus from Nazareth"; or adverbially, modifying ἦλθεν: "[Jesus] came from Nazareth" (see, Decker, *Mark 1–8*, 12).

23. ἀναβαίνων is an adverbial participle likely indicating time; the present tense indicates time contemporaneous with the action of the main verb (Wallace 623–27; BDF §418; *GNTG* §5.188): "while coming up."

24. σχιζομένους is likely an attributive participle (Wallace 617–18; BDF §413; *GNTG* §5.181), modifying τοὺς οὐρανούς: "being torn apart." Decker suggests it might serve as complement in an object-complement double accusative construction with τοὺς οὐρανοὺς as the object (*Mark 1–8*, 13; Wallace 181–89 [especially 2d]; BDF §157; *GNTG* §5.77): "the heavens, torn apart."

25. καταβαῖνον is an attributive participle (Wallace 617–18; BDF §413; *GNTG* §5.181), modifying περιστερὰν: "descending." Decker suggests it might serve as complement in an object-complement double accusative construction with περιστερὰν as the object (*Mark 1–8*, 13; Wallace 181–89 [especially 2d]; BDF §157; *GNTG* §5.77).

26. Mark appears to draw from Ps 2:7: Κύριος εἶπεν πρός με Υἱός μου εἶ σύ, ἐγὼ σήμερον γεγέννηκά σε. See §1.3 in this volume.

27. εὐδόκησα should likely be understood as a gnomic (or global) aorist that is used to indicate an act that is valid for all time (Wallace 562; BDF §333; *GNTG* §5.126). In this case the likely meaning is that God has been pleased with Jesus in the past and continues to be pleased in the present. Whitacre uses this verse as an illustration of the global aspect of the aorist tense (*GNTG* §5.122.b*); the statement is not simply about the past but carries implications into the present.

28. τεσσεράκοντα is an accusative of extent of time (Wallace 201; BDF §161; *GNTG* §5.82).

29. πειραζόμενος might be an adverbial participle indicating purpose (Wallace 635–37; BDF §418; *GNTG* §5.194): "to be tempted" (when πειράζω follows the controlling verb, it frequently indicates purpose [see Wallace 636 n. 60*]). Alternatively, it could be an imperfect periphrastic construction (the imperfect form of εἰμί plus the present participle);

14 Μετὰ δὲ τὸ παραδοθῆναι τὸν Ἰωάννην[30] ἦλθεν ὁ Ἰησοῦς εἰς τὴν Γαλιλαίαν κηρύσσων[31] τὸ εὐαγγέλιον τοῦ θεοῦ 15 καὶ λέγων[32] ὅτι[33] πεπλήρωται ὁ καιρὸς καὶ ἤγγικεν ἡ βασιλεία τοῦ θεοῦ· μετανοεῖτε καὶ πιστεύετε ἐν τῷ εὐαγγελίῳ.[34]

16 Καὶ παράγων[35] παρὰ τὴν θάλασσαν τῆς Γαλιλαίας εἶδεν Σίμωνα καὶ Ἀνδρέαν τὸν ἀδελφὸν Σίμωνος ἀμφιβάλλοντας[36] ἐν τῇ θαλάσσῃ· ἦσαν γὰρ ἁλιεῖς. 17 καὶ εἶπεν αὐτοῖς ὁ Ἰησοῦς· δεῦτε ὀπίσω μου, καὶ ποιήσω ὑμᾶς γενέσθαι[37] ἁλιεῖς ἀνθρώπων. 18 καὶ εὐθὺς ἀφέντες[38] τὰ

---

equivalent in function to the imperfect tense of the finite verb (Wallace 647–49; BDF §§352–53; *GNTG* §§5.184–85): "he was being tempted."

30. τὸ παραδοθῆναι τὸν Ἰωάννην: τὸ παραδοθῆναι is an articular infinitive going with Μετά; the aorist tense indicates that the action of the main verb comes after the infinitive (Wallace 611; BDF §402; *GNTG* §5.172*; BDAG 638): "after John was arrested." τὸν Ἰωάννην is the accusative subject of the infinitive.

31. κηρύσσων is an adverbial participle that might be indicating purpose (Wallace 635–37; BDF §418; *GNTG* §5.194): "to preach"; or it might be indicating manner (Wallace 627–28; BDF §418.5; *GNTG* §5.193): "preaching."

32. λέγων is likely a "redundant" or "pleonastic" participle (see n. 17; see also the discussion in Decker, *Mark 1–8*, 17).

33. ὅτι is a marker introducing direct discourse (BDAG 732.3; *GNTG* §5.218.c). Frequently it is left untranslated and quotation marks are inserted.

34. πιστεύετε ἐν τῷ εὐαγγελίῳ: πιστεύω with ἐν plus the dative has the sense of "to believe in" (BDAG 816.1.a.ε*; BDF §187.6*).

35. παράγων is an adverbial participle indicating time; the present tense indicates time contemporaneous with the action of the main verb (Wallace 623–27; BDF §418; *GNTG* §5.188): "while walking along."

36. ἀμφιβάλλοντας: the participle might be an attributive participle (Wallace 617–18; BDF §413; *GNTG* §5.181), modifying the compound accusative object, Σίμωνα καὶ Ἀνδρέαν: "who were casting"; it might be the complement in an object-complement double accusative with the compound accusative (Σίμωνα καὶ Ἀνδρέαν) as the object (Wallace 181–89 [especially 2d]; BDF §157; *GNTG* §5.77; see Decker, *Mark 1–8*, 20): "casting."

37. γενέσθαι is a complementary infinitive, going with ποιήσω (Wallace 598–99; BDF §392; *GNTG* §5.163). In this context, it likely means to experience a change in nature and to indicate entry into a new condition, "become something" (BDAG 198.5*): "I will turn you into fishers of people."

38. ἀφέντες might be an adverbial participle, likely indicating time; the aorist tense indicates time before that of the main verb (Wallace 623–27; BDF §418; *GNTG* §5.188): "after leaving." Alternatively, it could be an attendant circumstance participle, referring to an action that is parallel to the main verb (Wallace 640–45; *GNTG* §5.198): "they left . . . and."

δίκτυα ἠκολούθησαν αὐτῷ. 19 Καὶ προβὰς³⁹ ὀλίγον εἶδεν Ἰάκωβον τὸν τοῦ Ζεβεδαίου⁴⁰ καὶ Ἰωάννην τὸν ἀδελφὸν αὐτοῦ καὶ αὐτοὺς⁴¹ ἐν τῷ πλοίῳ καταρτίζοντας⁴² τὰ δίκτυα, 20 καὶ εὐθὺς ἐκάλεσεν αὐτούς. καὶ ἀφέντες⁴³ τὸν πατέρα αὐτῶν Ζεβεδαῖον ἐν τῷ πλοίῳ μετὰ τῶν μισθωτῶν ἀπῆλθον ὀπίσω αὐτοῦ.

Vocabulary

ἄγριος, ία, ον	wild, in a natural state, untamed
ἀκρίς, ίδος, ἡ	locust
ἁλιεύς, έως, ὁ	fisher
ἀμφιβάλλω	to cast a net. It occurs only here in the New Testament.
Ἀνδρέας, ου, ὁ	Andrew
ἄφεσις, έσεως, ἡ	forgiveness, release, remission, pardon, cancellation
βάπτισμα, ατος, τό	washing, baptism
βοάω	to cry out, call, shout
δερμάτινος, η, ον	made of skin, leather
δεῦτε, adv.	It serves as the plural of δεῦρο: **come here! come on!** Mostly as a hortatory particle with the plural. With ὀπίσω μου: "follow me" (BDAG 220*).

39. προβὰς is an adverbial participle, likely indicating time; the aorist tense indicates time before that of the main verb (Wallace 623–27; BDF §418; *GNTG* §5.188): "after going along."
40. τὸν τοῦ Ζεβεδαίου: a masculine, nongenitive, article is often used with a genitive proper name to indicate "son"; this is a genitive of relationship (Wallace 235; BDF §266.3; *GNTG* §5.39).
41. καὶ αὐτούς: the καὶ is epexegetical; it explains what Jesus saw James and John doing. αὐτούς, since it is plural, is likely the accusative direct object of an implied εἶδεν (Decker, *Mark 1–8*, 22; see the discussion in BDF §§479–83).
42. καταρτίζοντας might be an attributive participle (Wallace 617–18; BDF §413; *GNTG* §5.181), modifying the compound accusative object, Ἰάκωβον . . . καὶ Ἰωάννην: "who were mending." Alternatively, it might be the complement in an object-complement double accusative with the compound accusative (Ἰάκωβον . . . καὶ Ἰωάννην) as the object (Wallace 181–89 [especially 2d]; BDF §157; *GNTG* §5.77; see Decker, *Mark 1–8*, 22): "mending."
43. ἀφέντες might be an adverbial participle, likely indicating time; the aorist tense indicates time before that of the main verb (Wallace 623–27; BDF §418; *GNTG* §5.188): "after leaving." Alternatively, it might be an attendant circumstance participle, referring to an action that is parallel to the main verb (Wallace 640–45; *GNTG* §5.198): "they left . . . and."

διακονέω	to serve, wait on
δίκτυον, ου, τό	net; In New Testament, only used of fishnet (BDAG 250*).
ἐγγίζω	to come near, draw near
ἐκπορεύομαι	to go out, come out, go away
ἐνδύω	to wear; in the middle: to clothe oneself or put on, wear (BDAG 333.2*)
ἐξομολογέω	to confess, admit (BDAG 351.2*)
ἔρημος, ον	desolate; wilderness, desert (as a substantive, ἡ)
ἑτοιμάζω	to prepare
εὐδοκέω	to be well pleased, take delight, consent
εὐθύς, εῖα, ύ, gen. έως	straight; proper, right
Ζεβεδαῖος, ου, ὁ	Zebedee
ζώνη, ης, ἡ	belt, waistband
Ἡσαΐας, ου, ὁ	Isaiah
θηρίον, ου, τό	any animal, especially a wild animal
θρίξ, τριχός, ἡ	hair
Ἰάκωβος, ου, ὁ	James
Ἱεροσολυμίτης, ου, ὁ	Jerusalemite
ἱκανός, ή, όν	sufficient, able, worthy
ἱμάς, άντος, ὁ	thong, strap
Ἰορδάνης, ου, ὁ	Jordan
ἰσχυρός, ά, όν	strong, violent, mighty
κάμηλος, ου, ὁ and ἡ	camel
καταρτίζω	to mend, restore, create
κατασκευάζω	to prepare, make ready, construct, build
κύπτω	to stoop, bend down
μέλι, ιτος, τό	honey
μετανοέω	to change one's mind, to repent
μετάνοια, ας, ἡ	repentance
μισθωτός, οῦ, ὁ	hired laborer
Ναζαρά, ἡ, indecl.	Also Ναζαρέτ, Ναζαρέθ, Ναζαράτ, Ναζαράθ: Nazareth (BDAG 664*).
ὀλίγος, η, ον	little, few
ὀπίσω	(+ gen.) after (prep.); back (adv.)
ὀσφῦς, ύος, ἡ	waist, loins

παράγω	to move along; to bring in; to pass by
πειράζω	to tempt, test; to try
περιστερά, ᾶς, ἡ	dove, pigeon
ποταμός, οῦ, ὁ	river, stream
πρό	(+ gen.) before, above
προβαίνω	to move forward, to go on, advance
σατάν, ὁ, indecl.	Satan (Heb. adversary)
σχίζω	to split, divide, tear apart
τεσσεράκοντα, indecl.	forty
τρίβος, ου, ἡ	path, route
ὑπόδημα, ατος, τό	sandal
χώρα, ας, ἡ	land (in contrast with sea), region, country (in contrast with city)

Central Scenes from the Gospel of Mark

This selection from the central section of Mark's Gospel begins a transition in the narrative toward the lengthy presentation of Jesus's passion. Included here is Peter's confession that Jesus is Messiah, Jesus's initial teachings regarding his suffering and death, and the transfiguration. Also included in this selection are one of the few stories that appear only in Mark's Gospel (the healing of the blind man that requires two attempts) and an illustration of the so-called messianic secret.

8:22 Καὶ ἔρχονται[1] εἰς Βηθσαϊδάν. Καὶ φέρουσιν αὐτῷ τυφλὸν καὶ παρακαλοῦσιν[2] αὐτὸν ἵνα αὐτοῦ ἅψηται. 23 καὶ ἐπιλαβόμενος[3] τῆς χειρὸς[4] τοῦ τυφλοῦ ἐξήνεγκεν αὐτὸν ἔξω τῆς κώμης καὶ πτύσας[5] εἰς τὰ ὄμματα αὐτοῦ, ἐπιθεὶς[6] τὰς χεῖρας αὐτῷ ἐπηρώτα αὐτόν· εἴ[7] τι βλέπεις; 24 καὶ

1. The unstated subject of the verb is Jesus and the disciples.
2. παρακαλοῦσιν: παρακαλέω, with the accusative of person and ἵνα following (αὐτὸν ἵνα αὐτοῦ ἅψηται), means to beg someone earnestly to do something (BDAG 765.3*).
3. ἐπιλαβόμενος is either an adverbial participle indicating time; the aorist tense indicates time before that of the main verb (Wallace 623–27; BDF §418; *GNTG* §5.188): "after taking"; or an attendant circumstance participle, referring to an action that is parallel to the main verb (Wallace 640–45; *GNTG* §5.198): "he took . . . and."
4. τῆς χειρὸς is the genitive complement of ἐπιλαβόμενος (Wallace 131–32; BDF §170.2*; *GNTG* §5.36).
5. πτύσας is likely an adverbial participle indicating time; the aorist tense indicates time before that of the main verb (Wallace 623–27; BDF §418; *GNTG* §5.188): "after spitting."
6. ἐπιθεὶς is likely an adverbial participle indicating time; the aorist tense indicates time before that of the main verb (Wallace 623–27; BDF §418; *GNTG* §5.188): "after placing."
7. εἴ: in this context, εἴ is an interrogative particle marking a direct question (BDAG 278.5a*; Wallace 449–50*; BDF §440.3; *GNTG* §5.220).

ἀναβλέψας⁸ ἔλεγεν· βλέπω τοὺς ἀνθρώπους ὅτι⁹ ὡς δένδρα ὁρῶ περιπα-τοῦντας.¹⁰ 25 εἶτα πάλιν ἐπέθηκεν τὰς χεῖρας ἐπὶ τοὺς ὀφθαλμοὺς αὐτοῦ, καὶ διέβλεψεν καὶ ἀπεκατέστη¹¹ καὶ ἐνέβλεπεν τηλαυγῶς ἅπαντα. 26 καὶ ἀπέστειλεν αὐτὸν εἰς οἶκον αὐτοῦ λέγων·¹² μηδὲ εἰς τὴν κώμην εἰσέλθῃς.¹³

27 Καὶ ἐξῆλθεν¹⁴ ὁ Ἰησοῦς καὶ οἱ μαθηταὶ αὐτοῦ εἰς τὰς κώμας Καισα-ρείας τῆς Φιλίππου· καὶ ἐν τῇ ὁδῷ ἐπηρώτα τοὺς μαθητὰς αὐτοῦ λέγων¹⁵ αὐτοῖς· τίνα με λέγουσιν οἱ ἄνθρωποι εἶναι;¹⁶ 28 οἱ δὲ εἶπαν αὐτῷ λέγ-οντες¹⁷ ὅτι¹⁸ Ἰωάννην τὸν βαπτιστήν, καὶ ἄλλοι Ἠλίαν, ἄλλοι δὲ ὅτι εἷς

---

8. ἀναβλέψας is either an adverbial participle indicating time; the aorist tense indicates time before that of the main verb (Wallace 623–27; BDF §418; GNTG §5.188): "after looking up"; or an attendant circumstance participle, referring to an action that is parallel to the main verb (Wallace 640–45; GNTG §5.198): "he looked up . . . and. . . ."

9. ὅτι: here, ὅτι introduces the explanation of τοὺς ἀνθρώπους: "I see people: that is, I see." BDAG 731.2; Wallace 459–60; BDF §394; Decker, *Mark 1–8*, 218.

10. περιπατοῦντας is likely an attributive participle (Wallace 617–18; BDF §413; GNTG §5.181), modifying ἀνθρώπους (Wallace 617–18; BDF §412; GNTG §5.181; see Decker, *Mark 1–8*, 218 for the challenges of this verse): "walking."

11. ἀπεκατέστη: aor.-ind.-act.-3-sg. < ἀποκαθίστημι. Notice the double augment: it has two prepositional prefixes (ἀπό and κατά; Decker, *Mark 1–8*, 218).

12. λέγων is not a redundant participle of speaking because there is no verb of speaking associated with it (in contrast with v. 27). Although it is not aorist and it follows rather than precedes the verb it modifies, perhaps the participle is attendant circumstance, referring to an action that is parallel to the main verb (Wallace 640–45; GNTG §5.198): "[he sent] . . . and said" (see Decker, *Mark 1–8*, 219). It introduces direct discourse.

13. εἰσέλθῃς: prohibitive subjunctive with μηδὲ (Wallace 463 [2b], 487, 749; BDF §364; GNTG §5.141).

14. ἐξῆλθεν: a compound subject (ὁ Ἰησοῦς καὶ οἱ μαθηταὶ αὐτοῦ) can take a singular verb (Wallace 399–400; BDF §135; GNTG §5.26.b).

15. λέγων: verbs of speaking (ἐπηρώτα) will sometimes be supplemented with an adverbial participle. This participle is called "redundant" or "pleonastic"; it is a kind of participle of means (Wallace 649–50; BDF §420; GNTG §5.199). When the redundant participle introduces direct discourse, translators sometimes leave the participle untranslated; the presence of the participle in Greek is reflected in English by the use of quotation marks.

16. τίνα με λέγουσιν οἱ ἄνθρωποι εἶναι: Mark embeds indirect discourse (indicated by the use of the infinitive with the accusative as subject: με . . . εἶναι; see Wallace 603–5; BDF §§396, 397.3; GNTG §5.166) in direct discourse (τίνα . . . λέγουσιν οἱ ἄνθρωποι): "who do people say that I am?"

17. λέγοντες is a redundant participle (see n. 15).

18. ὅτι introduces direct discourse (Wallace 454–55; BDF §§397.3, 470; GNTG §5.218).

τῶν προφητῶν.[19] 29 καὶ αὐτὸς[20] ἐπηρώτα αὐτούς· ὑμεῖς δὲ τίνα με λέγετε εἶναι;[21] ἀποκριθεὶς[22] ὁ Πέτρος λέγει αὐτῷ· σὺ εἶ ὁ χριστός. 30 καὶ ἐπετίμησεν αὐτοῖς ἵνα[23] μηδενὶ λέγωσιν περὶ αὐτοῦ.

31 Καὶ ἤρξατο διδάσκειν[24] αὐτοὺς ὅτι δεῖ τὸν υἱὸν τοῦ ἀνθρώπου πολλὰ παθεῖν καὶ ἀποδοκιμασθῆναι ὑπὸ τῶν πρεσβυτέρων καὶ τῶν ἀρχιερέων καὶ τῶν γραμματέων καὶ ἀποκτανθῆναι καὶ μετὰ τρεῖς ἡμέρας ἀναστῆναι·[25] 32 καὶ παρρησίᾳ[26] τὸν λόγον ἐλάλει. καὶ προσλαβόμενος[27] ὁ Πέτρος αὐτὸν ἤρξατο ἐπιτιμᾶν[28] αὐτῷ. 33 ὁ δὲ ἐπιστραφεὶς[29] καὶ ἰδὼν[30] τοὺς μαθητὰς αὐτοῦ ἐπετίμησεν Πέτρῳ καὶ λέγει· ὕπαγε ὀπίσω μου, σατανᾶ, ὅτι οὐ φρονεῖς τὰ τοῦ θεοῦ ἀλλὰ τὰ τῶν ἀνθρώπων.[31]

19. Ἰωάννην τὸν βαπτιστήν, καὶ ἄλλοι Ἠλίαν, ἄλλοι δὲ ὅτι εἷς τῶν προφητῶν: the disciples' response is elliptical. The wording of the full response is embedded in Jesus's question in v. 27 and would have looked something like: λέγουσιν ἄλλοι σε εἶναι (see the discussion in BDF §§479–83; Decker, *Mark 1–8*, 220).

20. αὐτὸς is marking the change in subject (Wallace 321.1.a).

21. τίνα με λέγετε εἶναι: again, Mark embeds indirect discourse (indicated by the infinitive: με . . . εἶναι) in direct discourse (τίνα . . . λέγετε) (see n. 16).

22. ἀποκριθεὶς is a redundant participle (see n. 15).

23. ἵνα with ἐπιτιμάω introduces the content of the censure or warning (BDAG 384.1*; BDF §392.1.d; *GNTG* §5.145).

24. διδάσκειν is a complementary infinitive, going with ἤρξατο (Wallace 598–99; BDF §392; *GNTG* §5.163).

25. τὸν υἱὸν . . . ἀναστῆναι: infinitives (παθεῖν . . . ἀποδοκιμασθῆναι . . . ἀποκτανθῆναι . . . ἀναστῆναι) are used in impersonal expressions with verbs like δεῖ (BDF §393.1; Wallace describes this as a substantival use [600–601]; *GNTG* §5.164.b). τὸν υἱὸν is the accusative subject of the infinitives.

26. παρρησίᾳ is a dative of manner (Wallace 161–62; BDF §198.4*; *GNTG* §5.70): "with boldness," "boldly."

27. προσλαβόμενος is either an adverbial participle indicating time; the aorist tense indicates time before that of the main verb (Wallace 623–27; BDF §418; *GNTG* §5.188): "after taking him aside"; or an attendant circumstance participle, referring to an action that is parallel to the main verb (Wallace 640–45; *GNTG* §5.198): "he took him aside . . . and."

28. ἐπιτιμᾶν is a complementary infinitive, going with ἤρξατο (Wallace 598–99; BDF §392; *GNTG* §5.163).

29. ἐπιστραφεὶς is likely an adverbial participle indicating time; the aorist tense indicates time before that of the main verb (Wallace 623–27; BDF §418; *GNTG* §5.188): "after turning."

30. ἰδὼν is likely an adverbial participle indicating time; the aorist tense indicates time before that of the main verb (Wallace 623–27; BDF §418; *GNTG* §5.188): "after seeing."

31. τὰ τοῦ θεοῦ . . . τὰ τῶν ἀνθρώπων: the neuter plural article can be followed by a word or phrase in the genitive indicating "things" (Wallace 235 [5 (2)]; *GNTG* §5.15).

34 Καὶ προσκαλεσάμενος³² τὸν ὄχλον σὺν τοῖς μαθηταῖς αὐτοῦ εἶπεν αὐτοῖς· εἴ τις θέλει ὀπίσω μου ἀκολουθεῖν,³³ ἀπαρνησάσθω ἑαυτὸν καὶ ἀράτω τὸν σταυρὸν αὐτοῦ καὶ ἀκολουθείτω μοι. 35 ὃς γὰρ ἐὰν³⁴ θέλῃ τὴν ψυχὴν αὐτοῦ σῶσαι³⁵ ἀπολέσει αὐτήν· ὃς δ᾽ ἂν³⁶ ἀπολέσει τὴν ψυχὴν αὐτοῦ ἕνεκεν ἐμοῦ καὶ τοῦ εὐαγγελίου σώσει αὐτήν. 36 τί γὰρ ὠφελεῖ ἄνθρωπον κερδῆσαι τὸν κόσμον ὅλον καὶ ζημιωθῆναι³⁷ τὴν ψυχὴν αὐτοῦ; 37 τί γὰρ δοῖ ἄνθρωπος ἀντάλλαγμα³⁸ τῆς ψυχῆς αὐτοῦ; 38 ὃς γὰρ ἐὰν³⁹ ἐπαισχυνθῇ με καὶ τοὺς ἐμοὺς λόγους ἐν τῇ γενεᾷ ταύτῃ τῇ μοιχαλίδι καὶ ἁμαρτωλῷ, καὶ ὁ υἱὸς τοῦ ἀνθρώπου ἐπαισχυνθήσεται αὐτόν, ὅταν ἔλθῃ ἐν τῇ δόξῃ τοῦ πατρὸς αὐτοῦ μετὰ τῶν ἀγγέλων τῶν ἁγίων.

32. προσκαλεσάμενος is either an adverbial participle indicating time; the aorist tense indicates time before that of the main verb (Wallace 623–27; BDF §418; *GNTG* §5.188): "after calling"; or an attendant circumstance participle, referring to an action that is parallel to the main verb (Wallace 640–45; *GNTG* §5.198): "he called . . . and."

33. ἀκολουθεῖν is a complementary infinitive, going with θέλει (Wallace 598–99; BDF §392; *GNTG* §5.163).

34. ὃς . . . ἐάν: this is an indefinite relative clause (Wallace 478; 571*; *GNTG* §5.139*, 216*) or a conditional relative clause (BDF §380; *GNTG* §5.234) with the subjunctive (θέλῃ): "whoever." Such clauses suggest general assertions or suppositions rather than making assertions about concrete realities.

35. σῶσαι is a complementary infinitive, going with θέλει (Wallace 598–99; BDF §392; *GNTG* §5.163).

36. ὃς . . . ἄν: this appears to indicate the same idea as ὃς . . . ἐάν in the previous sentence. Though the use of ἄν with the future ἀπολέσει is unusual (Wallace 571*; BDF §380.2*; *GNTG* §5.237), ἄν with future or imperfect in the apodosis shows that the condition and its results are thought of as in the future (BDAG 56.1.b.α*).

37. ἄνθρωπον κερδῆσαι . . . ζημιωθῆναι: both infinitives are complementary going with ὠφελεῖ (Wallace 598–99; BDF §392; *GNTG* §5.163). ἄνθρωπον is the accusative subject of the infinitives.

38. τί γὰρ δοῖ ἄνθρωπος ἀντάλλαγμα: δοῖ is aor.-subjn.-act.-3-sg. < δίδωμι. It is a deliberative subjunctive (Wallace 465–68 [especially 467 2b]; BDF §366.1; *GNTG* §5.138). Some verbs (δοῖ) can take two accusatives. ἀντάλλαγμα is the complement in an object-complement double accusative construction with τί as the object (Wallace 181–89 [183 n. 24]; BDF §157; *GNTG* §5.77): "What can a person give in exchange for."

39. ὃς . . . ἐάν: this is an indefinite or conditional relative (see n. 34).

9:1 Καὶ ἔλεγεν αὐτοῖς· ἀμὴν λέγω ὑμῖν ὅτι εἰσίν τινες ὧδε τῶν ἐστη-κότων⁴⁰ οἵτινες οὐ μὴ γεύσωνται⁴¹ θανάτου⁴² ἕως ἂν⁴³ ἴδωσιν τὴν βασι-λείαν τοῦ θεοῦ ἐληλυθυῖαν⁴⁴ ἐν δυνάμει.

2 Καὶ μετὰ ἡμέρας ἓξ παραλαμβάνει ὁ Ἰησοῦς τὸν Πέτρον καὶ τὸν Ἰάκωβον καὶ τὸν Ἰωάννην καὶ ἀναφέρει αὐτοὺς εἰς ὄρος ὑψηλὸν κατ᾽ ἰδίαν μόνους.⁴⁵ καὶ μετεμορφώθη ἔμπροσθεν αὐτῶν, 3 καὶ τὰ ἱμάτια αὐτοῦ ἐγένετο στίλβοντα⁴⁶ λευκὰ λίαν, οἷα γναφεὺς ἐπὶ τῆς γῆς οὐ δύναται οὕτως λευκᾶναι.⁴⁷ 4 καὶ ὤφθη αὐτοῖς Ἠλίας σὺν Μωϋσεῖ καὶ ἦσαν συλ-λαλοῦντες⁴⁸ τῷ Ἰησοῦ. 5 καὶ ἀποκριθεὶς⁴⁹ ὁ Πέτρος λέγει τῷ Ἰησοῦ· ῥαββί, καλόν ἐστιν ἡμᾶς ὧδε εἶναι,⁵⁰ καὶ ποιήσωμεν⁵¹ τρεῖς σκηνάς, σοὶ μίαν

---

40. τῶν ἑστηκότων is a substantival participle (Wallace 619–21; BDF §413; *GNTG* §5.182): "who are standing."

41. οὐ μὴ γεύσωνται: the aorist subjunctive with the double negative indicates an emphatic negation, the strongest form of negation in Greek (Wallace 468–69; BDF §365; *GNTG* §5.136).

42. θανάτου is the genitive complement of γεύσωνται (Wallace 131–32; BDF §170.2; *GNTG* §5.36).

43. ἕως ἂν: "until" (BDAG 422.1.a.β*). With the subjunctive, it introduces an indefinite temporal clause (Wallace 479; BDF §383; *GNTG* §5.140c).

44. ἐληλυθυῖαν: pf.-ptc.-act.-fem.-acc.-sg. < ἔρχομαι. The participle is attributive (Wallace 617–18; BDF §413; *GNTG* §5.181), modifying βασιλείαν: "having come"; or "come."

45. κατ᾽ ἰδίαν μόνους: "by themselves" or "privately" (μόνους adds emphasis; BDAG 467.5*).

46. στίλβοντα is either an attributive participle (Wallace 617–18; BDF §413; *GNTG* §5.181), modifying τὰ ἱμάτια: "shining"; or, a periphrastic construction with ἐγένετο (Wallace 647–50; BDF §354; *GNTG* §§5.184–85; see the discussion in Rodney Decker, *Mark 9–16: A Handbook on the Greek Text*, BHGNT [Waco, TX: Baylor University Press, 2014], 2): "were shining."

47. λευκᾶναι is a complementary infinitive, going with δύναται (Wallace 598–99; BDF §392; *GNTG* §5.163).

48. συλλαλοῦντες is an imperfect periphrastic construction (the imperfect form of εἰμί plus the present participle); equivalent in function to the imperfect tense of the finite verb (Wallace 647–49; BDF §§352–53; *GNTG* §§5.184–85): "they were speaking together with."

49. ἀποκριθεὶς is a redundant participle (see n. 15).

50. ἡμᾶς ὧδε εἶναι: infinitives (εἶναι) are used in impersonal expressions with verbs like ἐστιν and an adjective (καλόν; BDF §393.1; Wallace describes this as a substantival use [600–601]; *GNTG* §5.164.b). ἡμᾶς is the accusative subject of the infinitive.

51. ποιήσωμεν is a hortatory subjunctive (Wallace 464–65; BDF §364; *GNTG* §5.137): "let us make."

καὶ Μωϋσεῖ μίαν καὶ Ἠλίᾳ μίαν. 6 οὐ γὰρ ᾔδει[52] τί ἀποκριθῇ,[53] ἔκφοβοι γὰρ ἐγένοντο. 7 καὶ ἐγένετο νεφέλη ἐπισκιάζουσα[54] αὐτοῖς, καὶ ἐγένετο φωνὴ ἐκ τῆς νεφέλης· οὗτός ἐστιν ὁ υἱός μου ὁ ἀγαπητός, ἀκούετε αὐτοῦ.[55] 8 καὶ ἐξάπινα περιβλεψάμενοι[56] οὐκέτι οὐδένα εἶδον ἀλλὰ τὸν Ἰησοῦν μόνον μεθ᾽ ἑαυτῶν.

9 Καὶ καταβαινόντων[57] αὐτῶν ἐκ τοῦ ὄρους διεστείλατο αὐτοῖς ἵνα[58] μηδενὶ ἃ εἶδον διηγήσωνται, εἰ μὴ[59] ὅταν[60] ὁ υἱὸς τοῦ ἀνθρώπου ἐκ νεκρῶν ἀναστῇ. 10 καὶ τὸν λόγον ἐκράτησαν πρὸς ἑαυτοὺς[61] συζη-τοῦντες[62] τί ἐστιν τὸ ἐκ νεκρῶν ἀναστῆναι.[63]

Vocabulary

| ἁμαρτωλός, όν | sinful, erroneous |
| ἀναβλέπω | to look up, to receive sight or regain sight |

52. ᾔδει: plpf.-ind.-act.-3-sg. < οἶδα.

53. τί ἀποκριθῇ: the subjunctive mood is used with the interrogative pronoun to indicate an indirect, deliberative question (Wallace 478; BDF §368; GNTG §5.138).

54. ἐπισκιάζουσα is either an attributive participle (Wallace 617–18; BDF §413; GNTG §5.181), modifying νεφέλη: "overshadowing"; an adverbial participle indicating result (Wallace 638; GNTG §5.195): "with the result that it overshadowed them"; or a periphrastic construction with ἐγένετο (Wallace 647–50; BDF §354; GNTG §§5.184–85; Decker, *Mark 9–16*, 5): "was overshadowing them."

55. αὐτοῦ is the genitive complement of ἀκούετε (Wallace 131–32; BDF §170.2; GNTG §5.36).

56. περιβλεψάμενοι is an adverbial participle indicating time; the aorist tense indicates time before that of the main verb (Wallace 623–27; BDF §418; GNTG §5.188): "after looking around."

57. καταβαινόντων is a genitive absolute with αὐτῶν (Wallace 654–55; BDF §423; GNTG §5.37). The present tense indicates time contemporaneous with the action of the main verb: "while they were coming down."

58. ἵνα: ἵνα with διεστείλατο introduces the content of the warning (BDAG 237*; BDF §392.1.d; GNTG §5.145).

59. εἰ μὴ: "except" (BDAG 278.6.i).

60. ὅταν: with the aorist subjunctive, "when" (BDAG730.1.a).

61. πρὸς ἑαυτοὺς: probably modifies ἐκράτησαν. Alternatively, it might modify συζητοῦντες (see the discussion in Decker, *Mark 9–16*, 7–8 for the preference for ἐκράτησαν; BDF indicates it could go with either [§239]).

62. συζητοῦντες is likely an adverbial participle indicating time; the present tense indicates time contemporaneous with the action of the main verb (Wallace 623–27; BDF §418; GNTG §5.188): "while discussing."

63. τὸ . . . ἀναστῆναι: the nominative article marks the infinitive as the subject of ἐστιν (BDF §399.1; GNTG §5.164; Decker, *Mark 9–16*, 8): "what is 'rising from the dead'?"

ἀναφέρω	to bring up, deliver, offer up, take up
ἀντάλλαγμα, ατος, τό	something given in exchange, item for exchange; with the gen. case.
ἀπαρνέομαι	to deny
ἅπας, ασα, αν	all, every (intensive form of πᾶς)
ἀποδοκιμάζω	to reject
ἀποκαθίστημι	to restore, bring back
ἅπτω	to touch, hold, grasp; to light
βαπτιστής, οῦ, ὁ	Baptist, Baptizer
Βηθσαϊδά(ν), ἡ, indecl.	Bethsaida. A place north of Lake Gennesaret, east of the Jordan, near where it empties into the lake (BDAG 175*).
γενεά, ᾶς, ἡ	generation, age, race, kind
γεύομαι	to taste, experience
γναφεύς, έως, ὁ	cloth refiner. A specialist in one or more of the processes in the treatment of cloth (BDAG 202*).
δένδρον, ου, τό	tree
διαβλέπω	to see clearly, look intently, open one's eyes wide
διαστέλλω	to order, command
διηγέομαι	to describe in detail; to tell, explain
εἶτα, adv.	then, next
ἐκφέρω	to carry out, bring out, carry away
ἔκφοβος, ον	terrified
ἐμβλέπω	to look at, gaze on; to consider
ἔμπροσθεν	(+ gen.) before, in front of
ἕνεκα	(+ gen.) because of, for the sake of, on account of
ἕξ, indecl.	six
ἐξάπινα, adv.	suddenly
ἐπαισχύνομαι	to be ashamed
ἐπιλαμβάνομαι	to take hold of; to arrest, seize, attack; to interrupt
ἐπισκιάζω	to overshadow, cover
ἐπιστρέφω	to turn back, return, turn around
ἐπιτίθημι	to lay on, place, put, add
ἐπιτιμάω	to rebuke
ζημιόω	to punish, lose

Ἠλίας, ου, ὁ	Elijah
Ἰάκωβος, ου, ὁ	James
Καισάρεια ἡ Φιλίππου	refers to a city at the foot of Mt. Hermon. It was rebuilt by Philip the Tetrarch and named Caesarea in honor of Tiberius Caesar (BDAG 499.1*).
κερδαίνω	to gain
κρατέω	to attain, hold, grasp; to keep to oneself a saying in order to occupy oneself with it later (BDAG 565.6.c*). BDF indicates this is a Latinism (§5.3.b*).
κώμη, ης, ἡ	village
λευκαίνω	to make white
λευκός, ή, όν	white, bright, shining
λίαν, adv.	exceedingly
μεταμορφόω	to change form, be transfigured or transformed
μοιχαλίς, ίδος, ἡ	adulteress
νεφέλη, ης, ἡ	cloud
οἷος, α, ον	such as, as; (adv.) for instance
ὄμμα, ατος, τό	eye
ὀπίσω	(+ gen.) after (prep.); back (adv.)
οὐκέτι, adv.	no longer
παραλαμβάνω	to take with/along, take over, receive, accept
παρρησία, ας, ἡ	boldness
πάσχω	to experience; to suffer, endure
περιβλέπω	to look around
προσκαλέω	to call, summon
προσλαμβάνω	to increase; to receive, accept; to bring along
πτύω	to spit
ῥαββί	Rabbi (Heb.: "my teacher")
σατάν, ὁ, indecl.	Satan
σκηνή, ῆς, ἡ	tent; tabernacle
σταυρός, οῦ, ὁ	cross

στίλβω	to shine
συζητέω	to discuss, argue, question
συλλαλέω	to speak with, discuss, converse
τηλαυγῶς, adv.	clearly
τυφλός, ή, όν	blind
ὑψηλός, ή, όν	high, proud
φρονέω	to think, have an opinion, set one's mind on
ὠφελέω	to benefit, help, accomplish

1.6. DIDACHE 7:1–4

On Baptism

The Didache, or The Teachings of the Twelve Apostles, was a popular text composed at the end of the first century CE or the beginning of the second century CE. The only complete Greek copy of this text is Codex Hierosolymitanus (H), from the eleventh century CE.[1] Fourth-century CE fragments were discovered among the Oxyrhynchus papyri.

The early chapters (1–6) describe "the two ways, one of life and one of death."[2] The later chapters (7–16) shift to a discussion of church practices. Chapter 7 considers the appropriate preparation for, and administration of, baptism.

Did. 7:1 Περὶ δὲ[3] τοῦ βαπτίσματος, οὕτω[4] βαπτίσατε· ταῦτα πάντα προειπόντες,[5] βαπτίσατε εἰς τὸ ὄνομα τοῦ πατρὸς καὶ τοῦ υἱοῦ καὶ τοῦ ἁγίου πνεύματος ἐν ὕδατι ζῶντι.[6] 2 ἐὰν[7] δὲ μὴ ἔχῃς ὕδωρ ζῶν,[8] εἰς

1. That codex also includes copies of the Epistle of Barnabas and 1 Clement (among other texts).
2. The "two ways" literary strategy also is used by the authors of the Epistle of Barnabas and the Shepherd of Hermas.
3. Περὶ δὲ is used to indicate a change in topic. The construction also appears in this volume in Did. 9:1, 3 (§1.8) and 1 Cor 12:1 (§3.4).
4. οὕτω is an alternative form of οὕτως.
5. προειπόντες is an adverbial participle indicating time; the aorist tense indicates time before that of the main verb (Wallace 623–27; BDF §418; *GNTG* §5.188): "after having said all things ahead of time."
6. ζῶντι is an attributive participle (Wallace 617–18; BDF §412; *GNTG* §5.181), modifying ὕδατι: "living water." A similar construction occurs in v. 2.
7. ἐὰν with the subjunctive (ἔχῃς) introduces the protasis of a third-class condition. The third-class condition can indicate something likely to occur in the future, something that might occur, or something that will not occur but hypothetically could (Wallace 469–71, 663, 696–99; BDF §§371, 373; *GNTG* §5.237).
8. ζῶν is an attributive participle (Wallace 617–18; BDF §412; *GNTG* §5.181), going with ὕδωρ: "living water."

ἄλλο ὕδωρ βάπτισον· εἰ δ᾽ οὐ δύνασαι ἐν ψυχρῷ, ἐν θερμῷ.⁹ 3 ἐὰν¹⁰ δὲ ἀμφότερα μὴ ἔχῃς, ἔκχεον εἰς τὴν κεφαλὴν τρὶς ὕδωρ εἰς ὄνομα πατρὸς καὶ υἱοῦ καὶ ἁγίου πνεύματος. 4 πρὸ δὲ τοῦ βαπτίσματος προνηστευσάτω¹¹ ὁ βαπτίζων καὶ ὁ βαπτιζόμενος¹² καὶ εἴ¹³ τινες ἄλλοι δύνανται. κελεύεις¹⁴ δὲ νηστεῦσαι τὸν βαπτιζόμενον¹⁵ πρὸ μιᾶς ἢ δύο.¹⁶

Vocabulary

ἀμφότεροι, αι, α	both; all
βαπτίζω	to baptize, wash, dip
βάπτισμα, ατου, τό	washing, baptism
δύο	two
ἐκχέω	to pour out; to bring forth, come forth
θερμός, ά, όν	warm, hot
κελεύω	to command
κεφαλή, ῆς, ἡ	head
νηστεύω	to fast

9. εἰ δ᾽ οὐ δύνασαι ἐν ψυχρῷ, ἐν θερμῷ: εἰ plus the indicative (δύνασαι) introduces the protasis of a first-class condition. The first-class condition assumes, for the sake of argument, that the protasis (the "if" statement) is true (Wallace 450–51, 663, 690–94; BDF §§371, 372; *GNTG* §5.235). This clause is exceedingly elliptical. The reader must supply several forms of the verb βαπτίζω: an implied complementary infinitive with δύνασαι; and an implied imperative before ἐν θερμῷ. ἐν ψυχρῷ, ἐν θερμῷ: the gender of the adjectives is neuter, to match the implied ὕδατι, which can be supplied from the end of the previous verse (see the discussion of ellipsis in BDF §§479–83).

10. ἐὰν with the subjunctive (ἔχῃς) introduces the protasis of a third-class condition. See n. 7 above.

11. προνηστευσάτω: the verb is singular because when multiple subjects are connected by καὶ, the verb will agree with the first subject if the verb stands before it (unless the group is basically conceived as a whole; Wallace 401; BDF §135.1.a).

12. ὁ βαπτίζων καὶ ὁ βαπτιζόμενος: the participles are substantival (Wallace 619–21; BDF §413; *GNTG* §5.182): "the one baptizing and the one being baptized."

13. εἰ plus the indicative (δύνανται) introduces the protasis of a first-class condition. See n. 9 above. The clause is elliptical; the reader must supply an imperative form of νηστεύω: "and if any others are able, [let them fast also]."

14. κελεύεις: the present indicative is surprising after the previous imperative verbs.

15. νηστεῦσαι τὸν βαπτιζόμενον: the infinitive νηστεῦσαι indicates indirect discourse (Wallace 603–5; BDF §§396, 397.3; *GNTG* §5.166). τὸν βαπτιζόμενον is a substantival participle (Wallace 619–21; BDF §413; *GNTG* §5.182): "the one being baptized"; it is the accusative subject of the infinitive.

16. πρὸ μιᾶς ἢ δύο: the gender of the adjectives is feminine, to agree with the implied ἡμέρας: "a day or two before" (BDF §213*).

πρό	(+ gen.) before, above
προλέγω	to say ahead of time; to foretell
προνηστεύω	to fast ahead of time
τρίς, adv.	three times
ὕδωρ, ατος, τό	water
ψυχρός, ά, όν	cold

1.7. DIDACHE 8:1–3

On Fasting and Prayer

In chapter 8, the author takes up the practices of fasting and prayer. He includes a version of the Lord's Prayer that appears to be influenced by the Gospel of Matthew.

Did. 8:1 Αἱ δὲ νηστεῖαι ὑμῶν μὴ ἔστωσαν[1] μετὰ τῶν ὑποκριτῶν· νηστεύουσι γὰρ δευτέρᾳ σαββάτων καὶ πέμπτῃ,[2] ὑμεῖς δὲ νηστεύσατε τετράδα καὶ παρασκευήν.[3] 2 μηδὲ προσεύχεσθε ὡς οἱ ὑποκριταί, ἀλλ᾽ ὡς ἐκέλευσεν ὁ κύριος ἐν τῷ εὐαγγελίῳ αὐτοῦ, οὕτως προσεύχεσθε·[4]

Πάτερ ἡμῶν ὁ ἐν τῷ οὐρανῷ,[5]
ἁγιασθήτω τὸ ὄνομά σου,
ἐλθέτω ἡ βασιλεία σου, γενηθήτω τὸ θέλημά σου ὡς ἐν οὐρανῷ καὶ ἐπὶ γῆς.
τὸν ἄρτον ἡμῶν τὸν ἐπιούσιον[6] δὸς ἡμῖν σήμερον,

1. ἔστωσαν: pres.-impv.-act.-3-pl. < εἰμί.
2. δευτέρᾳ σαββάτων . . . πέμπτῃ: the gender of the adjectives is feminine, to agree with the implied ἡμέρᾳ. They are in the dative case to indicate a particular point in time (Wallace 155–57; BDF §200; GNTG §5.66): "the second [day] of the week and the fifth [day]."
3. τετράδα καὶ παρασκευήν: the author switches to the accusative of time (Wallace 201–3; BDF §161; GNTG §5.82). Typically, as in the previous note, the dative is used to indicate the point in time when something happens. Occasionally, with ὥρα or with ἡμέρα, an author will use the accusative case (BDF §161.3).
4. This form of the Lord's Prayer is clearly influenced by the version found in Matt 6:9–13.
5. ὁ ἐν τῷ οὐρανῷ: The article changes the prepositional phrase into an attributive modifier of Πάτερ (Wallace 236; BDF §266; GNTG §5.16); it is nominative because the article does not have a distinctive vocative form: "who is in heaven."
6. ἐπιούσιον: the word appears only in the Lord's Prayer in the Gospels; nowhere else in the New Testament. Its meaning is not clear. BDAG provides the following glosses: (1) necessary for existence; (2) necessary for today; (3) for the following day; and several additional options (376*).

καὶ ἄφες ἡμῖν τὴν ὀφειλὴν ἡμῶν,[7] ὡς καὶ ἡμεῖς ἀφίεμεν τοῖς ὀφει-
λέταις ἡμῶν,
   καὶ μὴ εἰσενέγκῃς ἡμᾶς εἰς πειρασμόν,
   ἀλλὰ ῥῦσαι ἡμᾶς ἀπὸ τοῦ πονηροῦ·
   ὅτι σοῦ ἐστιν ἡ δύναμις καὶ ἡ δόξα εἰς τοὺς αἰῶνας.[8]
   3 Τρὶς τῆς ἡμέρας[9] οὕτω προσεύχεσθε.

Vocabulary

ἁγιάζω	to sanctify
ἄρτος, ου, ὁ	bread, loaf
ἀφίημι	to forgive, permit, free, neglect, abandon
βασιλεία, ας, ἡ	kingdom
δεύτερος, α, ον	second
εἰσφέρω	to bring in
εὐαγγέλιον, ου, τό	good news, gospel
θέλημα, ατος, τό	will, desire
κελεύω	to command
νηστεία, ας, ἡ	fast, fasting
νηστεύω	to fast
ὀφειλέτης, ου, ὁ	debtor
ὀφειλή, ῆς, ἡ	debt, duty
παρασκευή, ῆς, ἡ	preparation; preparation day; sixth day (Friday)
πειρασμός, οῦ, ὁ	temptation, test
πέμπτος, η, ον	fifth
προσεύχομαι	to pray
ῥύομαι	to deliver
σάββατον, ου, τό	sabbath, week
σήμερον, adv.	today
τετράς, άδος, ἡ	four; fourth day (Wednesday)
τρίς, adv.	three times
ὑποκριτής, οῦ, ὁ	hypocrite; interpreter; actor

7. ἄφες ἡμῖν τὴν ὀφειλὴν ἡμῶν: when used of forgiveness, ἀφίημι can take the dative of person and the accusative of the thing forgiven (BDAG 156.2): "forgive us our debt."
8. εἰς τοὺς αἰῶνας: "for eternity," "forever."
9. Τρὶς τῆς ἡμέρας: the genitive case indicates time within which (Wallace 122–25; BDF §186.2; *GNTG* §5.53): "three times during the day."

1.8. DIDACHE 9:1–5

On the Eucharist

In chapter 9, the author makes recommendations on the Eucharist. The discussion is distinctive to this text, differing from what one finds in the Synoptic Gospels. The Didache restricts the meal to those who have been baptized.

1 Περὶ δὲ[1] τῆς εὐχαριστίας, οὕτω[2] εὐχαριστήσατε.
2 Πρῶτον[3] περὶ τοῦ ποτηρίου·
    Εὐχαριστοῦμέν σοι, πάτερ ἡμῶν,
    ὑπὲρ τῆς ἁγίας ἀμπέλου Δαυὶδ τοῦ παιδός σου,
    ἧς[4] ἐγνώρισας ἡμῖν
    διὰ Ἰησοῦ τοῦ παιδός σου·
    σοὶ ἡ δόξα[5] εἰς τοὺς αἰῶνας.[6]
3 Περὶ δὲ[7] τοῦ κλάσματος·
    Εὐχαριστοῦμέν σοι, πάτερ ἡμῶν,
    ὑπὲρ τῆς ζωῆς καὶ γνώσεως, ἧς ἐγνώρισας ἡμῖν
    διὰ Ἰησοῦ τοῦ παιδός σου·
    σοὶ ἡ δόξα εἰς τοὺς αἰῶνας.

1. Περὶ δὲ is used to indicate a change in topic. The construction also appears in this volume in Did. 9:3 (§1.8), Did. 7:1 (§1.6), and 1 Cor 12:1 (§3.4).
2. οὕτω is an alternative form of οὕτως.
3. Πρῶτον is used as an adverb (BDAG 893.1.b.β).
4. ἧς is in the genitive case because of attraction to its antecedent (τῆς ἁγίας ἀμπέλου Δαυὶδ τοῦ παιδός σου). One expects it to be in the accusative case because it acts as the direct object of ἐγνώρισας. The attraction of the accusative case to the genitive is common (Wallace 338–39; BDF §294).
5. σοὶ ἡ δόξα: ἡ δόξα is the nominative subject of an implied form of εἰμί (Wallace 39–40; BDF §§127–28). σοὶ is a dative of possession (Wallace 149–51; BDF §189; GNTG §5.61).
6. εἰς τοὺς αἰῶνας: "for eternity," "forever."
7. Περὶ δὲ is used to indicate a change in topic (see n. 1).

4 Ὥσπερ ἦν τοῦτο τὸ κλάσμα διεσκορπισμένον[8] ἐπάνω τῶν ὀρέων καὶ συναχθὲν[9] ἐγένετο ἕν,

οὕτω συναχθήτω σου ἡ ἐκκλησία ἀπὸ τῶν περάτων τῆς γῆς εἰς τὴν σὴν βασιλείαν·

ὅτι σοῦ ἐστιν ἡ δόξα καὶ ἡ δύναμις διὰ Ἰησοῦ Χριστοῦ εἰς τοὺς αἰῶνας.

5 Μηδεὶς δὲ φαγέτω μηδὲ πιέτω ἀπὸ τῆς εὐχαριστίας ὑμῶν, ἀλλ᾽[10] οἱ βαπτισθέντες[11] εἰς ὄνομα κυρίου, καὶ[12] γὰρ περὶ τούτου εἴρηκεν ὁ κύριος· Μὴ δῶτε τὸ ἅγιον τοῖς κυσί.

Vocabulary

ἄμπελος, ου, ἡ	vine, vineyard
βαπτίζω	to baptize, wash, dip
βασιλεία, ας, ἡ	kingdom
γνωρίζω	to make known
γνῶσις, εως, ἡ	knowledge
Δαυίδ, ὁ, indecl.	David
διασκορπίζω	to scatter, squander
ἐπάνω	(+ gen.) over, above, upon, on
ἐσθίω	to eat
εὐχαριστέω	to give thanks
εὐχαριστία, ας, ἡ	thanksgiving, thankfulness; eucharist
κλάσμα, ατος, τό	fragment
κύων, κυνός, ὁ	dog
παῖς, παιδός, ὁ or ἡ	child; slave
πέρας, ατος, τό	end, finish; at length, at last
πίνω	to drink

8. ἦν . . . διεσκορπισμένον is a pluperfect periphrastic construction (the imperfect form of εἰμί plus the perfect participle); equivalent in function to the pluperfect tense of the finite verb (Wallace 647–49; BDF §§352–53; *GNTG* §§5.184–85): "had been scattered."

9. συναχθὲν is an adverbial participle indicating time; the aorist tense indicates time before that of the main verb (Wallace 623–27; BDF §418; *GNTG* §5.188): "after having been gathered together."

10. ἀλλ᾽ is functioning like εἰ μή: "except" (BDAG 45.1.b*; BDF §448.8*).

11. οἱ βαπτισθέντες is a substantival participle (Wallace 619–21; BDF §413; *GNTG* §5.182): "those who have been baptized."

12. καὶ functions here to intensify the clause: "also," "indeed" (BDAG 495.2).

ποτήριον, ου, τό	cup
σός, σή, σόν	your (sg.)
συνάγω	to gather, bring together; to compile
ὥσπερ, adv.	as, just as

1.9. DIDACHE 10:1–7

Additional Prayers

In chapter 10, the author continues the discussion of prayer. Here, he includes a prayer of thanksgiving to be said after the eucharistic meal.

1 Μετὰ δὲ τὸ ἐμπλησθῆναι¹ οὕτως εὐχαριστήσατε· 2 Εὐχαριστοῦμέν σοι, πάτερ ἅγιε,

ὑπὲρ τοῦ ἁγίου ὀνόματός σου οὗ² κατεσκήνωσας ἐν ταῖς καρδίαις ἡμῶν,

καὶ ὑπὲρ τῆς γνώσεως καὶ πίστεως καὶ ἀθανασίας ἧς³ ἐγνώρισας ἡμῖν διὰ Ἰησοῦ τοῦ παιδός σου·

σοὶ ἡ δόξα⁴ εἰς τοὺς αἰῶνας.

3   σύ, δέσποτα παντοκράτορ, ἔκτισας τὰ πάντα ἕνεκεν τοῦ ὀνόματός σου,

τροφήν τε καὶ ποτὸν ἔδωκας τοῖς ἀνθρώποις εἰς ἀπόλαυσιν,⁵

ἵνα σοι εὐχαριστήσωσιν

ἡμῖν δὲ ἐχαρίσω⁶ πνευματικὴν τροφὴν καὶ ποτόν,

1. Μετὰ δὲ τὸ ἐμπλησθῆναι: the articular infinitive with μετά indicates time before the main verb (Wallace 611; BDF §402.3; GNTG §5.172; BDAG 638): "after having been filled."
2. οὗ is in the genitive case because of attraction to its antecedent (τοῦ ἁγίου ὀνόματός σου). One expects it be in the accusative case because it acts as the direct object of κατεσκήνωσας. The attraction of the accusative case to the genitive is common (Wallace 338–39; BDF §294).
3. ἧς is in the genitive case because of attraction to its antecedent (τῆς γνώσεως καὶ πίστεως καὶ ἀθανασίας) (see n. 2).
4. σοὶ ἡ δόξα: ἡ δόξα is the nominative subject of an implied form of εἰμί (Wallace 39–40; BDF §§127–28). σοὶ is a dative of possession (Wallace 149–51; BDF §189; GNTG §5.61).
5. εἰς ἀπόλαυσιν: εἰς plus the accusative case, indicating purpose (BDAG 290.4.F): "to enjoy."
6. ἐχαρίσω: aor.-ind.-mid.-2-sg. < χαρίζομαι.

καὶ ζωὴν αἰώνιον διὰ τοῦ παιδός σου.

4   πρὸ πάντων[7] εὐχαριστοῦμέν σοι ὅτι δυνατὸς εἶ σύ· σοὶ ἡ δόξα[8] εἰς τοὺς αἰῶνας.

5   μνήσθητι, κύριε, τῆς ἐκκλησίας[9] σου,

τοῦ ῥύσασθαι αὐτὴν ἀπὸ παντὸς πονηροῦ καὶ τελειῶσαι[10] αὐτὴν ἐν τῇ ἀγάπῃ σου,

καὶ σύναξον αὐτὴν ἀπὸ τῶν τεσσάρων ἀνέμων, τὴν ἁγιασθεῖσαν,[11] εἰς τὴν σὴν βασιλείαν,

ἣν ἡτοίμασας αὐτῇ·

ὅτι σοῦ ἐστιν ἡ δύναμις καὶ ἡ δόξα εἰς τοὺς αἰῶνας.

6[12]   ἐλθέτω χάρις καὶ παρελθέτω ὁ κόσμος οὗτος.

ὡσαννὰ τῷ θεῷ Δαυίδ.

εἴ[13] τις ἅγιός ἐστιν, ἐρχέσθω·

εἴ τις οὐκ ἐστί,[14] μετανοείτω·

μαραναθά.[15] ἀμήν.

7 Τοῖς δὲ προφήταις[16] ἐπιτρέπετε εὐχαριστεῖν[17] ὅσα θέλουσιν.

---

7. πρὸ πάντων: "above all" (BDAG 864.3).

8. σοὶ ἡ δόξα: see n. 4.

9. τῆς ἐκκλησίας: the genitive object of μνήσθητι (Wallace 131–34; BDF §175).

10. τοῦ ῥύσασθαι . . . τελειῶσαι: the genitive articular infinitives indicate purpose (Wallace 590–92, 610; BDF §400; *GNTG* §5.161): "to rescue her . . . to perfect her."

11. τὴν ἁγιασθεῖσαν is an attributive participle (Wallace 617–18; BDF §412; *GNTG* §5.181), modifying αὐτὴν: "having been sanctified."

12. For the difficulties of this verse in terms of both content and its place in the chapter, see the discussion in Kurt Niederwimmer, *The Didache: A Commentary*, Hermeneia (Minneapolis: Fortress, 1998), 161–64.

13. εἰ plus the indicative (ἐστιν) introduces the protasis of a first-class condition. The first-class condition assumes, for the sake of argument, that the protasis (the "if" statement) is true (Wallace 450–51, 663, 690–94; BDF §§371, 372; *GNTG* §5.235).

14. This clause is elliptical; ἅγιός must be supplied from the previous clause (see the discussion in BDF §§479–83).

15. μαραναθά is an Aramaic expression that means "Lord, come!" The phrase appears to have been incorporated into some early Christian worship services. The phrase also occurs in 1 Cor 16:22 (BDAG 616*).

16. Τοῖς . . . προφήταις is the dative complement of ἐπιτρέπετε (BDAG 385.1).

17. εὐχαριστεῖν is a complementary infinitive going with ἐπιτρέπετε (BDAG 384.1; Wallace 598–99; BDF §392; *GNTG* §5.163).

Vocabulary

ἁγιάζω	to sanctify
ἀθανασία, ας, ἡ	immortality
αἰώνιος, ον	eternal
ἀμήν	amen (Heb: "truly")
ἄνεμος, ου, ὁ	wind
ἀπόλαυσις, εως, ἡ	enjoyment
βασιλεία, ας, ἡ	kingdom
γνωρίζω	to make known
γνῶσις, εως, ἡ	knowledge
Δαυίδ, ὁ, indecl.	David
δεσπότης, ου, ὁ	lord, master, owner
δυνατός, ή, όν	possible, strong, able
ἐμπίπλημι	to fill full
ἕνεκα	(+ gen.) because of, for the sake of
ἐπιτρέπω	to allow, entrust to, permit; to command
ἑτοιμάζω	to prepare
εὐχαριστέω	to give thanks
κατασκηνόω	to live, settle, nest
κτίζω	to create, build, found
μετανοέω	to change one's mind, repent, feel remorse
μιμνήσκομαι	to remember; to remind
παῖς, παιδός, ὁ or ἡ	child; slave
παντοκράτωρ, ορος, ὁ	all mighty; almighty
παρέρχομαι	to pass by, pass away
πνευματικός, ή, όν	spiritual
ποτός, ου, ὁ	drinking party
πρό	(+ gen.) before, above
ῥύομαι	to deliver
σός, σή, σόν	your (sg.)
συνάγω	to gather, bring together; to compile
τελειόω	to finish, make perfect
τέσσαρες	four
τροφή, ῆς, ἡ	food, provisions
χαρίζομαι	to give; to favor; to forgive
ὡσαννά	hosanna (Aramaic, a shout of praise)

The Angels of Righteousness and Wickedness

The Shepherd of Hermas was one of the most popular texts among the early churches. It was likely composed over a period of time during the early to middle years of the second century CE. The author (Hermas) identifies himself as a freedman who evidently was a member of the church in Rome. The shepherd is the primary angelic figure who interacts with Hermas. The book consists of three collections: five visions; twelve commandments (or mandates); and ten parables; there is considerable overlap of material between the sections. The sections of the Shepherd of Hermas contained in this reader are preserved in several Greek manuscripts. But certain sections near the end of the book are not found in any Greek manuscripts; these sections are only preserved in Latin translations. Two numbering systems are associated with these texts. The first numbers each vision, mandate, and parable sequentially from the beginning of the document (and so numbers 36 and 38 are included in this reader). The other system establishes numbers within each collection (and so Mandate 6.2 and 6.8 refer to the same places in the document).

In Mandate 6.2, the shepherd takes up the topic of faith and reveals that there are two angels, one of righteousness (δικαιοσύνης) and one of wickedness (πονηρίας) who try to direct a person down one path or the other. The concept of two ways is introduced in Mandate 6.1,[1] where the shepherd commands Hermas to "guard faith and fear and self-control." He explains to Hermas that there are two ways a person might take with

---

1. The "two ways" literary strategy is also used by the authors of the Didache and Epistle of Barnabas.

respect to each of these concerns: a way of righteousness (δίκαιον) and a way of unrighteousness (ἄδικον).

1 (Ἐντολὴ ϛ² 2) Ἄκουε νῦν, φησί, περὶ τῆς πίστεως. δύο εἰσὶν ἄγγελοι μετὰ τοῦ ἀνθρώπου, εἷς τῆς δικαιοσύνης καὶ εἷς τῆς πονηρίας. 2 Πῶς οὖν, φημί, κύριε, γνώσομαι τὰς αὐτῶν ἐνεργείας, ὅτι ἀμφότεροι ἄγγελοι μετ᾽ ἐμοῦ κατοικοῦσιν; 3 Ἄκουε, φησί, καὶ σύνιε³ αὐτάς. ὁ μὲν⁴ τῆς δικαιο- σύνης ἄγγελος τρυφερός ἐστι καὶ αἰσχυντηρὸς καὶ πραῢς καὶ ἡσύχιος. ὅταν⁵ οὖν οὗτος ἐπὶ τὴν καρδίαν σου ἀναβῇ, εὐθέως λαλεῖ μετὰ σοῦ περὶ δικαιοσύνης, περὶ ἁγνείας, περὶ σεμνότητος, περὶ αὐταρκείας, περὶ παντὸς ἔργου δικαίου καὶ περὶ πάσης ἀρετῆς ἐνδόξου. ταῦτα πάντα ὅταν εἰς τὴν καρδίαν σου ἀναβῇ,⁶ γίνωσκε ὅτι ὁ ἄγγελος τῆς δικαιοσύνης μετὰ σοῦ ἐστι. ταῦτα οὖν ἐστι τὰ ἔργα τοῦ ἀγγέλου τῆς δικαιοσύνης. τούτῳ οὖν πίστευε καὶ τοῖς ἔργοις αὐτοῦ. 4 ὅρα⁷ νῦν καὶ τοῦ ἀγγέλου τῆς πονηρίας τὰ ἔργα. πρῶτον πάντων ὀξύχολός ἐστι καὶ πικρὸς καὶ ἄφρων, καὶ τὰ ἔργα αὐτοῦ πονηρά,⁸ καταστρέφοντα⁹ τοὺς δούλους τοῦ θεοῦ· ὅταν οὖν οὗτος ἐπὶ τὴν καρδίαν σου ἀναβῇ, γνῶθι αὐτὸν ἀπὸ τῶν ἔργων αὐτοῦ.¹⁰ 5 Πῶς, φημί, κύριε, νοήσω αὐτόν, οὐκ ἐπίσταμαι. Ἄκουε, φησίν. ὅταν

2. ϛ: the ancient Greek letter digamma, which had dropped out of usage by the Koine period, was still used to indicate the number six. This section is the second chapter of the sixth commandment.

3. σύνιε: pres.-impv.-act.-2-sg. < συνίημι.

4. μέν is used to introduce a comparison or contrast. Frequently the item to be contrasted is introduced with δέ. Sometimes, as is the case here, δέ is dropped (see the discussion in BDF §447).

5. ὅταν: with the aorist subjunctive, the action of the subordinate clause precedes that of the main clause (BDAG 730.1a.β): "whenever." This construction occurs again in this verse and also in vv. 4 and 5.

6. ταῦτα πάντα . . . ἀναβῇ: the neuter plural subject frequently takes a singular verb (Wallace 399–400; BDF §133; *GNTG* §5.26.a).

7. ὅρα: pres.-impv.-act.-2-sg. < ὁράω.

8. πονηρά is a predicate adjective of an implied form of εἰμί (Wallace 39–40; BDF §§127–28): "[his works] are evil."

9. καταστρέφοντα is an attributive participle (Wallace 617–18; BDF §413; *GNTG* §5.181), modifying ἔργα: "overturning" or "destroying."

10. γνῶθι αὐτὸν ἀπὸ τῶν ἔργων αὐτοῦ: γινώσκω with its object in the accusative and ἀπό indicates acquiring information through some means (BDAG 200.2.d): "know him by his works."

ὀξυχολία σοί[11] τις[12] προσπέσῃ ἢ πικρία, γίνωσκε ὅτι αὐτός ἐστιν ἐν σοί·
εἶτα ἐπιθυμία πράξεων[13] πολλῶν καὶ πολυτέλεια ἐδεσμάτων πολλῶν[14]
καὶ μεθυσμάτων καὶ κραιπαλῶν πολλῶν καὶ ποικίλων τρυφῶν καὶ οὐ
δεόντων,[15] καὶ ἐπιθυμία γυναικῶν[16] καὶ πλεονεξία καὶ ὑπερηφανία καὶ
ἀλαζονεία, καὶ ὅσα τούτοις παραπλήσιά ἐστι καὶ ὅμοια. ταῦτα οὖν ὅταν
ἐπὶ τὴν καρδίαν σου ἀναβῇ, γίνωσκε ὅτι ὁ ἄγγελος τῆς πονηρίας ἐστὶ
μετὰ σοῦ. ὁ σὺ οὖν ἐπιγνοὺς[17] τὰ ἔργα αὐτοῦ ἀπόστα[18] ἀπ᾽ αὐτοῦ καὶ
μηδὲν αὐτῷ πίστευε, ὅτι τὰ ἔργα αὐτοῦ πονηρά εἰσι καὶ ἀσύμφορα τοῖς
δούλοις τοῦ θεοῦ. ἔχεις οὖν ἀμφοτέρων τῶν ἀγγέλων τὰς ἐνεργείας· σύνιε
αὐτὰς καὶ πίστευε τῷ ἀγγέλῳ τῆς δικαιοσύνης· 7 ἀπὸ δὲ τοῦ ἀγγέλου τῆς
πονηρίας ἀπόστηθι,[19] ὅτι ἡ διδαχὴ αὐτοῦ πονηρά ἐστι παντὶ ἔργῳ·[20] ἐὰν[21]
γὰρ ᾖ τις πιστὸς ἀνήρ, καὶ ἡ ἐνθύμησις τοῦ ἀγγέλου τούτου ἀναβῇ ἐπὶ τὴν
καρδίαν αὐτοῦ, δεῖ τὸν ἄνδρα ἐκεῖνον ἢ τὴν γυναῖκα[22] ἐξαμαρτῆσαί[23] τι.[24]

---

11. σοί is the dative complement of προσπέσῃ (BDAG 884.2*).

12. τις modifies ὀξυχολία . . . ἢ πικρία: "some angry temper . . . or bitterness."

13. πράξεων is an objective genitive (Wallace 116–19; BDF §163; *GNTG* §5.38) with ἐπιθυμία: "desires for much business" (BDAG 860.5*).

14. πολυτέλεια ἐδεσμάτων πολλῶν: "the luxury of many kinds of foods" (BDAG 850*).

15. οὐ δεόντων is an attributive participle (Wallace 617–18; BDF §413; *GNTG* §5.181), modifying τρυφῶν: "unnecessary" or "improper delights."

16. γυναικῶν is an objective genitive (Wallace 116–19; BDF §163; *GNTG* §5.38) with ἐπιθυμία: "desires for women."

17. ἐπιγνοὺς is likely an adverbial participle: it might be indicating time; the aorist tense indicates time before that of the main verb (Wallace 623–27; BDF §418; *GNTG* §5.188): "when you recognize"; it might be indicating cause (Wallace 631–32; BDF §418; *GNTG* §5.189): "since you recognize."

18. ἀπόστα: aor.-impv.-act.-2-sg. < ἀφίστημι (BDAG 157).

19. ἀπόστηθι: aor.-impv.-act.-2-sg. < ἀφίστημι.

20. παντὶ ἔργῳ (BDAG 851.1.a.β*): "in every way."

21. ἐὰν with the subjunctive (ᾖ . . . ἀναβῇ) introduces the protasis of a third-class condition. The third-class condition can indicate something likely to occur in the future, something that might occur, or something that will not occur but hypothetically could (Wallace 469–71, 663, 696–99; BDF §§371, 373; *GNTG* §5.237).

22. τὸν ἄνδρα . . . τὴν γυναῖκα are the accusative subjects of the infinitive.

23. ἐξαμαρτῆσαί: the infinitive is used in impersonal expressions with verbs like δεῖ (BDF §393.1; Wallace describes this as a substantival use [600–601]; *GNTG* §5.164.b).

24. τι: the indefinite pronoun is used to moderate ἐξαμαρτῆσαί (BDAG 1008.1.b.β.ℵ): "commit some sin" or "sin in some way."

8 ἐὰν²⁵ δὲ πάλιν²⁶ πονηρότατός τις ᾖ ἀνὴρ ἢ γυνή, καὶ ἀναβῇ ἐπὶ τὴν καρδίαν αὐτοῦ τὰ ἔργα τοῦ ἀγγέλου τῆς δικαιοσύνης, ἐξ ἀνάγκης δεῖ αὐτὸν
ἀγαθόν τι ποιῆσαι.²⁷ 9 βλέπεις οὖν, φησίν, ὅτι καλόν ἐστι τῷ ἀγγέλῳ²⁸
τῆς δικαιοσύνης ἀκολουθεῖν, τῷ δὲ ἀγγέλῳ τῆς πονηρίας ἀποτάξασθαι.²⁹
10 τὰ μὲν περὶ τῆς πίστεως³⁰ αὕτη ἡ ἐντολὴ δηλοῖ, ἵνα τοῖς ἔργοις τοῦ
ἀγγέλου τῆς δικαιοσύνης πιστεύσῃς, καὶ ἐργασάμενος³¹ αὐτὰ ζήσῃ³² τῷ
θεῷ. πίστευε δὲ ὅτι³³ τὰ ἔργα τοῦ ἀγγέλου τῆς πονηρίας χαλεπά³⁴ ἐστι·
μὴ ἐργαζόμενος³⁵ οὖν αὐτὰ ζήσῃ τῷ θεῷ.

Vocabulary

ἁγνεία, ας, ἡ	purity, chastity
αἰσχυντηρός, ά, όν	bashful, modest

25. ἐὰν with the subjunctive (ᾖ . . . ἀναβῇ) introduces the protasis of a third-class condition. See n. 21.

26. πάλιν: "on the other hand" (BDAG 753.4).

27. αὐτὸν ἀγαθόν τι ποιῆσαι: αὐτὸν is the accusative subject of the infinitive; ἀγαθόν is
the direct object of the infinitive. τι is an indefinite pronoun moderating ἀγαθόν (BDAG
1008.1.b.β.ℵ): "some good." ποιῆσαι: the infinitive is used in impersonal expressions with
verbs like δεῖ (BDF §393.1; Wallace describes this as a substantival use [600–601]; *GNTG*
§5.164.b).

28. τῷ ἀγγέλῳ is the dative complement of ἀκολουθεῖν (BDAG 816.1.b; Wallace 171–73;
BDF §187.6; *GNTG* §5.72).

29. ἀκολουθεῖν . . . ἀποτάξασθαι: the infinitive is used in impersonal expressions with
verbs like ἐστι and an adjective (BDF §393.1; Wallace describes this as a substantival use
[600–601]; *GNTG* §5.164.b): "it is good . . . to follow . . . to say goodbye to."

30. τὰ . . . περὶ τῆς πίστεως: the neuter plural article turns the prepositional phrase into
the accusative direct object of δηλοῖ (Wallace 236; BDF §266; *GNTG* §5.15): "makes clear
the things concerning faith."

31. ἐργασάμενος: is an adverbial participle that might be indicating time; the aorist tense
indicates time before that of the main verb (Wallace 623–27; BDF §418; *GNTG* §5.188):
"when you do them"; it might be indicating cause (Wallace 631–32; BDF §418; *GNTG*
§5.189): "because you do them"; it might also be indicating means (Wallace 627–28; BDF
§418; *GNTG* §5.193): "by doing them."

32. ζήσῃ: sometimes, a verb in the future tense follows a purpose clause (ἵνα plus the
subjunctive) to show some additional result (BDF §369.3*).

33. ὅτι indicates the content of what is to be believed (BDAG 816.1.a.β): "believe that."

34. χαλεπά: "evil" (BDAG 1076*).

35. μὴ ἐργασάμενος is an adverbial participle that might be indicating cause (Wallace
631–32; BDF §418; *GNTG* §5.189): "because you do not do them"; or it might be indicating
means (Wallace 627–28; BDF §418; *GNTG* §5.193): "by not doing them."

ἀκολουθέω	to follow, come after
ἀλαζονεία, ας, ἡ	boasting, boastfulness, arrogance, pretension
ἀμφότεροι, αι, α	both; all
ἀνάγκη, ης, ἡ	necessity; distress, calamity
ἀποτάσσω	to say goodbye; to renounce, give up
ἀρετή, ῆς, ἡ	moral excellence
ἀσύμφορος, ον	inconvenient, disagreeable, harmful, disadvantageous
αὐτάρκεια, ας, ἡ	self-sufficiency, independence, sufficient
ἀφίστημι	to withdraw, remove, depart, leave; to cause a revolt; to mislead
ἄφρων, ον, gen. ονος	foolish, ignorant
γυνή, αικός, ἡ	woman, wife
δέω	to bind, to tie
δηλόω	to make known, reveal, make clear; to explain
διδαχή, ῆς, ἡ	teaching, instruction
δύο	two
ἔδεσμα, ατος, τό	food
εἶτα, adv.	then, next
ἔνδοξος, ον	honored, distinguished; glorious, splendid
ἐνέργεια, ας, ἡ	working, action, energy, performance
ἐνθύμησις, εως, ἡ	idea, esteem, thought
ἐξαμαρτάνω	to miss a mark, sin; to cause to sin
ἐπιγινώσκω	to know; to recognize; to learn; to notice, perceive
ἐπίσταμαι	to understand; to know
εὐθέως, adv.	immediately, at once, suddenly
ἡσύχιος, ον	quiet
καταστρέφω	to overturn, overthrow; to destroy, ruin; to turn away, mislead
κραιπάλη, ης, ἡ	drunken excess; drunken headache
μεθύσμα, ατος, τό	strong drink
νοέω	to perceive, comprehend, understand, gain an insight into; to consider

ὅμοιος, οία, οιον	like, similar (+ dat.)
ὀξυχολία, ας, ἡ	irritability, bad temper, angry temper
ὀξύχολος, ον	irritable, ill-tempered
παραπλήσιος, ία, ιον	coming near, similar, resembling (+ dat.)
πικρία, ας, ἡ	bitterness, animosity, anger, harshness
πικρός, ά, όν	bitter, harsh
πιστός, ή, όν	faithful, dependable, trustworthy
πλεονεξία, ας, ἡ	greediness, avarice, insatiableness, covetousness
ποικίλος, η, ον	diverse, various kinds; many-colored
πολυτέλεια, ας, ἡ	extravagance, luxury, richness
πονηρία, ας, ἡ	wickedness, baseness, maliciousness
πρᾶξις, εως, ἡ	activity, function, deed, action
πραΰς, πραεῖα, πραΰ	gentle, humble, considerate, meek, mild
προσπίπτω	to come over (BDAG 884.2*); to fall down before; to fall upon, strike against
σεμνότης, τητος, ἡ	dignity, seriousness; reverence, holiness
συνίημι	to understand, comprehend
τρυφερός, ά, όν	delicate, gentle, subdued; effeminate, luxurious
τρυφή, ῆς, ἡ	delight; self-indulgence, softness, luxury, dainty
ὑπερηφανία, ας, ἡ	arrogance, haughtiness, pride

In What Areas Ought One Exercise Self-Control?

In Mandate 8, the shepherd discusses self-control, the third member of the trio introduced in 6.1 (faith, fear, self-control). Self-control can be thought of as having two aspects: things regarding which one ought to exercise self-control (πονηρός) and things regarding which one ought not (ἀγαθός).

1 (Ἐντολὴ ἡ) Εἶπόν σοι, φησίν, ὅτι τὰ κτίσματα τοῦ θεοῦ διπλᾶ ἐστι· καὶ γὰρ ἡ ἐγκράτεια διπλῆ ἐστιν. ἐπί τινων[1] γὰρ δεῖ ἐγκρατεύεσθαι,[2] ἐπί τινων δὲ οὐ δεῖ.[3] 2 Γνώρισόν μοι, φημί, κύριε, ἐπὶ τίνων[4] δεῖ ἐγκρα- τεύεσθαι, ἐπὶ τίνων δὲ οὐ δεῖ. Ἄκουε, φησί. τὸ πονηρὸν[5] ἐγκρατεύου, καὶ μὴ ποίει αὐτό· τὸ δὲ ἀγαθὸν μὴ ἐγκρατεύου, ἀλλὰ ποίει αὐτό. ἐὰν

---

1. ἐπί τινων: ἐπί with the genitive frequently follows ἐγκρατεύομαι (BDAG 274*; BDF §154): "in some things."

2. ἐγκρατεύεσθαι: the infinitive is used in impersonal expressions with verbs like δεῖ (BDF §393.1; Wallace describes this as a substantival use [600–601]; GNTG §5.164.b). The author repeats this construction eight times in vv. 2–8 (see n. 1). The author uses a variety of complements with the verb: ἐπί, ἀπό, the accusative case, the genitive case, and the infinitive (BDAG 274*).

3. οὐ δεῖ: the clause is elliptical; the reader must supply ἐγκρατεύεσθαι from the previous clause (see the discussion in BDF §§479–83). This syntax repeats in v. 2.

4. ἐπί τινων: the same construction as in v. 1, but the context requires a different English translation: "about the things."

5. τὸ πονηρὸν is an accusative of content (BDAG 274*): "with respect to evil."

γὰρ ἐγκρατεύσῃ[6] τὸ ἀγαθὸν μὴ ποιεῖν,[7] ἁμαρτίαν μεγάλην ἐργάζῃ· ἐὰν δὲ ἐγκρατεύσῃ[8] τὸ πονηρὸν μὴ ποιεῖν, δικαιοσύνην μεγάλην ἐργάζῃ. ἐγκράτευσαι οὖν ἀπὸ πονηρίας πάσης ἐργαζόμενος[9] τὸ ἀγαθόν. 3 Ποταπαί, φημί, κύριε, εἰσὶν αἱ πονηρίαι ἀφ᾽ ὧν ἡμᾶς[10] δεῖ ἐγκρατεύεσθαι; Ἄκουε, φησίν· ἀπὸ μοιχείας καὶ πορνείας, ἀπὸ μεθύσματος ἀνομίας, ἀπὸ τρυφῆς πονηρᾶς, ἀπὸ ἐδεσμάτων πολλῶν καὶ πολυτελείας πλούτου καὶ καυχήσεως καὶ ὑψηλοφροσύνης καὶ ὑπερηφανίας, καὶ ἀπὸ ψεύσματος καὶ καταλαλιᾶς καὶ ὑποκρίσεως, μνησικακίας καὶ πάσης βλασφημίας.[11] 4 ταῦτα τὰ ἔργα πάντων πονηρότατά[12] εἰσιν ἐν τῇ ζωῇ τῶν ἀνθρώπων. ἀπὸ τούτων οὖν τῶν ἔργων δεῖ ἐγκρατεύεσθαι τὸν δοῦλον[13] τοῦ θεοῦ. ὁ γὰρ μὴ ἐγκρατευόμενος[14] ἀπὸ τούτων οὐ δύναται ζῆσαι[15] τῷ θεῷ. ἄκουε οὖν καὶ τὰ ἀκόλουθα τούτων.[16] 5 Ἔτι[17] γάρ, φημί, κύριε, πονηρὰ ἔργα ἐστί; Καί γε πολλά,[18] φησίν, ἔστιν ἀφ᾽ ὧν δεῖ τὸν δοῦλον τοῦ θεοῦ ἐγκρατεύε-

6. ἐὰν . . . ἐγκρατεύσῃ: ἐὰν with the subjunctive introduces the protasis of a third-class condition. The third-class condition can indicate something likely to occur in the future, something that might occur, or something that will not occur but hypothetically could (Wallace 469–71, 663, 696–99: BDF §§371, 373; GNTG §5.237). Here, the future indicative is used instead of the subjunctive (see BDF §363 for connections between the future indicative and the subjunctive).

7. ποιεῖν: the infinitive might be indicating purpose (Wallace 590–92; BDF §390; GNTG §5.161) or result (Wallace 592–94; BDF 391.4*; GNTG §5.162).

8. ἐὰν . . . ἐγκρατεύσῃ: ἐὰν with the subjunctive introduces the protasis of a third-class condition (see n. 6).

9. ἐργαζόμενος might be an adverbial participle indicating purpose (Wallace 635–37; BDF §418.4; GNTG §5.194) or result (Wallace 592–94; BDF 391.4*; GNTG §5.162); it might be indicating means (Wallace 628–30; BDF §418; GNTG §5.192): "by means of doing good."

10. ἡμᾶς is the accusative subject of ἐγκρατεύεσθαι (Wallace 192–97; BDF §392; GNTG §5.79).

11. ἀπὸ μοιχείας . . . βλασφημίας: this sentence is elliptical; the reader must supply some form of ἐγκρατεύομαι (also see n. 1).

12. πάντων πονηρότατά: according to BDF, Hermas has confused the superlative with the comparative (§244.2*).

13. τὸν δοῦλον is the accusative subject of ἐγκρατεύεσθαι (Wallace 192–97; BDF §392; GNTG §5.79).

14. ὁ ἐγκρατευόμενος is a substantival participle (Wallace 619–21; BDF §413; GNTG §5.182): "the one who [does not] exercise self-control."

15. ζῆσαι is a complementary infinitive going with δύναται (Wallace 598–99; BDF §392; GNTG §5.163).

16. τὰ ἀκόλουθα τούτων: "what follows them" (BDAG 37*; BDF §182.1*).

17. Ἔτι: "Are there still [others]?" (BDAG 400.3).

18. πολλά is a predicate adjective with ἔστιν: "there are many [evils]."

σθαι· κλέμμα, ψεῦδος, ἀποστέρησις, ψευδομαρτυρία, πλεονεξία, ἐπιθυμία πονηρά, ἀπάτη, κενοδοξία, ἀλαζονεία, καὶ ὅσα τούτοις ὅμοια εἰσιν. 6 οὐ δοκεῖ σοι ταῦτα πονηρὰ εἶναι;[19] καὶ λίαν πονηρά, φησί, τοῖς δούλοις τοῦ θεοῦ. τούτων πάντων δεῖ ἐγκρατεύεσθαι τὸν δουλεύοντα[20] τῷ θεῷ. ἐγκράτευσαι οὖν ἀπὸ πάντων τούτων, ἵνα[21] ζήσῃ τῷ θεῷ καὶ ἐγγραφήσῃ μετὰ τῶν ἐγκρατευομένων[22] αὐτά. ἀφ᾽ ὧν μὲν οὖν δεῖ σε ἐγκρατεύεσθαι, ταῦτά ἐστιν. 7 ἃ δὲ δεῖ σε μὴ ἐγκρατεύεσθαι, φησίν, ἀλλὰ ποιεῖν,[23] ἄκουε. τὸ ἀγαθὸν μὴ ἐγκρατεύου, ἀλλὰ ποίει αὐτό. 8 Καὶ τῶν ἀγαθῶν[24] μοι, φημί, κύριε, δήλωσον τὴν δύναμιν, ἵνα πορευθῶ ἐν αὐτοῖς καὶ δουλεύσω αὐτοῖς, ἵνα ἐργασάμενος[25] αὐτὰ δυνηθῶ σωθῆναι.[26] Ἄκουε, φησί, καὶ τῶν ἀγαθῶν τὰ ἔργα, ἅ σε δεῖ ἐργάζεσθαι[27] καὶ μὴ ἐγκρατεύεσθαι. 9 πρῶτον[28] πάντων πίστις, φόβος κυρίου, ἀγάπη, ὁμόνοια, ῥήματα δικαιοσύνης, ἀλήθεια, ὑπομονή·[29] τούτων[30] ἀγαθώτερον οὐδέν ἐστιν ἐν τῇ ζωῇ τῶν ἀνθρώ- πων. ταῦτα ἐάν τις φυλάσσῃ καὶ μὴ ἐγκρατεύηται[31] ἀπ᾽ αὐτῶν, μακάριος

---

19. εἶναι is a complementary infinitive going with δοκεῖ (Wallace 598–99; BDF §392; *GNTG* §5.163).

20. τὸν δουλεύοντα is a substantival participle (Wallace 619–21; BDF §413; *GNTG* §5.182) serving as the accusative subject of the infinitive (Wallace 192–97; BDF §392; *GNTG* §5.79): "the one who serves."

21. Typically, ἵνα is used with the subjunctive to indicate purpose. It can also, as here, be used with the future indicative to indicate purpose (BDAG 474.1.b; Wallace 571; BDF §369).

22. τῶν ἐγκρατευομένων is a substantival participle (Wallace 619–21; BDF §413; *GNTG* §5.182) in the genitive case with μετὰ: "with those who exercise self-control."

23. ποιεῖν: the infinitive might be indicating purpose (Wallace 590–92; BDF §390; *GNTG* §5.161) or result (Wallace 592–94; BDF 391.4*; *GNTG* §5.162).

24. τῶν ἀγαθῶν goes with τὴν δύναμιν: "the power of good things."

25. ἐργασάμενος is an adverbial participle likely indicating means (Wallace 625–30; BDF §418; *GNTG* §5.192): "by doing."

26. σωθῆναι is a complementary infinitive going with δυνηθῶ (Wallace 598–99; BDF §392; *GNTG* §5.163).

27. ἐργάζεσθαι: the infinitive is used in impersonal expressions with verbs like δεῖ (BDF §393.1; Wallace describes this as a substantival use [600–601]; *GNTG* §5.164.b).

28. πρῶτον . . . εἶτα: πρῶτον introduces a list of things that Hermas appears to consider most important (BDAG 893.2). A second list is given in v. 10, introduced by εἶτα.

29. πίστις . . . ὑπομονή: predicate nominatives of an implied form of εἰμί (Wallace 39–40; BDF §§127–28): "there is faith."

30. τούτων is a genitive of comparison, going with ἀγαθώτερον (Wallace 110–12; BDF §185; *GNTG* §5.51).

31. ἐάν . . . φυλάσσῃ καὶ μὴ ἐγκρατεύηται: ἐάν with the subjunctive introduces the protasis of a third-class condition (see n. 6).

γίνεται ἐν τῇ ζωῇ αὐτοῦ. 10 εἶτα τούτων τὰ ἀκόλουθα³² ἄκουσον· χήραις ὑπηρετεῖν,³³ ὀρφανοὺς καὶ ὑστερουμένους ἐπισκέπτεσθαι, ἐξ ἀναγκῶν λυτροῦσθαι τοὺς δούλους τοῦ θεοῦ, φιλόξενον εἶναι (ἐν γὰρ τῇ φιλοξενίᾳ εὑρίσκεται ἀγαθοποίησίς ποτε),³⁴ μηδενὶ ἀντιτάσσεσθαι, ἡσύχιον εἶναι, ἐνδεέστερον γίνεσθαι πάντων ἀνθρώπων,³⁵ πρεσβύτας σέβεσθαι, δικαιοσύνην ἀσκεῖν, ἀδελφότητα συντηρεῖν, ὕβριν ὑποφέρειν, μακρόθυμον εἶναι, μνησικακίαν μὴ ἔχειν, κάμνοντας³⁶ τῇ ψυχῇ παρακαλεῖν, ἐσκανδαλισμένους³⁷ ἀπὸ τῆς πίστεως μὴ ἀποβάλλεσθαι ἀλλ᾽ ἐπιστρέφειν καὶ εὐθύμους ποιεῖν, ἁμαρτάνοντας³⁸ νουθετεῖν, χρεώστας μὴ θλίβειν καὶ ἐνδεεῖς, καὶ εἴ τινα³⁹ τούτοις ὅμοιά ἐστι. 11 δοκεῖ σοι, φησί, ταῦτα ἀγαθὰ εἶναι;⁴⁰ Τί γάρ,⁴¹ φημί, κύριε, τούτων ἀγαθώτερον; Πορεύου οὖν, φησίν, ἐν αὐτοῖς καὶ μὴ ἐγκρατεύου ἀπ᾽ αὐτῶν, καὶ ζήσῃ τῷ θεῷ. 12 φύλασσε οὖν τὴν ἐντολὴν ταύτην· ἐὰν τὸ ἀγαθὸν ποιῇς καὶ μὴ ἐγκρατεύσῃ⁴² ἀπ᾽ αὐτοῦ, ζήσῃ τῷ θεῷ, καὶ πάντες ζήσονται τῷ θεῷ οἱ οὕτω ποιοῦντες. καὶ πάλιν ἐὰν τὸ πονηρὸν μὴ ποιῇς καὶ ἐγκρατεύσῃ ἀπ᾽ αὐτοῦ, ζήσῃ τῷ θεῷ, καὶ πάντες ζήσονται τῷ θεῷ ὅσοι ἐὰν⁴³ ταύτας τὰς ἐντολὰς φυλάξωσι καὶ πορευθῶσιν ἐν αὐταῖς.

32. τούτων τὰ ἀκόλουθα: "what follows them" (BDAG 37; §182.1*).

33. ὑπηρετεῖν . . . ἐπισκέπτεσθαι . . . θλίβειν: all of the infinitives in this verse are likely substantival nominatives (Wallace 600–601; BDF §399; *GNTG* §5.164.a): "serving . . . looking after . . . rescuing."

34. ποτε (enclitic particle): "presumably" (BDAG 856.2*).

35. πάντων ἀνθρώπων is a genitive of comparison, going with ἐνδεέστερον (Wallace 110–12; BDF §185; *GNTG* §5.51): "needier than all human beings."

36. κάμνοντας is a substantival participle (Wallace 619–21; BDF §413; *GNTG* §5.182): "those who are sick."

37. ἐσκανδαλισμένους: pf.-ptc.-mid.-masc.-acc.-pl < σκανδαλίζω. The participle is a substantival (Wallace 619–21; BDF §413; *GNTG* §5.182): "those who have stumbled."

38. ἁμαρτάνοντας is a substantival participle (Wallace 619–21; BDF §413; *GNTG* §5.182): "those who sin."

39. εἴ τινα: "whatever" (BDAG 279.7).

40. εἶναι: verbs of perception (δοκεῖ) take the infinitive (BDF §397.2; Wallace treats it as a form of indirect discourse [603–5]; *GNTG* §5.166).

41. Τί γάρ introduces an elliptical question. The reader is likely intended to supply ἐστιν (BDAG 1007.1.a.β.ℵ): "What then? . . . Is there anything better than?"

42. ἐὰν . . . ποιῇς καὶ μὴ ἐγκρατεύσῃ: ἐὰν with the subjunctive introduces the protasis of a third-class condition (see n. 6).

43. ὅσοι ἐὰν: "all those who" or "whoever" (BDAG 729.2). ἐὰν with the subjunctive introduces the protasis of a third-class condition (see n. 6).

Vocabulary

ἀγαθοποίησις, εως, ἡ	doing good
ἀδελφότης, ητος, ἡ	brotherhood
ἀκόλουθος, ον	following; in conformity with
ἀλαζονεία, ας, ἡ	boasting, boastfulness
ἁμαρτάνω	to sin; to err
ἀνάγκη, ης, ἡ	necessity; distress, calamity
ἀνομία, ας, ἡ	lawlessness
ἀντιτάσσω	to oppose, resist
ἀπάτη, ης, ἡ	deceit, deceitfulness
ἀποβάλλω	to cast away, cast off
ἀποστέρησις, εως, ἡ	robbery, deprivation
ἀσκέω	to do one's best at, practice; to live as an ascetic
βλασφημία, ας, ἡ	abusive speech, blasphemy
γέ	yet, indeed, surely
γνωρίζω	to make known
δηλόω	to make clear, declare
διπλοῦς, ῆ, οῦν	double
δουλεύω	to serve as a slave
ἐγγράφω	to inscribe, write
ἐγκράτεια, ας, ἡ	self-control; abstinence, fasting
ἐγκρατεύομαι	to show self-control, restrain oneself
ἔδεσμα, ατος, τό	choice food
εἶτα, adv.	then, next
ἐνδεής, ες	in need, poor, impoverished
ἐπισκέπτομαι	to visit, care for
ἐπιστρέφω	to turn back, return, turn
εὔθυμος, ον	encouraged, cheerful
ἡ	numerical sign indicating 8; or eighth
ἡσύχιος, ον	quiet
θλίβω	to crush, compress; to oppress, trouble, annoy
κάμνω	to be sick; to be weary
καταλαλιά, ᾶς, ἡ	slander, defamation; evil speech
καύχησις, εως, ἡ	boasting, pride
κενοδοξία, ας, ἡ	conceit
κλέμμα, ατος, τό	theft, stolen object

κτίσμα, ατος, τό	what is created, creature
λίαν, adv.	exceedingly
λυτρόω	to ransom, redeem
μακάριος, α, ον	blessed, happy
μακρόθυμος, ον	patient, long-suffering, enduring
μεθύσμα, ατος, τό	strong drink
μνησικακία, ας, ἡ	grudge-bearing
μοιχεία, ας, ἡ	adultery
νουθετέω	to warn, admonish
ὅμοιος, α, ον	like, similar
ὁμόνοια, ας, ἡ	harmony
ὀρφανός, ή, όν	orphaned
παρακαλέω	to urge, exhort, comfort
πλεονεξία, ας, ἡ	greediness; lust; advantage, avarice
πλοῦτος, ου, ὁ	riches
πολυτέλεια, ας, ἡ	extravagance; great expense
πονηρία, ας, ἡ	wickedness
πορνεία, ας, ἡ	sexual immorality
ποταπός, ή, όν	what sort of? what kind of?
πρεσβύτης, ου, ὁ	old man, aged man; legate, ambassador
ῥῆμα, ατος, τό	word, thing
σέβω	to worship
σκανδαλίζω	to cause to stumble; to give offense
συντηρέω	to preserve
τρυφή, ῆς, ἡ	dainty; delight; luxury, self-indulgence
ὕβρις, εως, ἡ	insolence; insult; violence, injury
ὑπερηφανία, ας, ἡ	pride, arrogance
ὑπηρετέω	to serve
ὑπόκρισις, εως, τό	hypocrisy
ὑπομονή, ῆς, ἡ	endurance; staying
ὑποφέρω	to endure
ὑστερέω	to lack; to be late; to postpone
ὑψηλοφροσύνη, ης, ἡ	pride, snobbery, arrogance
φιλοξενία, ας, ἡ	hospitality
φιλόξενος, ον	hospitable
φόβος, ου, ὁ	fear, terror; reverence

χήρα, ας, ἡ	widow
χρεώστης, ου, ὁ	debtor
ψευδομαρτυρία, ας, ἡ	false testimony
ψεῦδος, ους, τό	lie; falsehood
ψεῦσμα, ατος, τό	untruthfulness

Texts Exhibiting More Challenging Greek

2.1. PSALM 21:1–32 LXX (22:1–31 MT)

The Psalmist Pleads for Salvation

The book of Psalms contains several collections of poetic prayers composed throughout the history of Israel. Many of the psalms are attributed to David, but other authors are represented as well; and some are anonymous. The MT and the LXX do not always agree on how the psalms ought to be divided. For example, Psalms 9 and 10 in the MT are a single psalm (9) in the LXX. As a result, Psalm 21 LXX is Psalm 22 in the MT (and therefore most English translations of TANAK).

This psalm is composed of thirty-two verses. Verses 1–22 constitute a lament from a person in dire distress; verses 23–32 constitute a song of praise to God who listens to those who ask for help.

The opening cry in verse 1 appears on the lips of Jesus in Mark 15:34 and Matt 27:46. Verses 7–8 evoke events at the end of the gospels (Matt 27:39–44; Mark 15:29–32; Luke 23:35–37). Verses 17–19 are reminiscent of events on the cross (Matt 27:35; Mark 15:24; Luke 23:34; John 19:23–24). Verse 23 is quoted in Heb 2:12.

1   Εἰς τὸ τέλος,[1] ὑπὲρ τῆς ἀντιλήμψεως[2] τῆς ἑωθινῆς·[3] ψαλμὸς τῷ Δαυιδ.

---

1. Εἰς τὸ τέλος is used as a header in numerous psalms; the meaning is unsure: "[looking forward] to the finish?" (*GELS* 676.b.iv). It is a peculiar translation of the Hebrew *lamnaṣṣēaḥ*: "for the choirmaster."

2. ὑπὲρ τῆς ἀντιλήμψεως: ὑπὲρ might indicate the cause or reason (BDAG 1031.A.2): "because of help"; or it might indicate content (BDAG 1031.A.3): "concerning help." The Hebrew appears to refer to the title of a musical tune (ʿal-ʾayyelet haššaḥar): "Deer of the Dawn." The LXX translator has apparently misunderstood this.

3. τῆς ἑωθινῆς is either an attributive genitive (genitive of quality [Wallace 86–88; BDF §165; *GNTG* §5.44]): "early morning help"; or, perhaps, a genitive of time (Wallace 122–24; BDF §186; *GNTG* §5.53): "help during the early morning."

2   Ὁ θεὸς ὁ θεός μου, πρόσχες μοι·[4] ἵνα τί[5] ἐγκατέλιπές με; μακρὰν ἀπὸ τῆς σωτηρίας μου οἱ λόγοι[6] τῶν παραπτω-μάτων μου.

3   ὁ θεός μου, κεκράξομαι[7] ἡμέρας,[8] καὶ οὐκ εἰσακούσῃ, καὶ νυκτός, καὶ οὐκ εἰς ἄνοιαν ἐμοί.[9]

4   σὺ δὲ ἐν ἁγίοις κατοικεῖς, ὁ ἔπαινος Ισραηλ.

5   ἐπὶ σοὶ ἤλπισαν οἱ πατέρες ἡμῶν, ἤλπισαν, καὶ ἐρρύσω[10] αὐτούς·

6   πρὸς[11] σὲ ἐκέκραξαν καὶ ἐσώθησαν, ἐπὶ σοὶ ἤλπισαν καὶ οὐ κατῃσχύνθησαν.

7   ἐγὼ δέ εἰμι σκώληξ καὶ οὐκ ἄνθρωπος, ὄνειδος ἀνθρώπου καὶ ἐξουδένημα λαοῦ.

8   πάντες οἱ θεωροῦντές[12] με ἐξεμυκτήρισάν με, ἐλάλησαν ἐν χείλεσιν,[13] ἐκίνησαν κεφαλήν[14]

9   Ἤλπισεν[15] ἐπὶ κύριον, ῥυσάσθω αὐτόν· σωσάτω αὐτόν, ὅτι θέλει αὐτόν.

10   ὅτι σὺ εἶ ὁ ἐκσπάσας[16] με ἐκ γαστρός,

---

4. μοι is the dative complement of προσέχω (BDAG 816.1.b; Wallace 171–73; BDF §187.6; *GNTG* §5.72).

5. ἵνα τί: "why" (BDAG 477).

6. οἱ λόγοι is the nominative subject of an implied εἰσίν (Wallace 39–40; BDF §§127–28): "The words . . . are."

7. κεκράξομαι: fut.-ind.-mid.-1-sg. < κράζω.

8. ἡμέρας (and νυκτός) is a genitive of time (Wallace 122–24; BDF §186; *GNTG* §5.53): "during the day."

9. καὶ οὐκ εἰς ἄνοιαν ἐμοί: this clause is elliptical; a verb must be supplied. Likely, some form of εἰμί or γίνομαι (Wallace 39–40; BDF §§127–28): "it is not folly for me"; or, "it does not become folly for me."

10. ἐρρύσω: aor.-ind.-mid.-2-sg. < ῥύομαι.

11. πρὸς here is used with a verb of speaking to indicate the addressee (BDAG 874.3.a.ε).

12. οἱ θεωροῦντές is a substantival participle (Wallace 619–21; BDF §413; *GNTG* §5.182); the present tense indicates time contemporaneous with the action of the main verb (which is aorist).

13. ἐλάλησαν ἐν χείλεσιν: "they spoke with their lips" (a derisive gesture; BDAG 1081.1*).

14. ἐκίνησαν κεφαλήν: "they moved their head back and forth" (another derisive gesture; BDAG 545.2*).

15. This is direct speech; the content of what "they spoke with their lips."

16. ὁ ἐκσπάσας is an attributive participle (Wallace 619–21; BDF §413; *GNTG* §5.182): "the one who drew me."

ἡ ἐλπίς¹⁷ μου ἀπὸ μαστῶν τῆς μητρός μου·
11 ἐπὶ σὲ ἐπερρίφην¹⁸ ἐκ μήτρας,
ἐκ κοιλίας μητρός μου θεός μου εἶ σύ.
12 μὴ ἀποστῆς ἀπ᾽ ἐμοῦ, ὅτι θλῖψις¹⁹ ἐγγύς,
ὅτι οὐκ ἔστιν ὁ βοηθῶν.²⁰
13 περιεκύκλωσάν με μόσχοι πολλοί,
ταῦροι πίονες περιέσχον με·
14 ἤνοιξαν ἐπ᾽ ἐμὲ τὸ στόμα αὐτῶν
ὡς λέων ὁ ἁρπάζων καὶ ὠρυόμενος.²¹
15 ὡσεὶ ὕδωρ ἐξεχύθην,
καὶ διεσκορπίσθη πάντα τὰ ὀστᾶ μου,
ἐγενήθη ἡ καρδία μου ὡσεὶ κηρὸς τηκόμενος²² ἐν μέσῳ²³
τῆς κοιλίας μου·
16 ἐξηράνθη ὡς ὄστρακον ἡ ἰσχύς μου,
καὶ ἡ γλῶσσά μου κεκόλληται τῷ λάρυγγί μου,
καὶ εἰς χοῦν θανάτου κατήγαγές με.
17 ὅτι ἐκύκλωσάν με κύνες πολλοί,
συναγωγὴ πονηρευομένων²⁴ περιέσχον με,
ὤρυξαν²⁵ χεῖράς μου καὶ πόδας.
18 ἐξηρίθμησα πάντα τὰ ὀστᾶ μου,
αὐτοὶ δὲ κατενόησαν καὶ ἐπεῖδόν²⁶ με.
19 διεμερίσαντο τὰ ἱμάτιά μου ἑαυτοῖς

17. ἡ ἐλπίς is the nominative subject of an implied ἐστίν (Wallace 39–40; BDF §§127–28): "my hope is."
18. ἐπερρίφην is aor.-ind.-pass.-1-sg. < ἐπιρρίπτω.
19. θλῖψις is the nominative subject of an implied ἐστίν (Wallace 39–40; BDF §§127–28): "affliction is."
20. ὁ βοηθῶν is a substantival participle (Wallace 619–21; BDF §413; *GNTG* §5.182); it is the nominative subject of the clause.
21. ὁ ἁρπάζων . . . ὠρυόμενος: the participles are attributive (Wallace 617–18; BDF §413; *GNTG* §5.181), modifying λέων: "a lion that snatches and roars."
22. τηκόμενος is an attributive participle (Wallace 617–18; BDF §413; *GNTG* §5.181), modifying κηρός: "wax melting."
23. ἐν μέσῳ: "within" (BDAG 635.1.b).
24. πονηρευομένων is a substantival participle (Wallace 619–21; BDF §413; *GNTG* §5.182).
25. ὤρυξαν: aor.-ind.-act.-3-sg. < ὀρύσσω: "to gouge" (*GELS* 507*).
26. ἐπεῖδόν: aor.-ind.-act.-3-pl. < ἐφοράω.

καὶ ἐπὶ τὸν ἱματισμόν μου²⁷ ἔβαλον κλῆρον.²⁸

20 σὺ δέ, κύριε, μὴ μακρύνῃς τὴν βοήθειάν μου,
εἰς τὴν ἀντίλημψίν μου πρόσχες.

21 ῥῦσαι ἀπὸ ῥομφαίας τὴν ψυχήν μου
καὶ ἐκ χειρὸς κυνὸς τὴν μονογενῆ²⁹ μου·

22 σῶσόν με ἐκ στόματος λέοντος
καὶ ἀπὸ κεράτων μονοκερώτων³⁰ τὴν ταπείνωσίν μου.

23 διηγήσομαι τὸ ὄνομά σου τοῖς ἀδελφοῖς μου,
ἐν μέσῳ ἐκκλησίας ὑμνήσω σε

24 Οἱ φοβούμενοι³¹ κύριον, αἰνέσατε αὐτόν,
ἅπαν τὸ σπέρμα Ιακωβ, δοξάσατε αὐτόν,
φοβηθήτωσαν αὐτὸν ἅπαν τὸ σπέρμα Ισραηλ,

25 ὅτι οὐκ ἐξουδένωσεν οὐδὲ προσώχθισεν τῇ δεήσει τοῦ

πτωχοῦ

οὐδὲ ἀπέστρεψεν τὸ πρόσωπον αὐτοῦ ἀπ᾽ ἐμοῦ
καὶ ἐν τῷ κεκραγέναι με³² πρὸς αὐτὸν εἰσήκουσέν μου.

26 παρὰ σοῦ ὁ ἔπαινός³³ μου ἐν ἐκκλησίᾳ μεγάλῃ,
τὰς εὐχάς μου ἀποδώσω³⁴ ἐνώπιον τῶν φοβουμένων³⁵

αὐτόν.

27 φάγονται³⁶ πένητες καὶ ἐμπλησθήσονται,
καὶ αἰνέσουσιν κύριον οἱ ἐκζητοῦντες³⁷ αὐτόν·
ζήσονται αἱ καρδίαι αὐτῶν εἰς αἰῶνα αἰῶνος.³⁸

---

27. ἐπὶ τὸν ἱματισμόν μου: with the accusative indicating the goal: "for my clothes" (BDAG 366.11).

28. ἔβαλον κλῆρον: "they cast lots" (BDAG 548*).

29. μονογενῆ: as a substantive, referring to one's soul or life (*GELS* 467*).

30. κεράτων μονοκερώτων: the Hebrew describes the horns of oxen (*ûmiqqarnê rēmîm*).

31. Οἱ φοβούμενοι is an attributive participle (Wallace 617–18; BDF §413; *GNTG* §5.181), modifying the implied subject of αἰνέσατε: "you who fear . . . praise."

32. ἐν τῷ κεκραγέναι με: the articular infinitive is used with ἐν to indicate time: "when I cried out" (Wallace 595; BDF §404; *GNTG* §5.172). με is the subject of the infinitive.

33. ὁ ἔπαινός is the nominative subject of an implied ἐστίν (Wallace 39–40; BDF §§127–28): "My praise is from you."

34. τὰς εὐχάς μου ἀποδώσω: "I will pay my vows" (BDAG 109.2.c).

35. τῶν φοβουμένων is a substantival participle (Wallace 619–21; BDF §413; *GNTG* §5.182).

36. φάγονται: fut.-ind.-mid.-3-pl. < ἐσθίω (see BDF §74.2 for this form).

37. οἱ ἐκζητοῦντες is a substantival participle (Wallace 619–21; BDF §413; *GNTG* §5.182).

38. εἰς αἰῶνα αἰῶνος: "for eternity" (BDAG 32.1.b).

28   μνησθήσονται καὶ ἐπιστραφήσονται³⁹ πρὸς κύριον
πάντα τὰ πέρατα τῆς γῆς
          καὶ προσκυνήσουσιν ἐνώπιόν σου πᾶσαι αἱ πατριαὶ τῶν
ἐθνῶν,
29   ὅτι τοῦ κυρίου ἡ βασιλεία,⁴⁰
          καὶ αὐτὸς δεσπόζει τῶν ἐθνῶν.⁴¹
30   ἔφαγον καὶ προσεκύνησαν πάντες οἱ πίονες τῆς γῆς,
          ἐνώπιον αὐτοῦ προπεσοῦνται πάντες οἱ καταβαίνοντες
εἰς τὴν γῆν.⁴²
          καὶ ἡ ψυχή μου αὐτῷ ζῇ,
31   καὶ τὸ σπέρμα μου δουλεύσει αὐτῷ·
          ἀναγγελήσεται τῷ κυρίῳ γενεὰ ἡ ἐρχομένη,⁴³
32   καὶ ἀναγγελοῦσιν τὴν δικαιοσύνην αὐτοῦ
          λαῷ τῷ τεχθησομένῳ,⁴⁴ ὅτι ἐποίησεν⁴⁵ ὁ κύριος.⁴⁶

Vocabulary

αἰνέω	to praise
ἀναγγέλλω	to announce; to report
ἄνοια, ας, ἡ	folly; madness
ἀντίλημψις, εως, ἡ	help
ἅπας, ασα, αν	all, everybody
ἁρπάζω	to snatch away
ἀφίστημι	to go away, withdraw; to keep away; to mislead

39. ἐπιστραφήσονται: in the LXX, the future and aorist passive forms tend to be used with active meanings (*GELS* 282–83): "they will turn."
40. τοῦ κυρίου ἡ βασιλεία: ἡ βασιλεία is the nominative subject of an implied ἐστίν (Wallace 39–40; BDF §§127–28): "The kingdom/kingship is the Lord's."
41. τῶν ἐθνῶν: verbs of ruling (δεσπόζει) generally take their object in the genitive (Wallace 131; BDF §177; BDAG 220).
42. οἱ καταβαίνοντες εἰς τὴν γῆν: the participle is substantival (Wallace 619–21; BDF §413; *GNTG* §5.182): "Those who descend into the earth" ("to Hades," *GELS* 367*).
43. ἡ ἐρχομένη: is an attributive participle (Wallace 617–18; BDF §413; *GNTG* §5.181), modifying γενεὰ: "the coming generation."
44. τῷ τεχθησομένῳ is an attributive participle (Wallace 617–18; BDF §413; *GNTG* §5.181), modifying λαῷ: "to the people who will be born."
45. ἐποίησεν is intransitive here: "acted" (*GELS* 568).
46. ὁ κύριος is inserted by the LXX translator; it is implied in the Hebrew.

βοήθεια, ας, ἡ	help, aid
βοηθέω	to help, furnish aid
γαστήρ, τρός, ἡ	belly, womb
δέησις, εως, ἡ	petition, prayer
δεσπόζω	to master, be master or lord
διαμερίζω	to divide
διασκορπίζω	to scatter, disperse; to waste, squander
διηγέομαι	to tell, describe
δουλεύω	to be a slave; to serve as a slave
ἐγκαταλείπω	to leave; to forsake, abandon
εἰσακούω	to listen, hear; to obey
ἐκζητέω	to seek out, search for
ἐκχέω	to pour out
ἐκμυκτηρίζω	to ridicule, deride, mock
ἐκσπάω	to draw out, pull off
ἐμπίπλημι	to cover, fill; to satisfy
ἐξαριθμέω	to count, number
ἐξουδένημα, ατος, τό	object of scorn
ἐξουδενόω	to treat with contempt; to scorn, despise
ἔπαινος, ου, ὁ	praise, approval, recognition
ἐπιρρίπτω	to throw on, throw at, add to
ἐπιστρέφω	to turn around, go back
ἐφοράω	to observe, watch over
ἑωθινός, ή, όν	in the morning, early
θλῖψις, εως, ἡ	distress, oppression, affliction, trouble
ἱματισμός, οῦ, ὁ	clothing
ἰσχύς, ύος, ἡ	strength, power, might
κατάγω	to lead/bring down
καταισχύνω	to dishonor, disgrace; to put to shame
κατανοέω	to consider, understand
κατοικέω	to live, dwell; to inhabit
κέρας, ατος, τό	horn
κηρός, οῦ, ὁ	wax
κινέω	to move, disturb
κοιλία, ας, ἡ	belly, stomach; womb; heart (the seat of the emotions)
κολλάω	to glue, join to

κράζω	to cry out, shriek; to call out
κυκλόω	to encircle, surround
κύων, κυνός, ὁ	dog
λάρυγξ, γγος, ὁ	throat
λέων, οντος, ὁ	lion
μακρύνω	to put away; to lengthen, delay, go far
μαστός, οῦ, ὁ	breast, chest
μήτρα, ας, ἡ	womb
μιμνήσκομαι	to remember; to remind; to call attention to
μονόκερως, ωτος, ὁ	unicorn
μόσχος, ου, ὁ	young bull or ox; calf
ξηραίνω	to dry up; to wither
ὄνειδος, ους, τό	disgrace, reproach, insult
ὀρύσσω	to dig, dig out
ὀστέον, οῦ, τό	bone
ὄστρακον, ου, τό	potsherd; earthenware
παράπτωμα, ατος, τό	trespass
πατριά, ᾶς, ἡ	family, clan
πένης, ητος	poor, needy
πέρας, ατος, τό	end, finish; at length, at last
περιέχω	to surround, encircle; to seize; contain
περικυκλόω	to surround
πίων, πῖον, gen. πίονος	fat, rich, fertile
πονηρεύομαι	to do evil; to behave wickedly
προπίπτω	to fall, bow down
προσέχω	to pay attention to; to be aware of
προσοχθίζω	to be angry
πτωχός, ή, όν	poor
ῥομφαία, ας, ἡ	sword
σκώληξ, ηκος, ὁ	worm; grub; maggot
ταπείνωσις, εως, ἡ	lowliness, humiliation, humble station
ταῦρος, ου, ὁ	bull
τίκτω	to give birth, bear; to produce
ὑμνέω	to sing in praise of/to, sing a hymn
χοῦς, χοός, acc. χοῦν, ὁ	dust; soil
ὠρύομαι	to roar
ὡσεί	as, like; about

2.2. ISAIAH 40:1–31

God Promises Peace to God's People

The book of Isaiah, as a whole, collects oracles associated with the eighth-century BCE prophet Isaiah ben Amoz but also includes material written for contexts that arose after Isaiah had died. Both of the selections included in this reader come from that section of the book scholars call Deutero-Isaiah. The context of the Babylonian exile appears to inform much of the material in this section of the book.

Chapter 40 introduces themes and motifs that can be found in subsequent chapters. In verses 1–11, the prophet offers God's comfort to the people: punishment is over, God's salvation will soon appear, and they will return to Zion with their God. Verses 12–31 enumerate the ways in which God is beyond comparison.

Verses 3–5 are quoted in Luke 3:4–6 (compare Matt 3:3; Mark 1:3; John 1:23). Verses 6–8 are quoted in 1 Pet 1:24–25.

1 Παρακαλεῖτε παρακαλεῖτε τὸν λαόν μου, λέγει ὁ θεός. 2 ἱερεῖς,[1] λαλήσατε εἰς τὴν καρδίαν Ιερουσαλημ, παρακαλέσατε αὐτήν· ὅτι[2] ἐπλήσθη ἡ ταπείνωσις αὐτῆς, λέλυται αὐτῆς ἡ ἁμαρτία· ὅτι ἐδέξατο ἐκ χειρὸς κυρίου διπλᾶ τὰ ἁμαρτήματα αὐτῆς. 3 φωνὴ βοῶντος[3] ἐν τῇ ἐρήμῳ Ἑτοιμάσατε τὴν ὁδὸν κυρίου, εὐθείας[4] ποιεῖτε τὰς τρίβους τοῦ θεοῦ ἡμῶν·

1. ἱερεῖς is an addition by the LXX translator. It is not in the MT.
2. ὅτι might be indicating the reason the prophet is to comfort the people (BDAG 732.4; this is how NETS glosses it): "because"; or it might be introducing the content of the speech (BDAG 732.1): "that."
3. βοῶντος is a substantival participle (Wallace 619–21; BDF §413; GNTG §5.182): "of one crying out."
4. εὐθείας: some verbs (ποιεῖτε) can take two accusatives. εὐθείας is the complement in an object-complement double accusative construction with τὰς τρίβους as the object (Wallace 181–89 [183 n. 24]; BDF §157; GNTG §5.77): "make straight the paths."

4 πᾶσα φάραγξ πληρωθήσεται καὶ πᾶν ὄρος καὶ βουνὸς ταπεινωθήσεται, καὶ ἔσται πάντα τὰ σκολιὰ εἰς εὐθεῖαν[5] καὶ ἡ τραχεῖα[6] εἰς πεδία· 5 καὶ ὀφθήσεται ἡ δόξα κυρίου, καὶ ὄψεται πᾶσα σάρξ[7] τὸ σωτήριον τοῦ θεοῦ· ὅτι κύριος ἐλάλησεν. 6 φωνὴ λέγοντος[8] Βόησον· καὶ εἶπα Τί βοήσω; Πᾶσα σὰρξ χόρτος, καὶ πᾶσα δόξα[9] ἀνθρώπου ὡς ἄνθος χόρτου· 7 ἐξηράνθη ὁ χόρτος, καὶ τὸ ἄνθος ἐξέπεσεν,[10] 8 τὸ δὲ ῥῆμα τοῦ θεοῦ ἡμῶν μένει εἰς τὸν αἰῶνα.[11] 9 ἐπ᾽ ὄρος ὑψηλὸν ἀνάβηθι, ὁ εὐαγγελιζόμενος[12] Σιων· ὕψωσον τῇ ἰσχύι[13] τὴν φωνήν σου, ὁ εὐαγγελιζόμενος Ιερουσαλημ· ὑψώσατε, μὴ φοβεῖσθε· εἰπὸν ταῖς πόλεσιν Ιουδα Ἰδοὺ ὁ θεὸς ὑμῶν. 10 ἰδοὺ κύριος μετὰ ἰσχύος ἔρχεται καὶ ὁ βραχίων[14] μετὰ κυριείας, ἰδοὺ ὁ μισθὸς αὐτοῦ μετ᾽ αὐτοῦ καὶ τὸ ἔργον[15] ἐναντίον αὐτοῦ. 11 ὡς ποιμὴν ποιμανεῖ τὸ ποίμνιον αὐτοῦ καὶ τῷ βραχίονι[16] αὐτοῦ συνάξει ἄρνας καὶ ἐν γαστρὶ ἐχούσας[17] παρακαλέσει.

5. ἔσται ... εἰς εὐθεῖαν: εἰμί with εἰς can mean "to become" (BDAG 285.6*): "will become straight." Alternatively, εἰς plus the accusative occasionally replaces the predicate nominative. This construction is a Hebraism (Conybeare & Stock §90.c; BDF §145.1; BDAG 291.8.a.β*).

6. ἡ τραχεῖα is the nominative subject of a clause with an elided verb to be supplied from context; the reader must supply ἔσται from the previous clause (see the discussion in BDF §§479–83).

7. πᾶσα σάρξ: "Every person" or "everyone" (BDAG 915.3.a*).

8. λέγοντος is a substantival participle (Wallace 619–21; BDF §413; *GNTG* §5.182).

9. σὰρξ ... δόξα: σὰρξ and δόξα are each the nominative subject of an implied ἐστίν (Wallace 39–40; BDF §§127–28).

10. LXX does not include 7b and 8a found in the MT (See the discussion in Joseph Blenkinsopp, *Isaiah 40–55: A New Translation and Commentary*, AB 19A [New York: Doubleday, 2002], 178 n. i).

11. εἰς τὸν αἰῶνα: when referring to time to come that has no end, "to eternity," "eternally" (BDAG 32.1.b*).

12. ὁ εὐαγγελιζόμενος is a substantival participle (Wallace 619–21; BDF §413; *GNTG* §5.182), specifying the subject of ἀνάβηθι: "you, who proclaim good news."

13. τῇ ἰσχύι is a dative of manner (Wallace 161–62; BDF §198; *GNTG* §5.70): "with strength."

14. ὁ βραχίων is the nominative subject of a clause with an elided verb to be supplied from the context; the reader should likely supply ἔρχεται from the previous clause (see the discussion in BDF §§479–83).

15. ὁ μισθὸς ... τὸ ἔργον are each the nominative subject of an implied ἐστίν (Wallace 39–40; BDF §§127–28).

16. τῷ βραχίονι is an instrumental dative (Wallace 162–63; BDF §195; *GNTG* §5.67): "with his arm."

17. ἐν γαστρὶ ἐχούσας: ἐχούσας is a substantival participle (Wallace 619–21; BDF §413; *GNTG* §5.182); ἐν γαστρὶ ἔχειν means "to be pregnant" (BDAG 190.2): "those who are pregnant."

12 Τίς ἐμέτρησεν τῇ χειρὶ[18] τὸ ὕδωρ καὶ τὸν οὐρανὸν σπιθαμῇ καὶ πᾶσαν τὴν γῆν δρακί; τίς ἔστησεν[19] τὰ ὄρη σταθμῷ καὶ τὰς νάπας ζυγῷ; 13 τίς ἔγνω νοῦν κυρίου, καὶ τίς αὐτοῦ σύμβουλος ἐγένετο, ὃς συμβιβᾷ[20] αὐτόν; 14 ἢ[21] πρὸς τίνα συνεβουλεύσατο καὶ συνεβίβασεν αὐτόν; ἢ τίς ἔδειξεν αὐτῷ κρίσιν; ἢ ὁδὸν συνέσεως τίς ἔδειξεν αὐτῷ;[22] 15 εἰ πάντα τὰ ἔθνη ὡς σταγὼν ἀπὸ κάδου καὶ ὡς ῥοπὴ ζυγοῦ ἐλογίσθησαν, καὶ ὡς σίελος λογισθήσονται· 16 ὁ δὲ Λίβανος[23] οὐχ ἱκανὸς εἰς καῦσιν, καὶ πάντα τὰ τετράποδα οὐχ ἱκανὰ εἰς ὁλοκάρπωσιν, 17 καὶ πάντα τὰ ἔθνη ὡς οὐδέν εἰσι καὶ εἰς οὐθὲν[24] ἐλογίσθησαν. 18 τίνι ὡμοιώσατε[25] κύριον καὶ τίνι ὁμοιώματι ὡμοιώσατε αὐτόν; 19 μὴ[26] εἰκόνα ἐποίησεν τέκτων, ἢ χρυσο-χόος χωνεύσας χρυσίον[27] περιεχρύσωσεν αὐτόν, ὁμοίωμα κατεσκεύασεν αὐτόν; 20 ξύλον γὰρ ἄσηπτον ἐκλέγεται τέκτων καὶ σοφῶς ζητεῖ πῶς στήσει αὐτοῦ εἰκόνα καὶ ἵνα μὴ σαλεύηται. 21 οὐ γνώσεσθε; οὐκ ἀκού-σεσθε; οὐκ ἀνηγγέλη ἐξ ἀρχῆς ὑμῖν; οὐκ ἔγνωτε τὰ θεμέλια τῆς γῆς; 22 ὁ κατέχων[28] τὸν γῦρον τῆς γῆς, καὶ οἱ ἐνοικοῦντες[29] ἐν αὐτῇ ὡς ἀκρίδες, ὁ

18. τῇ χειρὶ . . . σπιθαμῇ . . . δρακί . . . σταθμῷ . . . ζυγῷ are all instrumental datives (Wallace 162–63; BDF §195; *GNTG* §5.67).

19. ἔστησεν: when transitive, ἵστημι can mean "to establish" (BDAG 482.3), "to validate" (BDAG 482.4), or "to determine a monetary amount" (BDAG 482.6.b). In this context, with σταθμῷ and ζυγῷ, it likely means "to weigh."

20. συμβιβᾷ: fut.-ind.-act.-3-sg. < συμβιβάζω. In the LXX, the so-called Attic future appears regularly: the σ drops out and the vowels contract (Conybeare & Stock §§38–39 [21.b]).

21. ἢ is not the feminine nominative article but the disjunctive conjunction: "or" (Wallace 672; BDF §446; *GNTG* §§5.243–44).

22. The MT includes an additional line (for more information, see Blenkinsopp, *Isaiah 40–55*, 189 n. e).

23. ὁ . . . Λίβανος is the nominative subject of an implied ἐστίν (Wallace 39–40; BDF §§127–28).

24. εἰς οὐθὲν: here, εἰς plus the accusative substitutes for the predicate nominative (Wallace 47–48; BDF §145): "as nothing."

25. ὡμοιώσατε: aor.-ind.-act.-2-pl. < ὁμοιόω.

26. μὴ introduces a question that expects a negative answer (BDF §427; BDAG 646.3).

27. χωνεύσας χρυσίον: χωνεύσας is likely an adverbial participle indicating time; the aorist tense indicates time before that of the main verb (Wallace 623–27; BDF §418; *GNTG* §5.188): "after smelting gold."

28. ὁ κατέχων is a substantival participle (Wallace 619–21; BDF §413; *GNTG* §5.182); it is the nominative subject of an implied ἐστίν (Wallace 39–40; BDF §§127–28): "It is he who holds."

29. οἱ ἐνοικοῦντες is a substantival participle (Wallace 619–21; BDF §413; *GNTG* §5.182); it is the nominative subject of an implied εἰσίν (Wallace 39–40; BDF §§127–28): "those who dwell . . . are."

στήσας[30] ὡς καμάραν τὸν οὐρανὸν καὶ διατείνας[31] ὡς σκηνὴν κατοικεῖν,[32] 23 ὁ διδοὺς[33] ἄρχοντας εἰς οὐδὲν ἄρχειν,[34] τὴν δὲ γῆν ὡς οὐδὲν ἐποίησεν. 24 οὐ γὰρ μὴ σπείρωσιν οὐδὲ μὴ φυτεύσωσιν, οὐδὲ μὴ ῥιζωθῇ[35] εἰς τὴν γῆν ἡ ῥίζα αὐτῶν· ἔπνευσεν ἐπ᾽ αὐτοὺς καὶ ἐξηράνθησαν, καὶ καταιγὶς ὡς φρύγανα ἀναλήμψεται αὐτούς. 25 νῦν οὖν τίνι με ὡμοιώσατε καὶ ὑψωθήσομαι; εἶπεν ὁ ἅγιος. 26 ἀναβλέψατε εἰς ὕψος τοὺς ὀφθαλμοὺς[36] ὑμῶν καὶ ἴδετε· τίς κατέδειξεν πάντα ταῦτα; ὁ ἐκφέρων[37] κατὰ ἀριθμὸν τὸν κόσμον[38] αὐτοῦ πάντας ἐπ᾽ ὀνόματι καλέσει· ἀπὸ πολλῆς δόξης[39] καὶ ἐν κράτει ἰσχύος οὐδέν σε ἔλαθεν.

27 Μὴ γὰρ εἴπῃς, Ιακωβ, καὶ τί ἐλάλησας, Ισραηλ Ἀπεκρύβη ἡ ὁδός μου ἀπὸ τοῦ θεοῦ, καὶ ὁ θεός μου τὴν κρίσιν ἀφεῖλεν[40] καὶ ἀπέστη; 28 καὶ νῦν οὐκ ἔγνως εἰ μὴ ἤκουσας;[41] θεὸς αἰώνιος ὁ θεὸς ὁ κατασκευάσας[42] τὰ

30. ὁ στήσας is a substantival participle (Wallace 619–21; BDF §413; *GNTG* §5.182); it is the nominative subject of an implied ἐστίν (Wallace 39–40; BDF §§127–28): "He [is] the one who set up."

31. διατείνας is a substantival participle (Wallace 619–21; BDF §413; *GNTG* §5.182): "who stretched it out."

32. κατοικεῖν: the infinitive is indicating purpose (Wallace 590–92; BDF §390; *GNTG* §5.161): "to dwell in."

33. ὁ διδοὺς is a substantival participle (Wallace 619–21; BDF §413; *GNTG* §5.182); it is the nominative subject of an implied ἐστίν (Wallace 39–40; BDF §§127–28). With ἄρχοντας, δίδωμι means "to appoint" (BDAG 242.7): "it is he who appointed."

34. εἰς οὐδὲν ἄρχειν: εἰς οὐδὲν serves as the complement in an object-complement double accusative construction with ἄρχοντας as the object (Wallace 181–89 [especially 184.2c]; BDF §157.5; *GNTG* §5.77): "as nothing"; ἄρχειν is an infinitive indicating purpose (Wallace 590–92; BDF §390; *GNTG* §5.161): "to rule."

35. οὐ . . . μὴ σπείρωσιν . . . ῥιζωθῇ: οὐ μὴ plus the aorist subjunctive indicates emphatic negation (Wallace 468–69; BDF §365; *GNTG* §5.136): "they will in no way."

36. ἀναβλέψατε εἰς ὕψος τοὺς ὀφθαλμοὺς: an unusual construction. ἀναβλέψατε in LXX occasionally takes an accusative (*GELS* 36.1*): "lift up one's eyes"; "to look up."

37. ὁ ἐκφέρων is a substantival participle (Wallace 619–21; BDF §413; *GNTG* §5.182).

38. τὸν κόσμον: "decoration," "adornment" (BDAG 561.1).

39. ἀπὸ πολλῆς δόξης: ἀπὸ plus the genitive can indicate the cause of something (BDAG 106.5): "because of great glory."

40. ἀφεῖλεν: aor.-ind.-act.-3-sg. < ἀφαιρέω.

41. εἰ μὴ ἤκουσας: an unusual construction. Ottley offers several possible explanations for this wording (Richard R. Ottley, *The Book of Isaiah according to the Septuagint [Codex Alexandrinus]* [London: Cambridge University Press, 1904–1906], 2:301): "have you not heard?" It likely results from a very literal translation of the Hebrew.

42. ὁ κατασκευάσας is an attributive participle (Wallace 617–18; BDF §412; *GNTG* §5.181), modifying ὁ θεὸς: "who prepared."

ἄκρα τῆς γῆς, οὐ πεινάσει οὐδὲ κοπιάσει, οὐδὲ ἔστιν ἐξεύρεσις[43] τῆς φρο-
νήσεως αὐτοῦ· 29 διδοὺς[44] τοῖς πεινῶσιν[45] ἰσχὺν καὶ τοῖς μὴ ὀδυνωμένοις[46]
λύπην. 30 πεινάσουσιν γὰρ νεώτεροι,[47] καὶ κοπιάσουσιν νεανίσκοι, καὶ
ἐκλεκτοὶ ἀνίσχυες ἔσονται· 31 οἱ δὲ ὑπομένοντες[48] τὸν θεὸν ἀλλάξου-
σιν ἰσχύν, πτεροφυήσουσιν ὡς ἀετοί, δραμοῦνται[49] καὶ οὐ κοπιάσουσιν,
βαδιοῦνται[50] καὶ οὐ πεινάσουσιν.

Vocabulary

ἀετός, οῦ, ὁ	eagle, vulture
ἀκρίς, ίδος, ἡ	locust
ἄκρον, ου, τό	end; top
ἀλλάσσω	to change, exchange
ἁμάρτημα, ατος, τό	sin, transgression; error
ἀναβλέπω	to look up; to receive sight; to regain sight
ἀναγγέλλω	to report; to announce
ἀναλαμβάνω	to carry away; to take up
ἄνθος, ους, τό	flower; fragrance of flowers
ἄνισχυς, υ, gen. υος	without strength
ἀποκρύπτω	to hide, conceal; to keep secret
ἀρήν, ἀρνός, ὁ	lamb
ἄσηπτος, ον	not subject to rot
ἀφαιρέω	to take away
ἀφίστημι	to withdraw, go away
βαδίζω	to walk
βοάω	to cry out, shout

43. ἐξεύρεσις is a predicate nominative: "nor is there a searching out for."
44. διδοὺς is an attributive participle (Wallace 617–18; BDF §412; *GNTG* §5.181), modifying ὁ θεὸς (in v. 28): "giving."
45. τοῖς πεινῶσιν is a substantival participle (Wallace 619–21; BDF §413; *GNTG* §5.182).
46. τοῖς μὴ ὀδυνωμένοις is a substantival participle (Wallace 619–21; BDF §413; *GNTG* §5.182).
47. νεώτεροι is the comparative form of νέος and refers to young men (*GELS* 473).
48. οἱ δὲ ὑπομένοντες is a substantival participle (Wallace 619–21; BDF §413; *GNTG* §5.182).
49. δραμοῦνται: fut.-ind.-mid.-3-pl. < τρέχω.
50. βαδιοῦνται: fut.-ind.-act.-3-sg. < βαδίζω. In the LXX, the so-called Attic future appears regularly: the σ drops out and the vowels contract (Conybeare & Stock §§38–39 [21.b]).

βουνός, οῦ, ὁ	hill
βραχίων, ονος, ὁ	arm
ζυγός, οῦ, ὁ	scale; yoke
γῦρος, ὁ	circle, ring
διατείνω	to stretch out, extend; to exert oneself
διπλοῦς, ῆ, οῦν	double
δράξ, δρακός, ἡ	handful; hand
εἰκών, όνος, ἡ	image
ἐκλεκτός, ή, όν	chosen, elect
ἐκπίπτω	to fall; to drift; to change for the worse; to fail, weaken
ἐκφέρω	to carry/bring out
ἐνοικέω	to dwell in
ἐξεύρεσις, εως, ἡ	searching out; discovery
εὐαγγελίζω	to bring good news, announce good news; to proclaim good news
θεμέλιον, ου, τό	foundation, basis
ἱκανός, ή, όν	sufficient, competent, able
ἰσχύς, ύος, ἡ	strength, power
κάδος, ου, ὁ	jar, container (a Semitic word)
καμάρα, ας, ἡ	vault, vaulted room, arch
καταδείκνυμι	to discover and make known; to invent and teach, to introduce
καταιγίς, ίδος, ἡ	a sudden blast of wind
κατασκευάζω	to prepare, construct, build, create
κατέχω	to prevent, hinder, restrain; to hold fast; to possess; to confine
καῦσις, εως, ἡ	burning
κοπιάω	to become weary or tired; to work hard
κράτος, ους, τό	power, might
κρίσις, εως, ἡ	judgment
κυριεία, ἡ	authority, power
λανθάνω	to escape notice; to be hidden
Λίβανος, ου, ὁ	Lebanon
λύπη, ης, ἡ	grief, pain
λύω	to remove; to loosen, release
μετρέω	to measure; to give out

μισθός, οῦ, ὁ	reward, pay
νάπη, ης, ἡ	forest, wooded valley, glen
νεανίσκος, ου, ὁ	youth; young man
νέος, α, ον	young; new
νοῦς, νοός, νοΐ, νοῦν, ὁ	mind, thought, attitude
ξηραίνω	to dry up, wither
ξύλον, ου, τό	wood
ὀδυνάω	to suffer pain; to be in pain
ὁλοκάρπωσις, εως, ἡ	whole burnt offering
ὁμοιόω	to make like; to compare
ὁμοίωμα, ατος, τό	likeness; image, form
πεινάω	to hunger, be hungry
περιχρυσόω	to gold-plate
πνέω	to blow
ποιμαίνω	to shepherd, herd
ποιμήν, ένος, ὁ	shepherd
ποίμνιον, ου, τό	flock
πτεροφυέω	to grow feathers or wings
ῥίζα, ης, ἡ	root
ῥιζόω	to take root
ῥοπή, ῆς, ἡ	weight; influence
σαλεύω	to shake
σίελος, ου, ὁ	spit; spittle
σκολιός, ά, όν	curved, crooked, bent
σοφῶς, adv.	wisely
σπιθαμή, ῆς, ἡ	span (the distance between the little finger and the thumb)
σταγών, όνος, ἡ	drop
σταθμός, οῦ, ὁ	scale, balance; weight
συμβιβάζω	to advise; to conclude; to demonstrate; to unite
συμβουλεύω	to advise, counsel
σύμβουλος, ου, ὁ	adviser, counselor; advocate
ταπεινόω	to lower; to make humble, humiliate
ταπείνωσις, εως, ἡ	humiliation
τέκτων, ονος, ὁ	craftsman; builder, carpenter
τετράποδος, ον	four-footed (animals); quadrupeds
τραχύς, εῖα, ὑ	rough; uneven

τρέχω	to run
ὑπομένω	to wait for; to hold one's ground, endure; to remain
ὑψηλός, ή, όν	high, tall
ὑψόω	to lift up, raise up
φάραγξ, αγγος, ἡ	ravine, valley
φρόνησις, εως, ἡ	understanding; way of thinking
φρύγανον, ου, τό	pieces of dry wood, kindling; brush, shrub
φυτεύω	to plant
χόρτος, ου, ὁ	grass, hay
χρυσοχόος, ου, ὁ	goldsmith
χωνεύω	to cast (metal), smelt

2.3. ISAIAH 52:13–53:12

God's Suffering Servant

This selection is one of four that scholars sometimes identify as "servant songs" (see also 42:1–9; 49:1–13; 50:4–11). The servant, in most contexts in this section of the book of Isaiah, refers to the nation. That was likely the original referent here as well.

This selection had an enormous impact on the followers of Jesus as they attempted to understand Jesus's humiliation and death. Consider the following illustrations: 1 Pet 2:20–25 is influenced by 53:4, 5, 6, 9, 12; Luke 22:37 is influenced by 52:13; Acts 8:32–33 (and likely John 1:29) is likely influenced by 53:4–8; Paul likely has 53:10 in mind when he says that Christ died for our sins "according to the Scriptures" (1 Cor 15:3).

> 52:13 Ἰδοὺ συνήσει ὁ παῖς μου
> καὶ ὑψωθήσεται καὶ δοξασθήσεται σφόδρα.
> 14 ὃν τρόπον[1] ἐκστήσονται ἐπὶ σὲ[2] πολλοί
> οὕτως ἀδοξήσει ἀπὸ ἀνθρώπων[3] τὸ εἶδός σου
> καὶ ἡ δόξα[4] σου ἀπὸ τῶν ἀνθρώπων,[5]
> 15 οὕτως θαυμάσονται ἔθνη πολλὰ ἐπ᾽ αὐτῷ,
> καὶ συνέξουσιν βασιλεῖς τὸ στόμα αὐτῶν·

1. ὃν τρόπον: "in the manner in which"; "just as" (BDAG 1017.1).
2. ἐπὶ σὲ: the prepositional phrase goes with ἐκστήσονται (BDAG 350.2.b): "they will be amazed/astonished at you."
3. ἀπὸ ἀνθρώπων: with passive verbs, ἀπὸ can mean "by" (BDAG 107.5.e.β): "by human beings."
4. ἡ δόξα is the subject of a clause with an elided verb to be supplied from the context (see the discussion in BDF §§479–83); the reader must supply ἀδοξήσει from the previous clause or, perhaps, "will be absent" (which is what NETS supplies).
5. ἀπὸ τῶν ἀνθρώπων: the translation of ἀπὸ here will depend on the decision regarding which verb to supply.

ὅτι οἷς οὐκ ἀνηγγέλη⁶ περὶ αὐτοῦ, ὄψονται,
καὶ οἳ οὐκ ἀκηκόασιν, συνήσουσιν.
53:1 κύριε, τίς ἐπίστευσεν τῇ ἀκοῇ⁷ ἡμῶν;
καὶ ὁ βραχίων κυρίου τίνι ἀπεκαλύφθη;
2 ἀνέτειλε μὲν⁸ ἐναντίον αὐτοῦ ὡς παιδίον,
ὡς ῥίζα ἐν γῇ διψώσῃ,⁹
οὐκ ἔστιν εἶδος αὐτῷ¹⁰ οὐδὲ δόξα·
καὶ εἴδομεν αὐτόν, καὶ οὐκ εἶχεν εἶδος οὐδὲ κάλλος·
3 ἀλλὰ τὸ εἶδος¹¹ αὐτοῦ ἄτιμον ἐκλεῖπον παρὰ πάντας
ἀνθρώπους,¹²
ἄνθρωπος¹³ ἐν πληγῇ ὢν¹⁴ καὶ εἰδὼς φέρειν μαλακίαν,¹⁵
ὅτι ἀπέστραπται¹⁶ τὸ πρόσωπον αὐτοῦ,
ἠτιμάσθη καὶ οὐκ ἐλογίσθη.
4 οὗτος τὰς ἁμαρτίας ἡμῶν φέρει
καὶ περὶ ἡμῶν ὀδυνᾶται,

6. οἷς οὐκ ἀνηγγέλη: ἀνηγγέλη is aor.-ind.-pass.-3-sg. < ἀναγγέλλω: "those to whom it was not reported."

7. τῇ ἀκοῇ is the dative complement of ἐπίστευσεν (BDAG 816.1.a.δ).

8. ἀνέτειλε μὲν: this reading is a generally accepted conjectural reading. All of the surviving manuscripts read: ἀνηγγείλαμεν ("we announced"); this is the text included in Rahlfs's edition. This gloss makes little sense in context and is not close to the MT: *wayya'al*: "he grew up" (See the discussion and explanation in Karen H. Jobes and Moisés Silva, *Invitation to the Septuagint* [Grand Rapids: Baker Academic, 2000], 136 and 218 n. 27).

9. διψώσῃ: pres.-ptc.-act.-fem.-dat.-sg. < διψάω. It is an attributive participle (Wallace 617–18; BDF §412; *GNTG* §5.181), modifying γῇ: "a thirsty land."

10. αὐτῷ is a dative of possession: "he has."

11. τὸ εἶδος is the nominative subject of an implied ἦν (Wallace 39–40; BDF §§127–28).

12. ἐκλεῖπον παρὰ πάντας ἀνθρώπους: ἐκλεῖπον is pres.-ptc.-act.-neut.-nom.-sg. < ἐκλείπω. The participle is attributive (Wallace 617–18; BDF §412; *GNTG* §5.181), modifying τὸ εἶδος: "inferior to that of all human beings" (BDAG 306.4); or, "failing in comparison to all human beings" (Jobes and Silva, *Invitation*, 218).

13. ἄνθρωπος is the nominative subject of an implied form of εἰμί (Wallace 39–40; BDF §§127–28).

14. ἐν πληγῇ ὢν: ὢν is an attributive participle (Wallace 617–18; BDF §412; *GNTG* §5.181), modifying ἄνθρωπος: "struck down with misfortune" (BDAG 825.3*).

15. εἰδὼς φέρειν μαλακίαν: εἰδὼς is an attributive participle (Wallace 617–18; BDF §412; *GNTG* §5.181), modifying ἄνθρωπος. φέρειν is a complementary infinitive going with εἰδὼς (BDAG 694.3; Wallace 598–99; BDF §392.2; *GNTG* §5.163): "knowing how to endure sickness."

16. ἀπέστραπται: pf.-ind.-pass.-3-sg. < ἀποστρέφω.

καὶ ἡμεῖς ἐλογισάμεθα αὐτὸν εἶναι[17] ἐν πόνῳ
καὶ ἐν πληγῇ καὶ ἐν κακώσει.
5 αὐτὸς δὲ ἐτραυματίσθη διὰ τὰς ἀνομίας ἡμῶν
καὶ μεμαλάκισται διὰ τὰς ἁμαρτίας ἡμῶν·
παιδεία[18] εἰρήνης ἡμῶν[19] ἐπ᾽ αὐτόν,
τῷ μώλωπι[20] αὐτοῦ ἡμεῖς ἰάθημεν.
6 πάντες ὡς πρόβατα ἐπλανήθημεν,[21]
ἄνθρωπος τῇ ὁδῷ αὐτοῦ ἐπλανήθη·
καὶ κύριος παρέδωκεν αὐτὸν ταῖς ἁμαρτίαις ἡμῶν.[22]
7 καὶ αὐτὸς διὰ τὸ κεκακῶσθαι[23]
οὐκ ἀνοίγει τὸ στόμα·
ὡς πρόβατον ἐπὶ σφαγὴν[24] ἤχθη
καὶ ὡς ἀμνὸς ἐναντίον τοῦ κείροντος[25] αὐτὸν ἄφωνος[26]
οὕτως οὐκ ἀνοίγει τὸ στόμα αὐτοῦ.
8 ἐν τῇ ταπεινώσει ἡ κρίσις αὐτοῦ ἤρθη·
τὴν γενεὰν αὐτοῦ τίς διηγήσεται;
ὅτι αἴρεται ἀπὸ τῆς γῆς ἡ ζωὴ αὐτοῦ,
ἀπὸ τῶν ἀνομιῶν τοῦ λαοῦ μου[27] ἤχθη εἰς θάνατον.
9 καὶ δώσω τοὺς πονηροὺς ἀντὶ τῆς ταφῆς αὐτοῦ

17. εἶναι: verbs of believing (ἐλογισάμεθα) take the infinitive (BDF §397.2; Wallace treats it as a form of indirect discourse [Wallace 603–5]; GNTG §5.166; BDAG 597.1.b): "we regarded him as." αὐτὸν is the subject of the infinitive.

18. παιδεία is the nominative subject of an implied form of εἰμί (Wallace 39–40; BDF §§127–28).

19. εἰρήνης ἡμῶν: perhaps a genitive of purpose (Wallace 100–101; GNTG §5.57): "discipline for our peace."

20. τῷ μώλωπι is an instrumental dative (Wallace 162–63; BDF §195; GNTG §5.67): "by his wound."

21. ἐπλανήθημεν: passive but with an active sense (BDAG 821.2.b*).

22. παρέδωκεν αὐτὸν ταῖς ἁμαρτίαις ἡμῶν: "[the Lord] handed him over to our sins."

23. διὰ τὸ κεκακῶσθαι: the articular infinitive with διὰ normally indicates cause (Wallace 610; BDF §402.1; GNTG §5.173; BDAG 226.2.c): "because he has been afflicted."

24. ἐπὶ σφαγὴν: here, ἐπὶ indicates purpose, goal, result (BDAG 366.11): "to/for slaughter."

25. τοῦ κείροντος is a substantival participle (Wallace 619–21; BDF §413; GNTG §5.182): "the one who shears."

26. ἄφωνος is a predicate adjective with an implied form of εἰμί (Wallace 39–40; BDF §§127–28): "he was silent."

27. ἀπὸ τῶν ἀνομιῶν τοῦ λαοῦ μου: ἀπὸ can indicate cause (BDAG 107.5.a): "on account of the lawless deeds of my people."

καὶ τοὺς πλουσίους ἀντὶ τοῦ θανάτου αὐτοῦ·[28]
ὅτι ἀνομίαν οὐκ ἐποίησεν,
οὐδὲ εὑρέθη δόλος ἐν τῷ στόματι αὐτοῦ.
10 καὶ κύριος βούλεται
καθαρίσαι αὐτὸν τῆς πληγῆς·[29]
ἐὰν δῶτε περὶ ἁμαρτίας,[30]
ἡ ψυχὴ ὑμῶν ὄψεται σπέρμα μακρόβιον·
καὶ βούλεται κύριος ἀφελεῖν[31]
11 ἀπὸ τοῦ πόνου τῆς ψυχῆς αὐτοῦ,[32]
δεῖξαι[33] αὐτῷ φῶς καὶ πλάσαι[34] τῇ συνέσει,
δικαιῶσαι[35] δίκαιον εὖ δουλεύοντα[36] πολλοῖς,
καὶ τὰς ἁμαρτίας αὐτῶν αὐτὸς ἀνοίσει.[37]
12 διὰ τοῦτο αὐτὸς κληρονομήσει πολλοὺς
καὶ τῶν ἰσχυρῶν μεριεῖ σκῦλα,

28. τοὺς πλουσίους ἀντὶ τοῦ θανάτου αὐτοῦ: this clause is elliptical (see the discussion in BDF §§479–83); the reader must supply the verb from the previous clause (δώσω).

29. καθαρίσαι αὐτὸν τῆς πληγῆς: καθαρίσαι is a complementary infinitive, going with βούλεται (Wallace 598–99; BDF §392; *GNTG* §5.163). τῆς πληγῆς: the genitive case indicates that from which he is cleansed (BDAG 489.3.d).

30. ἐὰν δῶτε περὶ ἁμαρτίας: ἐὰν with the subjunctive introduces the protasis of a third-class condition. The third-class condition can indicate something likely to occur in the future, something that might occur, or something that will not occur but hypothetically could (Wallace 469–71, 663, 696–99; BDF §§371, 373; *GNTG* §5.5). δῶτε περὶ ἁμαρτίας: in this context, δῶτε means to give oneself to some purpose (BDAG 242.10): "if you offer yourselves for sin."

31. ἀφελεῖν is a complementary infinitive, going with βούλεται (Wallace 598–99; BDF §392; *GNTG* §5.163).

32. ἀπὸ τοῦ πόνου τῆς ψυχῆς αὐτοῦ: the prepositional phrase is complementary with ἀφελεῖν: "to take away from the pain of his soul."

33. δεῖξαι is a complementary infinitive, going with βούλεται in v. 10b (Wallace 598–99; BDF §392; *GNTG* §5.163).

34. πλάσαι is a complementary infinitive, going with the instance of βούλεται in v. 10b (Wallace 598–99; BDF §392; *GNTG* §5.163). πλάσαι ("to mold"), however, does not make much sense as a gloss of the Hebrew *yiśbāʿ* ("to be satisfied" or "filled"). πλῆσαι, aor.-inf.-act. < πίμπλημι ("to fill") has been conjectured as a more likely word (see Jobes and Silva, *Invitation*, 225 n. 42).

35. δικαιῶσαι is a complementary infinitive, going with βούλεται in v. 10b (Wallace 598–99; BDF §392; *GNTG* §5.163).

36. δουλεύοντα is an attributive participle (Wallace 617–18; BDF §412; *GNTG* §5.181), modifying δίκαιον: "a righteous man who serves."

37. ἀνοίσει: fut.-ind.-act.-3-sg. < ἀναφέρω.

ἀνθ᾽ ὧν[38] παρεδόθη εἰς θάνατον ἡ ψυχὴ αὐτοῦ,
καὶ ἐν τοῖς ἀνόμοις ἐλογίσθη·[39]
καὶ αὐτὸς ἁμαρτίας πολλῶν ἀνήνεγκεν
καὶ διὰ τὰς ἁμαρτίας αὐτῶν παρεδόθη.

Vocabulary

ἀδοξέω	to hold in low esteem, in contempt
ἀκοή, ῆς, ἡ	hearing, sound, report; rumor
ἀναγγέλλω	to report; to announce, proclaim, teach
ἀνατέλλω	to rise up, grow up
ἀναφέρω	to take up; to lead; to offer
ἀνομία, ας, ἡ	lawlessness; transgressions
ἀποκαλύπτω	to reveal, make known
ἀποστρέφω	to turn away
ἀτιμάζω	to dishonor
ἄτιμος, ον	unhonored, dishonored
ἀφαιρέω	to take away, remove
ἄφωνος, ον	silent, speechless
βραχίων, ονος, ὁ	arm, strength
δείκνυμι	to show, point out
δουλεύω	to be a slave, be subjected; to serve
διηγέομαι	to explain, describe
δικαιόω	to pronounce righteous, justify
διψάω	to thirst
δόλος, ου, ὁ	deceit, cunning, treachery
εἶδος, ους, τό	form, appearance
ἐκλείπω	to be inferior (BDAG 306.4*); to fail; to depart; to die out
ἐξίστημι	to astound, confuse, amaze
ἰσχυρός, ά, όν	strong
καθαρίζω	to clean, purify
κακόω	to cause harm, mistreat

---

38. ἀνθ᾽ ὧν: "because" (BDAG 88.4).
39. ἐν τοῖς ἀνόμοις ἐλογίσθη: this is a Semitic construction (BDF §145.2*): "he was reckoned among the lawless."

κάκωσις, εως, ἡ	suffering, affliction
κείρω	to cut, shave, shear
κληρονομέω	to inherit
λογίζομαι	to consider, think about; to calculate, reckon
μακρόβιος, ον	long-lived
μαλακία, ας, ἡ	sickness, disease, weakness
μαλακίζομαι	to be sick, weak
μερίζω	to divide, distribute
μώλωψ, ωπος, ὁ	wound
ὀδυνάω	to cause pain; to be in pain
παιδεία, ας, ἡ	discipline, instruction, correction
παῖς, παιδός, ὁ or ἡ	servant, slave, child
πίμπλημι	to fill
πλανάω	to cause to go astray, mislead, deceive; to wander, go astray
πλάσσω	to form, mold
πληγή, ῆς, ἡ	misfortune; blow, wound, bruise, plague
πόνος, ου, ὁ	pain, distress, affliction; labor, toil
σκῦλον, ου, τό	spoils, booty
συνέχω	to shut, stop; to hold together
συνίημι	to understand, comprehend
σφαγή, ῆς, ἡ	slaughter, butchery
σφόδρα, adv.	extremely, greatly
ταπείνωσις, εως, ἡ	humiliation
ταφή, ῆς, ἡ	burial place, burial
τραυματίζω	to wound
ὑψόω	to glorify, exalt; to lift up, raise up

2.4. MATTHEW 2:1–23

The Birth of Jesus in Herod's Kingdom

Most scholars consider Matthew to be the second of the Synoptic Gospels to be written. Papias refers to "logia" written by a Matthew in the "Hebrew dialect" (Eusebius, *Hist. eccl.* 3.39.16). The gospel as we have it, though, does not read like a translation from Hebrew. The gospel was written anonymously but was associated with Matthew the tax collector, a disciple of Jesus (10:3; 9:9), at an early date. The author has clearly made use of the Gospel of Mark. He also seems to be aware of the destruction of Jerusalem (see 22:7, for example). These considerations would likely set the time of writing sometime after 80 CE. The place of writing is frequently connected to Antioch in Syria, though other locations, such as somewhere in Galilee, have been suggested.

Chapter 2 is the opening narrative scene in the Gospel (following the genealogy). It connects Jesus to the time of Herod the Great and draws connections to events in the life of Moses. This narrative describes gentile priests/astrologers (μάγοι) bringing gifts to a newborn child whom they identify as a king; a massacre of infants initiated by Herod driving the family to Egypt until it is safe to return; and, finally, the family going to Nazareth in Galilee rather than returning to Bethlehem in Judea. This selection highlights Matthew's interest in gentile acknowledgment of Jesus and displays his concern for the ways in which the life of Jesus fulfilled scriptural prophecies.

The parallel birth narrative in the Gospel of Luke can be found in §3.1 of this reader.

1 Τοῦ δὲ Ἰησοῦ γεννηθέντος[1] ἐν Βηθλέεμ τῆς Ἰουδαίας ἐν ἡμέραις Ἡρῴδου τοῦ βασιλέως, ἰδοὺ μάγοι ἀπὸ ἀνατολῶν παρεγένοντο εἰς Ἱεροσόλυμα 2 λέγοντες[2]· ποῦ[3] ἐστιν ὁ τεχθεὶς βασιλεὺς[4] τῶν Ἰουδαίων; εἴδομεν γὰρ αὐτοῦ τὸν ἀστέρα ἐν τῇ ἀνατολῇ[5] καὶ ἤλθομεν προσκυνῆσαι[6] αὐτῷ. 3 ἀκούσας[7] δὲ ὁ βασιλεὺς Ἡρῴδης ἐταράχθη[8] καὶ πᾶσα Ἱεροσόλυμα μετ᾽ αὐτοῦ, 4 καὶ συναγαγὼν[9] πάντας τοὺς ἀρχιερεῖς καὶ γραμματεῖς τοῦ λαοῦ ἐπυνθάνετο παρ᾽ αὐτῶν ποῦ[10] ὁ χριστὸς γεννᾶται.[11] 5 οἱ δὲ εἶπαν αὐτῷ· ἐν Βηθλέεμ τῆς Ἰουδαίας· οὕτως γὰρ γέγραπται διὰ τοῦ προφήτου·[12]

6 καὶ σὺ Βηθλέεμ, γῆ Ἰούδα,

οὐδαμῶς ἐλαχίστη εἶ ἐν τοῖς ἡγεμόσιν Ἰούδα·

1. γεννηθέντος is a genitive absolute with Τοῦ δὲ Ἰησοῦ (Wallace 654–55; BDF §423; *GNTG* §5.197): "After Jesus was born."

2. λέγοντες is an adverbial participle of manner (Wallace 627–28; BDF §418; *GNTG* §5.193): "saying."

3. ποῦ introduces a direct question (BDAG 857.1.a*).

4. ὁ τεχθεὶς βασιλεὺς: the participle (τεχθεὶς) might be attributive (Wallace 617–18; BDF §413; *GNTG* §5.181), modifying βασιλεὺς: "king by birth"; or it might be substantival and the nominative subject in a double nominative subject-complement construction (see the discussion in Wesley G. Olmstead, *Matthew 1–14: A Handbook on the Greek Text*, BHGNT [Waco, TX: Baylor University Press, 2019], 21; *GNTG* §5.30): "the one who is born king."

5. ἐν τῇ ἀνατολῇ: the prepositional phrase can either be temporal ("at its rising") or locative ("in the east") (Wallace 372; *GNTG* §252).

6. προσκυνῆσαι is an infinitive indicating purpose (Wallace 590–92; BDF §390; *GNTG* §5.161).

7. ἀκούσας is an adverbial participle either indicating time; the aorist tense indicates time before that of the main verb (Wallace 623–27; BDF §418; *GNTG* §5.188): "When Herod heard"; or cause (Wallace 631–32; BDF 418; *GNTG* §5.189): "Because Herod heard."

8. ἐταράχθη: a compound subject (ὁ βασιλεὺς Ἡρῴδης ... καὶ πᾶσα Ἱεροσόλυμα) can take a singular verb (Wallace 399–402; BDF §135; *GNTG* §5.26.b).

9. συναγαγὼν is an adverbial participle indicating time; the aorist tense indicates time before that of the main verb (Wallace 623–27; BDF §418; *GNTG* §5.188): "after assembling."

10. παρ᾽ αὐτῶν ποῦ: παρ᾽ αὐτῶν is used with ἐπυνθάνετο to introduce indirect questions (BDAG 898.1*; BDF §173.3*). ποῦ introduces the indirect question (BDAG 857.1.b*): "he asked them where."

11. γεννᾶται is a futuristic present: the present tense is used for an event in the future to add connotations of immediacy or certainty (see Wallace 535–37; BDF §323; *GNTG* §5.102): "was to be born."

12. διὰ τοῦ προφήτου: "by the prophet" (BDAG 207.2.c). The quotation is primarily dependent on Micah 5:1: Καὶ σύ, Βηθλεεμ οἶκος τοῦ Εφραθα, ὀλιγοστὸς εἶ τοῦ εἶναι ἐν χιλιάσιν Ιουδα· ἐκ σοῦ μοι ἐξελεύσεται τοῦ εἶναι εἰς ἄρχοντα ἐν τῷ Ισραηλ, καὶ αἱ ἔξοδοι αὐτοῦ ἀπ᾽ ἀρχῆς ἐξ ἡμερῶν αἰῶνος.

ἐκ σοῦ γὰρ ἐξελεύσεται ἡγούμενος,[13]

ὅστις ποιμανεῖ τὸν λαόν μου τὸν Ἰσραήλ.[14]

7 Τότε Ἡρῴδης λάθρᾳ καλέσας[15] τοὺς μάγους ἠκρίβωσεν παρ᾽ αὐτῶν τὸν χρόνον τοῦ φαινομένου[16] ἀστέρος, 8 καὶ πέμψας[17] αὐτοὺς εἰς Βηθλέεμ εἶπεν· πορευθέντες[18] ἐξετάσατε ἀκριβῶς περὶ τοῦ παιδίου· ἐπὰν[19] δὲ εὕρητε, ἀπαγγείλατέ μοι, ὅπως[20] κἀγὼ ἐλθὼν[21] προσκυνήσω αὐτῷ. 9 Οἱ δὲ ἀκούσαντες[22] τοῦ βασιλέως[23] ἐπορεύθησαν καὶ ἰδοὺ ὁ ἀστήρ, ὃν εἶδον ἐν τῇ ἀνατολῇ,[24] προῆγεν αὐτούς, ἕως ἐλθὼν[25] ἐστάθη ἐπάνω

13. ἡγούμενος is a substantival participle (Wallace 619–21; BDF §413; *GNTG* §5.182); it is the nominative subject of ἐξελεύσεται: "a ruler."

14. This last clause is influenced by 2 Sam 5:2: καὶ εἶπεν κύριος πρὸς σέ Σὺ ποιμανεῖς τὸν λαόν μου τὸν Ισραηλ, καὶ σὺ ἔσει εἰς ἡγούμενον ἐπὶ τὸν Ισραηλ; or 1 Chr 11:2: καὶ εἶπεν κύριος ὁ θεός σού σοι Σὺ ποιμανεῖς τὸν λαόν μου τὸν Ισραηλ, καὶ σὺ ἔσῃ εἰς ἡγούμενον ἐπὶ Ισραηλ.

15. καλέσας is either an adverbial participle indicating time; the aorist tense indicates time before that of the main verb (Wallace 623–27; BDF §418; *GNTG* §5.188): "when he called"; or an attendant circumstance participle, referring to an action that is parallel to the main verb (Wallace 640–45; *GNTG* §5.198): "he called . . . and."

16. φαινομένου is an attributive participle (Wallace 617–18; BDF §413; *GNTG* §5.181), modifying τοῦ . . . ἀστέρος: "[the time] the star appeared" (BDAG 1046.1.b*).

17. πέμψας is likely an attendant circumstance participle, referring to an action that is parallel to the main verb (Wallace 640–45; *GNTG* §5.198): "he sent . . . and."

18. πορευθέντες is likely an attendant circumstance participle, referring to an action that is parallel to the main verb (Wallace 640–45; *GNTG* §5.198): "go and."

19. ἐπάν with the subjunctive mood (εὕρητε) introduces a temporal clause (BDAG 358*): "when you have found."

20. ὅπως with the subjunctive mood (προσκυνήσω) introduces a purpose clause (BDAG 718.2.b*).

21. ἐλθὼν is likely an attendant circumstance participle, referring to an action that is parallel to the main verb (Wallace 640–45; *GNTG* §5.198): "come and."

22. ἀκούσαντες: in context, this participle is likely adverbial, indicating time; the aorist tense indicates time before that of the main verb (Wallace 623–27; BDF §418; *GNTG* §5.188): "when they heard"; oἱ would then be the nominative subject of ἐπορεύθησαν. It could, though, be a substantival participle (Wallace 619–21; BDF §413; *GNTG* §5.182; Olmstead, *Matthew 1–14*, 27): "the ones who heard."

23. τοῦ βασιλέως is the genitive complement of ἀκούσαντες (Wallace 131–34; BDF §173; *GNTG* §5.36).

24. ἐν τῇ ἀνατολῇ: see n. 5.

25. ἐλθὼν is likely an attendant circumstance participle, referring to an action that is parallel to the main verb (Wallace 640–45; *GNTG* §5.198): "came and."

οὗ ἦν τὸ παιδίον. 10 ἰδόντες²⁶ δὲ τὸν ἀστέρα ἐχάρησαν χαρὰν²⁷ μεγάλην σφόδρα. 11 καὶ ἐλθόντες²⁸ εἰς τὴν οἰκίαν εἶδον τὸ παιδίον μετὰ Μαρίας τῆς μητρὸς αὐτοῦ, καὶ πεσόντες²⁹ προσεκύνησαν αὐτῷ καὶ ἀνοίξαντες³⁰ τοὺς θησαυροὺς αὐτῶν προσήνεγκαν αὐτῷ δῶρα, χρυσὸν καὶ λίβανον καὶ σμύρναν. 12 Καὶ χρηματισθέντες³¹ κατ᾽ ὄναρ³² μὴ ἀνακάμψαι³³ πρὸς Ἡρῴδην, δι᾽ ἄλλης ὁδοῦ ἀνεχώρησαν εἰς τὴν χώραν αὐτῶν.

13 Ἀναχωρησάντων³⁴ δὲ αὐτῶν ἰδοὺ ἄγγελος κυρίου φαίνεται κατ᾽ ὄναρ³⁵ τῷ Ἰωσὴφ λέγων·³⁶ ἐγερθεὶς³⁷ παράλαβε τὸ παιδίον καὶ τὴν μητέρα αὐτοῦ καὶ φεῦγε εἰς Αἴγυπτον καὶ ἴσθι³⁸ ἐκεῖ ἕως ἂν³⁹ εἴπω σοι· μέλλει

26. ἰδόντες is an adverbial participle either indicating time; the aorist tense indicates time before that of the main verb (Wallace 623–27; BDF §418; *GNTG* §5.188): "When they saw"; or cause: "Because they saw" (Wallace 631–32; BDF §418; *GNTG* §5.189).

27. χαρὰν μεγάλην σφόδρα: χαρὰν is a cognate accusative (Wallace 189–90*; BDF §153*); it includes the lexical root of the verb (ἐχάρησαν). With the modifiers μεγάλην σφόδρα, the construction is more emphatic: "they were very glad" (BDAG 1075.1*).

28. ἐλθόντες is an adverbial participle indicating time; the aorist tense indicates time before that of the main verb (Wallace 623–27; BDF §418; *GNTG* §5.188): "when they came."

29. πεσόντες is likely an attendant circumstance participle, referring to an action that is parallel to the main verb (Wallace 622–45; *GNTG* §5.198): "they fell down and."

30. ἀνοίξαντες is an adverbial participle indicating time; the aorist tense indicates time before that of the main verb (Wallace 623–27; BDF §418; *GNTG* §5.188): "after opening."

31. χρηματισθέντες is an adverbial participle either indicating time; the aorist tense indicates time before that of the main verb (Wallace 623–27; BDF §418; *GNTG* §5.188): "after they were warned"; or cause (Wallace 631–32; BDF §418; *GNTG* §5.189): "because they were warned."

32. κατ᾽ ὄναρ: "during a dream" or "in a dream" (BDAG 512.B.2.a*). Olmstead points out that this construction is similar to καθ᾽ ὕπνον, which occurs in the LXX and indicates the nature of an angelic appearance ("in a dream") (*Matthew 1–14*, 14).

33. ἀνακάμψαι: the infinitive is the complement of a verb of command (BDF §392.1.d*); it is indicating indirect discourse (Wallace 603–5; BDF §396; *GNTG* §5.166).

34. Ἀναχωρησάντων is a genitive absolute with αὐτῶν (Wallace 654–55; BDF §423; *GNTG* §5.197): "after they had gone."

35. κατ᾽ ὄναρ: see n. 32.

36. λέγων is an adverbial participle of manner (Wallace 627–28; BDF §418; *GNTG* §5.193); it is not a redundant participle of speaking because there is no verb of speaking associated with it. It introduces direct discourse.

37. ἐγερθεὶς is likely an attendant circumstance participle, referring to an action that is parallel to the main verb (Wallace 622–45; *GNTG* §5.198): "get up and."

38. ἴσθι: pres.-impv.-act.-2-sg. < εἰμί: "stay," "reside" (BDAG 284.3.a*).

39. ἕως ἂν with the aorist subjunctive: "until" (BDAG 422.1.a.β*).

γὰρ Ἡρῴδης ζητεῖν⁴⁰ τὸ παιδίον τοῦ ἀπολέσαι⁴¹ αὐτό. 14 ὁ⁴² δὲ ἐγερθεὶς⁴³
παρέλαβεν τὸ παιδίον καὶ τὴν μητέρα αὐτοῦ νυκτὸς⁴⁴ καὶ ἀνεχώρησεν
εἰς Αἴγυπτον, 15 καὶ ἦν ἐκεῖ ἕως τῆς τελευτῆς Ἡρῴδου· ἵνα πληρωθῇ τὸ
ῥηθὲν⁴⁵ ὑπὸ κυρίου διὰ τοῦ προφήτου λέγοντος·⁴⁶

  ἐξ Αἰγύπτου ἐκάλεσα τὸν υἱόν μου.⁴⁷

 16 Τότε Ἡρῴδης ἰδὼν⁴⁸ ὅτι⁴⁹ ἐνεπαίχθη ὑπὸ τῶν μάγων ἐθυμώθη
λίαν, καὶ ἀποστείλας⁵⁰ ἀνεῖλεν πάντας τοὺς παῖδας τοὺς ἐν Βηθλέεμ καὶ
ἐν πᾶσιν τοῖς ὁρίοις αὐτῆς⁵¹ ἀπὸ διετοῦς καὶ κατωτέρω, κατὰ τὸν χρόνον
ὃν ἠκρίβωσεν παρὰ τῶν μάγων. 17 τότε ἐπληρώθη τὸ ῥηθὲν⁵² διὰ Ἰερεμίου
τοῦ προφήτου λέγοντος·⁵³

  18 φωνὴ ἐν Ῥαμὰ ἠκούσθη,
    κλαυθμὸς καὶ ὀδυρμὸς πολύς·

40. ζητεῖν is a complementary infinitive going with μέλλει (Wallace 598–99; BDF §392; *GNTG* §5.163).

41. τοῦ ἀπολέσαι: the articular infinitive in the genitive indicates purpose (Wallace 590–92; BDF §390; *GNTG* §5.161).

42. ὁ is the masc.-nom. subject of παρέλαβεν (Wallace 211–16; BDF §251; *GNTG* §5.17), not the article of the participle.

43. ἐγερθεὶς is likely an attendant circumstance participle, referring to an action that is parallel to the main verb (Wallace 622–45; *GNTG* §5.198): "He got up and."

44. νυκτὸς is a genitive indicating duration of time (Wallace 122–24; BDF §186.2; *GNTG* §5.53): "during the night."

45. τὸ ῥηθὲν is a substantival participle (Wallace 619–21; BDF §413; *GNTG* §5.182) and the subject of πληρωθῇ: "what was spoken."

46. λέγοντος is an attributive participle (Wallace 617–18; BDF §413; *GNTG* §5.181), modifying τοῦ προφήτου: "the prophet who said/saying." Many translations treat it as redundant and do not translate it.

47. The quotation is from Hos 11:1: Διότι νήπιος Ισραηλ, καὶ ἐγὼ ἠγάπησα αὐτὸν καὶ ἐξ Αἰγύπτου μετεκάλεσα τὰ τέκνα αὐτοῦ.

48. ἰδὼν is an adverbial participle either indicating time; the aorist tense indicates time before that of the main verb (Wallace 623–27; BDF §418; *GNTG* §5.188): "when Herod saw"; or cause (Wallace 631–32; BDF §418; *GNTG* §5.189): "because Herod saw."

49. ὅτι introduces the clausal complement of ἰδὼν, reporting what Herod saw; it is similar to indirect discourse, which reports what was said (Wallace 456–58; BDF §396; *GNTG* §5.219a; cf. §5.166).

50. ἀποστείλας is likely an attendant circumstance participle, referring to an action that is parallel to the main verb (Wallace 622–45; *GNTG* §5.198): "he sent and."

51. τοὺς ἐν Βηθλέεμ καὶ ἐν πᾶσιν τοῖς ὁρίοις αὐτῆς: the article changes the prepositional phrases into attributive modifiers of παῖδας (Wallace 236; BDF §266; *GNTG* §5.16): "who were in Bethlehem and the whole region [around] it."

52. τὸ ῥηθὲν: see n. 45.

53. λέγοντος: see n. 46.

Ῥαχὴλ κλαίουσα[54] τὰ τέκνα αὐτῆς,

καὶ οὐκ ἤθελεν παρακληθῆναι,[55]

ὅτι οὐκ εἰσίν.[56]

19 Τελευτήσαντος[57] δὲ τοῦ Ἡρῴδου ἰδοὺ ἄγγελος κυρίου φαίνεται κατ᾽ ὄναρ[58] τῷ Ἰωσὴφ ἐν Αἰγύπτῳ 20 λέγων·[59] ἐγερθεὶς[60] παράλαβε τὸ παιδίον καὶ τὴν μητέρα αὐτοῦ καὶ πορεύου εἰς γῆν Ἰσραήλ· τεθνήκασιν γὰρ οἱ ζητοῦντες[61] τὴν ψυχὴν τοῦ παιδίου. 21 ὁ δὲ ἐγερθεὶς[62] παρέλαβεν τὸ παιδίον καὶ τὴν μητέρα αὐτοῦ καὶ εἰσῆλθεν εἰς γῆν Ἰσραήλ.

22 Ἀκούσας[63] δὲ ὅτι[64] Ἀρχέλαος βασιλεύει τῆς Ἰουδαίας[65] ἀντὶ τοῦ πατρὸς αὐτοῦ Ἡρῴδου ἐφοβήθη ἐκεῖ ἀπελθεῖν·[66] χρηματισθεὶς[67] δὲ κατ᾽

---

54. κλαίουσα is an attributive participle (Wallace 617–18; BDF §413; *GNTG* §5.181), modifying Ῥαχὴλ (Wallace 617–18; BDF §412; *GNTG* §5.181): "weeping."

55. παρακληθῆναι is a complementary infinitive going with ἤθελεν (Wallace 598–99; BDF §392; *GNTG* §5.163).

56. οὐκ εἰσίν: "they are no more" (BDAG 284.4*). The quotation is from Jer 38:15 LXX (31:15 MT): Οὕτως εἶπεν κύριος Φωνὴ ἐν Ραμα ἠκούσθη θρήνου καὶ κλαυθμοῦ καὶ ὀδυρμοῦ· Ραχηλ ἀποκλαιομένη οὐκ ἤθελεν παύσασθαι ἐπὶ τοῖς υἱοῖς αὐτῆς, ὅτι οὐκ εἰσίν.

57. Τελευτήσαντος is a genitive absolute with τοῦ Ἡρῴδου (Wallace 654–55; BDF §423; *GNTG* §5.197): "After Herod had died."

58. κατ᾽ ὄναρ: see n. 32.

59. λέγων is an adverbial participle of manner (Wallace 627–28; BDF §418; *GNTG* §5.193); it is not a redundant participle of speaking because there is no verb of speaking associated with it. It introduces direct discourse.

60. ἐγερθεὶς is likely an attendant circumstance participle, referring to an action that is parallel to the main verb (Wallace 622–45; *GNTG* §5.198): "Get up and."

61. οἱ ζητοῦντες is a substantival participle (Wallace 619–21; BDF §413; *GNTG* §5.182) and is the subject of τεθνήκασιν.

62. ὁ δὲ ἐγερθεὶς: ὁ is the masc.-nom. subject of παρέλαβεν, not the article of the participle (see n. 42).

63. Ἀκούσας is an adverbial participle, either indicating time; the aorist tense indicates time before that of the main verb (Wallace 623–27; BDF §418; *GNTG* §5.188): "When he heard"; or cause (Wallace 631–32; BDF §418; *GNTG* §5.189): "Because he heard."

64. ὅτι introduces indirect discourse (Wallace 456–58; BDF §396; *GNTG* §5.219a, cf. §5.166).

65. τῆς Ἰουδαίας: verbs of ruling generally take their objects in the genitive case; this is a genitive of subordination (Wallace 103–4; BDF §177; *GNTG* §§5.36, 5.41).

66. ἀπελθεῖν is a complementary infinitive going with ἐφοβήθη (BDAG 1061.1.a*; Wallace 598–99; BDF §392.1.b; *GNTG* §5.163).

67. χρηματισθεὶς is an adverbial participle, either indicating time; the aorist tense indicates time before that of the main verb (Wallace 623–27; BDF §418; *GNTG* §5.188): "after he was warned"; or cause (Wallace 631–32; BDF §418; *GNTG* §5.189): "because he was warned."

ὄναρ⁶⁸ ἀνεχώρησεν εἰς τὰ μέρη τῆς Γαλιλαίας, 23 καὶ ἐλθὼν⁶⁹ κατῴκησεν εἰς πόλιν λεγομένην⁷⁰ Ναζαρέτ· ὅπως⁷¹ πληρωθῇ τὸ ῥηθὲν⁷² διὰ τῶν προφητῶν ὅτι⁷³ Ναζωραῖος⁷⁴ κληθήσεται.

Vocabulary

Αἴγυπτος, ου, ἡ	Egypt
ἀκριβόω	to inquire diligently; to ascertain precisely
ἀκριβῶς, adv.	accurately, carefully, diligently, precisely
ἀναιρέω	to take away, destroy, kill
ἀνακάμπτω	to return
ἀνατολή, ῆς, ἡ	rising, sunrise; east
ἀναχωρέω	to go away, withdraw, return
ἀντί	(+ gen.) for, in place of, instead of
ἀπαγγέλλω	to tell, bring news, report
Ἀρχέλαος, ου, ὁ	Archelaus, the son of Herod I, ethnarch of Judea, Idumea, and Samaria from his father's death in 4 BCE to 6 CE, when he was deposed by Emperor Augustus; noted for his cruelty (BDAG 137*).

68. κατ᾽ ὄναρ: see n. 32.

69. ἐλθὼν is likely an attendant circumstance participle, referring to an action that is parallel to the main verb (Wallace 622–45; *GNTG* §5.198): "he came and."

70. λεγομένην is an attributive participle (Wallace 617–18; BDF §413; *GNTG* §5.181), modifying πόλιν: "the city called."

71. ὅπως with the subjunctive mood (πληρωθῇ) introduces a purpose clause.

72. τὸ ῥηθὲν: see n. 45.

73. ὅτι introduces either direct or indirect discourse; in this context, the choice is ambiguous (compare NRSV and ESV; see the discussion in Olmstead, *Matthew 1–14*, 39).

74. Ναζωραῖος κληθήσεται: verbs that can take a double accusative of object and complement in the active (καλέω) can end up with two nominatives when used as a passive. The word that would have been the accusative of object in the active becomes the subject in the passive (here it is the implied subject of κληθήσεται), and the accusative complement becomes a nominative complement (Ναζωραῖος; *GNTG* §5.30; Wallace suggests that καλέω can take a predicate nominative [40]). BDAG indicates that in the passive, καλέω comes close to meaning "to be" (503.1.d) and so would take a predicate nominative.

ἀστήρ, έρος, ὁ	star or planet
βασιλεύω	to rule; to be king; to make a king
Βηθλέεμ, ἡ, indecl.	Bethlehem
διετής, ές	two years old. Only in Matt 2:16.
δῶρον, ου, τό	gift, present
ἐλάχιστος, ίστη, ον	Used as the superlative of μικρός: least; very small; insignificant
ἐμπαίζω	to ridicule, mock, deceive or trick
ἐξετάζω	to scrutinize; to examine carefully
ἐπάν	(+ subjn.) when, as soon as
ἐπάνω	(+ gen.) over, above, upon, on
ἡγεμών, όνος, ὁ	governor, ruler
ἡγέομαι	to lead; to think or consider
Ἡρῴδης, ου, ὁ	Herod
θησαυρός, οῦ, ὁ	treasure, treasury
θνήσκω	to die
θυμόω	to make angry; in the passive: to be angry
Ἰερεμίας, ου, ὁ	Jeremiah
Ἰουδαία, ας, ἡ	Judea
Ἰούδας, α, ὁ	Judas; Judah
Ἰωσήφ, ὁ, indecl.	Joseph
κατοικέω	to settle, dwell, inhabit, reside
κατωτέρω, adv.	lower, below
κλαίω	to weep, cry
κλαυθμός, οῦ, ὁ	weeping, crying
λάθρᾳ, adv.	secretly
λίαν, adv.	exceedingly, very (much)
λίβανος, ου, ὁ	frankincense
μάγος, οὑ, ὁ	wise man and priest who was an expert in astrology, magician
Μαρία, ας, ἡ	Mary
μέρος, ους, τό	part
Ναζαρά, ἡ, indecl.	Also: Ναζαρέτ, Ναζαρέθ, Ναζαράτ, Ναζαράθ: Nazareth (BDAG 664*)
Ναζωραῖος, ου, ὁ	Nazarene
ὀδυρμός, οῦ, ὁ	mourning, lamentation
ὄναρ, τό	dream

ὅριον, ου, τό	boundary, border, region, district
οὗ	where, to where (really the gen. of ὅς, became an adv. of place; BDAG 732*)
οὐδαμῶς, adv.	by no means
παῖς, παιδός, ὁ or ἡ	child; slave
παραγίνομαι	to draw near, come, appear
παραλαμβάνω	to take, take with/along
ποιμαίνω	to shepherd, to nurture
ποῦ	where?
προάγω	to lead forward, go before; to elevate
προσφέρω	to bring, offer
πυνθάνομαι	to inquire, ask
Ῥαμά, ἡ, indecl.	Ramah. A city in the tribe of Benjamin, about 8 km north of Jerusalem (BDAG 903*).
Ῥαχήλ, ἡ, indecl.	Rachel
σμύρνα, ης, ἡ	myrrh. A resinous gum from a bush.
σφόδρα, adv.	very much
ταράσσω	to shake; to trouble; to stir up, disturb
τελευτάω	to come to an end, die
τελευτή, ῆς, ἡ	cease to exist, end; death
τίκτω	to give birth, produce
φαίνω	to appear, shine; to cause to shine
φεύγω	to flee, escape
χρηματίζω	to make known a divine warning; passive: to receive a warning
χρυσός, οῦ, ὁ	gold
χώρα, ας, ἡ	land (in contrast with sea), region, country (in contrast with city)

Opening of the Sermon on the Mount

This selection includes the opening verses of the so-called Sermon on the Mount. These words are part of Jesus's first discourse (Matthew includes five of these discourses in his gospel, perhaps alluding to the five books of Moses: 5:1–7:27; 10:5–42; 13:1–52; 18:1–35; 24:3–25:46). Verses 1–12 offer beatitudes; verses 13–16 include short teachings; verses 17–20 illustrate this gospel's distinctive concern for the role of Torah in the lives of Jesus's followers.

1 Ἰδὼν[1] δὲ τοὺς ὄχλους ἀνέβη εἰς τὸ ὄρος, καὶ καθίσαντος[2] αὐτοῦ προσῆλθαν αὐτῷ οἱ μαθηταὶ αὐτοῦ· 2 καὶ ἀνοίξας[3] τὸ στόμα αὐτοῦ ἐδί-δασκεν[4] αὐτοὺς λέγων·[5]

1. Ἰδὼν is an adverbial participle indicating time (Wallace 623–27; BDF §418; *GNTG* §5.188); the aorist tense indicates time before that of the main verb: "when he saw."
2. καθίσαντος is a genitive absolute with αὐτοῦ (Wallace 654–55; BDF §423*; *GNTG* §5.197). Genitive absolutes are frequently temporal; the aorist tense indicates time before that of the main verb: "after he sat down."
3. ἀνοίξας is either an adverbial participle indicating time (Wallace 623–27; BDF §418; *GNTG* §5.188); the aorist tense indicates time before that of the main verb: "after opening"; or an attendant circumstance participle, referring to an action that is parallel to the main verb (Wallace 640–45; *GNTG* §5.198): he opened his mouth . . . and."
4. ἐδίδασκεν: impf.-ind.-act.-3-sg. < διδάσκω.
5. λέγων: verbs of speaking (ἐδίδασκεν) will sometimes be supplemented with an adverbial participle. This participle is called "redundant" or "pleonastic"; it is a kind of participle of means (Wallace 649–50; BDF §420; *GNTG* §5.199). When the redundant participle introduces direct discourse, translators sometimes leave the participle untranslated; the presence of the participle in Greek is reflected in English by the use of quotation marks.

3   Μακάριοι⁶ οἱ πτωχοὶ τῷ πνεύματι,
    ὅτι αὐτῶν ἐστιν ἡ βασιλεία τῶν οὐρανῶν.

4   μακάριοι οἱ πενθοῦντες,⁷
    ὅτι αὐτοὶ παρακληθήσονται.⁸

5   μακάριοι οἱ πραεῖς,
    ὅτι αὐτοὶ κληρονομήσουσιν τὴν γῆν.

6   μακάριοι οἱ πεινῶντες καὶ διψῶντες⁹ τὴν δικαιοσύνην,
    ὅτι αὐτοὶ χορτασθήσονται.

7   μακάριοι οἱ ἐλεήμονες,
    ὅτι αὐτοὶ ἐλεηθήσονται.

8   μακάριοι οἱ καθαροὶ τῇ καρδίᾳ,
    ὅτι αὐτοὶ τὸν θεὸν ὄψονται.

9   μακάριοι οἱ εἰρηνοποιοί,
    ὅτι αὐτοὶ υἱοὶ¹⁰ θεοῦ κληθήσονται.

10 μακάριοι οἱ δεδιωγμένοι¹¹ ἕνεκεν δικαιοσύνης,
    ὅτι αὐτῶν ἐστιν ἡ βασιλεία τῶν οὐρανῶν.

11 μακάριοί ἐστε¹²

6. Μακάριοι is a predicate adjective in a clause with an implied εἰσίν (Wallace 39–40; BDF §§127–28): "blessed are"; or "happy are." Each of the beatitudes in vv. 3–10 uses this structure.

7. οἱ πενθοῦντες is a substantival participle (Wallace 619–21; BDF §413; *GNTG* §5.182) and the subject of the clause with the implied verb: "those who mourn."

8. παρακληθήσονται: this verb is likely a so-called divine passive: the implied agent of the verb is God (Wallace 437–38; BDF §§130.1, 313). Also, χορτασθήσονται (v. 6), ἐλεηθήσονται (v. 7), and κληθήσονται (v. 9).

9. οἱ πεινῶντες καὶ διψῶντες are substantival participles (Wallace 619–21; BDF §413; *GNTG* §5.182). The article is connected to both participles (Wallace 270–83): "those who hunger and thirst."

10. αὐτοὶ υἱοὶ θεοῦ κληθήσονται: verbs that can take a double accusative of object and complement in the active (καλέω) can end up with two nominatives when used as a passive. The word that would have been the accusative of object in the active becomes the subject in the passive (αὐτοὶ), and the accusative complement becomes a nominative complement (υἱοὶ; *GNTG* §5.30; Wallace suggests that καλέω can take a predicate nominative [40]). BDAG indicates that in the passive, καλέω comes close to meaning "to be" (503.1.d) and so would take a predicate nominative.

11. οἱ δεδιωγμένοι is a substantival participle (Wallace 619–21; BDF §413; *GNTG* §5.182); no agent is supplied.

12. μακάριοί ἐστε: notice the change from clauses with implied verbs to second-person plural declarative statements.

ὅταν[13] ὀνειδίσωσιν ὑμᾶς καὶ διώξωσιν καὶ εἴπωσιν πᾶν πονηρὸν καθ᾽[14] ὑμῶν ψευδόμενοι[15] ἕνεκεν ἐμοῦ.

12   χαίρετε καὶ ἀγαλλιᾶσθε, ὅτι ὁ μισθὸς[16] ὑμῶν πολὺς ἐν τοῖς οὐρανοῖς· οὕτως γὰρ ἐδίωξαν τοὺς προφήτας τοὺς πρὸ ὑμῶν.[17]

13 Ὑμεῖς ἐστε τὸ ἅλας τῆς γῆς· ἐὰν[18] δὲ τὸ ἅλας μωρανθῇ,[19] ἐν τίνι[20] ἀλισθήσεται; εἰς οὐδὲν ἰσχύει ἔτι[21] εἰ μὴ[22] βληθὲν[23] ἔξω καταπατεῖσθαι[24] ὑπὸ τῶν ἀνθρώπων.

13. ὅταν with the subjunctive introduces an indefinite temporal clause; the aorist tense indicates the action of the subordinate clause precedes the action of the main clause (BDAG 730.1.a.β*; Wallace 479; BDF §§381–82, 455; *GNTG* §§5.140, 228): "when."

14. καθ᾽ with the genitive and after verbs that express hostile action means "against" (BDAG 511.A.2.b.β*).

15. ψευδόμενοι is an adverbial participle likely indicating manner (Wallace 627–28; BDF §418; *GNTG* §5.193).

16. ὁ μισθὸς is the nominative subject of an implied ἐστίν (Wallace 39–40; BDF §§127–28).

17. τοὺς πρὸ ὑμῶν: the article changes the prepositional phrase into an attributive modifier of τοὺς προφήτας (Wallace 236; BDF §266; *GNTG* §§5.16, 251*): "who were before you."

18. ἐὰν with the subjunctive (μωρανθῇ) introduces the protasis of a third-class condition. The third-class condition can indicate something likely to occur in the future, something that might occur, or something that will not occur but hypothetically could (Wallace 469–71, 663, 696–99; BDF §§371, 373; *GNTG* §5.237).

19. μωραίνω typically means to make foolish or, in the passive, to become foolish (BDAG 663); here it likely means something like "become tasteless" (BDAG 663.2). For its meaning in this context, see the discussion in Olmstead, *Matthew 1–14*, 82.

20. ἐν τίνι is an instrumental prepositional phrase: "by what means" (BDAG 328.5*).

21. εἰς οὐδὲν ἰσχύει ἔτι: "it is no longer good for anything" (BDAG 484.2.a*).

22. εἰ μή: "except." We are likely to understand ἰσχύει as the implied finite verb for this clause (BDF §428.3*; §479; Olmstead, *Matthew 1–14*, 83).

23. βληθέν: aor.-ptc.-pass.-neut.-acc.-sg. < βάλλω. The participle might be an adverbial participle indicating time (Wallace 623–27; BDF §418; *GNTG* §5.188); the aorist tense indicates time before that of the main verb; or, it might be an attendant circumstance participle where the action of the participle is seen as parallel to that of the main verb (Wallace 640–45; *GNTG* §5.198). In either case, the translation will be something like: "to be thrown out . . . and . . . trampled on" (see the discussion in Olmstead, *Matthew 1–14*, 83).

24. καταπατεῖσθαι is likely a complementary infinitive going with an implied ἰσχύει (Wallace 598–99; BDF §392; *GNTG* §5.163; Olmstead, *Matthew 1–14*, 83). BDF suggests this particular infinite is an infinitive of purpose (§390.3*).

14 Ὑμεῖς ἐστε τὸ φῶς τοῦ κόσμου. οὐ δύναται πόλις κρυβῆναι²⁵ ἐπάνω ὄρους κειμένη·²⁶ 15 οὐδὲ καίουσιν²⁷ λύχνον καὶ τιθέασιν αὐτὸν ὑπὸ τὸν μόδιον ἀλλ᾽ ἐπὶ τὴν λυχνίαν, καὶ λάμπει πᾶσιν τοῖς ἐν τῇ οἰκίᾳ.²⁸ 16 οὕτως λαμψάτω τὸ φῶς ὑμῶν ἔμπροσθεν τῶν ἀνθρώπων, ὅπως²⁹ ἴδωσιν ὑμῶν τὰ καλὰ ἔργα καὶ δοξάσωσιν τὸν πατέρα ὑμῶν τὸν ἐν τοῖς οὐρανοῖς.³⁰

17 Μὴ νομίσητε³¹ ὅτι ἦλθον καταλῦσαι³² τὸν νόμον ἢ τοὺς προφήτας· οὐκ ἦλθον καταλῦσαι ἀλλὰ πληρῶσαι. 18 ἀμὴν γὰρ λέγω ὑμῖν· ἕως ἂν³³ παρέλθῃ³⁴ ὁ οὐρανὸς καὶ ἡ γῆ, ἰῶτα ἓν ἢ μία κεραία οὐ μὴ³⁵ παρέλθῃ ἀπὸ τοῦ νόμου, ἕως ἂν πάντα γένηται. 19 ὃς ἐὰν³⁶ οὖν λύσῃ μίαν τῶν ἐντολῶν τούτων τῶν ἐλαχίστων καὶ διδάξῃ οὕτως τοὺς ἀνθρώπους, ἐλάχιστος

25. κρυβῆναι is a complementary infinitive going with δύναται (Wallace 598–99; BDF §392; *GNTG* §5.163).

26. κειμένη could be an attributive participle (Wallace 617–18; BDF §413; *GNTG* §5.181), modifying πόλις: "a city set on a mountain"; or, an adverbial participle indicating condition (Wallace 632–33; BDF §418; *GNTG* §5.190): "a city, if it is set on a mountain."

27. καίουσιν is an indefinite plural; it has no expressed subject (Wallace 402–3; BDF §130): "[No one] lights."

28. πᾶσιν τοῖς ἐν τῇ οἰκίᾳ: πᾶσιν should probably be read as a substantive: "all." τοῖς ἐν τῇ οἰκίᾳ: the article changes the prepositional phrase into an attributive modifier of πᾶσιν (BDAG 782.1.b.β.ꜣ*; Wallace 236; BDF §266; *GNTG* §5.16; see the discussion in Olmstead, *Matthew 1–14*, 84): "to all who are in the house."

29. ὅπως with the subjunctive (ἴδωσιν) introduces a purpose clause (Wallace 676; BDF §369; *GNTG* §5.134, 229).

30. τὸν ἐν τοῖς οὐρανοῖς: the article changes the prepositional phrase into an attributive modifier of πατέρα (Wallace 236; BDF §266; *GNTG* §5.16): "who is in the heavens."

31. Μὴ νομίσητε: Μὴ with the aorist subjunctive creates the prohibitive subjunctive; a negative command (Wallace 469; BDF §364; *GNTG* §5.141).

32. καταλῦσαι . . . καταλῦσαι . . . πληρῶσαι: these infinitives indicate purpose (Wallace 590–92; BDF §390; *GNTG* §5.161).

33. ἕως ἂν with the subjunctive (παρέλθῃ) introduces an indefinite temporal clause (Wallace 479–80; BDF §383; *GNTG* §5.140, 228): "until."

34. παρέλθῃ: a compound subject (ὁ οὐρανὸς καὶ ἡ γῆ) can take a singular verb (Wallace 399–402; BDF §135; *GNTG* §5.26.b).

35. οὐ μὴ with the aorist subjunctive (παρέλθῃ) indicates an emphatic negation, the strongest form of negation in Greek (Wallace 468–69; BDF §365; *GNTG* §5.136).

36. ὃς ἐὰν introduces two indefinite relative clauses (Wallace 478–79, 571; BDF §380; *GNTG* §§5.139, 216); it is the subject of both λύσῃ and διδάξῃ. The whole clause (ὃς ἐὰν . . . ἀνθρώπους) is the subject of κληθήσεται (Olmstead, *Matthew 1–14*, 87).

κληθήσεται³⁷ ἐν τῇ βασιλείᾳ τῶν οὐρανῶν· ὃς δ’ ἂν³⁸ ποιήσῃ καὶ διδάξῃ,³⁹ οὗτος μέγας κληθήσεται ἐν τῇ βασιλείᾳ τῶν οὐρανῶν.⁴⁰

20 Λέγω γὰρ ὑμῖν ὅτι⁴¹ ἐὰν⁴² μὴ περισσεύσῃ ὑμῶν ἡ δικαιοσύνη πλεῖον⁴³ τῶν γραμματέων καὶ Φαρισαίων, οὐ μὴ⁴⁴ εἰσέλθητε εἰς τὴν βασιλείαν τῶν οὐρανῶν.

Vocabulary

ἀγαλλιάω	to exult, rejoice
ἅλας, ατος, τό	salt
ἁλίζω	to salt; passive: to be made salty

37. ἐλάχιστος κληθήσεται: verbs that can take a double accusative of object and complement in the active (καλέω) can end up with two nominatives when used as a passive. The word that would have been the accusative of object in the active becomes the subject in the passive (the relative clause [ὃς ἐὰν . . . ἀνθρώπους]), and the accusative complement becomes a nominative complement (ἐλάχιστος; *GNTG* §5.30; Wallace suggests that καλέω can take a predicate nominative [40]). BDAG indicates that in the passive, καλέω comes close to meaning "to be" (503.1.d) and so would take a predicate nominative. The structure repeats in the next clause. κληθήσεται is perhaps a divine passive (Wallace 437–38; BDF §§130.1, 313).

38. ὃς . . . ἂν is similar to, and not different in meaning from, ὃς ἐάν. ὃς . . . ἂν is the nominative subject of ποιήσῃ and διδάξῃ.

39. ποιήσῃ and διδάξῃ: have as an implied object (see the discussion in BDF §§479–83): μίαν τῶν ἐντολῶν τούτων τῶν ἐλαχίστων.

40. ὃς δ’ ἂν ποιήσῃ καὶ διδάξῃ, οὗτος μέγας κληθήσεται ἐν τῇ βασιλείᾳ τῶν οὐρανῶν. This clause is omitted in some manuscripts. See the discussion in Olmstead, *Matthew 1–14*, 88.

41. ὅτι could be introducing indirect discourse (as translated in the NIV 2011); or direct discourse (as translated in the NRSV). See the discussion in Wallace 456.

42. ἐάν with the subjunctive (περισσεύσῃ) introduces the protasis of a third-class condition. The third-class condition can indicate something likely to occur in the future, something that might occur, or something that will not occur but hypothetically could (Wallace 469–71, 663, 696–99; BDF §§371, 373; *GNTG* §5.237).

43. πλεῖον: the comparative adjective might be combined with τῶν γραμματέων καὶ Φαρισαίων as genitives of comparison: "greater than the Scribes and Pharisees" (Wallace 110–12; BDF §185; *GNTG* §5.51). It is also possible that the sentence is elliptical (with the reader being expected to supply τὴν δικαιοσύνην; see the discussion in BDF §§479–83). In this case, the comparative adjective would be functioning adverbially: "greatly" (see the discussion in Olmstead, *Matthew 1–14*, 89; BDAG 849.2.b.β*; BDF §185.1). BDF also indicates that πλεῖον with περισσεύσῃ heightens the comparison (§246*).

44. οὐ μὴ with the aorist subjunctive (εἰσέλθητε) indicates an emphatic negation, the strongest form of negation in Greek (Wallace 468–69; BDF §365; *GNTG* §5.136).

διψάω	to thirst
διώκω	to pursue, persecute
εἰρηνοποιός, οῦ, ὁ	peacemaker
ἐλάχιστος, ίστη, ον	least; very small; insignificant. The superlative of μικρός.
ἐλεέω	to show mercy; in the passive, find or be shown mercy (BDAG 315)
ἐλεήμων, ον, gen. -ονος	pitiful, merciful
ἔμπροσθεν	(+ gen.) before, in front of
ἕνεκα (ἕνεκεν)	(+ gen.) because of, for the sake of
ἐπάνω	(+ gen.) over, above, upon, on
ἰσχύω	to be able, be strong
ἰῶτα, τό	iota, smallest letter of the alphabet.
καθαρός, ά, όν	clean, pure, purity
καθίζω	to sit, set, place
καίω	to burn, kindle, light; to cauterize
καταλύω	to destroy, lodge
καταπατέω	to trample on, oppress
κεῖμαι	to lie down; to lie or be set on
κεραία	small stroke (of a letter). Anything that projects like a horn; a hook as part of a letter, a serif, or accents and breathings (BDAG 540).
κληρονομέω	to inherit
κρύπτω	to hide
λάμπω	to shine
λυχνία, ας, ἡ	lampstand, candlestick
λύχνος, ου, ὁ	lamp
λύω	to loosen, release; to melt
μισθός, οῦ, ὁ	wages; reward, recompense
μόδιος, ίου, ὁ	basket (for grain). A Latin loan word.
νομίζω	to think, suppose; to be customary
ὀνειδίζω	to reproach
παρέρχομαι	to pass by, pass away
πεινάω	to be hungry
πενθέω	to mourn
περισσεύω	to abound
πραΰς, πραεῖα, πραΰ	gentle, humble, meek

πρό	(+ gen.) before, above
πτωχός, ή, όν	poor
χορτάζω	to feed, fill
ψεύδομαι	to lie; to be wrong

2.6. ACTS 4:1–22

Peter's and John's Apology

The Acts of the Apostles is the second volume in a two-volume work attributed to Luke, the companion of Paul (Col 4:14; 2 Tim 4:11; Phlm 24). Both volumes address a certain Theophilus (Luke 1:3; Acts 1:1), and in the beginning of volume 2, the author refers to volume 1 (Acts 1:1). The place of composition is unknown. Because the author clearly uses the Gospel of Mark in composing his own gospel, and because he seems to be aware of the destruction of Jerusalem (see 19:41–44 and 21:20–24, for example), both volumes must have been written after that work.

This second volume illustrates events from the life of the first generation of Christ followers, focusing, in particular, on Peter and Paul. In chapter 4, we find Peter and John on trial before the religious leaders in Jerusalem. After their arrest, they are given a hearing and released with a warning against continuing to teach about Jesus. The details in this scene fulfill Jesus's prediction, found in Luke's Gospel, that the disciples would be put on trial but would be supplied with the words they needed to say by the Holy Spirit (12:11–12; §3.2 in this reader).

1 Λαλούντων δὲ αὐτῶν[1] πρὸς[2] τὸν λαὸν ἐπέστησαν αὐτοῖς οἱ ἱερεῖς καὶ ὁ στρατηγὸς τοῦ ἱεροῦ καὶ οἱ Σαδδουκαῖοι, 2 διαπονούμενοι[3] διὰ τὸ

---

1. Λαλούντων . . . αὐτῶν is a genitive absolute (Wallace 654–55; BDF §423; GNTG §197): "while they were speaking."
2. πρὸς is used here with a verb of speaking to indicate the addressee (BDAG 874.3.a.ε). Luke often uses this construction rather than the dative case (Martin M. Culy, Mikeal C. Parsons, and Joshua J. Stigall, *Luke: A Handbook on the Greek Text*, BHGNT [Waco, TX: Baylor University Press, 2010], 76, referencing p. 14).
3. διαπονούμενοι is an adverbial participle, indicating either cause, providing the reason the leaders arrest Peter and John (Wallace 631–32; BDF §418; GNTG §189): "because they

διδάσκειν αὐτοὺς τὸν λαὸν καὶ καταγγέλλειν⁴ ἐν τῷ Ἰησοῦ τὴν ἀνάστασιν τὴν ἐκ νεκρῶν,⁵ 3 καὶ ἐπέβαλον αὐτοῖς τὰς χεῖρας καὶ ἔθεντο εἰς τήρησιν εἰς τὴν αὔριον·⁶ ἦν γὰρ ἑσπέρα ἤδη. 4 πολλοὶ δὲ τῶν ἀκουσάντων⁷ τὸν λόγον ἐπίστευσαν καὶ ἐγενήθη ὁ ἀριθμὸς τῶν ἀνδρῶν ὡς⁸ χιλιάδες πέντε.

5 Ἐγένετο δὲ⁹ ἐπὶ τὴν αὔριον συναχθῆναι αὐτῶν τοὺς ἄρχοντας καὶ τοὺς πρεσβυτέρους καὶ τοὺς γραμματεῖς¹⁰ ἐν Ἰερουσαλήμ, 6 καὶ Ἄννας ὁ ἀρχιερεὺς καὶ Καϊάφας καὶ Ἰωάννης καὶ Ἀλέξανδρος καὶ ὅσοι ἦσαν ἐκ γένους ἀρχιερατικοῦ,¹¹ 7 καὶ στήσαντες¹² αὐτοὺς ἐν τῷ μέσῳ ἐπυνθάνοντο· ἐν ποίᾳ δυνάμει ἢ ἐν ποίῳ ὀνόματι¹³ ἐποιήσατε τοῦτο ὑμεῖς; 8 Τότε

---

were annoyed [on account of]"; or manner, expressing attitude or emotion (Wallace 627–28; BDF §418; *GNTG* §5.193): "annoyed."

4. διὰ τὸ διδάσκειν αὐτοὺς . . . καταγγέλλειν: the articular infinitives with διὰ are indicating cause (Wallace 596–97, 610; BDF §402; *GNTG* §5.173). αὐτοὺς is the accusative subject of the infinitives: "because they were teaching . . . and announcing."

5. τὴν ἐκ νεκρῶν: The article turns the prepositional phrase into an attributive modifier of τὴν ἀνάστασιν (Wallace 236; BDF §266; *GNTG* §5.16; Mikeal C. Parsons and Martin M. Culy, *Acts: A Handbook on the Greek Text*, BHGNT [Waco, TX: Baylor University Press, 2003], 64): "the resurrection from the dead."

6. εἰς τὴν αὔριον: "until tomorrow" (BDAG 289.2).

7. τῶν ἀκουσάντων is a substantival participle (Wallace 619–21; BDF §413; *GNTG* §5.182) and is a partitive genitive (Wallace 84–86; BDF §164; *GNTG* §5.47) going with πολλοὶ.

8. With numerals, ὡς indicates "about," "approximately," or "nearly" (BDAG 1105.6).

9. Ἐγένετο δὲ and, more frequently, καὶ ἐγένετο are influenced by Hebrew syntax that appears frequently in the LXX. The phrase occurs at the beginning of sentences to introduce a time-frame within which an event took place in the past (*GELS* 131.6; BDAG 198.4.f; BDF §442.5; *GNTG* §5.92.c.1). Older translations (cf. KJV) translated the phrase something like, "and it came to pass"; more recent translations (cf. NIV, NRSV) leave the phrase untranslated, only translating the temporal expression that follows; in this case: "on the next day."

10. συναχθῆναι αὐτῶν τοὺς ἄρχοντας καὶ τοὺς πρεσβυτέρους καὶ τοὺς γραμματεῖς: an infinitive clause is one type of construction that frequently follows ἐγένετο δὲ (BDAG 198.4.f). τοὺς ἄρχοντας καὶ τοὺς πρεσβυτέρους καὶ τοὺς γραμματεῖς is the compound accusative subject of the infinitive: "[on the next day,] their rulers and elders and scribes assembled."

11. Ἄννας . . . ἀρχιερατικοῦ: This whole clause is the nominative subject of ἐπυνθάνοντο.

12. στήσαντες is either an adverbial participle indicating time; the aorist tense indicates time before that of the main verb (Wallace 623–27; BDF §418; *GNTG* §5.188): "After making them stand"; or an attendant circumstance participle, referring to an action that is parallel to the main verb (Wallace 640–45; *GNTG* §5.198): "they made them stand and."

13. ἐν ποίᾳ δυνάμει ἢ ἐν ποίῳ ὀνόματι: "by whose/what authority or by whose name." The clause is direct discourse.

Πέτρος πλησθεὶς[14] πνεύματος ἁγίου εἶπεν πρὸς[15] αὐτούς· ἄρχοντες[16] τοῦ λαοῦ καὶ πρεσβύτεροι, 9 εἰ ἡμεῖς σήμερον ἀνακρινόμεθα ἐπὶ εὐεργεσίᾳ ἀνθρώπου[17] ἀσθενοῦς ἐν τίνι[18] οὗτος σέσωται, 10 γνωστὸν ἔστω πᾶσιν ὑμῖν καὶ παντὶ τῷ λαῷ Ἰσραὴλ ὅτι ἐν τῷ ὀνόματι Ἰησοῦ Χριστοῦ τοῦ Ναζωραίου ὃν ὑμεῖς ἐσταυρώσατε, ὃν ὁ θεὸς ἤγειρεν ἐκ νεκρῶν, ἐν τούτῳ[19] οὗτος[20] παρέστηκεν ἐνώπιον ὑμῶν ὑγιής.[21] 11 οὗτός[22] ἐστιν ὁ λίθος, ὁ ἐξουθενηθεὶς[23] ὑφ’ ὑμῶν τῶν οἰκοδόμων, ὁ γενόμενος[24] εἰς κεφαλὴν γωνίας.[25] 12 καὶ οὐκ ἔστιν ἐν ἄλλῳ οὐδενὶ[26] ἡ σωτηρία, οὐδὲ γὰρ ὄνομά ἐστιν ἕτερον ὑπὸ τὸν οὐρανὸν τὸ δεδομένον[27] ἐν ἀνθρώποις ἐν ᾧ δεῖ σωθῆναι ἡμᾶς.[28]

14. An adverbial participle indicating time; the aorist tense indicates time before that of the main verb (Wallace 623–27; BDF §418; *GNTG* §5.188): "after being filled" (a scenario like this event is predicted by Jesus in Luke 12; see §3.2 in this volume).

15. πρὸς here is used with a verb of speaking to indicate the addressee (see n. 2).

16. At this point, Luke moves to direct address through the end of v. 12.

17. ἐπὶ εὐεργεσίᾳ ἀνθρώπου: in this context, ἐπὶ indicates the basis for the examination (BDAG 365.6.a); ἀνθρώπου is an objective genitive (Wallace 117–18; BDF §163*; *GNTG* §5.38): "because of a good deed [done] to a man."

18. ἐν τίνι is introducing an indirect question: "by whom"; or "how" was this man saved (BDAG 329.6).

19. ἐν τούτῳ: the antecedent is likely τῷ ὀνόματι.

20. The antecedent of οὗτος is the man healed.

21. ὑγιής: predicate adjective: "This one stands before you, healthy."

22. The antecedent of οὗτός is Ἰησοῦ Χριστοῦ τοῦ Ναζωραίου.

23. ὁ ἐξουθενηθεὶς is either a substantival participle (Wallace 619–21; BDF §413; *GNTG* §5.182), in apposition to ὁ λίθος: "the stone, the one rejected"; or an attributive participle (Wallace 617–18; BDF §412; *GNTG* §5.181), modifying λίθος: "the stone rejected" (Parsons and Culy, *Acts*, 68).

24. ὁ γενόμενος is either a substantival participle (Wallace 619–21; BDF §413; *GNTG* §5.182), in apposition to ὁ λίθος: "the stone, the one that became"; or an attributive participle (Wallace 617–18; BDF §412; *GNTG* §5.181), modifying λίθος: "the stone that became" (Parsons and Culy, *Acts*, 68).

25. εἰς κεφαλὴν γωνίας: "the cornerstone" (BDAG 209). εἰς with γίνομαι indicates a change in nature and so a new condition (BDAG 198.5.a*).

26. ἐν ἄλλῳ οὐδενὶ: "in no one else."

27. τὸ δεδομένον is an attributive participle (Wallace 617–18; BDF §412; *GNTG* §5.181), modifying ὄνομά: "that has been given" or "given."

28. δεῖ σωθῆναι ἡμᾶς: the infinitive (σωθῆναι) is used in impersonal expressions with verbs like δεῖ (BDF §393.1; Wallace describes this as a substantival use (Wallace 600–601; *GNTG* §5.164.b). ἡμᾶς is the accusative subject of the infinitive.

13 Θεωροῦντες δὲ τὴν τοῦ Πέτρου παρρησίαν καὶ Ἰωάννου καὶ κατα-
λαβόμενοι²⁹ ὅτι ἄνθρωποι ἀγράμματοί εἰσιν καὶ ἰδιῶται, ἐθαύμαζον ἐπε-
γίνωσκόν τε αὐτοὺς ὅτι³⁰ σὺν τῷ Ἰησοῦ ἦσαν, 14 τόν τε ἄνθρωπον βλέπον-
τες³¹ σὺν αὐτοῖς ἑστῶτα³² τὸν τεθεραπευμένον³³ οὐδὲν εἶχον ἀντειπεῖν.³⁴
15 κελεύσαντες³⁵ δὲ αὐτοὺς ἔξω τοῦ συνεδρίου ἀπελθεῖν συνέβαλλον
πρὸς ἀλλήλους 16 λέγοντες·³⁶ τί³⁷ ποιήσωμεν τοῖς ἀνθρώποις τούτοις;
ὅτι μὲν³⁸ γὰρ γνωστὸν σημεῖον γέγονεν δι᾽ αὐτῶν πᾶσιν τοῖς κατοικοῦσιν

29. Θεωροῦντες . . . καταλαβόμενοι: both participles are likely adverbial participles indicating time; the aorist tense indicates time before that of the main verb (Wallace 623–27; BDF §418; *GNTG* §5.188): "When they saw . . . when they perceived"; it could be indicating cause (Wallace 631–32; BDF §418; *GNTG* §189): "Because they saw . . . because they perceived."

30. ὅτι is epexegetical; it explains αὐτούς: "they recognized them—that they were with Jesus" (Parsons and Culy, *Acts*, 70).

31. βλέποντες is likely an adverbial participle indicating time; the aorist tense indicates time before that of the main verb (Wallace 623–27; BDF §418; *GNTG* §5.188): "when they saw"; but it could also be indicating cause (Wallace 631–32; BDF §418; *GNTG* §189): "since/because they saw."

32. ἑστῶτα: the participle is substantival; without the article, it is likely the complement in an object-complement double accusative construction with ἄνθρωπον as the object (Wallace 181–89 [183 n. 24]; BDF §157; *GNTG* §5.77; see the explanation in Parsons and Culy, *Acts*, 71): "standing."

33. τὸν τεθεραπευμένον is an attributive participle (Wallace 617–18; BDF §412; *GNTG* §5.181), modifying ἄνθρωπον: "who had been healed."

34. εἶχον ἀντειπεῖν: in this context, εἶχον, followed by an infinitive might indicate the ability to do something (BDAG 421.5): "they were unable to respond"; or, it might mean: "they had nothing to say in response."

35. κελεύσαντες is an adverbial participle indicating time; the aorist tense indicates time before that of the main verb (Wallace 623–27; BDF §418; *GNTG* §5.188). κελεύω is typically followed by an aorist infinitive (in this case, ἀπελθεῖν) that indicates the action to be carried out; the person receiving the order is in the accusative case (BDAG 538*): "After they ordered them to go."

36. λέγοντες: Verbs of speaking (συνέβαλλον) will sometimes be supplemented with an adverbial participle. This participle is called "redundant" or "pleonastic." It is a kind of participle of means (Wallace 649–50; BDF §420; *GNTG* §5.199). Here introducing direct discourse. When the redundant participle introduces direct discourse, translators sometimes leave the participle untranslated; the presence of the participle in Greek is reflected in English by the use of quotation marks.

37. τί is an interrogative pronoun with the deliberative subjunctive (Wallace 465–68; BDF §366; *GNTG* §5.138): "What should we do?"

38. μὲν with ἀλλ᾽ in v. 17: "To be sure . . . but" (BDAG 630.1a.β).

Ἰερουσαλὴμ φανερὸν³⁹ καὶ οὐ δυνάμεθα ἀρνεῖσθαι·⁴⁰ 17 ἀλλ᾽ ἵνα μὴ ἐπὶ πλεῖον⁴¹ διανεμηθῇ εἰς τὸν λαὸν ἀπειλησώμεθα αὐτοῖς μηκέτι λαλεῖν⁴² ἐπὶ τῷ ὀνόματι τούτῳ μηδενὶ ἀνθρώπων.⁴³ 18 Καὶ καλέσαντες⁴⁴ αὐτοὺς παρήγγειλαν τὸ καθόλου μὴ φθέγγεσθαι μηδὲ διδάσκειν⁴⁵ ἐπὶ τῷ ὀνόματι τοῦ Ἰησοῦ. 19 ὁ δὲ Πέτρος καὶ Ἰωάννης ἀποκριθέντες⁴⁶ εἶπον πρὸς⁴⁷ αὐτούς· εἰ⁴⁸ δίκαιόν ἐστιν ἐνώπιον τοῦ θεοῦ ὑμῶν ἀκούειν⁴⁹ μᾶλλον ἢ τοῦ θεοῦ, κρίνατε·⁵⁰ 20 οὐ δυνάμεθα γὰρ ἡμεῖς ἃ εἴδαμεν καὶ ἠκούσαμεν

39. γνωστὸν σημεῖον γέγονεν δι᾽ αὐτῶν . . . φανερὸν: the clause is the subject of an implied ἐστίν; φανερὸν is the predicate nominative (Wallace 39–40; BDF §§127–28; Parsons and Culy, *Acts*, 71): "that a remarkable sign has been done through them . . . is evident."

40. ἀρνεῖσθαι is complementary going with δυνάμεθα (Wallace 598–99; BDF §392; *GNTG* §5.163).

41. ἐπὶ πλεῖον: "further" (BDAG 364.4.b.γ*).

42. ἀπειλησώμεθα αὐτοῖς μηκέτι λαλεῖν: ἀπειλησώμεθα is a hortatory subjunctive (Wallace 464–65; BDF §364; *GNTG* §5.137). λαλεῖν is a complementary infinitive going with ἀπειλησώμεθα (BDAG 100*; Wallace 598–99; BDF §392; *GNTG* §5.163); it also introduces indirect discourse (Wallace 603–5; BDF §§396–397.3; *GNTG* §166): "warn them no longer to speak."

43. ἀνθρώπων is a partitive genitive with μηδενὶ: "to any human being."

44. καλέσαντες is either an adverbial participle indicating time; the aorist tense indicates time before that of the main verb (Wallace 623–27; BDF §418; *GNTG* §5.188): "after they called"; or attendant circumstance participle, referring to an action that is parallel to the main verb (Wallace 640–45; *GNTG* §5.198): "they called . . . and."

45. τὸ καθόλου μὴ φθέγγεσθαι μηδὲ διδάσκειν: the infinitives are complementary going with παρήγγειλαν (Wallace 598–99; BDF §392; *GNTG* §5.163). παρήγγειλαν with an infinitive and μή means to forbid someone to do something (BDAG 760*). These infinitives also indicate indirect discourse (Wallace 603–5; BDF §§396–397.3; *GNTG* §5.166): "they forbade them to say anything at all or teach."

46. ἀποκριθέντες is a "redundant" or "pleonastic" participle (see n. 36).

47. πρὸς here is used with a verb of speaking to indicate the addressee (see n. 2).

48. εἰ is the marker of an indirect question with the present indicative (BDAG 278.5.b.α): "whether."

49. δίκαιόν ἐστιν . . . ὑμῶν ἀκούειν: the infinitive (ἀκούειν) is used in impersonal expressions with verbs like ἐστιν in combination with certain adjectives (δίκαιόν; BDF §393.1; Wallace describes this as a substantival use [600–601]; *GNTG* §5.164.b). ὑμῶν is the object of ἀκούειν (see Wallace 131–32; BDF §170.2): "[whether] it is right . . . to listen to you."

50. Peter's response is reminiscent of Socrates's response to his Athenian judges: "Much as I have affection and love for you, men of Athens; yet I shall obey the god rather than you; and so long as I have breath and am able, I shall not stop practicing philosophy and giving advice and explanations to whichever one of you I regularly bump into, saying the sort of thing I usually do" (Plato, *Apol.* 29D [Emlyn-Jones and Preddy]).

μὴ λαλεῖν.[51] 21 οἱ δὲ προσαπειλησάμενοι ἀπέλυσαν αὐτούς,[52] μηδὲν εὑρίσκοντες[53] τὸ πῶς[54] κολάσωνται αὐτούς, διὰ τὸν λαόν, ὅτι πάντες ἐδόξαζον τὸν θεὸν ἐπὶ τῷ γεγονότι· 22 ἐτῶν γὰρ ἦν πλειόνων τεσσεράκοντα[56] ὁ ἄνθρωπος ἐφ᾽ ὃν γεγόνει τὸ σημεῖον τοῦτο τῆς ἰάσεως.[57]

Vocabulary

ἀγράμματος, ον	unlearned, illiterate
Ἀλέξανδρος, ου, ὁ	Alexander, a member of Jerusalem's high priestly family.
ἀνακρίνω	to examine
ἀνάστασις, εως, ἡ	standing up, rising, insurrection, resurrection
Ἅννας, α, ὁ	Hannas or Annas. High priest from 6–15 CE; according to John 18:13, he was the father-in-law of Caiaphas (BDAG 84*).
ἀντιλέγω	to speak in response, speak against; to deny
ἀπειλέω	to threaten
ἀριθμός, οῦ, ὁ	number
ἀρνέομαι	to deny

51. λαλεῖν is a complementary infinitive, going with δυνάμεθα (Wallace 598–99; BDF §392; *GNTG* §5.163).

52. οἱ δὲ προσαπειλησάμενοι ἀπέλυσαν αὐτούς: οἱ is the subject of ἀπέλυσαν. When followed by δέ, the article functions like a personal pronoun (Wallace 211–12; BDF §251; *GNTG* §5.17). It is not the article of προσαπειλησάμενοι, which is an adverbial participle indicating time; the aorist tense indicates time before that of the main verb (Wallace 623–27; BDF §418; *GNTG* §5.188): "after threatening, they released them."

53. εὑρίσκοντες is likely an adverbial participle indicating cause; it provides the reason the leaders let Peter and John go (Wallace 631–32; BDF §418; *GNTG* §189).

54. πῶς introduces an indirect question with the deliberative subjunctive (κολάσωνται): "how" (BDAG 901.1.b.β). τὸ turns the indirect question into the object of κολάσωνται: "because they could not find a way to punish them."

55. In this context, ἐπί indicates the basis for the examination (BDAG 365.6.a): "because of what happened."

56. ἐτῶν ... πλειόνων τεσσεράκοντα: genitives of comparison: "more than forty years old." For a discussion of the problems of this phrase, see Parsons and Culy, *Acts*, 74.

57. ὁ ἄνθρωπος ἐφ᾽ ὃν γεγόνει τὸ σημεῖον τοῦτο τῆς ἰάσεως: the whole clause is the subject of ἦν.

ἀρχιερατικός, όν	high priestly
ἄρχων, οντος, ὁ	ruler
ἀσθενής, ές	weak; weakness
αὔριον	tomorrow
γένος, ους, τό	family, race, kind; offspring
γνωστός, ή, όν	remarkable, known; friend
γωνία, ας, ἡ	corner, leader
διανέμω	to distribute, apportion, spread
διαπονέομαι	to grieve
ἐξουθενέω	to despise
ἐπιβάλλω	to lay hands on, throw
ἐπιγινώσκω	to know; to look upon, witness; to recognize, decide
ἑσπέρα, ας, ἡ	evening
ἔτος, ους, τό	year
εὐεργεσία, ας, ἡ	service, act of kindness
ἐφίστημι	to set, set over, establish; to come upon
θαυμάζω	to marvel, wonder; to admire
θεραπεύω	to serve; take care of; to heal
ἴασις, εως, ἡ	healing, health
ἰδιώτης, ου, ὁ	unlearned, ignorant person; private person, common man
ἱερεύς, έως, ὁ	priest
καθόλου, adv.	completely, entirely, at all; generally
Καϊάφας, α, ὁ	Caiaphas, high priest from 18–36 CE. According to John 18:13, he was the son-in-law of Annas (BDAG 496*).
καταγγέλλω	to announce, declare, preach
καταλαμβάνω	to take, overtake, reach
κατοικέω	to settle, dwell, inhabit
κελεύω	to command
κολάζω	to punish
μηκέτι, adv.	no longer, no more
Ναζωραῖος, ου, ὁ	Nazarene
οἰκοδόμος, ου, ὁ	builder
παραγγέλλω	to command
παρίστημι	to present, stand by

παρρησία, ας, ἡ	boldness
πέντε, indecl.	five
πίμπλημι	to fill, fulfill
ποῖος, α, ον	what kind of?
προσαπειλέω	to threaten further
πυνθάνομαι	to inquire
Σαδδουκαῖος, ου, ὁ	Sadducee
σήμερον	today
σταυρόω	to crucify
στρατηγός, οῦ, ὁ	captain, commander; chief magistrate
συμβάλλω	to meet; to consider, compare
συνέδριον, ου, τό	council; Sanhedrin
σωτηρία, ας, ἡ	salvation
τεσσεράκοντα, indecl.	forty
τήρησις, εως, ἡ	keeping, custody
ὑγιής, ές	whole, healthy
φανερός, ά, όν	known, plain
φθέγγομαι	to speak, utter
χιλιάς, άδος, ἡ	group of a thousand

2.7. ACTS 9:1–19

Saul's Call and Baptism

Saul was introduced to the readers of Acts in 8:3 as an attendant at the stoning of Stephen. This selection describes Saul's mission to Damascus to round up followers of Jesus, here identified as belonging to "the Way." On his journey to Damascus, Saul encounters the risen Lord; readers are introduced to Ananias, who will baptize Saul; Saul begins to proclaim Jesus as son of God and Messiah. This event is so important to Luke that he will narrate it two more times (22:1–21; 26:2–23).

1 Ὁ δὲ Σαῦλος ἔτι ἐμπνέων[1] ἀπειλῆς καὶ φόνου εἰς τοὺς μαθητὰς[2] τοῦ κυρίου, προσελθὼν[3] τῷ ἀρχιερεῖ 2 ᾐτήσατο παρ᾽ αὐτοῦ ἐπιστολὰς εἰς Δαμασκὸν πρὸς τὰς συναγωγάς, ὅπως[4] ἐάν[5] τινας εὕρῃ τῆς ὁδοῦ ὄντας,[6] ἄνδρας τε καὶ γυναῖκας, δεδεμένους[7] ἀγάγῃ εἰς Ἰερουσαλήμ.

1. ἐμπνέων is likely an attributive participle (Wallace 617–18; BDF §412; GNTG §5.181), modifying Σαῦλος: "breathing." It takes its object in the genitive case (ἀπειλῆς καὶ φόνου).
2. εἰς τοὺς μαθητὰς: in this context, indicating hostility (BDAG 290.4.c.α): "against the disciples."
3. προσελθὼν is likely an attendant circumstance participle, referring to an action that is parallel to the main verb (Wallace 640–45; GNTG §5.198): "went to . . . and."
4. ὅπως, with the subjunctive mood (ἀγάγῃ), introduces a purpose clause (BDAG 718.2): "so that . . . he could bring."
5. ἐάν with the subjunctive mood (εὕρῃ) introduces the protasis of a third-class condition. The third-class condition can indicate something likely to occur in the future, something that might occur, or something that will not occur but hypothetically could (Wallace 469–71, 663, 696–99; BDF §§371, 373; GNTG §5.237): "if he found."
6. ὄντας is an attributive participle (Wallace 617–18; BDF §412; GNTG §5.181), modifying τινας. BDF describes ὄντας as a supplemental participle going with εὕρῃ (a verb of cognition; §416.2*). In this context, it means to belong to someone or something and takes its object in the genitive case (BDAG 285.9): "any who belong to the way."
7. δεδεμένους is either an attributive participle (Wallace 617–18; BDF §412; GNTG §5.181), modifying ἄνδρας τε καὶ γυναῖκας: "bound"; or the complement in an object-complement

3 Ἐν δὲ τῷ πορεύεσθαι ἐγένετο αὐτὸν ἐγγίζειν τῇ Δαμασκῷ,⁸ ἐξαίφνης τε αὐτὸν περιήστραψεν φῶς ἐκ τοῦ οὐρανοῦ 4 καὶ πεσὼν⁹ ἐπὶ τὴν γῆν ἤκουσεν φωνὴν λέγουσαν¹⁰ αὐτῷ· Σαοὺλ Σαούλ, τί με διώκεις; 5 εἶπεν δέ· τίς εἶ, κύριε; ὁ δέ·¹¹ ἐγώ εἰμι Ἰησοῦς ὃν σὺ διώκεις· 6 ἀλλ᾽¹² ἀνάστηθι¹³ καὶ εἴσελθε εἰς τὴν πόλιν καὶ λαληθήσεταί σοι ὅ τί σε δεῖ ποιεῖν.¹⁴ 7 οἱ δὲ ἄνδρες οἱ συνοδεύοντες¹⁵ αὐτῷ εἱστήκεισαν ἐνεοί,¹⁶ ἀκούοντες μὲν¹⁷

double accusative construction with ἄνδρας τε καὶ γυναῖκας as the compound object (Wallace 181–89 [183 n. 24]; BDF §157; *GNTG* §5.77; Parsons and Culy, *Acts*, 170): "bound."

8. Ἐν δὲ . . . Δαμασκῷ: ἐγένετο (both with δὲ and, more frequently, καὶ) is influenced by Hebrew syntax that appears frequently in the LXX. The phrase occurs at the beginning of sentences to introduce a time frame within which an event took place in the past (*GELS* 131.6; BDAG 198.4.f; BDF §442.5; *GNTG* §5.92.c.1). Older translations translated the phrase something like, "and it came to pass"; more recent translations leave the phrase untranslated, only translating the temporal expression that follows; in this case: Ἐν δὲ τῷ πορεύεσθαι. Here, the articular infinitive is used with ἐν to indicate contemporaneous time: "while they were going along" (Wallace 595; BDF §404; *GNTG* §5.172; Parsons and Culy, *Acts*, 170). αὐτὸν ἐγγίζειν τῇ Δαμασκῷ: An infinitive clause is one type of construction that frequently follows ἐγένετο δὲ: "he drew near to Damascus." αὐτὸν is the subject of the infinitive.

9. πεσὼν is either an adverbial participle indicating time; the aorist tense indicates time before that of the main verb (Wallace 623–27; BDF §418; *GNTG* §5.188): "after he fell"; or an attendant circumstance participle, referring to an action that is parallel to the main verb (Wallace 640–45; *GNTG* §5.198): "he fell . . . and."

10. λέγουσαν is either an attributive participle (Wallace 617–18; BDF §412; *GNTG* §5.181), modifying φωνὴν: "saying"; or the complement in an object-complement double accusative construction with φωνὴν as the object (Wallace 181–89 [183 n. 24]; BDF §157; *GNTG* §5.77; Parsons and Culy, *Acts*, 171): "a voice, saying."

11. ὁ δέ: when followed by δέ, the article functions like a personal pronoun (Wallace 211–12; BDF §251; *GNTG* §5.17). Here it is the subject of a clause with an elided verb to be supplied from the context; the reader must supply εἶπεν from the previous clause (see the discussion in BDF §§479–83).

12. Parsons and Culy suggest that ἀλλ᾽ likely indicates that what follows goes against what Saul is expecting (*Acts*, 17).

13. ἀνάστηθι: aor.-impv.-mid.-2-sg. < ἀνίστημι.

14. ὅ τί σε δεῖ ποιεῖν: here, ὅ likely serves as the masculine singular article and turns the clause into the subject of λαληθήσεταί: "what is necessary for you to do will be told to you." It could also be interpreted as the neuter accusative relative pronoun serving as the direct object of ποιεῖν (Parsons and Culy, *Acts*, 172).

15. οἱ συνοδεύοντες is an attributive participle (Wallace 617–18; BDF §412; *GNTG* §5.181), modifying οἱ . . . ἄνδρες: "The men traveling with him."

16. ἐνεοί is a predicate adjective, modifying οἱ . . . ἄνδρες: "speechless."

17. μὲν . . . δὲ: "on the one hand . . . on the other hand" (see the discussion in BDAG 629).

τῆς φωνῆς μηδένα δὲ θεωροῦντες.¹⁸ 8 ἠγέρθη δὲ Σαῦλος ἀπὸ τῆς γῆς, ἀνεῳγμένων δὲ τῶν ὀφθαλμῶν αὐτοῦ¹⁹ οὐδὲν ἔβλεπεν· χειραγωγοῦντες²⁰ δὲ αὐτὸν εἰσήγαγον εἰς Δαμασκόν. 9 καὶ ἦν ἡμέρας τρεῖς²¹ μὴ βλέπων²² καὶ οὐκ ἔφαγεν οὐδὲ ἔπιεν.

10 Ἦν δέ τις μαθητὴς ἐν Δαμασκῷ ὀνόματι²³ Ἀνανίας, καὶ εἶπεν πρὸς²⁴ αὐτὸν ἐν ὁράματι ὁ κύριος· Ἀνανία. ὁ δὲ²⁵ εἶπεν· ἰδοὺ ἐγώ,²⁶ κύριε. 11 ὁ δὲ κύριος²⁷ πρὸς²⁸ αὐτόν· ἀναστὰς²⁹ πορεύθητι ἐπὶ τὴν ῥύμην τὴν καλουμένην³⁰ Εὐθεῖαν καὶ ζήτησον³¹ ἐν οἰκίᾳ Ἰούδα Σαῦλον ὀνόματι Ταρσέα·³² ἰδοὺ γὰρ προσεύχεται 12 καὶ εἶδεν ἄνδρα ἐν ὁράματι Ἀνανίαν

18. ἀκούοντες . . . θεωροῦντες: the participles are likely adverbial participles indicating cause (Wallace 631–32; BDF §418; *GNTG* §189): "since/because they heard . . . but they did not see."

19. ἀνεῳγμένων δὲ τῶν ὀφθαλμῶν αὐτοῦ is a genitive absolute (Wallace 654–55; BDF §423; *GNTG* §197). In this context, it could be concessive: "although his eyes were open"; or it could temporal: "when he opened his eyes, he saw nothing."

20. χειραγωγοῦντες is likely an adverbial participle indicating means (Wallace 625–30*; BDF §418; *GNTG* §192): "[by means of] leading him by the hand."

21. ἡμέρας τρεῖς is accusative indicating extent of time (Wallace 201; BDF §161; *GNTG* §5.82): "for three days."

22. βλέπων is an imperfect periphrastic construction (the imperfect form of εἰμί plus the present participle); equivalent in function to the imperfect tense of the finite verb (Wallace 647–49; BDF §§352–53; *GNTG* §§5.184–85): "he was not seeing."

23. ὀνόματι is a dative of possession (the verb of being is omitted in this construction; BDF §128.3; Wallace 149–51; BDF §189; *GNTG* §5.61): "his name was."

24. πρὸς here is used with a verb of speaking to indicate the addressee (BDAG 874.3.a.ε). Luke often uses this construction rather than the dative case (Curly, Parsons, Stigall, *Luke*, 76, referencing p. 14).

25. ὁ δὲ: when followed by δέ, the article functions like a personal pronoun (Wallace 211–12; BDF §251; *GNTG* §5.17).

26. ἰδοὺ ἐγώ: an idiomatic expression: "here I am" (BDAG 468.2*).

27. ὁ δὲ κύριος is the subject of a clause with an elided verb to be supplied from the context; the reader must supply εἶπεν from the previous clause (see the discussion in BDF §§479–83).

28. πρὸς here is used with a verb of speaking to indicate the addressee (see n. 24).

29. ἀναστὰς is likely an attendant circumstance participle, referring to an action that is parallel to the main verb (Wallace 640–45; *GNTG* §5.198): "get up! . . . and."

30. καλουμένην is an attributive participle (Wallace 617–18; BDF §412; *GNTG* §5.181), modifying ῥύμην: "the road called."

31. ζήτησον: aor.-impv.-act.-2-sg. < ζητέω: "look for," "search out" (BDAG 428.1.c*).

32. Σαῦλον ὀνόματι Ταρσέα: Ταρσέα is the accusative object of ζήτησον. Σαῦλον is in apposition to Ταρσέα. ὀνόματι is a dative of possession (the verb of being is omitted in this construction; BDF §128.3; Wallace 149–51; BDF §189; *GNTG* §5.61): "whose name is Saul."

ὀνόματι[33] εἰσελθόντα καὶ ἐπιθέντα[34] αὐτῷ τὰς χεῖρας ὅπως[35] ἀναβλέψῃ.
13 ἀπεκρίθη δὲ Ἀνανίας· κύριε, ἤκουσα ἀπὸ πολλῶν περὶ τοῦ ἀνδρὸς
τούτου ὅσα κακὰ τοῖς ἁγίοις σου ἐποίησεν ἐν Ἰερουσαλήμ· 14 καὶ ὧδε ἔχει
ἐξουσίαν παρὰ τῶν ἀρχιερέων δῆσαι[36] πάντας τοὺς ἐπικαλουμένους τὸ
ὄνομά σου. 15 εἶπεν δὲ πρὸς αὐτὸν ὁ κύριος· πορεύου, ὅτι σκεῦος ἐκλογῆς[37] ἐστίν μοι[38] οὗτος τοῦ βαστάσαι[39] τὸ ὄνομά μου ἐνώπιον ἐθνῶν τε
καὶ βασιλέων υἱῶν τε Ἰσραήλ·[40] 16 ἐγὼ γὰρ ὑποδείξω αὐτῷ ὅσα δεῖ αὐτὸν
ὑπὲρ τοῦ ὀνόματός μου παθεῖν.[41] 17 Ἀπῆλθεν δὲ Ἀνανίας καὶ εἰσῆλθεν
εἰς τὴν οἰκίαν καὶ ἐπιθεὶς[42] ἐπ᾽ αὐτὸν τὰς χεῖρας εἶπεν· Σαοὺλ ἀδελφέ, ὁ
κύριος ἀπέσταλκέν με, Ἰησοῦς ὁ ὀφθείς[43] σοι ἐν τῇ ὁδῷ ᾗ ἤρχου,[44] ὅπως[45]

33. ὀνόματι is a dative of possession (the verb of being is omitted in this construction; BDF §§128.3, 189; Wallace 149–51; *GNTG* §5.61): "whose name is Ananias."

34. εἰσελθόντα καὶ ἐπιθέντα: the participles might be attributive (Wallace 617–18; BDF §412; *GNTG* §5.181), modifying ἄνδρα: who came in and placed his hands on him; or they might be complements in an object-complement double accusative construction with ἄνδρα as the object (Wallace 181–89 [183 n. 24]; BDF §157; *GNTG* §5.77; Parsons and Culy, *Acts*, 175): "coming in and placing."

35. ὅπως, with the subjunctive mood (ἀναβλέψῃ), introduces a purpose clause (BDAG 718.2): "so that he might see again."

36. δῆσαι is an epexegetical infinitive explaining ἐξουσίαν (Parsons and Culy, *Acts*, 175; see Wallace 607; BDF §394; *GNTG* §5.167).

37. ἐκλογῆς is an attributive genitive (Wallace 86–88*; BDF §165*; *GNTG* §5.44): "chosen vessel."

38. μοι is a dative of possession (Wallace 149–51; BDF §189; *GNTG* §5.61): "my chosen vessel."

39. τοῦ βαστάσαι: the articular infinitive (τοῦ βαστάσαι) might be in apposition to ἐκλογῆς (Wallace 606*; *GNTG* §5.168): "namely, carrying"; or it might be indicating purpose (Wallace 590–92; BDF §390; *GNTG* §5.161; see Parsons and Culy, *Acts*, 176): "to carry."

40. ἐνώπιον ἐθνῶν τε καὶ βασιλέων υἱῶν τε Ἰσραήλ: "before nations and kings and the sons of Israel."

41. ὅσα δεῖ αὐτὸν . . . παθεῖν: the infinitive (παθεῖν) is used in impersonal expressions with verbs like δεῖ (BDF §393.1; Wallace describes this as a substantival use [600–601]; *GNTG* §5.164.b); αὐτὸν is the subject of the infinitive: "how much he must suffer."

42. ἐπιθεὶς is either an adverbial participle indicating time; the aorist tense indicates time before that of the main verb (Wallace 623–27; BDF §418; *GNTG* §5.188): "after placing his hands"; or an attendant circumstance participle, referring to an action that is parallel to the main verb (Wallace 640–45; *GNTG* §5.198): he placed his hands . . . and."

43. ὁ ὀφθείς is an attributive participle (Wallace 617–18; BDF §412; *GNTG* §5.181), modifying Ἰησοῦς: "who appeared."

44. ἤρχου: impf.-ind.-mid.-2-sg. < ἔρχομαι. With ᾗ: "on which you came."

45. ὅπως, with the subjunctive mood (ἀναβλέψῃς . . . πλησθῇς), introduces a purpose clause (BDAG 718.2): "so that you might see again and be filled."

ἀναβλέψῃς καὶ πλησθῇς πνεύματος ἁγίου. 18 καὶ εὐθέως ἀπέπεσαν αὐτοῦ ἀπὸ τῶν ὀφθαλμῶν ὡς λεπίδες,[46] ἀνέβλεψέν τε καὶ ἀναστὰς[47] ἐβαπτίσθη 19 καὶ λαβὼν[48] τροφὴν ἐνίσχυσεν.

Vocabulary

ἀναβλέπω	to regain sight; to receive sight
Ἀνανίας, ου, ὁ	Ananias
ἀπειλή, ῆς, ἡ	threatening, threat
ἀποπίπτω	to fall
βαστάζω	to bear
Δαμασκός, οῦ, ἡ	Damascus
δέω	to bind, stop
διώκω	to pursue, persecute
ἐγγίζω	to bring near, come near
εἰσάγω	to bring in
ἐκλογή, ῆς, ἡ	election, choice; selection, extract
ἐμπνέω	to breathe, breathe out; to be alive
ἐνεός, ά, όν	speechless
ἐνισχύω	to regain strength; to grow strong
ἐξαίφνης, adv.	suddenly, immediately; unexpectedly
ἐπικαλέω	to call on
ἐπιστολή, ῆς, ἡ	letter, epistle
ἐπιτίθημι	to lay on, place, put, add
εὐθέως, adv.	immediately, at once, suddenly
εὐθύς, εῖα, ύ, gen. έως	straight; proper, right
λεπίς, ίδος, ἡ	flake, scale
ὅραμα, ατος, τό	vision; sight
πάσχω	to experience; to suffer, endure

46. ἀπέπεσαν αὐτοῦ ἀπὸ τῶν ὀφθαλμῶν ὡς λεπίδες: the subject of the comparison is left unstated: "they fell from him—that is, from his eyes like scales" (Parsons and Culy, *Acts*, 178). Perhaps: "things like scales fell from his eyes."

47. ἀναστὰς is either an adverbial participle indicating time; the aorist tense indicates time before that of the main verb (Wallace 623–27; BDF §418; *GNTG* §5.188): "after getting up"; or an attendant circumstance participle, referring to an action that is parallel to the main verb (Wallace 640–45; *GNTG* §5.198): "he got up . . . and."

48. λαβὼν is likely an adverbial participle indicating time; the aorist tense indicates time before that of the main verb (Wallace 623–27; BDF §418; *GNTG* §5.188): "after taking."

περιαστράπτω	to flash around
πίμπλημι	to fill, fulfill
ῥύμη, ης, ἡ	street
Σαούλ, ὁ, indecl.	Shaul; Saul. This form of the name is found in the LXX (BDAG 913.2*).
Σαῦλος, ου, ὁ	Saul. This is the Greek form of the name (BDAG 917*).
σκεῦος, ους, τό	object, vessel
συνοδεύω	to travel with
Ταρσεύς, έως, ὁ	Tarsean; from Tarsus
τροφή, ῆς, ἡ	food, provisions, forage
ὑποδείκνυμι	to show, inform
φόνος, ου, ὁ	murder; slaughter
χειραγωγέω	to lead by the hand

The Throne Room of God

The author identifies himself as a prophet named John. Tradition connected him to the apostle John and assigned to him the gospel and three letters that bear that name. The literary relationship between these documents is complex. The Semitic features of this book have suggested to some scholars that the author was originally from Judea or Galilee and moved to Asia Minor. John says that he writes the book on the island of Patmos, off the western coast of modern-day Turkey. The book was likely written toward the end of Domitian's reign as emperor (81–96 CE), but this date is debated.

In this selection, the reader is shown the throne room of God. The visual imagery is heavily influenced by Exodus, Isaiah, Ezekiel, and Daniel. Stylistically, the chapter contains very few indicative verbs. Much of the writing consists of verbless clauses, sometimes with nouns or adjectives in the nominative case, sometimes in the accusative case. The emphasis in chapter 4 is on description, not action (see the discussion in David L. Matthewson, *Revelation: A Handbook on the Greek Text*, BHGNT [Waco, TX: Baylor University Press, 2016], 58–59).

1 Μετὰ ταῦτα εἶδον, καὶ ἰδοὺ[1] θύρα[2] ἠνεῳγμένη[3] ἐν τῷ οὐρανῷ, καὶ ἡ

---

1. εἶδον, καὶ ἰδοὺ is a formula in Revelation. John repeatedly uses ἰδοὺ after εἶδον (BDAG 468.2*). Here it introduces a series of clauses with implied verbs that point to what it is that John saw. ἰδοὺ can be left untranslated and some form of εἰμί introduced: "there was" or "there are," depending on the context (cf. NET, NIV).

2. θύρα is the nominative subject of an implied form of εἰμί (Wallace 39–40; BDF §§127–28). John uses the nominative case after ἰδοὺ (Matthewson, *Revelation*, 59).

3. ἠνεῳγμένη is an attributive participle (Wallace 617–18; BDF §412; *GNTG* §5.181), modifying θύρα: "that was open."

φωνὴ ἡ πρώτη[4] ἣν ἤκουσα ὡς[5] σάλπιγγος λαλούσης[6] μετ᾽ ἐμοῦ λέγων·[7] ἀνάβα ὧδε, καὶ δείξω σοι ἃ δεῖ γενέσθαι[8] μετὰ ταῦτα.

2 Εὐθέως ἐγενόμην ἐν πνεύματι,[9] καὶ ἰδοὺ θρόνος[10] ἔκειτο[11] ἐν τῷ οὐρανῷ, καὶ ἐπὶ τὸν θρόνον καθήμενος,[12] 3 καὶ ὁ καθήμενος ὅμοιος

4. ἡ φωνὴ ἡ πρώτη: ἡ φωνὴ is the nominative subject of an implied form of εἰμί (Wallace 39–40; BDF §§127–28): "There was the first voice [that I heard]." It refers back to the voice first described in Rev 1:10: ἤκουσα ὀπίσω μου φωνὴν μεγάλην ὡς σάλπιγγος.

5. ὡς σάλπιγγος: ὡς can be used in ellipsis where the missing word is supplied from the context (BDAG 1103–4.1.b.α; 2.c.β*). Here, either φωνὴ ("as [the voice] of a trumpet") or a form of ἀκούω ("as [hearing] a trumpet"; with σάλπιγγος in the genitive case as the object of ἀκούω) could be supplied.

6. λαλούσης is likely an attributive participle (Wallace 617–18; BDF §412; *GNTG* §5.181). The genitive case here is peculiar (the same construction [σάλπιγγος λαλούσης] is used in 1:10–11). We would expect either the nominative case modifying φωνὴ (this is how most modern translations handle the participle), or the accusative case, modifying ἣν (both changes are reflected in the manuscript tradition); Matthewson suggests reading it as modifying σάλπιγγος (*Revelation*, 59): "like a trumpet, speaking."

7. λέγων: The masculine gender is peculiar since what is speaking is φωνὴ. BDF identifies this use of λέγων as a distinctive feature of Revelation, influenced by LXX usage (§136.4*).

8. ἃ . . . γενέσθαι: the infinitive is used in impersonal expressions with verbs like δεῖ (BDF §393.1; Wallace describes this as a substantival use [600–601]; *GNTG* §5.164.b). ἃ is the accusative subject of the infinitive: "what must happen."

9. ἐγενόμην ἐν πνεύματι: ἐγενόμην with ἐν indicates a state of being: "I was in the spirit" (BDAG 198.5.c*).

10. θρόνος: as in v. 1, the nominative follows ἰδοὺ. Matthewson indicates that John uses a pattern in which the first time an image is introduced into the narrative, it appears anarthrous; subsequent references are articular (vv. 2, 3, 4, 5, 6, 9, 10). This usage of the article is called "anaphoric": the article points backward (Matthewson, *Revelation*, 60–61; see Wallace 217–20; BDF §252; *GNTG* §5.12.b).

11. ἔκειτο: impf.-ind.-mid.-3-sg. < κεῖμαι: in this context, "was standing" (BDAG 537.2*).

12. καθήμενος is a substantival participle (Wallace 619–21; BDF §413; *GNTG* §5.182). It is likely anarthrous because this is the first time this entity has been introduced into the narrative. Subsequent uses include the anaphoric use of the article (vv. 3, 9, 10). The participle is the nominative subject of an implied form of εἰμί (Wallace 39–40; BDF §§127–28): "There was someone sitting."

ὁράσει¹³ λίθῳ ἰάσπιδι καὶ σαρδίῳ, καὶ ἶρις¹⁴ κυκλόθεν τοῦ θρόνου ὅμοιος ὁράσει σμαραγδίνῳ. 4 Καὶ κυκλόθεν τοῦ θρόνου θρόνους¹⁵ εἴκοσι τέσσαρες, καὶ ἐπὶ τοὺς θρόνους εἴκοσι τέσσαρας πρεσβυτέρους καθημένους¹⁶ περιβεβλημένους¹⁷ ἐν ἱματίοις λευκοῖς καὶ ἐπὶ τὰς κεφαλὰς αὐτῶν στεφάνους χρυσοῦς. 5 Καὶ ἐκ τοῦ θρόνου ἐκπορεύονται ἀστραπαὶ καὶ φωναὶ¹⁸ καὶ βρονταί, καὶ ἑπτὰ λαμπάδες πυρὸς¹⁹ καιόμεναι²⁰ ἐνώπιον τοῦ θρόνου, ἅ εἰσιν τὰ ἑπτὰ πνεύματα τοῦ θεοῦ, 6 καὶ ἐνώπιον τοῦ θρόνου ὡς θάλασσα ὑαλίνη²¹ ὁμοία κρυστάλλῳ. Καὶ ἐν μέσῳ τοῦ θρόνου καὶ κύκλῳ τοῦ θρόνου²² τέσσαρα ζῷα²³ γέμοντα ὀφθαλμῶν²⁴ ἔμπροσθεν καὶ

13. ὁ καθήμενος ὅμοιος ὁράσει: ὁ καθήμενος is a substantival participle (Wallace 619–21; BDF §413; *GNTG* §5.182); the article is anaphoric (pointing back to v. 2); the participle is the nominative subject of an implied form of εἰμί (Wallace 39–40; BDF §§127–28). ὅμοιος, taking the dative case (BDAG 706.a*), means "similar . . . to." ὁράσει is a dative of respect/reference (Wallace 144–46; BDF §197; *GNTG* §5.43): "The one sitting was similar in appearance to."

14. ἶρις is the nominative subject of an implied form of εἰμί (Wallace 39–40; BDF §§127–28): "There was a rainbow."

15. θρόνους . . . πρεσβυτέρους . . . στεφάνους: the accusatives are likely to be understood as the objects of an implied εἶδον (see the discussion in BDF §§479–83; Matthewson, *Revelation*, 62): "[I saw] thrones . . . elders . . . crowns."

16. καθημένους is likely an attributive participle (Wallace 617–18; BDF §412; *GNTG* §5.181), modifying πρεσβυτέρους: "seated."

17. περιβεβλημένους is likely an attributive participle (Wallace 617–18; BDF §412; *GNTG* §5.181), modifying πρεσβυτέρους: "clothed."

18. φωναὶ: sounds associated with a storm (BDAG 1071.1*). Many modern translations gloss this as "rumblings" (cf. ESV, NET, NRSV).

19. ἑπτὰ λαμπάδες πυρός: λαμπάδες is the nominative subject of an implied form of εἰμί (Wallace 39–40; BDF §§127–28). πυρὸς is an attributive genitive (Wallace 86–88; BDF §165; *GNTG* §5.44), modifying λαμπάδες: "There were seven flaming lamps."

20. καιόμεναι is an attributive participle (Wallace 617–18; BDF §412; *GNTG* §5.181), modifying λαμπάδες: "burning.

21. ὡς θάλασσα ὑαλίνη: ὡς plus the nominative in some contexts can take the place of a substantive (BDAG 1104.2.c.α.ℵ*). Here, it functions as the subject of an implied form of εἰμί (Wallace 39–40; BDF §§127–28): "There was [something] like a glass sea."

22. ἐν μέσῳ τοῦ θρόνου καὶ κύκλῳ τοῦ θρόνου: the combination of ἐν μέσῳ ("in the midst") with κύκλῳ ("around") is difficult to imagine. Matthewson suggests the language portrays the creatures close to (ἐν μέσῳ) the throne and all around it (*Revelation*, 64).

23. ζῷα is the nominative subject of an implied form of εἰμί (Wallace 39–40; BDF §§127–28): "There were four living creatures."

24. γέμοντα ὀφθαλμῶν: γέμοντα is an attributive participle (Wallace 617–18; BDF §412; *GNTG* §5.181), modifying ζῷα. ὀφθαλμῶν is the genitive object of the participle (BDAG 191.a): "full of eyes."

ὄπισθεν. 7 καὶ τὸ ζῷον²⁵ τὸ πρῶτον ὅμοιον λέοντι καὶ τὸ δεύτερον ζῷον ὅμοιον μόσχῳ καὶ τὸ τρίτον ζῷον ἔχων τὸ πρόσωπον²⁶ ὡς ἀνθρώπου καὶ τὸ τέταρτον ζῷον ὅμοιον ἀετῷ πετομένῳ.²⁷ 8 καὶ τὰ τέσσαρα ζῷα,²⁸ ἓν καθ᾿ ἕν²⁹ αὐτῶν ἔχων³⁰ ἀνὰ³¹ πτέρυγας ἕξ, κυκλόθεν καὶ ἔσωθεν γέμουσιν ὀφθαλμῶν, καὶ ἀνάπαυσιν οὐκ ἔχουσιν ἡμέρας καὶ νυκτὸς³² λέγοντες·³³
ἅγιος ἅγιος ἅγιος κύριος ὁ θεὸς ὁ παντοκράτωρ,³⁴
ὁ ἦν καὶ ὁ ὢν καὶ ὁ ἐρχόμενος.³⁵

25. τὸ ζῷον is the nominative subject of an implied form of εἰμί (Wallace 39–40; BDF §§127–28): "The [first] living creature was." The construction occurs four times in this verse.

26. ἔχων τὸ πρόσωπον: the use of the masculine is puzzling given that ζῷον is neuter. Perhaps this is an instance where the participle is being used as an indicative (Wallace 653*; BDF §136; *GNTG* §5.201; see the discussion in Matthewson, *Revelation*, 64): "had a face."

27. πετομένῳ is an attributive participle (Wallace 617–18; BDF §412; *GNTG* §5.181), modifying ἀετῷ: "flying eagle."

28. τὰ τέσσαρα ζῷα is the nominative subject of γέμουσιν.

29. ἓν καθ᾿ ἕν: "each one" (BDAG 293.5.e*).

30. ἔχων: as in v. 7, the use of the masculine is puzzling given that ζῷον and ἕν are neuter. It is possible that the participle is functioning attributively (Wallace 617–18; BDF §412; *GNTG* §5.181), modifying ἕν: "each one having" (this is the way the NRSV reads the clause). Perhaps this is an instance where the participle is being used as an indicative (Wallace 653*; BDF §136; *GNTG* §5.201; the NET and NIV read the clause this way): "each one . . . had." See the discussion in Matthewson, *Revelation*, 64.

31. ἀνὰ: with numbers, ἀνὰ has a distributive connotation: "apiece" (BDF §204*; BDAG 58.3*).

32. ἡμέρας καὶ νυκτὸς are genitives of time (Wallace 122–24; BDF §186.2; *GNTG* §5.53): "day and night."

33. λέγοντες is likely an adverbial participle indicating manner (Wallace 627–28; BDF §418; *GNTG* §5.193): "saying." But it presents the same challenges as λέγων in v. 1 (see n. 7). BDAG suggests a translation of this last clause as "they say without ceasing" (BDAG 69*).

34. κύριος ὁ θεὸς ὁ παντοκράτωρ: κύριος is the nominative subject of an implied form of εἰμί (Wallace 39–40; BDF §§127–28). ὁ θεὸς and ὁ παντοκράτωρ are both in apposition to κύριος.

35. ὁ ἦν καὶ ὁ ὢν καὶ ὁ ἐρχόμενος: this clause is in apposition to κύριος. ὁ ἐρχόμενος refers to one coming in the future (BDAG 394.4.a.β*).

9 Καὶ ὅταν³⁶ δώσουσιν τὰ ζῷα δόξαν καὶ τιμὴν καὶ εὐχαριστίαν τῷ καθημένῳ³⁷ ἐπὶ τῷ θρόνῳ τῷ ζῶντι³⁸ εἰς τοὺς αἰῶνας τῶν αἰώνων,³⁹ 10 πεσοῦνται οἱ εἴκοσι τέσσαρες πρεσβύτεροι ἐνώπιον τοῦ καθημένου⁴⁰ ἐπὶ τοῦ θρόνου καὶ προσκυνήσουσιν τῷ ζῶντι⁴¹ εἰς τοὺς αἰῶνας τῶν αἰώνων καὶ βαλοῦσιν τοὺς στεφάνους αὐτῶν ἐνώπιον τοῦ θρόνου λέγοντες·⁴²

11 ἄξιος εἶ, ὁ κύριος καὶ ὁ θεὸς⁴³ ἡμῶν,
λαβεῖν⁴⁴ τὴν δόξαν καὶ τὴν τιμὴν καὶ τὴν δύναμιν,
ὅτι σὺ ἔκτισας⁴⁵ τὰ πάντα
καὶ διὰ τὸ θέλημά σου ἦσαν⁴⁶ καὶ ἐκτίσθησαν.

Vocabulary

ἀετός, οῦ, ὁ	eagle, vulture
ἀνάπαυσις, εως, ἡ	rest
ἄξιος, ία, ον	worthy; worth, value, dignity
ἀστραπή, ῆς, ἡ	lightning
βροντή, ῆς, ἡ	thunder
γέμω	to be full
δείκνυμι	to show
δεύτερος, α, ον	second
εἴκοσι, indecl.	twenty
ἐκπορεύομαι	to go, come out

36. ὅταν plus the future (δώσουσιν): "whenever" (BDF §382.4*; BDAG 731.1.b.α*): "whenever [the living creatures] give." Though there is debate about whether the construction indicates a simple event in the future or a repeated event (see Matthewson, *Revelation*, 66).
37. τῷ καθημένῳ is a substantival participle (Wallace 619–21; BDF §413; GNTG §5.182): "to the one who sits."
38. τῷ ζῶντι is an attributive participle (Wallace 617–18; BDF §412; GNTG §5.181), modifying τῷ καθημένῳ: "who lives."
39. εἰς τοὺς αἰῶνας τῶν αἰώνων: "forevermore" (BDAG 32.1.b*).
40. τοῦ καθημένου is a substantival participle (Wallace 619–21; BDF §413; GNTG §5.182).
41. τῷ ζῶντι is a substantival participle (Wallace 619–21; BDF §413; GNTG §5.182); it is the dative complement of προσκυνήσουσιν (Wallace 171–73*; BDF §187.6; GNTG §5.72).
42. λέγοντες is likely an adverbial participle indicating manner (Wallace 627–28; BDF §418; GNTG §5.192): "saying."
43. ὁ κύριος καὶ ὁ θεὸς are nominatives used for the vocative (Wallace 56–59; BDF §147.3*; GNTG §5.28).
44. λαβεῖν is an epexegetical infinitive explaining ἄξιος (Wallace 607; BDF §394; GNTG §5.167).
45. ἔκτισας: aor.-ind.-act.-2-sg. < κτίζω.
46. ἦσαν: "they existed."

ἔμπροσθεν	(+ gen.) before, in front of
ἕξ, indecl.	six
ἔσωθεν, adv.	within, inside, from within
εὐθέως, adv.	immediately, at once, suddenly
εὐχαριστία, ας, ἡ	thanksgiving, thankfulness; eucharist
ζῷον, ου, τό	living being; animal; (zodiacal) sign; life
θύρα, ας, ἡ	door; doorway, gate, entrance
ἴασπις, ιδος, ἡ	jasper
ἶρις, ιδος, ἡ	rainbow; iris plant
καίω	to burn, kindle, light; to cauterize
κεῖμαι	to lie down; to be valid for
κρύσταλλος, ου, ὁ	crystal, ice
κτίζω	to create, build, found
κυκλόθεν	(+ gen.) about, all around
κύκλῳ	(+ gen.) round (prep.); in a circle (adv.)
λαμπάς, άδος, ἡ	lamp
λευκός, ή, όν	white
λέων, οντος, ὁ	lion
μόσχος, ου, ὁ	calf
ὅμοιος, οία, οιον	like, similar
ὄπισθεν	(+ gen.) behind (prep.); from behind (adv.)
ὅρασις, εως, ἡ	appearance; sight; vision
παντοκράτωρ, ορος, ὁ	all mighty; almighty
περιβάλλω	to put on, clothe
πέτομαι	to fly
πτέρυξ, υγος, ἡ	wing
σάλπιγξ, ιγγος, ἡ	trumpet
σάρδιον, ου, τό	sardius, carnelian; a reddish, precious stone
σμαράγδινος, η, ον	made of emerald
στέφανος, ου, ὁ	crown
τέσσαρες, α	four
τέταρτος, η, ον	fourth
τιμή, ῆς, ἡ	honor
ὑάλινος, η, ον	made of glass
χρυσοῦς, ῆ, οῦν	golden

Circumcision, Abraham, and Jesus

The Epistle of Barnabas was popular in some circles of early Christians. It was bound together with other "biblical" texts in Codex Sinaiticus (fourth century CE). Though the document was written anonymously, it came to be associated with the early traveling companion of the apostle Paul. The book was written sometime between 70 CE and 135 CE. It has traditionally been associated with Alexandria in Egypt. The oldest complete Greek manuscript of the epistle is preserved in Codex Sinaiticus. It is also included, along with the Didache and 1 Clement, in Codex Hierosolymitanus (eleventh century CE).

The text is anti-Jewish in its arguments and is concerned to show that it is followers of Jesus who are the true heirs to the patriarchal promises. In this section of the document, the author takes up the rite of circumcision. He argues that God has abolished circumcision of the flesh. He offers prooftexts showing God's desire that the heart be circumcised and interprets Genesis 17 as a reference to Jesus on the cross.

1 Λέγει γὰρ πάλιν περὶ τῶν ὠτίων, πῶς περιέτεμεν[1] ἡμῶν τὴν καρδίαν. λέγει κύριος ἐν τῷ προφήτῃ·[2] Εἰς ἀκοὴν ὠτίου[3] ὑπήκουσάν μου.[4] καὶ

---

1. περιέτεμεν: aor.-ind.-act.-3-sg. < περιτέμνω.
2. The quotation appears to be from Ps 18:44 (17:45 LXX): εἰς ἀκοὴν ὠτίου ὑπήκουσέν μοι; this is similar to 2 Sam 22:45: εἰς ἀκοὴν ὠτίου ἤκουσάν μου·
3. Εἰς ἀκοὴν ὠτίου: "as soon as they heard" (BDAG 36.2*).
4. μου is the genitive complement of ὑπήκουσάν (Wallace 131–34; BDF §173; *GNTG* §5.36).

πάλιν λέγει·[5] Ἀκοῇ ἀκούσονται[6] οἱ πόρρωθεν,[7] ἃ ἐποίησα γνώσονται· καί· Περιτμήθητε, λέγει κύριος,[8] τὰς καρδίας ὑμῶν. 2 καὶ πάλιν λέγει·[9] Ἄκουε, Ἰσραήλ, ὅτι τάδε λέγει κύριος ὁ θεός σου. καὶ πάλιν τὸ πνεῦμα κυρίου προφητεύει·[10] Τίς ἐστιν ὁ θέλων[11] ζῆσαι[12] εἰς τὸν αἰῶνα;[13] ἀκοῇ ἀκου-σάτω τῆς φωνῆς[14] τοῦ παιδός μου. 3 καὶ πάλιν λέγει·[15] Ἄκουε οὐρανέ, καὶ ἐνωτίζου γῆ, ὅτι κύριος ἐλάλησεν ταῦτα εἰς μαρτύριον. καὶ πάλιν λέγει· Ἀκούσατε λόγον κυρίου,[16] ἄρχοντες τοῦ λαοῦ τούτου. καὶ πάλιν λέγει·[17]

5. The reference appears to depend on Isa 33:13: ἀκούσονται οἱ πόρρωθεν ἃ ἐποίησα, γνώσονται οἱ ἐγγίζοντες τὴν ἰσχύν μου.

6. Ἀκοῇ ἀκούσονται: Ἀκοῇ is a cognate dative; the force of this dative is to emphasize the action of the verb (Wallace 168–69; BDF §198.6; the construction is found frequently in LXX; Conybeare & Stock §61): "they will listen" or "they will listen attentively" (BDAG 36.2*). The author also might be using Ἀκοῇ as a dative of means (Wallace 162–63; BDF §195): "will hear with their ear." A similar construction occurs in v. 2.

7. οἱ πόρρωθεν: the article turns the adverb into the nominative subject of the clause (BDF §266): "those who are far away."

8. This reference appears to depend on Jer 4:4: περιτμήθητε τῷ θεῷ ὑμῶν καὶ περιτέμεσθε τὴν σκληροκαρδίαν ὑμῶν.

9. The reference appears to be to Jer 7:2–3: Ἀκούσατε λόγον κυρίου, πᾶσα ἡ Ιουδαία· τάδε λέγει κύριος ὁ θεὸς Ισραηλ.

10. This reference appears to be influenced by both Ps 34:12 (33:13 LXX): τίς ἐστιν ἄνθρωπος ὁ θέλων ζωὴν ἀγαπῶν ἡμέρας ἰδεῖν ἀγαθάς; and Isa 50:10: Τίς ἐν ὑμῖν ὁ φοβούμενος τὸν κύριον; ἀκουσάτω τῆς φωνῆς τοῦ παιδὸς αὐτοῦ·

11. ὁ θέλων is a substantival participle (Wallace 619–21; BDF §413; *GNTG* §5.182).

12. ζῆσαι is a complementary infinitive going with θέλων (Wallace 598–99; BDF §392; *GNTG* §5.163).

13. εἰς τὸν αἰῶνα: "forever" (BDAG 32.1.b).

14. τῆς φωνῆς is the genitive complement of ἀκουσάτω (Wallace 131–34; BDF §173; *GNTG* §5.36).

15. The reference appears to be influenced by both Isa 1:2: Ἄκουε, οὐρανέ, καὶ ἐνωτίζου, γῆ, ὅτι κύριος ἐλάλησεν· υἱοὺς ἐγέννησα καὶ ὕψωσα, αὐτοὶ δέ με ἠθέτησαν; and Mic 1:2: Ἀκούσατε, λαοί, λόγους, καὶ προσεχέτω ἡ γῆ καὶ πάντες οἱ ἐν αὐτῇ, καὶ ἔσται κύριος ἐν ὑμῖν εἰς μαρτύριον, κύριος ἐξ οἴκου ἁγίου αὐτοῦ·

16. Ἀκούσατε λόγον κυρίου is a stock phrase that occurs repeatedly in the prophetic litera-ture (e.g., Hos 4:1; Isa 1:10; Jer 2:4; Ezek 6:3). This particular reference is perhaps influenced by Isa 28:14: διὰ τοῦτο ἀκούσατε λόγον κυρίου, ἄνδρες τεθλιμμένοι καὶ ἄρχοντες τοῦ λαοῦ τούτου τοῦ ἐν Ιερουσαλημ.

17. This reference does not exactly match a specific passage in the LXX, but it is clearly informed by Isa 40:3: φωνὴ βοῶντος ἐν τῇ ἐρήμῳ (see §2.2 in this volume).

Ἀκούσατε, τέκνα, φωνῆς βοῶντος[18] ἐν τῇ ἐρήμῳ. 4 οὐκοῦν περιέτεμεν[19] ἡμῶν τὰς ἀκοάς, ἵνα ἀκούσαντες[20] λόγον πιστεύσωμεν ἡμεῖς.

Ἀλλὰ καὶ[21] ἡ περιτομὴ ἐφ᾽ ᾗ πεποίθασιν[22] κατήργηται, περιτομὴν γὰρ εἴρηκεν οὐ σαρκὸς γενηθῆναι.[23] ἀλλὰ παρέβησαν, ὅτι ἄγγελος πονηρὸς ἐσόφιζεν[24] αὐτούς. 5 λέγει[25] πρὸς αὐτούς·[26] Τάδε λέγει κύριος ὁ θεὸς ὑμῶν (ὧδε εὑρίσκω ἐντολήν)· Μὴ σπείρητε ἐπ᾽ ἀκάνθαις, περιτμήθητε τῷ κυρίῳ ὑμῶν.[27] καὶ τί λέγει;[28] Περιτμήθητε τὴν σκληροκαρδίαν ὑμῶν, καὶ τὸν τράχηλον ὑμῶν οὐ σκληρυνεῖτε.[29] λάβε πάλιν·[30] Ἰδού, λέγει κύριος,

18. φωνῆς βοῶντος: φωνῆς is the genitive complement of Ἀκούσατε (Wallace 131–34; BDF §173; *GNTG* §5.36). βοῶντος is an adjectival participle and, in this context, could be either attributive (Wallace 617–18; BDF §412; *GNTG* §5.181), modifying φωνῆς: "a voice crying"; or substantival (Wallace 619–21; BDF §413; *GNTG* §65.182): "voice of one crying." In Isaiah 40, the participle is substantival.

19. περιέτεμεν: aor.-ind.-act.-3-sg. < περιτέμνω.

20. ἀκούσαντες is likely an adverbial participle indicating time; the aorist tense indicates time before that of the main verb (Wallace 623–27; BDF §418; *GNTG* §5.188): "when we hear."

21. Ἀλλὰ καὶ: καὶ intensifies Ἀλλὰ. Barnabas uses this expression twice more in 9:6.

22. ἐφ᾽ ᾗ πεποίθασιν: "in which they have trusted."

23. περιτομὴν . . . οὐ σαρκὸς γενηθῆναι: περιτομὴν is the accusative subject of the infinitive (γενηθῆναι). σαρκὸς is in the genitive case but its precise function is difficult to state. It might be characterized as a kind of genitive of relationship (BDF §162.7; BDAG 199.9; see also Wallace 83–84; *GNTG* §39): circumcision was not instituted [as a matter of/ belonging to] the flesh. γενηθῆναι: the infinitive indicates indirect discourse following a verb of speaking (Wallace 603–5; BDF §397.3; *GNTG* §5.166).

24. ἐσόφιζεν: the author appears to be using the verb sarcastically.

25. The first two references in what follows are to Jer 4:3–4: ὅτι **τάδε λέγει κύριος** τοῖς ἀνδράσιν Ιουδα καὶ τοῖς κατοικοῦσιν Ιερουσαλημ Νεώσατε ἑαυτοῖς νεώματα καὶ **μὴ σπείρητε ἐπ᾽ ἀκάνθαις. περιτμήθητε τῷ θεῷ ὑμῶν** καὶ **περιτέμεσθε τὴν σκληροκαρδίαν ὑμῶν**, ἄνδρες Ιουδα καὶ οἱ κατοικοῦντες Ιερουσαλημ.

26. πρὸς αὐτούς: πρὸς is used here with a verb of speaking to indicate the addressee (BDAG 874.3.a.ε).

27. περιτμήθητε τῷ κυρίῳ ὑμῶν: "let yourselves be circumcised for your Lord" (BDAG 807.b.β*).

28. The reference is to Deut 10:16: καὶ περιτεμεῖσθε τὴν σκληροκαρδίαν ὑμῶν καὶ τὸν τράχηλον ὑμῶν οὐ σκληρυνεῖτε ἔτι.

29. σκληρυνεῖτε is an imperatival future indicating a command (Wallace 452, 569; BDF §362; *GNTG* §5.108): "you will [not] harden."

30. The reference that follows is influenced by Jer 9:25–26 (9:24–25 LXX): **ἰδοὺ** ἡμέραι ἔρχονται, **λέγει κύριος**, καὶ ἐπισκέψομαι ἐπὶ πάντας περιτετμημένους ἀκροβυστίας αὐτῶν . . . **πάντα τὰ ἔθνη ἀπερίτμητα σαρκί, καὶ πᾶς οἶκος Ισραηλ ἀπερίτμητοι καρδίας** αὐτῶν.

πάντα τὰ ἔθνη ἀπερίτμητα ἀκροβυστίαν, ὁ δὲ λαὸς οὗτος[31] ἀπερίτμητος καρδίας.

6 Ἀλλ᾽ ἐρεῖς· Καὶ μὴν[32] περιτέτμηται ὁ λαὸς εἰς σφραγίδα. ἀλλὰ καὶ πᾶς Σύρος καὶ Ἄραψ καὶ πάντες οἱ ἱερεῖς τῶν εἰδώλων·[33] ἄρα οὖν[34] κἀκεῖνοι ἐκ τῆς διαθήκης αὐτῶν εἰσίν; ἀλλὰ καὶ οἱ Αἰγύπτιοι ἐν περιτομῇ εἰσίν.

7 Μάθετε οὖν, τέκνα ἀγάπης, περὶ πάντων πλουσίως,[35] ὅτι Ἀβραάμ, πρῶτος περιτομὴν δούς,[36] ἐν πνεύματι προβλέψας[37] εἰς τὸν Ἰησοῦν περιέτεμεν,[38] λαβὼν τριῶν γραμμάτων δόγματα.[39] 8 λέγει γάρ· Καὶ περιέτεμεν Ἀβραὰμ ἐκ τοῦ οἴκου αὐτοῦ ἄνδρας δεκαοκτὼ καὶ τριακοσίους.[40] τίς οὖν

---

31. πάντα τὰ ἔθνη . . . ὁ . . . λαὸς οὗτος: both are nominative subjects of clauses with elided verbs to be supplied from the context (see the discussion in BDF §§479–83): "All the nations [have] . . . This people [has]."

32. Καὶ μὴν introduces an emphatic statement (LSJ 1127.II.2): "well, surely."

33. πᾶς Σύρος καὶ Ἄραψ καὶ πάντες οἱ ἱερεῖς τῶν εἰδώλων are the nominative subjects of a clause with an elided verb to be supplied from the context; the reader must likely supply περιτέτμηται from the previous sentence (see the discussion in BDF §§479–83).

34. ἄρα οὖν: "So then" (BDAG 127.2.b).

35. Μάθετε . . . πλουσίως: the adverb is displaced to the end of the clause, likely for emphasis: "learn abundantly."

36. περιτομὴν δούς: δούς is an attributive participle (Wallace 617–18; BDF §412; *GNTG* §5.181), modifying Ἀβραάμ. In combination with περιτομὴν: "who [first] instituted circumcision" (BDAG 243.14*).

37. προβλέψας is an adverbial participle; likely indicating time; the aorist tense indicates time before that of the main verb (Wallace 623–25; BDF §418; *GNTG* §5.188): "when he looked forward."

38. περιέτεμεν: "practiced circumcision."

39. λαβὼν τριῶν γραμμάτων δόγματα: λαβὼν is an adverbial participle, indicating either time; the aorist tense indicates time before that of the main verb (Wallace 623–25; BDF §418; *GNTG* §5.188): "after receiving the teaching of the three letters"; or indicating cause (Wallace 631–32; BDF §418.1; *GNTG* §5.189): "because he received the teaching of the three letters."

40. The reference to the number of men comes from Abraham's mission to rescue Lot described in Gen 14:14: ἠρίθμησεν τοὺς ἰδίους **οἰκογενεῖς** αὐτοῦ, **τριακοσίους δέκα καὶ ὀκτώ**. But Abraham does not circumcise them in that narrative. The reference to Abraham circumcising men is influenced by Gen 17:17: Καὶ **ἔλαβεν Αβρααμ** Ισμαηλ τὸν υἱὸν αὐτοῦ καὶ **πάντας τοὺς οἰκογενεῖς αὐτοῦ** καὶ πάντας τοὺς ἀργυρωνήτους καὶ πᾶν ἄρσεν τῶν ἀνδρῶν τῶν ἐν τῷ οἴκῳ Αβρααμ καὶ **περιέτεμεν** τὰς ἀκροβυστίας αὐτῶν ἐν τῷ καιρῷ τῆς ἡμέρας ἐκείνης, καθὰ ἐλάλησεν αὐτῷ ὁ θεός. For the first part of the Gen 17 narrative, see §1.1.

ἡ δοθεῖσα⁴¹ αὐτῷ γνῶσις;⁴² μάθετε⁴³ ὅτι τοὺς δεκαοκτὼ πρώτους, καὶ διάστημα ποιήσας⁴⁴ λέγει τριακοσίους. τὸ δεκαοκτὼ,⁴⁵ Ι δέκα, Η ὀκτώ·⁴⁶ ἔχεις Ἰησοῦν. ὅτι δὲ ὁ σταυρὸς ἐν τῷ Τ ἤμελλεν⁴⁷ ἔχειν⁴⁸ τὴν χάριν, λέγει καὶ τριακοσίους. δηλοῖ οὖν τὸν μὲν Ἰησοῦν ἐν τοῖς δυσὶ γράμμασιν, καὶ ἐν τῷ ἑνὶ τὸν σταυρόν. 9 οἶδεν ὁ τὴν ἔμφυτον δωρεὰν⁴⁹ τῆς διαθήκης αὐτοῦ θέμενος⁵⁰ ἐν ἡμῖν. οὐδεὶς γνησιώτερον ἔμαθεν ἀπ᾽ ἐμοῦ λόγον,⁵¹ ἀλλὰ οἶδα ὅτι ἄξιοί ἐστε ὑμεῖς.

Vocabulary

Ἀβραάμ, ὁ, indecl.	Abraham
Αἰγύπτιος, ία, ιον	Egyptian
ἄκανθα, ης, ἡ	thorn; thorny plant
ἀκοή, ῆς, ἡ	hearing; obedience; ear
ἀκροβυστία, ας, ἡ	foreskin; uncircumcision
ἄξιος, ία, ον	worthy; worth, fit, deserving
ἀπερίτμητος, ον	uncircumcised
ἄρα	then, therefore
Ἄραψ, βος, ὁ	Arabian, Arab
ἄρχων, οντος, ὁ	ruler; leader, official
βοάω	to cry out

41. δοθεῖσα is an attributive participle (Wallace 617–18; BDF §412; *GNTG* §5.181), modifying γνῶσις: "that was given."

42. ἡ . . . γνῶσις is the nominative subject of an implied form of εἰμί (Wallace 39–40; BDF §§127–28): "[What therefore] is the knowledge."

43. μάθετε: perhaps, "notice" in this context.

44. διάστημα ποιήσας: ποιήσας is an adverbial participle; likely indicating time; the aorist tense indicates time before that of the main verb (Wallace 623–25; BDF §418; *GNTG* §5.188): "after creating an interval."

45. τὸ δεκαοκτὼ is an accusative of respect (Wallace 203–4; BDF §160; *GNTG* §5.81) or, perhaps, pendent accusative (Wallace 198): "With respect to the eighteen."

46. Ι δέκα, Η ὀκτώ: "I is the Greek letter used to indicate the number 10, H is the Greek letter used to indicate the number 8." They are also, the first two letters of Ἰησοῦν.

47. ἤμελλεν: "destined" (BDAG 628.2).

48. ἔχειν is a complementary infinitive, going with ἤμελλεν (Wallace 598–99; BDF §392; *GNTG* §5.163).

49. τὴν ἔμφυτον δωρεὰν: the accusative direct object of θέμενος.

50. ὁ . . . θέμενος: aor.-ptc.-mid.-masc.-sg.-neut. < τίθημι. The participle is substantival (Wallace 619–21; BDF §413; *GNTG* §65.182): "The one who placed."

51. γνησιώτερον . . . λόγον: "a more reliable teaching" (BDAG 202.2*).

γνήσιος, α, ον	legitimate, genuine
γνῶσις, εως, ἡ	knowledge
γράμμα, ατος, τό	character; letter (of alphabet); epistle
δέκα, indecl.	ten
δεκαοκτώ, indecl.	eighteen
δηλόω	to make clear, declare
διαθήκη, ης, ἡ	last will and testament; covenant; contract
διάστημα, ατος, τό	interval
δόγμα, ατος, τό	teaching, opinion, judgment, decree; dogma, doctrine
δωρεάν, adv.	freely
εἴδωλον, ου, τό	phantom; image; cultic image, idol
ἔμφυτος, ον	implanted
ἐνωτίζομαι	to pay close attention to
ἔρημος, ον	desolate; wilderness, desert
ἤ	8
ἱ	10
ἱερεύς, έως, ὁ	priest
κἀκεῖνος, η, ο	and that one; even that one
καταργέω	to use up, exhaust, waste; to make powerless; to abolish, wipe out
μανθάνω	to learn
μαρτύριον, ου, τό	testimony; martyrdom
μήν	indeed, surely
ὅδε, ἥδε, τόδε	this, here; he, she, it
ὀκτώ, indecl.	eight
οὐκοῦν	so, then, accordingly
παῖς, παιδός, ὁ or ἡ	child; slave
παραβαίνω	to disobey, deviate, transgress
πείθω	to persuade; to believe; to trust
περιτέμνω	to circumcise; in the passive, to be circumcised or allow oneself to be circumcised
περιτομή, ῆς, ἡ	circumcision
πλουσίως, adv.	richly, abundantly
πόρρωθεν, adv.	from afar, at a distance
προβλέπω	to foresee, to provide

προφητεύω	to prophesy
σκληροκαρδία, ας, ἡ	hard-heartedness, stubbornness
σκληρύνω	to harden; to make stubborn
σοφίζω	to give wisdom; to make wise
σπείρω	to sow
σταυρός, οῦ, ὁ	cross
Σύρος, ου, ὁ	Syrian, Aramean
σφραγίς, ῖδος, ἡ	seal
τ´	300
τράχηλος, ου, ὁ	neck, throat
τριακόσιοι, αι, α	three hundred
ὑπακούω	to obey; to hear, listen
ὠτίον, ου, τό	ear

Examples of Faith: Peter, Paul, and Women

This letter was written anonymously by someone from the church in Rome to the church in Corinth. It came to be associated with Clement, who was a leader of the Roman church toward the end of the first century CE. The date of the epistle is traditionally assigned to the mid-90s of the common era. That the text was viewed as influential is demonstrated by the fact that it was bound together with other "biblical" documents in Codex Alexandrinus (fifth century CE). It was also bound together with the Didache and the Epistle of Barnabas in Codex Hierosolymitanus (eleventh century CE).

The overarching purpose of the letter was to eliminate factionalism present in the Corinthian church and to get the church to reinstate presbyters who had been removed from their roles. In this section of the letter, the author provides illustrations of individuals who suffered because of jealousy (ζῆλος). In chapter 4, he provided examples from TANAK. In chapter 5, he discusses recent followers of Christ: Peter and Paul; in chapter 6, he discusses women.

5:1 Ἀλλ' ἵνα τῶν ἀρχαίων ὑποδειγμάτων[1] παυσώμεθα, ἔλθωμεν ἐπὶ τοὺς ἔγγιστα γενομένους[2] ἀθλητάς· λάβωμεν τῆς γενεᾶς ἡμῶν τὰ γενναῖα ὑποδείγματα. 2 διὰ ζῆλον καὶ φθόνον οἱ μέγιστοι καὶ δικαιότατοι στῦλοι ἐδιώχθησαν καὶ ἕως θανάτου ἤθλησαν. 3 λάβωμεν πρὸ ὀφθαλμῶν

---

1. τῶν . . . ὑποδειγμάτων is a genitive of separation going with παυσώμεθα (Wallace 107–9; BDF §180.6; *GNTG* §5.50): "in order that we might cease from ancient examples."

2. τοὺς ἔγγιστα γενομένους is a substantival participle (Wallace 619–21; BDF §413; *GNTG* §5.182): "who lived nearest [to us]."

ἡμῶν³ τοὺς ἀγαθοὺς ἀποστόλους· 4 Πέτρον,⁴ ὃς διὰ ζῆλον ἄδικον οὐχ
ἕνα οὐδὲ δύο ἀλλὰ πλείονας ὑπήνεγκεν πόνους, καὶ οὕτω μαρτυρήσας⁵
ἐπορεύθη εἰς τὸν ὀφειλόμενον τόπον τῆς δόξης.⁶ 5 διὰ ζῆλον καὶ ἔριν
Παῦλος ὑπομονῆς βραβεῖον⁷ ὑπέδειξεν, 6 ἑπτάκις δεσμὰ φορέσας, φυγα-
δευθείς, λιθασθείς, κῆρυξ γενόμενος⁸ ἔν τε τῇ ἀνατολῇ καὶ ἐν τῇ δύσει,⁹
τὸ γενναῖον τῆς πίστεως αὐτοῦ κλέος¹⁰ ἔλαβεν, 7 δικαιοσύνην διδάξας
ὅλον τὸν κόσμον¹¹ καὶ ἐπὶ τὸ τέρμα τῆς δύσεως ἐλθών·¹² καὶ μαρτυρήσας¹³

3. λάβωμεν πρὸ ὀφθαλμῶν ἡμῶν: "let us place before our eyes (BDAG 744.2*).

4. Πέτρον is an accusative of respect (Wallace 203–4; BDF §160; *GNTG* §5.81), or, perhaps, pendent accusative (Wallace 198): "With respect to Peter."

5. μαρτυρήσας is an adverbial participle that might be indicating cause (Wallace 631–32; BDF §418.1; *GNTG* §5.189): "because he gave his testimony"; or, perhaps more likely, time (Wallace 623–25; BDF §418; *GNTG* §5.188): "after giving his testimony."

6. τὸν ὀφειλόμενον τόπον τῆς δόξης: τὸν ὀφειλόμενον is an attributive participle (Wallace 617–18; BDF §412; *GNTG* §5.181), modifying τόπον. τῆς δόξης is an attributive genitive (Wallace 86–88; BDF §165; *GNTG* §5.44): "the glorious place he deserved" (BDAG 743.2.α*).

7. ὑπομονῆς βραβεῖον: "reward for endurance" (BDAG 183.b*).

8. φορέσας . . . γενόμενος: these participles are adverbial; they might be indicating cause (Wallace 631–32; BDF §418.1; *GNTG* §5.189): "because he wore chains"; or, more likely, time; the aorist tense indicates time before that of the main verb (Wallace 623–25; BDF §418; *GNTG* §5.188): "after he wore chains."

9. ἔν τε τῇ ἀνατολῇ καὶ ἐν τῇ δύσει: this clause (along with the second clause of the next verse) might indicate that Paul was set free from his initial imprisonment in Rome and was able to travel west.

10. τὸ γενναῖον τῆς πίστεως αὐτοῦ κλέος: "the glorious renown for his faith" (BDAG 193*).

11. δικαιοσύνην . . . κόσμον: verbs of teaching (διδάξας) can take a double accusative of a person (τὸν κόσμον) and thing (δικαιοσύνην; Wallace 181–89; BDF §155.1; *GNTG* §5.76): "having taught the whole world, righteousness"; or, more smoothly in English, "righteousness to the whole world."

12. διδάξας . . . ἐλθών: these are adverbial participles; they might be indicating cause (Wallace 631–32; BDF §418.1; *GNTG* §5.189): "because he taught"; or, more likely, time; the aorist tense indicates time before that of the main verb (Wallace 623–25; BDF §418; *GNTG* §5.188): "after he taught."

13. μαρτυρήσας is an adverbial participle that might be indicating cause (Wallace 631–32; BDF §418.1; *GNTG* §5.189): "because he gave witness"; or, more likely, time; the aorist tense indicates time before that of the main verb (Wallace 623–25; BDF §418; *GNTG* §5.188): "after he gave witness."

ἐπὶ τῶν ἡγουμένων,[14] οὕτως ἀπηλλάγη τοῦ κόσμου[15] καὶ εἰς τὸν ἅγιον τόπον ἐπορεύθη, ὑπομονῆς γενόμενος[16] μέγιστος ὑπογραμμός.

6:1 Τούτοις τοῖς ἀνδράσιν ὁσίως πολιτευσαμένοις[17] συνηθροίσθη πολὺ πλῆθος[18] ἐκλεκτῶν, οἵτινες πολλαῖς αἰκίαις καὶ βασάνοις[19] διὰ ζῆλος παθόντες,[20] ὑπόδειγμα κάλλιστον ἐγένοντο ἐν ἡμῖν. 2 διὰ ζῆλος διωχθεῖσαι[21] γυναῖκες, Δαναΐδες καὶ Δίρκαι,[22] αἰκίσματα δεινὰ καὶ ἀνόσια παθοῦσαι[23] ἐπὶ τὸν τῆς πίστεως βέβαιον δρόμον κατήντησαν[24] καὶ ἔλαβον γέρας γενναῖον αἱ ἀσθενεῖς τῷ σώματι.[25] 3 ζῆλος ἀπηλλοτρίωσεν γαμετὰς ἀνδρῶν[26] καὶ ἠλλοίωσεν τὸ ῥηθὲν[27] ὑπὸ τοῦ πατρὸς ἡμῶν Ἀδάμ· Τοῦτο[28] νῦν ὀστοῦν ἐκ τῶν ὀστέων μου καὶ σὰρξ ἐκ τῆς σαρκὸς μου.[29] 4 ζῆλος καὶ ἔρις πόλεις μεγάλας κατέστρεψεν καὶ ἔθνη μεγάλα ἐξερίζωσεν.

14. τῶν ἡγουμένων is a substantival participle (Wallace 619–21; BDF §413; *GNTG* §5.182): "those who rule."

15. τοῦ κόσμου is a genitive of separation going with ἀπηλλάγη (Wallace 107–9; BDF §180.1; *GNTG* §5.50): "he departed from the world" (BDAG 96.2*).

16. γενόμενος is an attributive participle (Wallace 617–18; BDF §412; *GNTG* §5.181), modifying the implied subject of ἐπορεύθη: "having become."

17. πολιτευσαμένοις is an attributive participle (Wallace 617–18; BDF §412; *GNTG* §5.181), modifying ἀνδράσιν: "to these men who lived holy lives."

18. πολὺ πλῆθος is the nominative subject of συνηθροίσθη.

19. πολλαῖς . . . βασάνοις: these are likely instrumental datives (Wallace 162–63; BDF §195; *GNTG* §5.67) indicating the means by which these people suffered (BDAG 785.3.a.β*).

20. παθόντες is an attributive participle (Wallace 617–18; BDF §412; *GNTG* §5.181), modifying οἵτινες: "These ones who suffered."

21. διωχθεῖσαι is an attributive participle (Wallace 617–18; BDF §412; *GNTG* §5.181), modifying γυναῖκες: "Women who were persecuted."

22. Δαναΐδες καὶ Δίρκαι are in apposition to γυναῖκες as illustrations of women who suffered.

23. παθοῦσαι is an attributive participle (Wallace 617–18; BDF §412; *GNTG* §5.181), modifying γυναῖκες: "who suffered."

24. ἐπὶ τὸν τῆς πίστεως βέβαιον δρόμον κατήντησαν: "steadfastly finished the course of faith" (BDAG 172.2*).

25. αἱ ἀσθενεῖς τῷ σώματι: "These women weak in body."

26. ἀνδρῶν is a genitive of separation (Wallace 107–9; BDF §180.1; *GNTG* §5.50): "from husbands."

27. τὸ ῥηθὲν is a substantival participle (Wallace 619–21; BDF §413; *GNTG* §5.182): "what was spoken."

28. Τοῦτο is the nominative subject of an implied ἐστίν (Wallace 39–40; BDF §§127–28): "This is."

29. The author quotes Gen 2:23 LXX: Τοῦτο νῦν ὀστοῦν ἐκ τῶν ὀστέων μου καὶ σὰρξ ἐκ τῆς σαρκός μου·

Vocabulary

Ἀδάμ, ὁ, indecl.	Adam
ἄδικος, ον	unjust; unrighteous
ἀθλέω	to compete (BDAG 24*)
ἀθλητής, οῦ, ὁ	athlete; prizefighter
αἰκία, ίας, ἡ	outrage, torture, suffering
αἴκισμα, ατος, τό	torment
ἀλλοιόω	to change (so that it becomes null and void [BDAG 46*]), alter, reject, alienate
ἀνατολή, ῆς, ἡ	sunrise; east
ἀνόσιος, ον	unholy
ἀπαλλάσσω	to set free, remove, put away
ἀπαλλοτριόω	to estrange, alienate, be a stranger
ἀρχαῖος, αία, αῖον	old, ancient
ἀσθενής, ές	weak; weakness
βάσανος, ου, ἡ	torment, torture
βέβαιος, α, ον	sure, firm, certain
βραβεῖον, ου, τό	prize
γαμετή, ῆς, ἡ	wife
γενεά, ᾶς, ἡ	generation
γενναῖος, α, ον	noble, renowned, illustrious
γέρας, ως, τό	prize, reward
Δαναΐδες, ων, αἱ	Danaids were daughters of Danaus (all but one of whom killed their husbands on their wedding night). They are said to suffer punishment by filling leaky jars with water, but the traditions vary (see the entry in BDAG 212*).
δεινός, ή, όν	terrible, dreadful; skillful; formidable
δεσμός, οῦ, ὁ	bond, chain, imprisonment; bundle
Δίρκη, ης, ἡ	Dirce was the wife of the Theban king Lycus; she was dragged to death by a wild bull (BDAG 252*).
διώκω	to pursue, persecute
δρόμος, ου, ὁ	race-course, race; circuit
δύσις, εως, ἡ	setting (of sun); west

ἐγγύς	(+ gen.) near
ἐκλεκτός, ή, όν	elect, chosen
ἐκριζόω	to uproot
ἑπτάκις	seven times
ἔρις, ιδος, ἡ	strife
ἕως	until; when, up to, as far as
ζῆλος, ου, ὁ	zeal; jealousy
ἡγέομαι	to lead, consider, count, regard
καταντάω	to come, arrive; to reach, meet, attain
καταστρέφω	to overthrow; to be subdued; to be ended
κῆρυξ, υκος, ὁ	herald, preacher
κλέος, ους, τό	honor; report; fame
λιθάζω	to stone
μαρτυρέω	to bear witness; to suffer martyrdom
ὁσίως, adv.	in a holy manner
ὀστέον, ου	bone
ὀφείλω	to be obligated
παύω	to cease, stop
πλῆθος, ους, τό	multitude
πολιτεύομαι	to live, live as a citizen
πόνος, ου, ὁ	labor, toil; pain
πρό	(+ gen.) before, above
στῦλος, ου, ὁ	pillar
συναθροίζω	to gather; to link with others in a common experience, unite with, be joined to (BDAG 964.2*)
τέρμα, ατος, τό	limit, end
ὑπογραμμός, οῦ, ὁ	example; outline
ὑπόδειγμα, ατος, τό	example, pattern
ὑποδείκνυμι	to show, inform
ὑπομονή, ῆς, ἡ	endurance; staying
ὑποφέρω	to endure
φθόνος, ου, ὁ	envy
φορέω	to wear; to bear
φυγαδεύω	to become an exile; to send away; to flee

2.11. 1 CLEMENT 25:1–26:3

The Phoenix and Resurrection

In this section of the letter, the author illustrates that attentive persons can see "resurrection" all around them. In the previous chapter, the author pointed to natural phenomena that illustrate resurrection. In chapters 25–26, he points to the mythical bird, the phoenix.

25:1 Ἴδωμεν τὸ παράδοξον σημεῖον τὸ γινόμενον[1] ἐν τοῖς ἀνατο-λικοῖς τόποις, τουτέστιν τοῖς περὶ τὴν Ἀραβίαν.[2] 2 ὄρνεον γάρ ἐστιν, ὁ προσονομάζεται φοῖνιξ· τοῦτο μονογενὲς ὑπάρχον[3] ζῇ ἔτη πεντακόσια· γενόμενόν[4] τε ἤδη πρὸς ἀπόλυσιν[5] τοῦ ἀποθανεῖν αὐτό,[6] σηκὸν ἑαυτῷ ποιεῖ ἐκ λιβάνου καὶ σμύρνης καὶ τῶν λοιπῶν ἀρωμάτων, εἰς ὃν πληρω-θέντος[7] τοῦ χρόνου εἰσέρχεται καὶ τελευτᾷ. 3 σηπομένης[8] δὲ τῆς σαρκὸς σκώληξ τις γεννᾶται, ὃς ἐκ τῆς ἰκμάδος τοῦ τετελευτηκότος[9] ζῴου ἀνα-

1. τὸ γινόμενον is an attributive participle (Wallace 617–18; BDF §412; *GNTG* §5.181), modifying σημεῖον: "that happens."
2. τοῖς περὶ τὴν Ἀραβίαν: the article changes the prepositional phrases into an attributive modifier of τόποις (Wallace 236; BDF §266; *GNTG* §5.16): "in the places around Arabia."
3. ὑπάρχον is an attributive participle (Wallace 617–18; BDF §412; *GNTG* §5.181), modifying τοῦτο: "this [bird] being."
4. γενόμενόν is an adverbial participle indicating time; the aorist tense indicates time before that of the main verb (Wallace 623–25; BDF §418; *GNTG* §5.188): "when [it comes time]."
5. πρὸς ἀπόλυσιν: πρὸς indicates a goal (BDAG 874.3.c.): "for the release."
6. τοῦ ἀποθανεῖν αὐτό: the articular infinitive is epexegetical; it explains ἀπόλυσιν (Wallace 610; BDF §400.8; *GNTG* §5.167); αὐτό is the accusative subject of τοῦ ἀποθανεῖν (BDF §406.3*): "that is, for it to die."
7. πληρωθέντος, with τοῦ χρόνου, is a genitive absolute (Wallace 654–55; BDF §423; *GNTG* §5.197): "when its time has completed" (BDAG 828.2*).
8. σηπομένης, with τῆς σαρκὸς, is a genitive absolute (Wallace 654–55; BDF §423; *GNTG* §5.197): "as its flesh decays" (BDAG 922*).
9. τοῦ τετελευτηκότος is an attributive participle (Wallace 617–18; BDF §412; *GNTG* §5.181), modifying ζῴου: "of the dead animal."

τρεφόμενος[10] πτεροφυεῖ· εἶτα γενναῖος γενόμενος[11] αἴρει τὸν σηκὸν
ἐκεῖνον ὅπου τὰ ὀστᾶ τοῦ προγεγονότος[12] ἐστίν, καὶ ταῦτα βαστάζων[13]
διανύει ἀπὸ τῆς Ἀραβικῆς χώρας ἕως[14] τῆς Αἰγύπτου εἰς τὴν λεγομένην
Ἡλιούπολιν.[15] 4 καὶ ἡμέρας,[16] βλεπόντων[17] πάντων, ἐπιπτὰς[18] ἐπὶ τὸν
τοῦ ἡλίου βωμὸν τίθησιν αὐτά, καὶ οὕτως εἰς τοὐπίσω ἀφορμᾷ.[19] 5 οἱ οὖν
ἱερεῖς ἐπισκέπτονται τὰς ἀναγραφὰς τῶν χρόνων καὶ εὑρίσκουσιν αὐτὸν
πεντακοσιοστοῦ ἔτους πεπληρωμένου ἐληλυθέναι.[20]

26:1 Μέγα καὶ θαυμαστὸν οὖν νομίζομεν εἶναι,[21] εἰ ὁ δημιουργὸς
τῶν ἁπάντων ἀνάστασιν ποιήσεται τῶν ὁσίως αὐτῷ δουλευσάντων[22]
ἐν πεποιθήσει πίστεως ἀγαθῆς, ὅπου καὶ δι᾽ ὀρνέου δείκνυσιν ἡμῖν τὸ

---

10. ἀνατρεφόμενος is an attributive participle (Wallace 617–18; BDF §412; *GNTG* §5.181), modifying ὅς: "which, being nourished."

11. γενναῖος γενόμενος: γενόμενος is likely an adverbial participle indicating time; the aorist tense indicates time before that of the main verb (Wallace 623–25; BDF §418; *GNTG* §5.183): "after becoming strong" (BDAG 193*).

12. προγεγονότος is a substantival participle (Wallace 619–21; BDF §413; *GNTG* §5.182). Here, προγίνομαι means "the former one," "predecessor" (BDAG 866*).

13. βαστάζων is likely an adverbial participle indicating time; the present tense indicates time contemporaneous with that of the main verb (Wallace 623–25; BDF §418; *GNTG* §5.188): "while carrying."

14. ἕως with the genitive is indicating the limit reached: "to Egypt" (BDAG 423.3.a).

15. τὴν λεγομένην Ἡλιούπολιν: λεγομένην frequently precedes a proper name and is placed after the term that it is specifying (BDF §412.2: BDAG 590.4). Here that term is implied: "[the city] called Heliopolis."

16. ἡμέρας is a genitive of time (Wallace 122–24; BDF §186.2; *GNTG* §5.53): "during the day."

17. βλεπόντων, with πάντων, is a genitive absolute (Wallace 654–55; BDF §423; *GNTG* §5.197): "while everyone is looking."

18. ἐπιπτὰς is an adverbial participle indicating time; the aorist tense indicates time before that of the main verb (Wallace 623–25; BDF §418; *GNTG* §5.188): "after flying in."

19. εἰς τοὐπίσω ἀφορμᾷ: ἀφορμᾷ is pres.-ind.-act.-3-sg. < ἀφορμάω: "he starts back" (BDAG 715.1*).

20. αὐτὸν πεντακοσιοστοῦ ἔτους πεπληρωμένου ἐληλυθέναι: αὐτὸν is the accusative subject of the infinitive (ἐληλυθέναι). πεντακοσιοστοῦ ἔτους πεπληρωμένου is a genitive absolute (Wallace 654–55; BDF §423; *GNTG* §5.197): "after the five hundredth year had been completed." ἐληλυθέναι is likely indicating indirect discourse (Wallace 603–5; BDF §396; *GNTG* §166), relating the content of what was found in the Scriptures: "that he had come."

21. εἶναι indicates indirect discourse following a verb of believing (νομίζομεν; Wallace 603–5; BDF §397.2; *GNTG* §5.166): "do we think that it is."

22. τῶν . . . δουλευσάντων is a substantival participle (Wallace 619–21; BDF §413; *GNTG* §5.182).

μεγαλεῖον τῆς ἐπαγγελίας αὐτοῦ; 2 λέγει γάρ που·²³ Καὶ ἐξαναστήσεις με, καὶ ἐξομολογήσομαί σοι, καί·Ἐκοιμήθην καὶ ὕπνωσα, ἐξηγέρθην, ὅτι σὺ μετ᾽ ἐμοῦ εἶ.²⁴ 3 καὶ πάλιν Ἰὼβ λέγει·²⁵ Καὶ ἀναστήσεις τὴν σάρκα μου ταύτην τὴν ἀναντλήσασαν²⁶ ταῦτα πάντα.

Vocabulary

Αἴγυπτος, ου, ἡ	Egypt
αἴρω	to take up
ἀναγραφή, ῆς, ἡ	record
ἀναντλέω	to go through, endure
ἀνάστασις, εως, ἡ	standing up, rising, insurrection, resurrection
ἀνατολικός, ή, όν	eastern
ἀνατρέφω	to nourish, bring up, educate
ἀνίστημι	to raise up, set up, resist, restore, arise
ἅπας, ασα, αν	all, every
ἀποθνήσκω	to die
ἀπόλυσις, εως, ἡ	release, deliverance; dismissal
Ἀραβία, ας, ἡ	Arabia
Ἀραβικός, ή, όν	Arabic
ἄρωμα, ατος, τό	spices
ἀφορμάω	to start out
βαστάζω	to bear
βωμός, οῦ, ὁ	altar
γενναῖος, α, ον	noble, renowned, strong
γεννάω	to be father of, bear, beget; to engender
δείκνυμι	to show
δημιουργός, οῦ, ὁ	builder, maker, creator; demiurge
διανύω	to travel; to arrive; to complete

23. Perhaps the author has Ps 28:7 (27:7 LXX) in mind: καὶ ἀνέθαλεν ἡ σάρξ μου· / καὶ ἐκ θελήματός μου ἐξομολογήσομαι αὐτῷ.

24. Perhaps the author is thinking of Ps 3:6: ἐγὼ ἐκοιμήθην καὶ ὕπνωσα· / ἐξηγέρθην, ὅτι κύριος ἀντιλήμψεταί μου.

25. Job 19:26: ἀναστῆσαι τὸ δέρμα μου τὸ ἀνατλῶν ταῦτα.

26. τὴν ἀναντλήσασαν is an attributive participle (Wallace 617–18; BDF §412; *GNTG* §5.181), modifying σάρκα: "which has endured."

δουλεύω	to serve as a slave
εἰσέρχομαι	to enter
εἶτα, adv.	then, next
ἐξανίστημι	to raise up, rise up
ἐξεγείρω	to raise up, wake up, arise, revive (passive with the intransitive sense: woke up [BDAG 346.1*])
ἐξομολογέω	to confess, admit
ἐπαγγελία, ας, ἡ	promise; notification; indication
ἐπιπέτομαι	to fly onto
ἐπισκέπτομαι	to look at, examine, inspect; to visit, care for
ἔτος, ους, τό	year
ζῷον, ου, τό	living being; animal; (zodiacal) sign; life
ἤδη, adv.	now, already
ἥλιος, ου, ὁ	sun
Ἡλιούπολις, εως, ἡ	Heliopolis
θαυμαστός, ή, όν	marvelous, wonderful
ἱερεύς, έως, ὁ	priest
ἰκμάς, άδος, ἡ	moisture
Ἰώβ, ὁ, indecl.	Job
κοιμάω	to go to bed; to sleep; to calm (only in the passive in our literature [BDAG 551*])
λίβανος, ου, ὁ	frankincense
μεγαλεῖος, α, ον	mighty, magnificent; mighty act
μονογενής, ές	only, unique
νομίζω	to think, suppose; to be customary
ὀπίσω	(+ gen.) after (prep.); back (adv.)
ὅπου, adv.	where, whereas; insofar as, since
ὄρνεον, ου, τό	bird
ὁσίως, adv.	in a holy manner
ὀστέον, ου, τό	bone
παράδοξος, ον	remarkable; unusual; paradoxical
πεντακόσιοι, αι, α	five hundred
πεντακοσιοστός, ή, όν	five hundredth
πεποίθησις, εως, ἡ	confidence

πληρόω	to fill; to fulfill
πού, adv.	somewhere
προγίνομαι	to happen previously
προσονομάζω	to call by name, give a name
πτεροφυέω	to grow feathers/wings
σηκός, οῦ, ὁ	nest, tomb (BDAG 920*).
σημεῖον, ου, τό	sign, miracle
σήπω	to rot, decay
σκώληξ, ηκος, ὁ	worm; grub; maggot
σμύρνα, ης, ἡ	myrrh
τελευτάω	to die
τουτέστιν	that is
ὑπάρχω	to be, exist; to possess, have advantage
ὕπνόω	to sleep
φοῖνιξ, ικος, ὁ	palm tree, palm branch; date-palm, date; fabulous bird
χρόνος, ου, ὁ	time
χώρα, ας, ἡ	place, land, country

Texts Exhibiting More Sophisticated Greek

The Birth of Jesus in the Roman Empire

This gospel is volume one in a two-volume work attributed to Luke, the companion of Paul (Col 4:14; 2 Tim 4:11; Phlm 24). Both volumes address a certain Theophilus (Luke 1:3; Acts 1:1), and in the beginning of volume 2, the author refers to volume 1 (Acts 1:1). The place of composition is unknown. Because the author clearly uses the Gospel of Mark in composing his own gospel, and because he seems to be aware of the destruction of Jerusalem (see 19:41–44 and 21:20–24, for example), both volumes must have been written after that work.

Luke begins his gospel alternating stories about the birth of John and the birth of Jesus. Chapter 2 sets Jesus's birth in the context of both the Roman Empire (mentioning Roman governmental officials) and Herod the Great (specified in 1:5). Mary and Joseph go to Bethlehem where the child is born in a humble setting and his birth is announced by shepherds. This narrative concludes with illustrations of Mary's and Joseph's piety: they fulfill the requirements given in Torah for the birth a of male child. This selection displays Luke's interest to highlight God's concern for people not in power and his interest in prophecy and prophets.

The parallel birth narrative in the Gospel of Matthew can be found in §2.4.

1 Ἐγένετο δὲ[1] ἐν ταῖς ἡμέραις ἐκείναις ἐξῆλθεν δόγμα παρὰ Καίσαρος Αὐγούστου ἀπογράφεσθαι[2] πᾶσαν τὴν οἰκουμένην.[3] 2 αὕτη ἀπογραφὴ πρώτη[4] ἐγένετο ἡγεμονεύοντος τῆς Συρίας Κυρηνίου.[5] 3 καὶ ἐπορεύοντο πάντες ἀπογράφεσθαι,[6] ἕκαστος εἰς τὴν ἑαυτοῦ πόλιν. 4 Ἀνέβη δὲ καὶ[7] Ἰωσὴφ ἀπὸ τῆς Γαλιλαίας ἐκ πόλεως Ναζαρὲθ εἰς τὴν Ἰουδαίαν εἰς πόλιν

1. Ἐγένετο δὲ and, more frequently, καὶ ἐγένετο (see v. 15) are influenced by Hebrew syntax that appears frequently in the LXX. The phrase occurs at the beginning of sentences to introduce a time-frame within which an event took place in the past (*GELS* 131.6; BDAG 198.4.f*; BDF §§442.5, 472.2*; *GNTG* §5.92.c.1). Older translations translated the phrase something like, "And it came to pass" (cf. KJV); more recent translations leave the phrase untranslated, only translating the temporal expression that follows (cf. NIV and NRSV); in this case: "In those days."

2. ἀπογράφεσθαι: the infinitive might be indirect discourse, reporting the content of the decree (Wallace 603–5; BDF §396; *GNTG* §166); it could also be epexegetical (Wallace 607; BDF §394; *GNTG* §5.167; Culy, Parsons, and Stigall, *Luke*, 64), explaining δόγμα; or, it could indicate the purpose of the decree (Wallace 590–92; BDF §390; *GNTG* §5.161): "that the [whole empire] was to be registered."

3. τὴν οἰκουμένην: this feminine substantival participle was used to indicate the inhabited world or the world as an administrative unit of the Roman Empire (BDAG 699.1–2; see Culy, Parsons, and Stigall, *Luke*, 64).

4. αὕτη ἀπογραφὴ πρώτη might be interpreted in three different ways: (1) αὕτη is read as the nominative subject of ἐγένετο and ἀπογραφὴ πρώτη is the predicate nominative: "This was the first census"; (2) alternatively, αὕτη ἀπογραφὴ is read as the subject, and πρώτη is the predicate adjective: "This census was the first"; (3) finally, αὕτη ἀπογραφὴ πρώτη is read as the subject: "This first census came about." A noun modified by a demonstrative pronoun normally has the article when it is the subject. When the nominative substantive is the predicate, though, the article is normally not present. This points toward option (1); there is strong evidence in the textual tradition, however, to suggest that many ancient scribes read ἀπογραφὴ as the subject, taking πρώτη as the predicate adjective; thus suggesting reading (2) as the more likely. See discussion in Culy, Parsons, and Stigall, *Luke*, 64–65; also Wallace 304–5.

5. ἡγεμονεύοντος . . . Κυρηνίου is a genitive absolute (Wallace 654–55; BDF §423; *GNTG* §5.197): "when Quirinius was governor of Syria."

6. ἀπογράφεσθαι: the infinitive is indicating purpose (Wallace 590–92; BDF §390; *GNTG* §5.161).

7. Luke likes to use δὲ καὶ for emphasis (see the discussion in Culy, Parsons, and Stigall, *Luke*, 66).

Δαυὶδ ἥτις καλεῖται Βηθλέεμ,⁸ διὰ τὸ εἶναι αὐτὸν⁹ ἐξ οἴκου καὶ πατριᾶς Δαυίδ, 5 ἀπογράψασθαι¹⁰ σὺν Μαριὰμ τῇ ἐμνηστευμένῃ¹¹ αὐτῷ, οὔσῃ¹² ἐγκύῳ. 6 Ἐγένετο δὲ ἐν τῷ εἶναι αὐτοὺς¹³ ἐκεῖ ἐπλήσθησαν αἱ ἡμέραι τοῦ τεκεῖν¹⁴ αὐτήν, 7 καὶ ἔτεκεν τὸν υἱὸν αὐτῆς τὸν πρωτότοκον, καὶ ἐσπαργάνωσεν αὐτὸν καὶ ἀνέκλινεν αὐτὸν ἐν φάτνῃ, διότι οὐκ ἦν αὐτοῖς¹⁵ τόπος ἐν τῷ καταλύματι.¹⁶

8. Βηθλέεμ, although indeclinable, is likely to be read as nominative here. Verbs that can take a double accusative of object and complement in the active (καλέω) can end up with two nominatives when used as a passive. The word that would have been the accusative of object in the active becomes the subject in the passive (ἥτις), and the accusative complement becomes a nominative complement (Βηθλέεμ; *GNTG* §5.30; Wallace suggests that καλέω can take a predicate nominative [40]). BDAG indicates that in the passive, καλέω comes close to meaning "to be" (503.1.d) and so would take a predicate nominative.
9. διὰ τὸ εἶναι αὐτὸν: the articular infinitive with διὰ is indicating cause (Wallace 596–97, 610; BDF §402; *GNTG* §5.173); αὐτὸν is the subject of the infinitive: "because he was."
10. ἀπογράψασθαι: the infinitive is indicating purpose (Wallace 590–92; BDF §390; *GNTG* §5.161).
11. τῇ ἐμνηστευμένῃ is an attributive participle (Wallace 617–18; BDF §413; *GNTG* §5.181), modifying Μαριὰμ: "who was betrothed."
12. οὔσῃ is an attributive participle (Wallace 617–18; BDF §412; *GNTG* §5.181), modifying Μαριὰμ: "who was."
13. Ἐγένετο δὲ ἐν τῷ εἶναι αὐτοὺς: for Ἐγένετο δὲ, see n. 1. The articular infinitive (τῷ εἶναι) is used with ἐν to indicate contemporaneous time (Wallace 595; BDF §404; *GNTG* §5.172; Culy, Parsons, and Stigall, *Luke*, 67): "while they were."
14. τοῦ τεκεῖν: the genitive, articular infinitive is likely epexegetical (Wallace 607, 610; BDF §§394, 400.8; *GNTG* §5.167), explaining αἱ ἡμέραι: "the days of her giving birth"; "the time for her to give birth."
15. αὐτοῖς is a dative of possession (Wallace 149–51; BDF §189; *GNTG* §5.61): "there was no place for them"; "they had no place."
16. τῷ καταλύματι probably does not indicate an "inn" but rather a guest room (for relatives or friends). This is clearly its meaning in 22:11. Contrast 10:34 where Luke uses πανδοχεῖον, which is the more common word for "inn." See Stephen C. Carlson, "The Accommodations of Joseph and Mary in Bethlehem: Κατάλυμα in Luke 2.7," *New Testament Studies* 56 (2010): 326–42, DOI:10.1017/S0028688509990282.

8 Καὶ ποιμένες ἦσαν ἐν τῇ χώρᾳ τῇ αὐτῇ ἀγραυλοῦντες[17] καὶ φυλάσσοντες φυλακὰς[18] τῆς νυκτὸς[19] ἐπὶ τὴν ποίμνην αὐτῶν. 9 καὶ ἄγγελος
κυρίου ἐπέστη[20] αὐτοῖς καὶ δόξα κυρίου περιέλαμψεν αὐτούς, καὶ ἐφοβήθησαν φόβον[21] μέγαν. 10 καὶ εἶπεν αὐτοῖς ὁ ἄγγελος· μὴ φοβεῖσθε,
ἰδοὺ γὰρ εὐαγγελίζομαι ὑμῖν χαρὰν μεγάλην ἥτις ἔσται παντὶ τῷ λαῷ,
11 ὅτι[22] ἐτέχθη[23] ὑμῖν σήμερον σωτὴρ ὅς ἐστιν χριστὸς κύριος ἐν πόλει
Δαυίδ. 12 καὶ τοῦτο[24] ὑμῖν τὸ σημεῖον, εὑρήσετε βρέφος ἐσπαργανωμένον[25]

17. ἀγραυλοῦντες could be either an attributive participle (Wallace 617–18; BDF §412;
GNTG §5.181), modifying ποιμένες: "Shepherds who were living"; or an imperfect periphrastic construction (the imperfect form of εἰμί plus the present participle); equivalent
in function to the imperfect tense of the finite verb (Wallace 647–49; BDF §§352–53;
GNTG §§5.184–85; see the discussion in Culy, Parsons, and Stigall, *Luke*, 70): "Shepherds
were living."

18. φυλάσσοντες φυλακὰς: φυλάσσοντες could be either an attributive participle (Wallace
617–18; BDF §412; *GNTG* §5.181), modifying ποιμένες: "shepherds who were keeping
watch"; or, an imperfect periphrastic construction (the imperfect form of εἰμί plus the
present participle); equivalent in function to the imperfect tense of the finite verb (Wallace
647–49; BDF §§352–53; *GNTG* §§5.184–85; see the discussion in Culy, Parsons, and Stigall,
Luke, 70): "Shepherds were keeping watch." φυλακὰς is a cognate accusative (Wallace
189–90; BDF §153); it includes the lexical root of the verb (φυλάσσοντες). Unless there is
a modifier, this accusative functions merely as a direct object.

19. τῆς νυκτὸς is either a genitive of time (Wallace 122–24; BDF §186.2; *GNTG* §5.53):
"during the night"; or attributive genitive (Wallace 86–88; BDF §167; *GNTG* §5.44): "night
watches."

20. ἐπέστη: aor.-ind.-act.-3-sg. < ἐφίστημι.

21. φόβον is a cognate accusative (Wallace 189–90; BDF §153); it includes the lexical root
of the verb (ἐφοβήθησαν). With the modifier μέγαν, the construction is more emphatic:
"they were very much afraid" (BDAG 1061.1.a*).

22. Culy, Parsons, and Stigall suggest ὅτι introduces an epexegetical clause explaining χαρὰν μεγάλην. They argue that because εὐαγγελίζομαι has a complement (χαρὰν
μεγάλην), ὅτι cannot introduce another complement (indirect discourse). See Culy, Parsons, and Stigall, *Luke*, 71–72.

23. ἐτέχθη: aor.-ind.-pass.-3-sg. < τίκτω. The aorist tense here is likely used to indicate an
event that has just now happened (Wallace 564–65).

24. τοῦτο is the subject of an implied form of εἰμί (Wallace 39–40; BDF §§127–28); probably
future since εὑρήσετε (which follows) is future: "this will be."

25. ἐσπαργανωμένον: pf.-ptc.-pass.-neut.-acc.-sg. < σπαργανόω. Both participles,
ἐσπαργανωμένον and κείμενον, are either attributive (Wallace 617–18; BDF §412; *GNTG*
§5.181), modifying βρέφος; or complements in an object-complement double accusative
construction with βρέφος as the object (Wallace 181–89 [183 n. 24]; BDF §157; *GNTG*
§5.77; see the discussion in Culy, Parsons, and Stigall, *Luke*, 72).

καὶ κείμενον ἐν φάτνῃ. 13 καὶ ἐξαίφνης ἐγένετο σὺν τῷ ἀγγέλῳ πλῆθος στρατιᾶς οὐρανίου αἰνούντων τὸν θεὸν καὶ λεγόντων·[26]

14   δόξα[27] ἐν ὑψίστοις θεῷ
          καὶ ἐπὶ γῆς εἰρήνη
          ἐν ἀνθρώποις εὐδοκίας.[28]

15 Καὶ[29] ἐγένετο ὡς ἀπῆλθον ἀπ᾽ αὐτῶν εἰς τὸν οὐρανὸν οἱ ἄγγελοι, οἱ ποιμένες ἐλάλουν πρὸς ἀλλήλους· διέλθωμεν δὴ[30] ἕως Βηθλέεμ καὶ ἴδωμεν τὸ ῥῆμα[31] τοῦτο τὸ γεγονὸς[32] ὃ[33] ὁ κύριος ἐγνώρισεν ἡμῖν. 16 καὶ ἦλθαν σπεύσαντες[34] καὶ ἀνεῦραν[35] τήν τε Μαριὰμ καὶ τὸν Ἰωσὴφ καὶ[36]

---

26. αἰνούντων . . . λεγόντων are attributive participles (Wallace 617–18; BDF §412; *GNTG* §5.181), modifying στρατιᾶς. Even though στρατιᾶς is singular, the participles are plural on the principle of *constructio ad sensum*: a singular noun that contains a plurality of persons is taken as if it is plural (Wallace 400–401; on the concept of *constructio ad sensum*, see the discussion in BDF §134).

27. δόξα . . . εἰρήνη are each the subject of an implied form of εἰμί (Wallace 39–40; BDF §§127–28).

28. ἀνθρώποις εὐδοκίας: according to BDAG, the phrase is often understood to mean: men characterized by good will (404.1); Culy, Parsons, and Stigall suggest the phrase reflects a common first-century Jewish expression: "those upon whom God's favor rests (*Luke*, 73).

29. καὶ ἐγένετο is influenced by Hebrew syntax that appears frequently in the LXX (see n. 1). Leave the phrase untranslated and translate the temporal expression that follows: "When the angels went away" (BDAG 1105.8).

30. δὴ is a particle used with exhortations or commands, to give them greater urgency (BDAG 222.2; Wallace 673, 761; BDF §451.4): "certainly," or "indeed."

31. τὸ ῥῆμα: in this context, "thing" (BDAG 902.2).

32. τὸ γεγονὸς: pf.-ptc.-act.-neut.-acc.-sg. < γίνομαι. The participle is attributive (Wallace 617–18; BDF §412; *GNTG* §5.181), modifying τὸ ῥῆμα: "that has happened."

33. ὃ is neut.-acc.-sg.; the direct object of ἐγνώρισεν.

34. σπεύσαντες is likely a participle of manner modifying ἦλθαν (Wallace 627–28; BDF §418; *GNTG* §5.193): "they left as quickly as possible" (BDAG 937.1.a*).

35. ἀνεῦραν: aor.-ind.-act.-3-pl. < ἀνευρίσκω.

36. τε . . . καὶ . . . καὶ: "both . . . and . . . and."

τὸ βρέφος κείμενον³⁷ ἐν τῇ φάτνῃ· 17 ἰδόντες³⁸ δὲ ἐγνώρισαν³⁹ περὶ τοῦ
ῥήματος τοῦ λαληθέντος⁴⁰ αὐτοῖς περὶ τοῦ παιδίου τούτου. 18 καὶ πάντες
οἱ ἀκούσαντες ἐθαύμασαν περὶ τῶν λαληθέντων⁴¹ ὑπὸ τῶν ποιμένων
πρὸς⁴² αὐτούς· 19 ἡ δὲ Μαριὰμ πάντα συνετήρει τὰ ῥήματα ταῦτα συμ-
βάλλουσα⁴³ ἐν τῇ καρδίᾳ αὐτῆς. 20 καὶ ὑπέστρεψαν οἱ ποιμένες δοξάζοντες καὶ αἰνοῦντες⁴⁴ τὸν θεὸν ἐπὶ⁴⁵ πᾶσιν οἷς⁴⁶ ἤκουσαν καὶ εἶδον καθὼς
ἐλαλήθη πρὸς⁴⁷ αὐτούς.

37. κείμενον is either an attributive participle (Wallace 617–18; BDF §412; GNTG §5.181),
modifying τὸ βρέφος; or the complement in an object-complement double accusative
construction with τὸ βρέφος as the object (Wallace 181–89 [183 n. 24]; BDF §157; GNTG
§5.77; see the discussion in Culy, Parsons, and Stigall, *Luke*, 75).
38. ἰδόντες is either an adverbial participle indicating time; the aorist tense indicates time
before that of the main verb (Wallace 623–27; BDF §418; GNTG §5.188): "when they saw";
or "after they saw"; or an attendant circumstance participle, referring to an action that is
parallel to the main verb (Wallace 640–45; GNTG §5.198): "they saw and."
39. ἐγνώρισαν has no direct object, but περὶ often occurs with verbs of speaking or
knowing. It means "concerning" (BDF §229). It is ambiguous to whom the shepherds
made known this information (see discussion in Culy, Parsons, and Stigall, *Luke*, 75):
"they made known the word (or thing)."
40. τοῦ λαληθέντος is an attributive participle (Wallace 617–18; BDF §412; GNTG §5.181),
modifying τοῦ ῥήματος: "the thing that had been said."
41. τῶν λαληθέντων is a substantival participle (Wallace 619–21; BDF §413; GNTG §5.182):
"[at] what was said."
42. πρὸς here is used with a verb of speaking to indicate the addressee (BDAG 874.3.a.ε).
Luke often uses this construction rather than the dative case (Culy, Parsons, and Stigall,
Luke, 76, referencing p. 14).
43. συμβάλλουσα might be an attendant circumstance participle, referring to an action
that is parallel to the main verb (Wallace 640–45; GNTG §5.198): "was treasuring . . . and
considered" (Culy, Parsons, and Stigall, *Luke*, 76); it might be a participle of manner
(Wallace 627–28; BDF §418; GNTG §5.193): "was treasuring . . . considering." In this context, συμβάλλουσα means something like "to give careful thought to, consider, ponder"
(BDAG 956.2*).
44. δοξάζοντες καὶ αἰνοῦντες are likely adverbial participles indicating manner (Wallace
627–28; BDF §418; GNTG §5.193).
45. After verbs that express feelings, opinions, ἐπὶ can mean "because of" (BDAG 364.6.c).
46. οἷς is dative by attraction to πᾶσιν. We would expect a neuter accusative since it is the
direct object of ἤκουσαν καὶ εἶδον (Culy, Parsons, and Stigall, *Luke*, 77).
47. πρὸς here is used with a verb of speaking to indicate the addressee (BDAG 874.3.a.ε).
See n. 42.

21 Καὶ ὅτε ἐπλήσθησαν ἡμέραι ὀκτὼ τοῦ περιτεμεῖν αὐτὸν[48] καὶ[49] ἐκλήθη τὸ ὄνομα αὐτοῦ Ἰησοῦς,[50] τὸ κληθὲν[51] ὑπὸ τοῦ ἀγγέλου πρὸ τοῦ συλλημφθῆναι[52] αὐτὸν ἐν τῇ κοιλίᾳ.

22 Καὶ ὅτε ἐπλήσθησαν αἱ ἡμέραι τοῦ καθαρισμοῦ αὐτῶν κατὰ τὸν νόμον Μωϋσέως,[53] ἀνήγαγον αὐτὸν εἰς Ἱεροσόλυμα παραστῆσαι[54] τῷ κυρίῳ, 23 καθὼς γέγραπται ἐν νόμῳ κυρίου ὅτι πᾶν ἄρσεν διανοῖγον[55] μήτραν ἅγιον[56] τῷ κυρίῳ κληθήσεται,[57] 24 καὶ τοῦ δοῦναι[58] θυσίαν κατὰ τὸ εἰρημένον[59] ἐν τῷ νόμῳ κυρίου, ζεῦγος τρυγόνων ἢ δύο νοσσοὺς[60] περιστερῶν.[61]

48. τοῦ περιτεμεῖν αὐτὸν: Culy, Parsons, and Stigall suggest the genitive, articular infinitive is epexegetical, explaining ἡμέραι (*Luke*, 77; see Wallace 607; BDF §394; *GNTG* §5.167); BDF suggests the infinitive has the sense of result (§400.2*): the completion of the days results in the circumcision. αὐτὸν is the object of περιτεμεῖν: "when eight days were completed [and] he was circumcised."

49. καὶ is likely introducing the apodosis of the temporal clause because of influence from LXX syntax (BDAG 494.1.b.δ); it can be omitted from translation.

50. Ἰησοῦς: verbs that can take a double accusative of object and complement in the active (καλέω) can end up with two nominatives when used as a passive. See n. 8.

51. κληθὲν: aor.-ptc.-pass.-neut.-nom.-sg. < καλέω. The participle is substantival (Wallace 619–21; BDF §413; *GNTG* §5.182) and in apposition to τὸ ὄνομα: "the name given."

52. συλλημφθῆναι: the infinitive is used with πρὸ τοῦ to indicate subsequent time (Wallace 596; BDF §§395, 403; *GNTG* §5.172): "before he was conceived."

53. The expectations for a woman who has given birth to a son are set out in Lev 12:2–4.

54. παραστῆσαι: the infinitive indicates purpose (Wallace 590–92; BDF §390; *GNTG* §5.161).

55. διανοῖγον: pres.-ptc.-act.-neut.-nom.-sg. < διανοίγω. The participle is attributive (Wallace 617–18; BDF §412; *GNTG* §5.181), modifying ἄρσεν: "who opens."

56. ἅγιον: verbs that can take a double accusative of object and complement in the active (καλέω) can end up with two nominatives when used as a passive. See n. 8.

57. This statement points to Exod 13:2: Ἁγίασόν μοι πᾶν πρωτότοκον πρωτογενὲς διανοῖγον πᾶσαν μήτραν (see also vv. 12, 15).

58. τοῦ δοῦναι: the infinitive indicates purpose (Wallace 590–92, 610; BDF §§390, 400.5; *GNTG* §5.161). With θυσία, "to offer a sacrifice."

59. τὸ εἰρημένον: pf.-ptc.-pass.-neut.-acc.-sg. < λέγω; it is substantival (Wallace 619–21; BDF §413; *GNTG* §5.182): "according to what has been said."

60. ζεῦγος . . . δύο νοσσοὺς are both accusatives in apposition to θυσίαν (Culy, Parsons, and Stigall, *Luke*, 81).

61. This is a quotation of Lev 12:8 LXX: ἐὰν δὲ μὴ εὑρίσκῃ ἡ χεὶρ αὐτῆς τὸ ἱκανὸν εἰς ἀμνόν, καὶ λήμψεται δύο **τρυγόνας ἢ δύο νεοσσοὺς περιστερῶν**.

25 Καὶ ἰδοὺ ἄνθρωπος ἦν ἐν Ἰερουσαλὴμ ᾧ⁶² ὄνομα⁶³ Συμεὼν καὶ ὁ ἄνθρωπος οὗτος⁶⁴ δίκαιος καὶ εὐλαβὴς προσδεχόμενος⁶⁵ παράκλησιν τοῦ Ἰσραήλ, καὶ πνεῦμα ἦν ἅγιον ἐπ᾽ αὐτόν· 26 καὶ ἦν αὐτῷ κεχρηματισμέ-νον⁶⁶ ὑπὸ τοῦ πνεύματος τοῦ ἁγίου μὴ ἰδεῖν⁶⁷ θάνατον πρὶν ἢ ἂν⁶⁸ ἴδῃ τὸν χριστὸν κυρίου. 27 καὶ ἦλθεν ἐν τῷ πνεύματι εἰς τὸ ἱερόν· καὶ ἐν τῷ εἰσαγαγεῖν⁶⁹ τοὺς γονεῖς τὸ παιδίον Ἰησοῦν τοῦ ποιῆσαι αὐτοὺς⁷⁰ κατὰ τὸ εἰθισμένον⁷¹ τοῦ νόμου περὶ αὐτοῦ 28 καὶ αὐτὸς ἐδέξατο αὐτὸ⁷² εἰς τὰς ἀγκάλας καὶ εὐλόγησεν τὸν θεὸν καὶ εἶπεν·

29   νῦν ἀπολύεις τὸν δοῦλόν σου,⁷³ δέσποτα,
           κατὰ τὸ ῥῆμά σου ἐν εἰρήνη·
30   ὅτι εἶδον οἱ ὀφθαλμοί μου τὸ σωτήριόν σου,
           31   ὃ ἡτοίμασας⁷⁴ κατὰ πρόσωπον ⁷⁵ πάντων τῶν
λαῶν,

62. ᾧ is a dative of possession (Wallace 149–51; BDF §189; *GNTG* §5.61): "whose."

63. ὄνομα is the nominative subject of an implied ἦν (Wallace 39–40; BDF §§127–28).

64. ὁ ἄνθρωπος οὗτος is the nominative subject of an implied ἦν (Wallace 39–40; BDF §§127–28): "this man was."

65. προσδεχόμενος is likely an attributive participle (Wallace 617–18; BDF §413; *GNTG* §5.181) in apposition to δίκαιος καὶ εὐλαβὴς: "looking forward to."

66. κεχρηματισμένον is a pluperfect periphrastic construction (the imperfect form of εἰμί plus the perfect participle); equivalent in function to the pluperfect tense of the finite verb (Wallace 647–49; BDF §§352–53; *GNTG* §§5.184–85): "it had been revealed to him."

67. ἰδεῖν: the infinitive is indicating indirect discourse (Wallace 603–5; BDF §§396, 397.3; *GNTG* §5.166): "that he would not see."

68. πρὶν ἢ plus ἂν with the subjunctive is classical Attic usage (BDF §383.3): "before he would see."

69. τῷ εἰσαγαγεῖν: the infinitive is used with ἐν to indicate contemporaneous time (Wallace 595; BDF §404; *GNTG* §5.172; Culy, Parsons, and Stigall, *Luke*, 83): "as/when the parents led."

70. τοῦ ποιῆσαι αὐτοὺς: the genitive articular infinitive indicates purpose (Wallace 590–92, 610; BDF §§390, 400.5; *GNTG* §5.161); αὐτοὺς is the accusative subject of ποιῆσαι: "so that they could do."

71. εἰθισμένον: pf.- ptc.-pass.-neut.-acc.-sg. < ἐθίζω. The participle is substantival (Wallace 619–21; BDF §413; *GNTG* §5.182): "according to the custom of" (BDAG 276).

72. αὐτὸς ἐδέξατο αὐτὸ: αὐτὸς is the nominative subject of ἐδέξατο; the antecedent is Simeon. αὐτὸ is the accusative direct object of ἐδέξατο; it is neuter because the antecedent is τὸ παιδίον.

73. ἀπολύεις τὸν δοῦλόν σου: ἀπολύεις can be used as a euphemism for letting someone die (BDAG 118.3*).

74. ὃ is the neuter accusative direct object of ἡτοίμασας, not the article of a participle. ἡτοίμασας: aor.-ind.-act.-2-sg. < ἑτοιμάζω.

75. κατὰ πρόσωπον: "before" or "in the presence of" (BDAG 888.1.b.β.ꓶ).

32 φῶς εἰς ἀποκάλυψιν ἐθνῶν[76]
  καὶ δόξαν[77] λαοῦ[78] σου Ἰσραήλ.

33 καὶ ἦν ὁ πατὴρ αὐτοῦ καὶ ἡ μήτηρ θαυμάζοντες[79] ἐπὶ τοῖς λαλουμένοις[80] περὶ αὐτοῦ. 34 καὶ εὐλόγησεν αὐτοὺς Συμεὼν καὶ εἶπεν πρὸς Μαριὰμ τὴν μητέρα αὐτοῦ· ἰδοὺ οὗτος κεῖται εἰς πτῶσιν καὶ ἀνάστασιν πολλῶν ἐν τῷ Ἰσραὴλ καὶ εἰς σημεῖον ἀντιλεγόμενον[81] 35 καὶ σοῦ δὲ αὐτῆς[82] τὴν ψυχὴν διελεύσεται ῥομφαία ὅπως ἂν[83] ἀποκαλυφθῶσιν ἐκ πολλῶν καρδιῶν διαλογισμοί.

36 Καὶ ἦν Ἅννα προφῆτις, θυγάτηρ Φανουήλ, ἐκ φυλῆς Ἀσήρ· αὕτη προβεβηκυῖα ἐν ἡμέραις πολλαῖς,[84] ζήσασα[85] μετὰ ἀνδρὸς ἔτη ἑπτὰ[86] ἀπὸ τῆς παρθενίας[87] αὐτῆς 37 καὶ αὐτὴ[88] χήρα ἕως ἐτῶν ὀγδοήκοντα

---

76. εἰς plus the accusative indicating purpose: "for a revelation" (BDAG 290.4.F). ἐθνῶν is a genitive of reference (Wallace 126; *GNTG* §5.43): "for the nations."

77. φῶς . . . δόξαν are accusatives in apposition to σωτήριόν.

78. λαοῦ is a genitive of reference (Wallace 126; *GNTG* §5.43): "for your people."

79. θαυμάζοντες is an imperfect periphrastic construction (the imperfect form of εἰμί plus the present participle); equivalent in function to the imperfect tense of the finite verb (Wallace 647–49; BDF §§352–53; *GNTG* §§5.184–85): "were marveling." ἦν is singular with a compound subject (ὁ πατὴρ αὐτοῦ καὶ ἡ μήτηρ; Wallace 399–400; BDF §135; *GNTG* §5.26.b).

80. τοῖς λαλουμένοις is a substantival participle (Wallace 619–21; BDF §413; *GNTG* §5.182): "at what was said."

81. ἀντιλεγόμενον is an attributive participle (Wallace 617–18; BDF §412; *GNTG* §5.181), modifying σημεῖον: "a sign [that will be] rejected" (BDAG 89.2*).

82. αὐτῆς is intensive: "your own soul also."

83. ὅπως ἂν with the subjunctive indicates purpose (Wallace 676; BDF §369.5): "in order that."

84. προβεβηκυῖα ἐν ἡμέραις πολλαῖς: προβεβηκυῖα is pf.-ptc.-act.-fem.-nom.-sg. < προβαίνω. Culy, Parsons, and Stigall suggest the participle is a pluperfect periphrastic construction (the imperfect form of εἰμί plus the perfect participle); equivalent in function to the pluperfect tense of the finite verb (Wallace 647–49; BDF §§352–53; *GNTG* §§5.184–85); Luke introduced Anna with the verb ἦν and so, perhaps did not feel the need to repeat it with the participle (Culy, Parsons, and Stigall, *Luke*, 89). The clause is idiomatic: "she was advanced in years" (BDAG 865.2*).

85. ζήσασα is likely an adverbial participle indicating cause; it provides the reason she was advanced in age (Wallace 631–32; BDF §418; *GNTG* §5.189; Culy, Parsons, and Stigall, *Luke*, 89): "because she lived."

86. ἔτη ἑπτὰ is an accusative of extent of time (Wallace 201; BDF §161; *GNTG* §5.82).

87. παρθενίας here marks the time of her marriage (BDAG 777*).

88. αὐτὴ is the nominative subject of an implied ἦν (Wallace 39–40; BDF §§127–28): "she was."

τεσσάρων,⁸⁹ ἣ⁹⁰ οὐκ ἀφίστατο τοῦ ἱεροῦ⁹¹ νηστείαις καὶ δεήσεσιν⁹²
λατρεύουσα⁹³ νύκτα καὶ ἡμέραν.⁹⁴ 38 καὶ αὐτῇ τῇ ὥρᾳ⁹⁵ ἐπιστᾶσα⁹⁶ ἀνθω-
μολογεῖτο τῷ θεῷ καὶ ἐλάλει περὶ αὐτοῦ πᾶσιν τοῖς προσδεχομένοις
λύτρωσιν Ἰερουσαλήμ.

Vocabulary

ἀγκάλη, ης, ἡ	arm
ἀγραυλέω	to live outdoors
αἰνέω	to praise
ἀνάγω	to take up, raise, offer up, bring
ἀνακλίνω	to sit down, recline
ἀνάστασις, εως, ἡ	standing up, rising, insurrection, resurrection
ἀνευρίσκω	to discover, seek
ἀνθομολογέομαι	to confess openly, sing praise, give thanks
Ἄννα, ας, ἡ	Hannah, Anna
ἀντιλέγω	to speak in response, speak against; to deny

89. ἕως ἐτῶν ὀγδοήκοντα τεσσάρων: the construction is ambiguous. It might mean that she has been a widow until her current age, which is 84; or it might mean that she has been a widow for 84 years (Culy, Parsons, and Stigall, *Luke*, 89).

90. ἣ is the nominative subject of ἀφίστατο.

91. τοῦ ἱεροῦ is the genitive complement of ἀφίστημι (BDAG 157.2.a).

92. νηστείαις . . . δεήσεσιν are datives of means going with λατρεύουσα.

93. λατρεύουσα might be an adverbial participle indicating manner (Wallace 627–28; BDF §418; *GNTG* §5.193): "serving"; it might be an attendant circumstance participle, referring to an action that is parallel to the main verb (Wallace 640–45; *GNTG* §5.198): "she did not leave . . . and served."

94. νύκτα . . . ἡμέραν are accusatives of extent of time (Wallace 201; BDF §161; *GNTG* §5.82).

95. αὐτῇ τῇ ὥρᾳ: the dative case is indicating a particular point in time (Wallace 155–57; BDF §§200–201; *GNTG* §5.66).

96. ἐπιστᾶσα: aor.-ptc.-act.-fem.-nom.-sg. < ἐφίστημι. It is either an adverbial participle indicating time; the aorist tense indicates time before that of the main verb (Wallace 623–27; BDF §418; *GNTG* §5.188): "after she came up"; or an attendant circumstance participle, referring to an action that is parallel to the main verb (Wallace 640–45; *GNTG* §5.198): "she came up and was giving thanks."

ἀπογραφή, ῆς, ἡ	registration, census, list, enrollment, inventory
ἀπογράφω	to register, enroll
ἀποκαλύπτω	to reveal
ἀποκάλυψις, εως, ἡ	revelation, disclosure
ἄρσην, εν, gen. ενος	male, man
Ἀσήρ, ὁ, indecl.	Asher
Αὔγουστος, ου, ὁ	Augustus. The title given to Octavian by the Senate in 27 BCE (BDAG 150*).
ἀφίστημι	to withdraw, remove, depart, leave; to revolt
Βηθλέεμ, ἡ, indecl.	Bethlehem
βρέφος, ους, τό	baby, infant; unborn child
γνωρίζω	to make known
γονεύς, έως, ὁ	parent (only plural in NT [BDAG 205*]: οἱ γονεῖς, έων)
δέησις, εως, ἡ	entreaty, request, prayer
δεσπότης, ου, ὁ	master, lord, slaveowner
δή	indeed, then, therefore, now
διαλογισμός, οῦ, ὁ	thought, opinion, discussion, reasoning, dispute
διανοίγω	to open up, reveal
διέρχομαι	to pass through
διότι	because, for, therefore
δόγμα, ατος, τό	command, decree; opinion, dogma, doctrine
ἔγκυος, ον	pregnant
ἐθίζω	to accustom, use
εἰσάγω	to bring in
ἐξαίφνης, adv.	suddenly, immediately
ἑτοιμάζω	to prepare
ἔτος, ους, τό	year
εὐδοκία, ας, ἡ	good pleasure, good will, approval; satisfaction
εὐλαβής, ές	devout, reverent
εὐλογέω	to bless
ἐφίστημι	to set, set over, establish; to come upon

ζεῦγος, ους, τό	yoke of beasts
ἡγεμονεύω	to govern
θαυμάζω	to marvel, wonder; to admire
θυγάτηρ, τρός, ἡ	daughter
θυσία, ας, ἡ	sacrifice
Ἰουδαία, ας, ἡ	Judea
Ἰωσήφ, ὁ, indecl.	Joseph
καθαρισμός, οῦ, ὁ	cleansing, purification
Καῖσαρ, αρος, ὁ	Caesar; the name given to Gaius Octavius when he was adopted as Julius's heir.
κατάλυμα, ατος, τό	a lodging place, guest room
κεῖμαι	to be appointed or destined for; to lie down; to be valid for
κοιλία, ας, ἡ	stomach, womb
Κυρήνιος, ου, ὁ	Quirinius, imperial governor of Syria
λατρεύω	to serve, worship
λύτρωσις, εως, ἡ	redemption, ransoming, releasing
Μαριάμ, ἡ, indecl.	Miriam; Mary
μήτρα, ας, ἡ	womb
μνηστεύω	to become betrothed, engaged for marriage
Ναζαρά, ἡ, indecl.	Also: Ναζαρέτ, Ναζαρέθ, Ναζαράτ, Ναζαράθ: Nazareth
νηστεία, ας, ἡ	fast, fasting
νοσσός, οῦ, ὁ	the young (of a bird)
ὀγδοήκοντα, indecl.	eighty
οἰκουμένη, ης, ἡ	world
ὀκτώ, indecl.	eight
οὐράνιος, ον	heavenly
παράκλησις, εως, ἡ	encouragement, appeal, request, comfort
παρθενία, ας, ἡ	virginity
παρίστημι	to present, stand by
πατριά, ᾶς, ἡ	family, people
περιλάμπω	to shine around
περιστερά, ᾶς, ἡ	dove, pigeon

περιτέμνω	to circumcise; in the passive, to be circumcised or allow oneself to be circumcised
πίμπλημι	to fill, fulfill
πλῆθος, ους, τό	multitude
ποιμήν, ένος, ὁ	shepherd
ποίμνη, ης, ἡ	flock
πρίν	before; (adv.) formerly
πρό	(+ gen.) before, above
προβαίνω	to go on, advance; to be old
προσδέχομαι	to receive; to wait for
προφῆτις, ιδος, ἡ	prophet
πρωτότοκος, ον	firstborn
πτῶσις, εως, ἡ	fall; disaster
ῥομφαία, ας, ἡ	sword
σήμερον, adv.	today
σπαργανόω	to wrap in baby cloths
σπεύδω	to hasten
στρατιά, ᾶς, ἡ	army
συλλαμβάνω	to seize; to help; to conceive, become pregnant
συμβάλλω	to meet; to consider, compare
Συμεών, ὁ, indecl.	Simeon
συντηρέω	to preserve; keep in mind; treasure
Συρία, ας, ἡ	Syria
σωτήρ, ῆρος, ὁ	savior, deliverer, preserver
σωτήριος, ον	salvation; peace-offering
τέσσαρες	four
τίκτω	to bear children
τρυγών, όνος, ἡ	turtledove, small pigeon
ὑποστρέφω	to return
ὕψιστος, η, ον	highest; most high; Most High
Φανουήλ, ὁ, indecl.	Phanuel
φάτνη, ης, ἡ	manger, feeding trough, stall
φόβος, ου, ὁ	fear, terror; reverence
φυλακή, ῆς, ἡ	guard, watch, prison
φυλάσσω	to guard, keep

φυλή, ῆς, ἡ	tribe
χήρα, ας, ἡ	widow
χρηματίζω	to deal with; to warn, direct, reveal; to be titled, called
χώρα, ας, ἡ	place, land, country

Jesus Teaches the Disciples

Chapter 12 is in a lengthy block of material where Luke is using his own sources to supplement the narrative he has been using from Mark (9:51–19:27). Verses 1–12 offer warnings against hypocrisy, exhortations that the disciples should not be afraid, and a prediction that they will be brought before rulers at which time the Holy Spirit will assist in their defense. This prediction is fulfilled in Acts 4 (§2.6). Verses 13–34 illustrate Luke's interest in how people think about, and use, their possessions: Jesus tells the parable of the rich landowner and offers exhortations that the hearers should not worry about possessions.

1'Εν¹ οἷς ἐπισυναχθεισῶν τῶν μυριάδων τοῦ ὄχλου,² ὥστε³ καταπατεῖν ἀλλήλους, ἤρξατο λέγειν⁴ πρὸς⁵ τοὺς μαθητὰς αὐτοῦ πρῶτον·⁶ προσέχετε ἑαυτοῖς⁷ ἀπὸ τῆς ζύμης, ἥτις ἐστὶν ὑπόκρισις, τῶν Φαρισαίων.

1. Ἐν can be used with the dative relative pronoun (singular or plural) with the meaning "meanwhile" or "as long as" (BDAG 330.10.c; Culy, Parsons, and Stigall, *Luke*, 410).
2. ἐπισυναχθεισῶν . . . τοῦ ὄχλου is a genitive absolute (Wallace 127–28; BDF §423; *GNTG* §5.197): "when many thousands of the crowd had gathered."
3. ὥστε with an infinitive (καταπατεῖν) forms a result clause (Wallace 593; BDF §391; *GNTG* §5.162): "with the result that they trampled."
4. λέγειν is a complementary infinitive, going with ἤρξατο (Wallace 598–99; BDF §392; *GNTG* §5.163).
5. πρὸς is used here with a verb of speaking to indicate the addressee (BDAG 874.3.a.ε). Luke often uses this construction rather than the dative case (Culy, Parsons, and Stigall, *Luke*, 76, referencing p. 14).
6. πρῶτον probably modifies λέγειν rather than προσέχετε (Culy, Parsons, and Stigall, *Luke*, 410).
7. προσέχετε ἑαυτοῖς followed by ἀπό τινος means to beware of or to be on one's guard against something (BDAG 879.10): "Be on your guard against the leaven."

2 Οὐδὲν δὲ συγκεκαλυμμένον⁸ ἐστὶν ὃ⁹ οὐκ ἀποκαλυφθήσεται καὶ κρυπτὸν¹⁰ ὃ οὐ γνωσθήσεται. 3 ἀνθ᾽¹¹ ὧν ὅσα ἐν τῇ σκοτίᾳ εἴπατε ἐν τῷ φωτὶ ἀκουσθήσεται, καὶ ὃ πρὸς τὸ οὖς ἐλαλήσατε¹² ἐν τοῖς ταμείοις κηρυχθήσεται ἐπὶ τῶν δωμάτων.¹³

4 Λέγω δὲ ὑμῖν τοῖς φίλοις μου, μὴ φοβηθῆτε ἀπὸ τῶν ἀποκτεινόν-των¹⁴ τὸ σῶμα καὶ μετὰ ταῦτα μὴ ἐχόντων περισσότερόν τι ποιῆσαι.¹⁵ 5 ὑποδείξω δὲ ὑμῖν τίνα φοβηθῆτε·¹⁶ φοβήθητε¹⁷ τὸν μετὰ¹⁸ τὸ ἀποκτεῖναι ἔχοντα¹⁹ ἐξουσίαν ἐμβαλεῖν²⁰ εἰς τὴν γέενναν. ναὶ λέγω ὑμῖν, τοῦτον φοβήθητε. 6 οὐχὶ πέντε στρουθία πωλοῦνται ἀσσαρίων δύο;²¹ καὶ ἓν

8. συγκεκαλυμμένον either serves as a predicate adjective (Wallace 617–19; BDF §414; GNTG §5.181): "nothing is hidden"; or, a perfect periphrastic construction (the present tense of εἰμί plus the perfect participle); equivalent in function to the perfect tense of the finite verb (Wallace 647–49; BDF §§352–53; GNTG §§5.184–85), which is how Culy, Parsons, and Stigall read this verse (*Luke*, 411): "has been hidden."

9. ὃ is the subject of ἀποκαλυφθήσεται: "that."

10. κρυπτὸν is the predicate adjective of a clause with an elided verb to be supplied by the reader; the context suggests ἐστὶν (see the discussion in BDF §§479–83).

11. ἀντί plus the genitive relative pronoun can indicate either result (which is how BDAG glosses the verse, 88.5*): "Therefore," "So then"; or purpose (which is how Culy, Parsons, and Stigall read this verse, *Luke*, 411; cf. BDAG 88.4): "In order that."

12. ὃ πρὸς τὸ οὖς ἐλαλήσατε: literally, to speak something into someone's ear; it is an idiomatic expression that means to say something in confidence or to whisper (BDAG 739.1*).

13. κηρυχθήσεται ἐπὶ τῶν δωμάτων is an idiomatic expression that means to proclaim something publicly (BDAG 266*).

14. μὴ φοβηθῆτε ἀπὸ τῶν ἀποκτεινόντων: φοβηθῆτε with μὴ forms the prohibitive sub-junctive (Wallace 463.2b, 487, 749; BDF §364; GNTG §5.141). Verbs of fearing take ἀπὸ to show the cause of the fear (BDAG 106.5.c*). τῶν ἀποκτεινόντων is a substantival participle (Wallace 619–21; BDF §413; GNTG §5.182).

15. μὴ ἐχόντων περισσότερόν τι ποιῆσαι: the participle is substantival (Wallace 619–21; BDF §413; GNTG §5.182). When combined with an infinitive, ἔχω can indicate ability: "are not able to do anything more" (BDAG 421.5*).

16. φοβηθῆτε is a deliberative subjunctive (Wallace 465–68; BDF §366; GNTG §5.138): "(what) you should fear" (it answers the question "what should I fear?").

17. φοβήθητε: aor.-impv.-pass.-2-pl. < φοβέω (not subjunctive: note the accent is different from the previous word).

18. μετὰ with the articular infinitive (τὸ ἀποκτεῖναι) indicates time before the main verb (Wallace 594, 611; BDF 402.3; GNTG §5.172): "after killing."

19. τὸν . . . ἔχοντα is a substantival participle (Wallace 619–21; BDF §413; GNTG §5.182): "the one who has." The article brackets the articular infinitive.

20. ἐμβαλεῖν: the infinitive is epexegetical explaining ἐξουσίαν (Wallace 607; BDF §394; GNTG §5.167).

21. ἀσσαρίων δύο is a genitive of price (Wallace 122; BDF §179; GNTG §5.52).

ἐξ αὐτῶν οὐκ ἔστιν ἐπιλελησμένον²² ἐνώπιον τοῦ θεοῦ.²³ 7 ἀλλὰ καὶ²⁴
αἱ τρίχες τῆς κεφαλῆς ὑμῶν πᾶσαι ἠρίθμηνται.²⁵ μὴ φοβεῖσθε· πολλῶν
στρουθίων διαφέρετε.²⁶

8 Λέγω δὲ ὑμῖν, πᾶς ὃς ἂν²⁷ ὁμολογήσῃ²⁸ ἐν ἐμοὶ ἔμπροσθεν τῶν
ἀνθρώπων, καὶ ὁ υἱὸς τοῦ ἀνθρώπου ὁμολογήσει ἐν αὐτῷ ἔμπροσθεν
τῶν ἀγγέλων τοῦ θεοῦ· 9 ὁ δὲ ἀρνησάμενός²⁹ με ἐνώπιον τῶν ἀνθρώπων
ἀπαρνηθήσεται ἐνώπιον τῶν ἀγγέλων τοῦ θεοῦ.

10 Καὶ πᾶς ὃς ἐρεῖ³⁰ λόγον εἰς τὸν υἱὸν³¹ τοῦ ἀνθρώπου, ἀφεθήσεται³²
αὐτῷ· τῷ δὲ εἰς τὸ ἅγιον πνεῦμα³³ βλασφημήσαντι³⁴ οὐκ ἀφεθήσεται.

---

22. ἐπιλελησμένον is a perfect periphrastic construction (the present tense of εἰμὶ plus the perfect participle); equivalent in function to the perfect tense of the finite verb (Wallace 647–49; BDF §§352–53; *GNTG* §§5.184–85): "has been forgotten"; or "is forgotten."

23. ἐνώπιον τοῦ θεοῦ: "in God's sight" (BDAG 342.2.b*).

24. ἀλλὰ καὶ means "but also" (BDAG 45.3; Culy, Parsons, and Stigall, *Luke*, 414).

25. ἠρίθμηνται is likely a divine passive (Wallace 437–38; BDF §§130.1, 313).

26. διαφέρετε with the genitive of comparison: "to be worth more or superior to" (BDAG 239.4; Wallace 110–12; BDF §185; *GNTG* §5.51).

27. πᾶς ὃς ἂν: ὃς ἂν with the subjunctive introduces an indefinite relative clause (Wallace 478, 571; BDF 380; *GNTG* §5.216). Such clauses suggest general assertions or suppositions rather than making assertions about concrete realties: "whoever."

28. ὁμολογέω normally takes the accusative. Its use with ἐν perhaps reflects a semitic original (BDAG 709.4.b; BDF §220.2; Culy, Parsons, and Stigall, *Luke*, 416): "confesses me."

29. ὁ . . . ἀρνησάμενός is a substantival participle (Wallace 619–21; BDF §413; *GNTG* §5.182).

30. πᾶς ὃς ἐρεῖ: there does not appear to be any difference in nuance between the use of the future indicative here and the aorist subjunctive used in the similar phrase in v. 8 (see Wallace 571; Culy, Parsons, and Stigall, *Luke*, 417).

31. εἰς τὸν υἱὸν: in this context, indicating hostility (BDAG 290.4.c.α): "against the son of man."

32. ἀφίημι takes a dative of person when referring to forgiveness and the thing forgiven (if specified) is in the accusative case (BDAG 156.2). Likely a divine passive (Wallace 437–38; BDF §§130.1, 313): "it will be forgiven him [by God]." More smoothly in English: "he will be forgiven."

33. εἰς τὸ ἅγιον πνεῦμα: in this context, indicating hostility (BDAG 290.4.c.α): "against the Holy Spirit."

34. τῷ . . . βλασφημήσαντι is a substantival participle (Wallace 619–21; BDF §413; *GNTG* §5.182); it is a dative of person going with ἀφεθήσεται.

11 Ὅταν³⁵ δὲ εἰσφέρωσιν ὑμᾶς ἐπὶ τὰς συναγωγὰς³⁶ καὶ τὰς ἀρχὰς καὶ τὰς ἐξουσίας, μὴ μεριμνήσητε³⁷ πῶς ἢ τί³⁸ ἀπολογήσησθε ἢ τί εἴπητε·³⁹ 12 τὸ γὰρ ἅγιον πνεῦμα διδάξει ὑμᾶς ἐν αὐτῇ τῇ ὥρᾳ⁴⁰ ἃ δεῖ εἰπεῖν.⁴¹

13 Εἶπεν δέ τις ἐκ τοῦ ὄχλου αὐτῷ· διδάσκαλε, εἰπὲ τῷ ἀδελφῷ μου μερίσασθαι⁴² μετ᾽ ἐμοῦ τὴν κληρονομίαν. 14 ὁ δὲ εἶπεν αὐτῷ· ἄνθρωπε, τίς με κατέστησεν κριτὴν ἢ μεριστὴν⁴³ ἐφ᾽ ὑμᾶς;⁴⁴ 15 Εἶπεν δὲ πρὸς⁴⁵ αὐτούς· ὁρᾶτε καὶ φυλάσσεσθε⁴⁶ ἀπὸ πάσης πλεονεξίας, ὅτι οὐκ ἐν τῷ περισσεύειν τινὶ ἡ ζωὴ αὐτοῦ ἐστιν ἐκ τῶν ὑπαρχόντων αὐτῷ.⁴⁷

35. Ὅταν, when used with the present subjunctive, frequently indicates repeated action: "whenever," "as often as," "every time that" (BDAG 730.1.a.α; Wallace 479).

36. ἐπὶ τὰς συναγωγὰς: In this context, ἐπὶ points to a legal context; therefore, with the accusative, it means "before" (BDAG 365.10*).

37. μεριμνήσητε with μὴ forms the prohibitive subjunctive (Wallace 463[2b], 487, 749; BDF §364; *GNTG* §5.141).

38. πῶς ἢ τί: πῶς (with the deliberative subjunctive) and pronoun (τί) introduce an indirect question (BDF §436; Culy, Parsons, and Stigall, *Luke*, 418): "how or what."

39. ἀπολογήσησθε ἢ τί εἴπητε: ἀπολογήσησθε and εἴπητε are deliberative subjunctives (Wallace 465–68; BDF §366; *GNTG* §5.138): "[how or what] you will say in defense or what you will say."

40. ἐν αὐτῇ τῇ ὥρᾳ: αὐτῇ τῇ is similar to a demonstrative: "in that very hour" (BDAG 152.1.g; Culy, Parsons, and Stigall, *Luke*, 356).

41. δεῖ εἰπεῖν: infinitives (εἰπεῖν) are used in impersonal expressions with verbs like δεῖ (BDF §393.1; Wallace describes this as a substantival use [600–601]; *GNTG* §5.164.b).

42. μερίσασθαι is an infinitive indicating indirect discourse (Wallace 603–5; BDF §§396, 397.3; *GNTG* §5.166): "to divide."

43. με . . . κριτὴν ἢ μεριστὴν: some verbs (κατέστησεν) can take two accusatives. κριτὴν ἢ μεριστὴν are complements in an object-complement double accusative construction with με as the object (Wallace 181–89 [183 n. 24]; BDF §157; *GNTG* §5.77): "[who] made me judge or arbitrator."

44. ἐφ᾽ ὑμᾶς: in this context, ἐφ᾽ is a marker of power, authority, control of, or over, someone or something (BDAG 365.9.c): "over you."

45. πρὸς here is used with a verb of speaking to indicate the addressee (see n. 5).

46. φυλάσσω in the middle with ἀπὸ can mean: "to be on one's guard against," "look out for," "avoid" (BDAG 1068.3).

47. οὐκ ἐν τῷ περισσεύειν τινὶ ἡ ζωὴ αὐτοῦ ἐστιν ἐκ τῶν ὑπαρχόντων αὐτῷ. The articular infinitive (τῷ περισσεύειν) is used with ἐν to indicate contemporaneous time (Wallace 595; BDF §404; *GNTG* §5.172; Culy, Parsons, and Stigall, *Luke*, 420). ὑπαρχόντων is a substantival participle (Wallace 619–21; BDF §413; *GNTG* §5.182); when used with dative of person (αὐτῷ) it can indicate possession (BDAG 1029.1). Literally: "not while it abounds to someone is his life from his possessions." We might translate this something like: "a person's life does not consist in the increasing of possessions."

16 Εἶπεν δὲ παραβολὴν πρὸς[48] αὐτοὺς λέγων·[49] ἀνθρώπου τινὸς πλουσίου εὐφόρησεν ἡ χώρα. 17 καὶ διελογίζετο ἐν ἑαυτῷ λέγων·[50] τί ποιήσω, ὅτι οὐκ ἔχω ποῦ συνάξω τοὺς καρπούς μου;[51] 18 καὶ εἶπεν· τοῦτο ποιήσω, καθελῶ μου τὰς ἀποθήκας καὶ μείζονας οἰκοδομήσω καὶ συνάξω ἐκεῖ πάντα τὸν σῖτον καὶ τὰ ἀγαθά μου 19 καὶ ἐρῶ τῇ ψυχῇ μου· ψυχή, ἔχεις πολλὰ ἀγαθὰ κείμενα[52] εἰς[53] ἔτη πολλά· ἀναπαύου, φάγε, πίε, εὐφραίνου. 20 εἶπεν δὲ αὐτῷ ὁ θεός· ἄφρων, ταύτῃ τῇ νυκτὶ[54] τὴν ψυχήν σου ἀπαιτοῦσιν[55] ἀπὸ σοῦ· ἃ δὲ ἡτοίμασας,[56] τίνι[57] ἔσται; 21 οὕτως ὁ θησαυρίζων ἑαυτῷ καὶ μὴ εἰς θεὸν πλουτῶν.[58]

48. πρὸς is used here with a verb of speaking to indicate the addressee (see n. 5).

49. λέγων: verbs of speaking (Εἶπεν) will sometimes be supplemented with an adverbial participle. This participle is called "redundant" or "pleonastic." It is a kind of participle of means (Wallace 649–50; BDF §420; *GNTG* §5.199). When the redundant participle introduces direct discourse, translators sometimes leave the participle untranslated; the presence of the participle in Greek is reflected in English by the use of quotation marks.

50. λέγων is a "redundant" or "pleonastic" participle (see n. 49), introducing direct speech.

51. ποῦ συνάξω τοὺς καρπούς μου: This interrogative clause (an indirect question) serves as the direct object of ἔχω (Culy, Parsons, and Stigall, *Luke*, 421). Literally, "where I will store my fruit." We might translate something like: "I do not have [a place] where I can store my crops."

52. κείμενα: pf.-ptc.-pass.-neut.-acc.-pl. < κεῖμαι. The participle is attributive (Wallace 617–18; BDF §412; *GNTG* §5.181), modifying ἀγαθά: "goods stored up."

53. εἰς plus the accusative indicates the duration of time (BDAG 289.2.b): "for many years."

54. ταύτῃ τῇ νυκτὶ: the dative case is indicating a particular point in time (Wallace 155–57; BDF §§200–201; *GNTG* §5.66).

55. ἀπαιτοῦσιν: active voice. Greek authors sometimes use plural active verbs without specifying the subjects explicitly when we would expect a passive verb in English (see the discussion and references in Culy, Parsons, and Stigall, *Luke*, 423; BDAG 96.1*; BDF suggests this as a strategy to avoid using the name of God [72.2*]): "your soul will be required of you."

56. ἃ . . . ἡτοίμασας: serves as the subject of ἔσται: "who will have what you prepared?"

57. τίνι is a dative of possession (Wallace 149–51; BDF §189; *GNTG* §5.61).

58. ὁ θησαυρίζων . . . καὶ μὴ . . . πλουτῶν: the participles are substantival (Wallace 619–21; BDF §413; *GNTG* §5.182); each is the nominative subject of an implied form of εἰμί (Wallace 39–40; BDF §§127–28): "Thus it is for the one who stores up riches for himself but is not wealthy toward God."

22 Εἶπεν δὲ πρὸς⁵⁹ τοὺς μαθητὰς αὐτοῦ· διὰ τοῦτο λέγω ὑμῖν· μὴ μεριμνᾶτε τῇ ψυχῇ⁶⁰ τί φάγητε,⁶¹ μηδὲ τῷ σώματι τί ἐνδύσησθε. 23 ἡ γὰρ ψυχὴ πλεῖόν ἐστιν τῆς τροφῆς⁶² καὶ τὸ σῶμα τοῦ ἐνδύματος.⁶³ 24 κατανοήσατε τοὺς κόρακας ὅτι οὐ σπείρουσιν οὐδὲ θερίζουσιν, οἷς⁶⁴ οὐκ ἔστιν ταμεῖον οὐδὲ ἀποθήκη, καὶ ὁ θεὸς τρέφει αὐτούς· πόσῳ μᾶλλον⁶⁵ ὑμεῖς διαφέρετε τῶν πετεινῶν.⁶⁶ 25 τίς δὲ ἐξ ὑμῶν μεριμνῶν⁶⁷ δύναται ἐπὶ τὴν ἡλικίαν αὐτοῦ προσθεῖναι⁶⁸ πῆχυν;⁶⁹ 26 εἰ οὖν οὐδὲ⁷⁰ ἐλάχιστον⁷¹ δύνασθε, τί περὶ τῶν λοιπῶν μεριμνᾶτε; 27 κατανοήσατε τὰ κρίνα πῶς⁷² αὐξάνει·⁷³ οὐ κοπιᾷ οὐδὲ νήθει· λέγω δὲ ὑμῖν, οὐδὲ Σολομὼν ἐν πάσῃ τῇ δόξῃ αὐτοῦ περιεβάλετο ὡς ἓν τούτων. 28 εἰ δὲ ἐν ἀγρῷ τὸν χόρτον

59. πρὸς is here used with a verb of speaking to indicate the addressee (see n. 5).

60. τῇ ψυχῇ is a dative of advantage (Wallace 142–44; BDF §188; *GNTG* §5.60), going with μεριμνᾶτε (BDAG 632.1*): "do not be anxious for your life."

61. φάγητε is a deliberative subjunctive (Wallace 465–68; BDF §366; *GNTG* §5.138): "what you will eat."

62. τῆς τροφῆς is a genitive of comparison (BDAG 239.4; Wallace 110–12; BDF §185; *GNTG* §5.51): "more than nourishment."

63. τὸ σῶμα τοῦ ἐνδύματος: this clause is elliptical. Luke does not repeat πλεῖόν ἐστιν; the reader can supply the phrase from the context (see the discussion in BDF §§479–83).

64. οἷς is a dative of possession (Wallace 149–51; BDF §189; *GNTG* §5.61): "they do not have."

65. πόσῳ μᾶλλον: "how much more" (BDAG 855.1).

66. τῶν πετεινῶν is a genitive of comparison (BDAG 239.4; Wallace 110–12; BDF §185; *GNTG* §5.51): "than birds."

67. μεριμνῶν is an adverbial participle of means (Wallace 625–30; BDF §418; *GNTG* §5.192): "by worrying."

68. προσθεῖναι is a complementary infinitive, going with δύναται (Wallace 598–99; BDF §392; *GNTG* §5.163).

69. ἡλικίαν . . . πῆχυν: ἡλικίαν can either point to age or to stature/height. πῆχυν refers to the forearm and then a length—a cubit; it does not appear to be used for time. Many translations suggest: "add an hour to his age" (cf. NIV, NRSV). A more likely reading is: "to add a cubit to his height" (cf. the note to this verse in NET; see the discussion in Culy, Parsons, and Stigall, *Luke*, 426–27).

70. οὐδὲ: "not even" (BDAG 734.3).

71. ἐλάχιστον is the accusative object of an implied complementary infinitive (see the discussion in BDF §§479–83; Culy, Parsons, and Stigall, *Luke*, 427): "To do the smallest thing."

72. πῶς introduces an indirect question that is epexegetical to κρίνα (BDAG 900.1.b.α; Culy, Parsons, and Stigall, *Luke*, 428): "how."

73. αὐξάνει . . . κοπιᾷ . . . νήθει: neuter plural subjects frequently take singular verbs (Wallace 399–400; BDF §133; *GNTG* §5.26.a).

ὄντα⁷⁴ σήμερον καὶ αὔριον εἰς κλίβανον βαλλόμενον⁷⁵ ὁ θεὸς οὕτως ἀμφιέζει, πόσῳ μᾶλλον ὑμᾶς,⁷⁶ ὀλιγόπιστοι. 29 καὶ ὑμεῖς μὴ ζητεῖτε τί φάγητε καὶ τί πίητε⁷⁷ καὶ μὴ μετεωρίζεσθε·⁷⁸ 30 ταῦτα γὰρ πάντα⁷⁹ τὰ ἔθνη τοῦ κόσμου ἐπιζητοῦσιν, ὑμῶν δὲ ὁ πατὴρ οἶδεν ὅτι χρῄζετε τούτων.⁸⁰ 31 πλὴν ζητεῖτε⁸¹ τὴν βασιλείαν αὐτοῦ, καὶ ταῦτα προστεθήσεται ὑμῖν. 32 Μὴ φοβοῦ, τὸ μικρὸν ποίμνιον, ὅτι εὐδόκησεν ὁ πατὴρ ὑμῶν δοῦναι⁸² ὑμῖν τὴν βασιλείαν.

33 Πωλήσατε τὰ ὑπάρχοντα⁸³ ὑμῶν καὶ δότε ἐλεημοσύνην· ποιήσατε ἑαυτοῖς βαλλάντια μὴ παλαιούμενα,⁸⁴ θησαυρὸν ἀνέκλειπτον⁸⁵ ἐν τοῖς οὐρανοῖς, ὅπου κλέπτης οὐκ ἐγγίζει οὐδὲ σὴς διαφθείρει· 34 ὅπου γὰρ ἐστιν ὁ θησαυρὸς ὑμῶν, ἐκεῖ καὶ ἡ καρδία ὑμῶν ἔσται.

Vocabulary

ἀγρός, οῦ, ὁ	field, farm, country
ἀμφιέζω	to clothe

74. ὄντα is an attributive participle (Wallace 617–18; BDF §412; *GNTG* §5.181), modifying χόρτον: "grass, which is in the field today."

75. βαλλόμενον is an attributive participle (Wallace 617–18; BDF §412; *GNTG* §5.181), modifying χόρτον: "thrown."

76. πόσῳ μᾶλλον ὑμᾶς: πόσῳ μᾶλλον (see n. 65). This clause is elliptical. ὑμᾶς is the accusative direct object of an implied ἀμφιέζει; the reader supplies both the subject and verb from the previous clause (see the discussion in BDF §§479–83): "how much more will [God clothe] you."

77. τί φάγητε καὶ τί πίητε: τί plus the deliberative subjunctive (Wallace 465–68; BDF §366; *GNTG* §5.138) introduces indirect questions (Wallace 478; BDF §366; *GNTG* §5.145) that are the direct object of ζητεῖτε (Culy, Parsons, and Stigall, *Luke*, 429).

78. μετεωρίζεσθε typically means "to be lifted up"; or "to be elevated." In the context, it likely means "do not be anxious, worried" (BDAG 643*).

79. πάντα could modify either ταῦτα or τὰ ἔθνη (see discussion in Culy, Parsons, and Stigall, *Luke*, 429).

80. χρῄζετε τούτων: χρῄζετε takes its object in the genitive (BDAG 1089).

81. πλὴν ζητεῖτε: in contrast with μὴ ζητεῖτε from v. 29: "instead."

82. δοῦναι is a complementary infinitive, goingwith εὐδόκησεν (Wallace 598–99; BDF §392; *GNTG* §5.163).

83. τὰ ὑπάρχοντα is a substantival participle (Wallace 619–21; BDF §413; *GNTG* §5.182): "your possessions" (BDAG 1029.1*).

84. παλαιούμενα is an attributive participle (Wallace 617–18; BDF §412; *GNTG* §5.181), modifying βαλλάντια: "purses that do not wear out."

85. θησαυρὸν ἀνέκλειπτον: accusative in apposition to βαλλάντια (Culy, Parsons, and Stigall, *Luke*, 431): "unfailing treasure."

ἀναπαύω	to stop, rest, refresh; to die
ἀνέκλειπτος, ον	unfailing
ἀντί	(+ gen.) for, in place of, instead of
ἀπαιτέω	to demand back, ask again
ἀπαρνέομαι	to deny, renounce
ἀποθήκη, ης, ἡ	barn, storehouse
ἀποκαλύπτω	to reveal
ἀπολογέομαι	to defend oneself
ἀριθμέω	to number
ἀρνέομαι	to deny
ἀσσάριον, ου, τό	assarion (Roman copper coin)
αὐξάνω	to grow; to cause to grow
αὔριον, adv.	tomorrow
ἄφρων, ον, gen. ονος	foolish
βαλλάντιον, ου, τό	money bag, purse
βλασφημέω	to verbally abuse, blaspheme
γέεννα, ης, ἡ	hell, gehenna
διαλογίζομαι	to reason, discuss, consider
διαφέρω	to be worth more than, be superior to (with the genitive of comparison)
διαφθείρω	to destroy, ruin; to lose, forget
δῶμα, ατος, τό	roof, housetop
ἐγγίζω	to bring near, come near
εἰσφέρω	to bring in
ἐλάχιστος, ίστη, ον	least; very small; insignificant
ἐλεημοσύνη, ης, ἡ	pity; alms
ἐμβάλλω	to throw in, lay in, set
ἔμπροσθεν	(+ gen.) before, in front of
ἔνδυμα, ατος, τό	clothing
ἐνδύω	to wear, put on
ἐπιζητέω	to seek after
ἐπιλανθάνομαι	to forget
ἐπισυνάγω	to gather together; to narrow
ἑτοιμάζω	to prepare
ἔτος, ους, τό	year
εὐδοκέω	to be well pleased, consent, enjoy
εὐφορέω	to produce good crops
εὐφραίνω	to cheer, rejoice

ζύμη, ης, ἡ	yeast, leaven
ἡλικία, ας, ἡ	time of life, life span, height
θερίζω	to reap
θησαυρίζω	to store up treasure
θησαυρός, οῦ, ὁ	treasure, treasury
θρίξ, τριχός, ἡ	hair, thread, bristle
καθαιρέω	to take down, destroy; overthrow
καθίστημι	to put down, bring to, put in charge, make
κατανοέω	to understand, consider
καταπατέω	to trample on, oppress
κεῖμαι	to lie down; to be valid for. Of goods: to be laid up, be stored up (BDAG 537.2*)
κλέπτης, ου, ὁ	thief
κληρονομία, ας, ἡ	inheritance
κλίβανος, ου, ὁ	oven, furnace
κοπιάω	to toil, grow tired, be weary
κόραξ, ακος, ὁ	raven; hook
κρίνον, ου, τό	lily
κριτής, οῦ, ὁ	judge
κρυπτός, ή, όν	hidden
μερίζω	to divide, distribute
μεριμνάω	to be anxious for
μεριστής, οῦ, ὁ	divider
μετεωρίζομαι	to soar on high, rise up; to worry
μικρός, ά, όν	small, little
μυριάς, άδος, ἡ	myriad, ten thousand; countless thousands
ναί	yes
νήθω	to spin
οἰκοδομέω	to build
ὀλιγόπιστος, ον	of little faith
ὁμολογέω	to confess, praise; to acknowledge
οὖς, ὠτός, τό	ear
παλαιόω	to make or become old, wear out
πέντε, indecl.	five
περιβάλλω	to put on, clothe

περισσεύω	to abound
περισσός, ή, όν	more, remaining, excessive, to the full
πετεινόν, οῦ, τό	bird
πῆχυς, εως, ὁ	arm; cubit
πλεονεξία, ας, ἡ	greediness; lust; advantage
πλήν	(+ gen.) only, except (prep.); but, nevertheless (conj.)
πλούσιος, ία, ιον	rich
πλουτέω	to be rich
ποίμνιον, ου, τό	flock
πόσος	how much, how many?
ποῦ	where?
προσέχω	to pay attention to
προστίθημι	to put; to add
πωλέω	to sell
σήμερον, adv.	today
σής, σητός, ὁ	moth
σῖτος, ου, ὁ	grain
σκοτία, ας, ἡ	darkness
Σολομών, ῶνος, ὁ	Solomon
στρουθίον, ου, τό	small sparrow; ostrich
συγκαλύπτω	to cover up
ταμεῖον, ου, τό	inner room
τρέφω	to feed
τροφή, ῆς, ἡ	food, provisions, forage
ὑποδείκνυμι	to show, inform
ὑπόκρισις, εως, ἡ	hypocrisy
φίλος, η, ον	friend, beloved; friendly, agreeable, dear, pleasant, welcome
φυλάσσω	to guard, keep
χόρτος, ου, ὁ	grass
χρήζω	to have need
χώρα, ας, ἡ	place, land, country

Abraham and the Righteousness of Faith

Paul's letter to the Romans is one of those the authorship of which scholars do not dispute. Paul writes to this church (a church he did not establish and to which he has never been), likely from Corinth, around the year 58 CE. He is preparing to take the collection taken up from his gentile churches to the church in Jerusalem. Once he has done this, he intends to come to Rome on his way to Spain.

While the letter is long and complex, much of the first part of the letter (1:18–11:36) argues for the righteousness of God in God's dealings with both Jew and non-Jew. Chapter 4 brings to conclusion the opening argument of the letter (1:18–4:25). Paul introduces Abraham (also discussed in Gal 3) as an illustration of a person who trusts God and as someone whose relationship with God can assist the audience in thinking about righteousness. Although Paul makes use of material found in Genesis 17 (§1.1), he emphasizes God's promise to Abraham found in Romans 15 where God considers Abraham righteous before requiring Abraham and his male descendants to become circumcised.

Paul's discussion of faith and works can be compared with James's discussion (§3.6). The discussion of Abraham connects to James (§3.6), to Barnabas (§2.9), and to Genesis 17 (§1.1).

1 Τί οὖν ἐροῦμεν εὑρηκέναι Ἀβραὰμ τὸν προπάτορα ἡμῶν κατὰ σάρκα;¹ 2 εἰ γὰρ Ἀβραὰμ ἐξ ἔργων² ἐδικαιώθη, ἔχει καύχημα, ἀλλ᾽ οὐ πρὸς θεόν. 3 τί γὰρ ἡ γραφὴ λέγει;³ ἐπίστευσεν δὲ Ἀβραὰμ τῷ θεῷ⁴ καὶ ἐλογίσθη αὐτῷ εἰς δικαιοσύνην.⁵ 4 τῷ δὲ ἐργαζομένῳ⁶ ὁ μισθὸς οὐ λογίζεται

1. Τί οὖν ἐροῦμεν εὑρηκέναι Ἀβραὰμ τὸν προπάτορα ἡμῶν κατὰ σάρκα: this verse presents several challenges. A compelling reading would require more analysis than can be accomplished in this note. The following are the key issues that must be resolved. Although εὑρηκέναι is absent in a few manuscripts (and is the basis for the translation in the RSV), most scholars today accept it as part of the text (see Bruce M. Metzger, *A Textual Commentary on the Greek New Testament*, 2nd ed. [Stuttgart: Deutsche Bibelgesellschaft, 1994], 450). εὑρηκέναι is indicating indirect discourse (Wallace 603–5; BDF §396; *GNTG* §5.166). But what is its subject, and does it have an object? Many interpreters take Ἀβραὰμ as the accusative subject of the infinitive: "What then shall we say that Abraham . . . found" (cf. NASB, NET, and NIV). However, with respect to verbs of speaking that indicate the content of what is being said, "If the subject of the infinitive is the same as the governing verb, it is not expressed" (BDF §397; cf. Wallace 192; and *GNTG* §5.169.a). Given this consideration, we have at least two other grammatical options: (1) Richard Hays has persuaded some that the sentence should be repunctuated: Τί οὖν ἐροῦμεν; εὑρηκέναι Ἀβραὰμ τὸν προπάτορα ἡμῶν κατὰ σάρκα; Such a proposal reads Ἀβραὰμ as the accusative direct object of the infinitive; the subject would be implied from ἐροῦμεν: "What then shall we say? That we have found Abraham [to be] our forefather." ("'Have We Found Abraham to Be Our Forefather according to the Flesh?': A Reconsideration of Rom 4:1," *Novum Testamentum* 27 [1985]: 76–98, DOI:10.2307/1560852). (2) Another option would be to read Ἀβραὰμ as the accusative subject of an implied copulative infinitive suggested by εὑρηκέναι. This reading would not require repunctuating the sentence: "What then shall we say that we have found Abraham . . . to be? Finally, does the prepositional phrase κατὰ σάρκα modify Ἀβραὰμ τὸν προπάτορα ἡμῶν or εὑρηκέναι? Most translations read it as modifying Ἀβραὰμ τὸν προπάτορα ἡμῶν: "our forefather according to the flesh."

2. ἐξ ἔργων: ἐξ provides the reason for ἐδικαιώθη: "by works" or "because of works" (BDAG 297.e*).

3. He cites Gen 15:6 (LXX): καὶ ἐπίστευσεν Αβραμ τῷ θεῷ, καὶ ἐλογίσθη αὐτῷ εἰς δικαιοσύνην.

4. τῷ θεῷ is the dative complement of πιστεύω (BDAG 816.1.b; Wallace 171–73; BDF §187.6; *GNTG* §5.72*).

5. ἐλογίσθη αὐτῷ εἰς δικαιοσύνην: λογίζομαι in the passive with the dative and εἰς plus the accusative means to credit something to someone as something (BDAG 597.1.a*): "it was credited to him as righteousness." εἰς plus the accusative (δικαιοσύνην) can substitute for a predicate nominative (Wallace 47–48*; also BDF §145.2*). Similar constructions with λογίζομαι occur in vv. 5, 9, and 22.

6. τῷ . . . ἐργαζομένῳ is a substantival participle (Wallace 619–21; BDF §413; *GNTG* §5.182); dative because of λογίζεται. This construction occurs again in v. 5.

κατὰ χάριν ἀλλὰ κατὰ ὀφείλημα,⁷ 5 τῷ δὲ μὴ ἐργαζομένῳ πιστεύοντι δὲ ἐπὶ τὸν δικαιοῦντα⁸ τὸν ἀσεβῆ λογίζεται ἡ πίστις αὐτοῦ εἰς δικαιοσύνην· 6 καθάπερ καὶ Δαυὶδ λέγει τὸν μακαρισμὸν τοῦ ἀνθρώπου⁹ ᾧ ὁ θεὸς λογίζεται δικαιοσύνην χωρὶς ἔργων·

    7 μακάριοι¹⁰ ὧν ἀφέθησαν αἱ ἀνομίαι

        καὶ ὧν ἐπεκαλύφθησαν αἱ ἁμαρτίαι·

    8 μακάριος¹¹ ἀνὴρ οὗ οὐ μὴ λογίσηται κύριος ἁμαρτίαν.¹²

    9 Ὁ μακαρισμὸς¹³ οὖν οὗτος ἐπὶ τὴν περιτομὴν ἢ καὶ ἐπὶ τὴν ἀκροβυστίαν; λέγομεν γάρ· ἐλογίσθη τῷ Ἀβραὰμ ἡ πίστις εἰς δικαιοσύνην. 10 πῶς οὖν ἐλογίσθη; ἐν περιτομῇ ὄντι ἢ ἐν ἀκροβυστίᾳ;¹⁴ οὐκ¹⁵ ἐν περιτομῇ ἀλλ᾽ ἐν ἀκροβυστίᾳ· 11 καὶ σημεῖον ἔλαβεν περιτομῆς σφραγῖδα¹⁶ τῆς

---

7. λογίζεται κατὰ χάριν . . . ὀφείλημα: λογίζεται followed by κατὰ plus the accusative, indicates how an accounting entry is labeled (BDAG 597.1.a*): "is [not] credited as a gift . . . as wages."

8. πιστεύοντι δὲ ἐπὶ τὸν δικαιοῦντα: the participles are substantival (Wallace 619–21; BDF §413; *GNTG* §5.182). Here, the object of trust is given with ἐπί and accusative case (BDAG 817.1.a. δ*).

9. λέγει τὸν μακαρισμὸν τοῦ ἀνθρώπου: "speaks [about] the blessedness of the human being." The reference is to Ps 32:1–2a (31:1–2a LXX): Μακάριοι ὧν ἀφέθησαν αἱ ἀνομίαι / καὶ ὧν ἐπεκαλύφθησαν αἱ ἁμαρτίαι· / μακάριος ἀνήρ, οὗ οὐ μὴ λογίσηται κύριος ἁμαρτίαν.

10. μακάριοι is the predicate adjective of an implied εἰσίν (Wallace 39–40; BDF §§127–28); the subject is the implied antecedent of the relative pronoun (ὧν): "Blessed are those whose."

11. μακάριος is the predicate adjective of an implied ἐστίν (Wallace 39–40; BDF §§127–28); the subject is ἀνὴρ: "Blessed is the man."

12. οὗ οὐ μὴ λογίσηται: here, λογίσηται places the person against whom something is reckoned into the genitive case (BDAG 597.1.a*). οὐ μὴ plus the aorist subjunctive indicates emphatic negation (Wallace 468*; BDF §365.3*; [though BDF suggests the combination here is a simple negation]; *GNTG* §5.136): "against whom the Lord will never reckon sin."

13. Ὁ μακαρισμὸς is the nominative subject of an implied verb; here, perhaps, some form of λέγεται (BDF §481*): "Is this blessedness spoken over?"

14. ἐν περιτομῇ ὄντι ἢ ἐν ἀκροβυστίᾳ: ἐν with the dative is marking the circumstance or condition under which the reckoning took place (BDAG 329.7). ὄντι is an attributive participle (Wallace 617–18; BDF §413; *GNTG* §5.181), modifying τῷ Ἀβραὰμ: "while he was circumcised or uncircumcised?" The question is elliptical; the reader must bring forward the verb from the first question, at the beginning of the verse. This kind of ellipsis is common in imitation of ordinary speech (BDF §481).

15. This response to the question is elliptical; the reader must bring forward the verb from the first question, at the beginning of the verse (see n. 14).

16. σφραγῖδα: some verbs (ἔλαβεν) can take two accusatives. σφραγῖδα could be the complement in an object-complement double accusative construction with σημεῖον as

δικαιοσύνης τῆς πίστεως τῆς ἐν τῇ ἀκροβυστίᾳ,[17] εἰς τὸ εἶναι αὐτὸν[18] πατέρα πάντων τῶν πιστευόντων[19] δι᾽ ἀκροβυστίας, εἰς τὸ λογισθῆναι καὶ αὐτοῖς τὴν δικαιοσύνην,[20] 12 καὶ πατέρα[21] περιτομῆς τοῖς οὐκ ἐκ περιτομῆς[22] μόνον ἀλλὰ καὶ τοῖς στοιχοῦσιν[23] τοῖς ἴχνεσιν[24] τῆς ἐν ἀκροβυστίᾳ πίστεως τοῦ πατρὸς ἡμῶν Ἀβραάμ.[25]

13 Οὐ γὰρ διὰ νόμου ἡ ἐπαγγελία[26] τῷ Ἀβραὰμ ἢ τῷ σπέρματι αὐτοῦ, τὸ κληρονόμον αὐτὸν εἶναι[27] κόσμου, ἀλλὰ διὰ δικαιοσύνης πίστεως.

---

the object (Wallace 181–89 [183 n. 24]; BDF §157; *GNTG* §5.76): "he received the sign . . . as a seal"; or, it could be a direct object in apposition to σημεῖον: "the sign . . . , a seal."

17. τῆς ἐν τῇ ἀκροβυστίᾳ: the article changes the prepositional phrases into an attributive modifier of πίστεως (Wallace 236; BDF §266; *GNTG* §5.16): "while he was uncircumcised."

18. εἰς τὸ εἶναι αὐτὸν: the articular infinitive with εἰς indicates purpose (Wallace 590–92*, 610; BDF §402.2*; *GNTG* §5.174): "in order that he might be"; αὐτὸν is the accusative subject of the infinitive.

19. τῶν πιστευόντων is a substantival participle (Wallace 619–21; BDF §413; *GNTG* §5.182).

20. εἰς τὸ λογισθῆναι . . . τὴν δικαιοσύνην: the articular infinitive with εἰς indicates purpose (Wallace 590–92*, 610; BDF §402.2*; *GNTG* §5.174); τὴν δικαιοσύνην is the accusative subject of the infinitive: "in order that righteousness might be credited."

21. πατέρα is a predicate accusative of εἰς τὸ εἶναι from v. 11: "he [αὐτὸν] might be father."

22. τοῖς οὐκ ἐκ περιτομῆς: the article changes the prepositional phrase into a substantive dative of advantage (Wallace 236; BDF §266; *GNTG* §5.16).

23. τοῖς στοιχοῦσιν is a substantival participle (Wallace 619–21; BDF §413; *GNTG* §5.182). The presence of the article is puzzling. It suggests that this is a second group of people from the one introduced by the dative article in v. 12a. See the discussion in the major commentaries.

24. τοῖς ἴχνεσιν is the dative complement of τοῖς στοιχοῦσιν (BDAG 946).

25. τῆς ἐν ἀκροβυστίᾳ πίστεως τοῦ πατρὸς ἡμῶν Ἀβραάμ: ἐν with the dative is marking the circumstance or condition under which the faith took place (BDAG 329.7): "the faith our father Abraham had while he was uncircumcised."

26. ἡ ἐπαγγελία is the nominative subject of an implied verb (see the discussion in BDF §§479–83). Perhaps a form of γίνομαι: "The promise did not come"; or a form of βεβαιόω: "The promise was not established." In favor of the latter is the use of βεβαίαν in v. 16 and βεβαιῶσαι τὰς ἐπαγγελίας (Rom 15:8). Or a form of δίδωμι (Gal 3:22): ἵνα ἡ ἐπαγγελία ἐκ πίστεως Ἰησοῦ Χριστοῦ **δοθῇ** τοῖς πιστεύουσιν. Gal 3:16: τῷ δὲ Ἀβραὰμ **ἐρρέθησαν** αἱ ἐπαγγελίαι καὶ τῷ σπέρματι αὐτοῦ.

27. τὸ κληρονόμον αὐτὸν εἶναι: αὐτὸν is the accusative subject of the infinitive (Wallace 196*; BDF §399.1*). The infinitive might be epexegetical (Wallace 607; BDF §§394, 399.1*; *GNTG* §5.167), explaining ἡ ἐπαγγελία; it might be indicating indirect discourse (Wallace 603–5; BDF §396; *GNTG* §5.166), if ἡ ἐπαγγελία suggests something spoken: "promise [that] he would be"; it might be indicating purpose/result (Wallace 590–92; BDF §390; *GNTG* §5.161): "promise . . . so that it might be."

14 εἰ γὰρ οἱ ἐκ νόμου κληρονόμοι,[28] κεκένωται ἡ πίστις καὶ κατήργηται ἡ ἐπαγγελία· 15 ὁ γὰρ νόμος ὀργὴν κατεργάζεται· οὗ[29] δὲ οὐκ ἔστιν νόμος οὐδὲ παράβασις. 16 Διὰ τοῦτο[30] ἐκ πίστεως,[31] ἵνα[32] κατὰ χάριν, εἰς τὸ εἶναι βεβαίαν τὴν ἐπαγγελίαν[33] παντὶ τῷ σπέρματι, οὐ τῷ ἐκ τοῦ νόμου μόνον ἀλλὰ καὶ τῷ ἐκ πίστεως Ἀβραάμ,[34] ὅς ἐστιν πατὴρ πάντων ἡμῶν, 17 καθὼς γέγραπται[35] ὅτι πατέρα[36] πολλῶν ἐθνῶν τέθεικά σε, κατέναντι οὗ ἐπίστευσεν θεοῦ[37] τοῦ ζῳοποιοῦντος τοὺς νεκροὺς καὶ καλοῦντος[38]

28. οἱ ἐκ νόμου κληρονόμοι: The article changes the prepositional phrase into the nominative subject (Wallace 236; BDF §266; *GNTG* §5.16) of an implied εἰσίν (Wallace 39–40; BDF §§127–28); it is not the article for κληρονόμοι: "[if] those who are from the law are heirs."
29. οὗ is the adverb, "where"; not the relative pronoun.
30. Διὰ τοῦτο: "therefore," "for this reason" (BDAG 225.B.2.b); it likely refers to the preceding argument.
31. The initial clause of the verse is elliptical; the reader must supply some form of εἰμί (Wallace 39–40; BDF §§127–28): "It is on the basis of faith."
32. ἵνα: with the subjunctive is introducing a purpose clause; the clause is elliptical but implies either the subjunctive of εἰμί or γίνομαι (Wallace 39–40; BDF §§127–28): "so that it might be."
33. εἰς τὸ εἶναι βεβαίαν τὴν ἐπαγγελίαν: εἰς plus the articular infinitive can indicate purpose (Wallace 603–5; BDF §396; *GNTG* §5.166) or result (Wallace 592–94; BDF §402.2*; *GNTG* §5.162). Here, it likely indicates result. τὴν ἐπαγγελίαν is the accusative subject of the infinitive: "with the result that the promise may be guaranteed."
34. τῷ ἐκ τοῦ νόμου . . . τῷ ἐκ πίστεως Ἀβραάμ: the article changes each of the prepositional phrases into a substantive dative of advantage (Wallace 236; BDF §266; *GNTG* §5.16): "[not only] for the one from the law . . . [but also] for the one from the faith of Abraham."
35. The quotation is from Gen 17:5: ὅτι πατέρα πολλῶν ἐθνῶν τέθεικά σε. For the larger context of the text, see §1.1 in this volume.
36. πατέρα: some verbs (τέθεικά) can take two accusatives. πατέρα is the complement in an object-complement double accusative construction with σε as the object (Wallace 181–89 [183 n. 24]; BDF §157; *GNTG* §5.77): "I have made you the father."
37. κατέναντι οὗ ἐπίστευσεν θεοῦ: BDAG suggests that Paul's syntax is the equivalent of κατέναντι θεοῦ ᾧ ἐπίστευσεν (818.1.b; also BDF §294.2*). θεοῦ is in the genitive case by attraction to its antecedent rather than in the dative case, which one typically expects with ἐπίστευσεν.
38. τοῦ ζῳοποιοῦντος . . . καλοῦντος: the participles are substantival (Wallace 619–21; BDF §413; *GNTG* §5.182).

τὰ μὴ ὄντα ὡς ὄντα.³⁹ 18 Ὃς⁴⁰ παρ᾽ ἐλπίδα⁴¹ ἐπ᾽ ἐλπίδι⁴² ἐπίστευσεν εἰς τὸ γενέσθαι αὐτὸν πατέρα⁴³ πολλῶν ἐθνῶν κατὰ τὸ εἰρημένον·⁴⁴ οὕτως ἔσται τὸ σπέρμα σου, 19 καὶ μὴ ἀσθενήσας⁴⁵ τῇ πίστει⁴⁶ κατενόησεν τὸ ἑαυτοῦ σῶμα ἤδη νενεκρωμένον,⁴⁷ ἑκατονταετής που ὑπάρχων,⁴⁸ καὶ τὴν νέκρωσιν⁴⁹ τῆς μήτρας Σάρρας· 20 εἰς δὲ τὴν ἐπαγγελίαν⁵⁰ τοῦ θεοῦ οὐ διεκρίθη τῇ ἀπιστίᾳ ἀλλ᾽ ἐνεδυναμώθη τῇ πίστει, δοὺς⁵¹ δόξαν τῷ

39. τὰ μὴ ὄντα ὡς ὄντα: with καλοῦντος: "who calls into existence things that do not exist" (BDAG 504.4*); or, "who summons things that do not exist as if they did."

40. Ὃς: the antecedent is Ἀβραάμ (v. 16).

41. παρ᾽ ἐλπίδα: παρά marks something that goes against what is expected (BDAG 758.6): "against hope."

42. ἐπ᾽ ἐλπίδι: ἐπί marks the basis for an action (BDAG 364.6): "on the basis of hope."

43. εἰς τὸ γενέσθαι αὐτὸν πατέρα: εἰς plus the articular infinitive can indicate purpose (Wallace 603–5; BDF §396; *GNTG* §5.166) or result (Wallace 592–94; BDF §402.2*; *GNTG* §5.162). Here, it likely indicates result: "with the result that he became the father" (*GNTG* §5.78c*). αὐτὸν is the accusative subject of the infinitive.

44. κατὰ τὸ εἰρημένον: εἰρημένον is pf.-ptc.-pass.-neut.-acc.-sg. < λέγω. The participle is substantival (Wallace 619–21; BDF §413): "according to the thing spoken"; "according to what was spoken."

45. ἀσθενήσας is an attributive participle (Wallace 617–18; BDF §413; *GNTG* §5.181), modifying the implied subject of κατενόησεν: "without growing weak . . . he considered."

46. τῇ πίστει is a dative of respect (Wallace 144–46*; BDF §197; *GNTG* §5.68).

47. νενεκρωμένον is likely an adjectival participle (Wallace 619–21; BDF §413; *GNTG* §5.182) serving as a predicate adjective with σῶμα as the accusative object (Wallace 190–91; BDF §157; *GNTG* §5.78): "as dead."

48. ἑκατονταετής που ὑπάρχων: this participle is likely an adverbial participle indicating cause (Wallace 631–32; BDF §418.1; *GNTG* §189). που means "approximately" (BDF §103): "since he was approximately one hundred years old."

49. τὴν νέκρωσιν is a second accusative object of κατενόησεν (he considered [1] his own body and [2] the deadness of Sarah's womb).

50. εἰς . . . τὴν ἐπαγγελίαν: εἰς goes with διεκρίθη, indicating "that 'toward' which he did not waver." (BDAG 231.6*): "he did not doubt the promise."

51. δοὺς might be indicating action pragmatically equal to the main verb: "he became strengthened in faith and gave thanks"; it might be an adverbial participle indicating manner (Wallace 627–28; BDF §418.5; *GNTG* §5.193); or result (Wallace 637–39; *GNTG* §5.195).

θεῷ 21 καὶ πληροφορηθεὶς[52] ὅτι ὃ[53] ἐπήγγελται δυνατός ἐστιν καὶ ποιῆσαι.[54] 22 διὸ καὶ ἐλογίσθη αὐτῷ εἰς δικαιοσύνην. 23 Οὐκ ἐγράφη δὲ δι᾽
αὐτὸν μόνον ὅτι ἐλογίσθη αὐτῷ 24 ἀλλὰ καὶ δι᾽ ἡμᾶς, οἷς μέλλει λογίζεσθαι,[55] τοῖς πιστεύουσιν[56] ἐπὶ τὸν ἐγείραντα[57] Ἰησοῦν τὸν κύριον ἡμῶν
ἐκ νεκρῶν, 25 ὃς παρεδόθη διὰ τὰ παραπτώματα ἡμῶν καὶ ἠγέρθη διὰ
τὴν δικαίωσιν ἡμῶν.

Vocabulary

ἀκροβυστία, ας, ἡ	foreskin, uncircumcision
ἀνομία, ας, ἡ	lawlessness
ἀπιστία, ας, ἡ	unbelief
ἀσεβής, ές	ungodly
ἀσθενέω	to be weak
βέβαιος, α, ον	sure, firm, certain
διακρίνω	to evaluate, consider, doubt
δικαιόω	to pronounce righteous, justify
δικαίωσις, εως, ἡ	justification
δυνατός, ή, όν	possible, strong, able
ἑκατονταετής, ές	hundred years old
ἐνδυναμόω	to be strong
ἐπαγγέλλομαι	to promise; to profess
ἐπικαλύπτω	to cover
ἐργάζομαι	to work
ζῳοποιέω	to make alive, keep alive
ἴχνος, ους, τό	footprint, track
καθάπερ	as, just as, like

52. πληροφορηθεὶς is likely an adverbial participle indicating manner (Wallace 627–28; BDF §418.5; *GNTG* §5.193); or result (Wallace 637–39; *GNTG* §5.195).
53. ὃ is either the nominative subject of ἐπήγγελται, if the verb is read as passive: "what was promised"; or the accusative object of the verb, if it is read as middle: "what he promised."
54. ποιῆσαι is a complementary infinitive going with δυνατός (Wallace 598–99; BDF §392; *GNTG* §5.163).
55. λογίζεσθαι is a complementary infinitive going with μέλλει (Wallace 598–99; BDF §392; *GNTG* §5.163).
56. τοῖς πιστεύουσιν is a substantival participle (Wallace 619–21; BDF §413; *GNTG* §5.182) and in apposition to the relative pronoun.
57. ἐπὶ τὸν ἐγείραντα: ἐπὶ here marking the object of πιστεύουσιν. The participle is sub-stantival (Wallace 619–21; BDF §413; *GNTG* §5.182).

κατανοέω	to understand, consider
καταργέω	to leave idle, occupy, make of no effect, nullify
κατέναντι	(+ gen.) opposite, before, in the presence of
κατεργάζομαι	to work, prepare, make, oppress, subdue
καύχημα, ατος, τό	object of boasting, pride
κενόω	to make of no effect, make empty
κληρονόμος, ου, ὁ	heir
λογίζομαι	to count, think, calculate
μακαρισμός, οῦ, ὁ	blessedness, happiness
μήτρα, ας, ἡ	womb
μισθός, οῦ, ὁ	wages; reward, recompense
νεκρόω	to put to death
νέκρωσις, εως, ἡ	deadness, death
ὀργή, ῆς, ἡ	wrath; anger
οὗ	where, to where
ὀφείλημα, ατος, τό	debt
παράβασις, εως, ἡ	disobedience
παράπτωμα, ατος, τό	trespass
περιτομή, ῆς, ἡ	circumcision
πληροφορέω	to be set on; to assure fully
πού, adv.	somewhere, about (with numbers)
προπάτωρ, ορος, ὁ	forefather, ancestor
Σάρρα, ας, ἡ	Sarah
σπέρμα, ατος, τό	seed, offspring
στοιχέω	to walk, live; prosper
σφραγίς, ῖδος, ἡ	seal
χωρίς	(+ gen.) without (prep.); separately (adv.)

3.4. 1 CORINTHIANS 12:1–31A

The Body of Christ

Paul's "first" letter to Corinth (though this letter was not actually the first letter to this church; he mentions a previous letter in 5:9) is one of those the authorship of which scholars do not dispute. The precise year in which Paul wrote the letter is unknown; most scholars suggest 53–54 CE. Paul writes to this church, which he himself had established, from Ephesus. He is responding to a letter the Corinthians have sent him (7:1) and to reports he had received about problems in the church (1 Cor 1:11).

In this section of the letter, Paul is responding to issues raised by the Corinthians in their letter to him. Chapter 12 introduces the topic of spiritual gifts that will run through the end of chapter 14. In chapter 12, Paul emphasizes the variety of gifts, that each gift is necessary and comes from the same source, and he compares the variety of gifts to the different parts that make up a human body.

1 Περὶ δὲ[1] τῶν πνευματικῶν,[2] ἀδελφοί, οὐ θέλω ὑμᾶς ἀγνοεῖν.[3]
2 Οἴδατε ὅτι ὅτε ἔθνη ἦτε πρὸς τὰ εἴδωλα τὰ ἄφωνα ὡς ἂν[4] ἤγεσθε

---

1. Περὶ δὲ is used to indicate a change in topic. Paul uses it, on occasion, in this letter to indicate when he is taking up topics they have written to him about (see 1 Cor 7:1). The construction also appears in this volume in Did. 7:1 (§1.6) and 9:1, 3 (§1.8).

2. τῶν πνευματικῶν: if this adjective is neuter: "spiritual things"; if masculine: "spiritual people." See the discussion in Timothy A. Brookins and Bruce W. Longenecker, *1 Corinthians 10–16: A Handbook on the Greek Text*, BHGNT (Waco, TX: Baylor University Press, 2016), 62.

3. ὑμᾶς ἀγνοεῖν: ἀγνοεῖν is a complementary infinitive, going with θέλω (Wallace 598–99; BDF §392; *GNTG* §5.163); ὑμᾶς is the accusative subject of the infinitive.

4. ὡς ἂν: under certain conditions, ἂν indicates repeated action in past time (BDAG 56.1.a.α*; BDF §367*): "whenever."

ἀπαγόμενοι.⁵ 3 διὸ γνωρίζω ὑμῖν ὅτι οὐδεὶς ἐν πνεύματι⁶ θεοῦ λαλῶν⁷ λέγει· Ἀνάθεμα Ἰησοῦς,⁸ καὶ οὐδεὶς δύναται εἰπεῖν·⁹ Κύριος Ἰησοῦς, εἰ μὴ¹⁰ ἐν πνεύματι ἁγίῳ.

4 Διαιρέσεις δὲ χαρισμάτων εἰσίν, τὸ δὲ αὐτὸ πνεῦμα·¹¹ 5 καὶ διαιρέσεις διακονιῶν εἰσιν, καὶ ὁ αὐτὸς κύριος· 6 καὶ διαιρέσεις ἐνεργημάτων εἰσίν, ὁ δὲ αὐτὸς θεὸς ὁ ἐνεργῶν¹² τὰ πάντα ἐν πᾶσιν. 7 ἑκάστῳ δὲ δίδοται ἡ φανέρωσις τοῦ πνεύματος πρὸς τὸ συμφέρον.¹³ 8 ᾧ μὲν¹⁴ γὰρ διὰ τοῦ πνεύματος δίδοται λόγος σοφίας, ἄλλῳ δὲ λόγος γνώσεως κατὰ τὸ

5. ἀπαγόμενοι is probably an imperfect periphrastic participle going with an implied ἦτε (Wallace 647–49; also BDF §§352–56): "you were being led astray." It agrees with ἔθνη in case and number but not gender; therefore it is *constructio ad sensum* (on the concept of *constructio ad sensum*, see the discussion in BDF §134). See Brookins and Longenecker for grammatical problems in this verse (*1 Corinthians 10–16*, 63). Of the five options suggested by Brookins and Longenecker, the first two seem to me most plausible: (1) ἦτε needs to be repeated with the participle: "When you were gentiles, at whatever time you might have been led, [you were] led." (2) It might be that ἦτε properly belongs with ἀπαγόμενοι, and it is ὅτε ἔθνη that contains an ellipsis: "When [you were] gentiles, you were being led away" (*1 Corinthians 10–16*, 63).

6. ἐν πνεύματι: the prepositional phrase could be: (1) instrumental ("by means of the spirit"); (2) locative ("in the spirit"); or (3) manner ("spiritually"; Brookins and Longenecker, *1 Corinthians 10–16*, 64).

7. λαλῶν: this participle might be attributive (Wallace 617–18; BDF §412; *GNTG* §5.181), modifying οὐδεὶς: "no one who speaks"; it might be an adverbial participle indicating time; the present tense indicates time contemporaneous with the action of the main verb (Wallace 623–27; BDF §418; *GNTG* §5.188): "while speaking ἐν πνεύματι θεοῦ."

8. Ἀνάθεμα Ἰησοῦς: Ἀνάθεμα is the predicate nominative of an implied form of εἰμί (Wallace 39–40; BDF §§127–28).

9. εἰπεῖν is a complementary infinitive going with δύναται (Wallace 598–99; BDF §392; *GNTG* §5.163).

10. εἰ μὴ: "Except" (BDAG 278.6.i.α).

11. τὸ δὲ αὐτὸ πνεῦμα: αὐτός used with a noun in the attributive position means "the same" (*GNTG* §5.7). τὸ . . . πνεῦμα is the nominative subject of an implied form of εἰμί (Wallace 39–40; BDF §§127–28): "it is the same spirit." Paul repeats this syntax, using εἰσίν in the first clause but omitting the verb in the second, in vv. 5–6.

12. ὁ ἐνεργῶν is an attributive participle (Wallace 617–18; BDF §412; *GNTG* §5.181), modifying ὁ . . . θεὸς: "The same God who produces" (BDAG 335.2*).

13. πρὸς τὸ συμφέρον: the participle is substantival (Wallace 619–21; BDF §413; *GNTG* §5.182). It serves as the accusative object of πρὸς: "for [someone's] advantage" (BDAG 960.2.b.γ). Whose advantage must be determined from the larger context of the paragraph. Since the discussion in this section of the letter is the importance of the individual for the whole, most translators translate the prepositional phrase as: "for the advantage/benefit of all."

14. ᾧ μὲν . . . ἄλλῳ δὲ: "To the one . . . to another" (BDAG 727.2.b*). Paul begins to illustrate what he meant by the general statement in v. 7: ἑκάστῳ δὲ δίδοται ἡ φανέρωσις τοῦ

αὐτὸ πνεῦμα, 9 ἑτέρῳ πίστις¹⁵ ἐν τῷ αὐτῷ πνεύματι, ἄλλῳ δὲ χαρίσματα¹⁶ ἰαμάτων ἐν τῷ ἑνὶ πνεύματι, 10 ἄλλῳ δὲ ἐνεργήματα¹⁷ δυνάμεων, ἄλλῳ δὲ προφητεία,¹⁸ ἄλλῳ δὲ διακρίσεις¹⁹ πνευμάτων, ἑτέρῳ γένη²⁰ γλωσσῶν, ἄλλῳ δὲ ἑρμηνεία²¹ γλωσσῶν· 11 πάντα δὲ ταῦτα ἐνεργεῖ τὸ ἓν καὶ τὸ αὐτὸ πνεῦμα²² διαιροῦν²³ ἰδίᾳ²⁴ ἑκάστῳ καθὼς βούλεται.

12 Καθάπερ γὰρ τὸ σῶμα ἕν ἐστιν καὶ μέλη πολλὰ ἔχει, πάντα δὲ τὰ μέλη τοῦ σώματος πολλὰ ὄντα²⁵ ἕν ἐστιν σῶμα, οὕτως καὶ ὁ Χριστός·²⁶ 13 καὶ γὰρ ἐν ἑνὶ πνεύματι ἡμεῖς πάντες εἰς ἓν σῶμα ἐβαπτίσθημεν, εἴτε Ἰουδαῖοι εἴτε Ἕλληνες εἴτε δοῦλοι εἴτε ἐλεύθεροι,²⁷ καὶ πάντες ἓν πνεῦμα ἐποτίσθημεν.²⁸ 14 Καὶ γὰρ τὸ σῶμα οὐκ ἔστιν ἓν μέλος ἀλλὰ πολλά.

πνεύματος. The first statement in v. 8 includes the verb that the reader must supply for each of the nominative subjects that follow through the end of v. 10: δίδοται.

15. πίστις is the nominative subject of a clause with an elided verb to be supplied by the reader; the context suggests δίδοται (see the discussion in BDF §§479–83).

16. χαρίσματα is the nominative subject of a clause with an elided verb to be supplied by the reader; the context suggests δίδοται (see the discussion in BDF §§479–83).

17. ἐνεργήματα is the nominative subject of a clause with an elided verb to be supplied by the reader; the context suggests δίδοται (see the discussion in BDF §§479–83).

18. προφητεία is the nominative subject of a clause with an elided verb to be supplied by the reader; the context suggests δίδοται (see the discussion in BDF §§479–83).

19. διακρίσεις is the nominative subject of a clause with an elided verb to be supplied by the reader; the context suggests δίδοται (see the discussion in BDF §§479–83).

20. γένη is the nominative subject of a clause with an elided verb to be supplied by the reader; the context suggests δίδοται (see the discussion in BDF §§479–83).

21. ἑρμηνεία is the nominative subject of a clause with an elided verb to be supplied by the reader; the context suggests δίδοται (see the discussion in BDF §§479–83).

22. τὸ . . . πνεῦμα is the nominative subject of ἐνεργεῖ.

23. διαιροῦν: pres.-ptc.-act.-neut.-nom.-sg. < διαιρέω. The participle might be an adverbial participle indicating manner (the manner in which the spirit accomplishes all these things; Wallace 627–28; BDF §418; *GNTG* §5.193); it might be an attributive participle (Wallace 617–18; BDF §412; *GNTG* §5.181), modifying τὸ . . . πνεῦμα: "the Spirit, who distributes."

24. ἰδίᾳ is an adverbial dative (BDAG 467.5*): "privately"; "individually" (see the discussion in Brookins and Longenecker, *1 Corinthians 10–16*, 71–72).

25. ὄντα is likely an adverbial participle indicating concession (Wallace 634–35; BDF §418.3; *GNTG* §5.191): "although being."

26. ὁ Χριστός is the nominative subject of an implied ἐστίν (Wallace 39–40; BDF §§127–28).

27. εἴτε Ἰουδαῖοι εἴτε Ἕλληνες εἴτε δοῦλοι εἴτε ἐλεύθεροι: all of these nominatives provide examples of what Paul means by ἡμεῖς πάντες.

28. ἓν πνεῦμα ἐποτίσθημεν: in the passive, with an accusative of thing: to be given something to drink (BDAG 857.1.a*): "we have all been given to drink the same Spirit."

15 ἐὰν²⁹ εἴπῃ ὁ πούς· ὅτι³⁰ οὐκ εἰμὶ χείρ, οὐκ εἰμὶ ἐκ τοῦ σώματος, οὐ παρὰ τοῦτο οὐκ³¹ ἔστιν ἐκ τοῦ σώματος; 16 καὶ ἐὰν³² εἴπῃ τὸ οὖς· ὅτι οὐκ εἰμὶ ὀφθαλμός, οὐκ εἰμὶ ἐκ τοῦ σώματος, οὐ παρὰ τοῦτο οὐκ ἔστιν ἐκ τοῦ σώματος; 17 εἰ³³ ὅλον τὸ σῶμα³⁴ ὀφθαλμός, ποῦ ἡ ἀκοή;³⁵ εἰ ὅλον³⁶ ἀκοή, ποῦ ἡ ὄσφρησις;³⁷ 18 νυνὶ δὲ ὁ θεὸς ἔθετο τὰ μέλη, ἓν ἕκαστον³⁸ αὐτῶν ἐν τῷ σώματι καθὼς ἠθέλησεν. 19 εἰ³⁹ δὲ ἦν τὰ πάντα ἓν μέλος, ποῦ τὸ

29. ἐὰν with the subjunctive (εἴπῃ) introduces the protasis of a third-class condition. The third-class condition can indicate something likely to occur in the future, something that might occur, or something that will not occur but hypothetically could (Wallace 469–71, 663, 696–99; BDF §§371, 373; *GNTG* §5.237).

30. ὅτι is introducing direct discourse; it need not be translated (BDAG 732.3).

31. οὐ παρὰ τοῦτο οὐκ: this prepositional phrase introduces the apodosis of the third-class condition. παρὰ in this context is a marker of causality: "because of this." The double negative here strengthens the affirmative: is it for this reason not a part of the body? (BDAG 758.C.5*; see the discussion in Brookins and Longenecker, *1 Corinthians 10–16*, 75–76).

32. ἐὰν with the subjunctive (εἴπῃ) introduces the protasis of a third-class condition (see n. 29).

33. εἰ plus the indicative can introduce either a first-class condition or a second-class (contrary-to-fact) condition. The second-class condition introduces, for the sake of argument, the assumption of something that is not true (Wallace 694–96; BDF §§360, 371.3; *GNTG* §236). The fact that Paul omits the verb in this sentence complicates making a decision on which kind of conditional statement he is setting up; the second-class condition uses secondary tense verbs in both the protasis and the apodosis. As Brookins and Longenecker indicate, the context and the evidence from v. 19 (the presence of ἦν) suggest that here, εἰ is introducing a condition of the second class. The absence of ἄν, while often included in second-class conditions, is not necessary (*1 Corinthians 10–16*, 76).

34. ὅλον τὸ σῶμα is the nominative subject of an implied form of εἰμί (Wallace 39–40; BDF §§127–28). ἦν should likely be supplied on the basis of reading the conditional statement as second class: "if the whole body were."

35. ἡ ἀκοή is the nominative subject of an implied ἄν ἦν as the expected apodosis in a second-class condition (Brookins and Longenecker, *1 Corinthians 10–16*, 76): "where would the hearing be?"

36. εἰ ὅλον: εἰ introduces another second-class condition. ὅλον (along with an implied τὸ σῶμα) is the nominative subject of an implied form of εἰμί; ἦν should likely be supplied on the basis of reading the conditional statement as second class.

37. ἡ ὄσφρησις is the nominative subject of an implied ἄν ἦν as the expected apodosis in a second-class condition.

38. ἓν ἕκαστον is in apposition to τὰ μέλη: "every single one" (BDAG 298.b*).

39. εἰ introduces a second-class condition (see n. 33).

σῶμα;⁴⁰ 20 νῦν δὲ πολλὰ μὲν μέλη,⁴¹ ἓν δὲ σῶμα.⁴² 21 οὐ δύναται δὲ ὁ ὀφθαλμὸς εἰπεῖν⁴³ τῇ χειρί· χρείαν σου οὐκ ἔχω, ἢ πάλιν ἡ κεφαλὴ⁴⁴ τοῖς ποσίν· χρείαν ὑμῶν οὐκ ἔχω· 22 ἀλλὰ πολλῷ μᾶλλον⁴⁵ τὰ δοκοῦντα⁴⁶ μέλη τοῦ σώματος ἀσθενέστερα ὑπάρχειν⁴⁷ ἀναγκαῖά ἐστιν, 23 καὶ ἃ⁴⁸ δοκοῦμεν ἀτιμότερα εἶναι⁴⁹ τοῦ σώματος τούτοις⁵⁰ τιμὴν περισσοτέραν περιτίθεμεν, καὶ τὰ ἀσχήμονα⁵¹ ἡμῶν εὐσχημοσύνην περισσοτέραν ἔχει,⁵² 24 τὰ δὲ εὐσχήμονα ἡμῶν οὐ χρείαν ἔχει. Ἀλλ᾽ ὁ θεὸς συνεκέρασεν τὸ σῶμα τῷ ὑστερουμένῳ⁵³ περισσοτέραν δοὺς⁵⁴ τιμήν, 25 ἵνα μὴ ᾖ σχίσμα ἐν τῷ σώματι ἀλλὰ τὸ αὐτὸ ὑπὲρ ἀλλήλων μεριμνῶσιν⁵⁵ τὰ μέλη. 26 καὶ

40. τὸ σῶμα is the nominative subject of an implied ἂν ἦν as the expected apodosis in a second-class condition.

41. πολλὰ . . . μέλη is the nominative subject of an implied ἐστίν (Wallace 39–40; BDF §§127–28).

42. ἓν . . . σῶμα is the nominative subject of an implied ἐστίν (Wallace 39–40; BDF §§127–28).

43. εἰπεῖν is a complementary infinitive, going with δύναται (Wallace 598–99; BDF §392; *GNTG* §5.163); it introduces direct discourse.

44. ἡ κεφαλὴ is the nominative subject of a clause with an elided verb to be supplied by the reader; the context suggests οὐ δύναται εἰπεῖν (see the discussion in BDF §§479–83).

45. πολλῷ μᾶλλον: the dative of degree of difference with the comparative adverb of μάλα (BDAG 849.2.a.כ*; also, Brookins and Longenecker, *1 Corinthians 10–16*, 78): "to a much greater degree."

46. τὰ δοκοῦντα is likely an attributive participle (Wallace 617–18; BDF §412; *GNTG* §5.181), modifying μέλη: "that seem."

47. ὑπάρχειν: verbs of perception (δοκοῦντα) take the infinitive (BDF §397.2; Wallace treats it as a form of indirect discourse [603–5]; *GNTG* §5.166). It is unusual for the articular participle to be complemented by an infinitive, but it does occur elsewhere (Rom 8:18; Gal 3:23; 2 Pet 3:2; Brookins and Longenecker, *1 Corinthians 10–16*, 79).

48. ἃ is the accusative direct object of δοκοῦμεν.

49. εἶναι: verbs of perception (δοκοῦμεν) take the infinitive (BDF §397.2; Wallace treats it as a form of indirect discourse [603–5]; *GNTG* §5.166).

50. τούτοις is the dative complement to περιτίθεμεν (BDAG 807.2*): "to these we show."

51. τὰ ἀσχήμονα can be a euphemism for the genitalia (BDAG 147*).

52. ἔχει is likely singular because neuter plural subjects (τὰ ἀσχήμονα) frequently take singular verbs (Wallace 399–400; BDF §133; *GNTG* §5.26.a).

53. τῷ ὑστερουμένῳ is a substantival participle (Wallace 619–21; BDF §413; *GNTG* §5.182). In context, the reader should supply something like τῷ μέλῳ: "to the lesser members."

54. δοὺς is likely an adverbial participle indicating means (Wallace 625–30; BDF §418; *GNTG* §5.192): "by giving."

55. τὸ αὐτὸ . . . μεριμνῶσιν: "show the same concern for one another" (BDAG 632.2*).

εἴτε πάσχει ἓν μέλος, συμπάσχει πάντα τὰ μέλη· εἴτε[56] δοξάζεται ἓν μέλος, συγχαίρει πάντα τὰ μέλη. 27 Ὑμεῖς δέ ἐστε σῶμα Χριστοῦ καὶ μέλη ἐκ μέρους.[57] 28 Καὶ οὓς[58] μὲν[59] ἔθετο ὁ θεὸς ἐν τῇ ἐκκλησίᾳ πρῶτον ἀποστόλους, δεύτερον προφήτας, τρίτον διδασκάλους, ἔπειτα δυνάμεις, ἔπειτα χαρίσματα ἰαμάτων, ἀντιλήμψεις, κυβερνήσεις, γένη γλωσσῶν. 29 μὴ[60] πάντες[61] ἀπόστολοι; μὴ πάντες προφῆται; μὴ πάντες διδάσκαλοι; μὴ πάντες δυνάμεις; 30 μὴ[62] πάντες χαρίσματα ἔχουσιν ἰαμάτων; μὴ πάντες γλώσσαις λαλοῦσιν; μὴ πάντες διερμηνεύουσιν; 31 ζηλοῦτε δὲ τὰ χαρίσματα τὰ μείζονα.

Vocabulary

ἀγνοέω	to be ignorant; to ignore
ἀκοή, ῆς, ἡ	hearing, sound, report
ἀναγκαῖος, α, ον	necessary
ἀνάθεμα, ατος, τό	accursed
ἀντίλημψις, εως, ἡ	help
ἀπάγω	to lead away, carry off; to withdraw
ἀσθενής, ές	weak; weakness
ἀσχήμων, ον	unpresentable, shameful, unworthy
ἄτιμος, ον	dishonored; insignificant
ἄφωνος, ον	speechless; unsounded, unvoiced; consonant
βούλομαι	to will, want
γένος, ους, τό	family, race, kind; offspring

56. εἴτε ... εἴτε: "if ... if" (BDAG 279.6.o).

57. ἐκ μέρους: "in part"; "individually" (BDAG 633.1.c*).

58. οὓς: some verbs (ἔθετο) can take two accusatives. οὓς is the accusative direct object in a double accusative of object and complement construction (Wallace 181–89 [183 n. 24]; BDF §157; GNTG §5.77). The complements are: ἀποστόλους ... προφήτας ... διδασκάλους, and δυνάμεις ... χαρίσματα ... ἀντιλήμψεις ... κυβερνήσεις ... γένη (see the discussion in Brookins and Longenecker, *1 Corinthians 10–16*, 83): "some God has appointed in the church as."

59. μὲν is awkward in that it does not appear to be resolved by a δὲ. It is likely that, as Brookins and Longenecker suggest, the ἔπειτα string introduced later in this verse continues the thought introduced by μὲν (*1 Corinthians 10–16*, 82–83; BDF §447.2*).

60. μὴ introduces a rhetorical question expecting the answer, "no" (BDF §427.2).

61. πάντες is the nominative subject of an implied εἰσίν (Wallace 39–40; BDF §§127–28).

62. μὴ introduces a rhetorical question expecting the answer, "no."

γνωρίζω	to make known
γνῶσις, εως, ἡ	knowledge
δείκνυμι	to show
δεύτερος, α, ον	second
διαίρεσις, εως, ἡ	diversity
διαιρέω	to divide, separate
διακονία, ας, ἡ	service, ministry
διάκρισις, εως, ἡ	dispute, dissolution
διερμηνεύω	to explain, interpret
εἴδωλον, ου, τό	false god, idol; ghost, phantom
ἐλεύθερος, έρα, ον	free
Ἕλλην, ηνος, ὁ	Greek person; gentile
ἐνεργέω	to work
ἐνέργημα, ατος, τό	operation
ἔπειτα, adv.	then
ἑρμηνεία, ας, ἡ	interpretation, explanation, translation
εὐσχημοσύνη, ης, ἡ	modesty, propriety, presentability
εὐσχήμων, ον, gen. ονος	respected, presentable, graceful
ζηλόω	to strive, desire; to be jealous
ἴαμα, ατος, τό	healing; remedy
καθάπερ	as, just as, like
κυβέρνησις, εως, ἡ	ability to lead; leadership; administration
μέλος, ους, τό	body part, member
μεριμνάω	to be anxious for
μέρος, ους, τό	part
νυνί, adv.	now
ὄσφρησις, εως, ἡ	sense of smell
οὖς, ὠτός, τό	ear
πάσχω	to experience; to suffer, endure
περισσός, ή, όν	extraordinary, remarkable; abundant, profuse
περιτίθημι	to put on
πνευματικός, ή, όν	spiritual
ποτίζω	to give a drink
ποῦ	where?
προφητεία, ας, ἡ	prophecy

συγκεράννυμι	to compose; to blend, unite
συγχαίρω	to rejoice with
συμπάσχω	to suffer together
σχίσμα, ατος, τό	division
τιμή, ῆς, ἡ	honor
ὑπερβολή, ῆς, ἡ	exceeding quality; excess
ὑστερέω	to be inferior, less than; to lack; to be late
φανέρωσις, εως, ἡ	manifestation, disclosure
χάρισμα, ατος, τό	gift
χρεία, ας, ἡ	need, use, duty

3.5. PHILIPPIANS 2:1–30

Thinking and Acting Like Christ

Paul's letter to the Philippians is one of those the authorship of which scholars do not dispute. There is much debate about the year and location for this letter. Paul indicates that he writes from prison but does not say which one. It has historically been connected with Paul's imprisonment in Rome and therefore assigned to a year toward the end of his life. More recently, some scholars have suggested that Ephesus makes better sense; this location would move the year of composition into the middle of his writing career. Although some scholars believe the letter to consist of multiple letters written by Paul to this church, it seems best to understand the letter as unified.

Paul writes to thank the Philippians for support that he has recently received; he discusses the circumstances of his imprisonment and shows concern for divisions within the church. Chapter 2 forms the centerpiece of the letter, including the so-called Christ hymn. The statements about Christ ground the ethical instructions that follow in vv. 12–18. Verses 19–30 illustrate, in the persons of Timothy and Epaphroditus, certain characteristics attributed to Christ in vv. 6–11.

1¹ Εἴ τις οὖν παράκλησις² ἐν Χριστῷ, εἴ τι παραμύθιον³ ἀγάπης, εἴ τις κοινωνία⁴ πνεύματος, εἴ τις σπλάγχνα καὶ οἰκτιρμοί,⁵ 2 πληρώσατέ μου τὴν χαρὰν ἵνα τὸ αὐτὸ φρονῆτε,⁶ τὴν αὐτὴν ἀγάπην ἔχοντες,⁷ σύμψυχοι,⁸ τὸ ἓν φρονοῦντες,⁹ 3 μηδὲν¹⁰ κατ᾽ ἐριθείαν μηδὲ κατὰ κενοδοξίαν¹¹

1. Verses 1–4 constitute one long sentence.
2. τις . . . παράκλησις is the nominative subject of an implied ἐστίν (Wallace 39–40; BDF §§127–28): "[if] there is any encouragement."
3. τι παραμύθιον is the nominative subject of an implied ἐστίν (Wallace 39–40; BDF §§127–28).
4. τις κοινωνία is the nominative subject of an implied ἐστίν (Wallace 39–40; BDF §§127–28).
5. τις σπλάγχνα καὶ οἰκτιρμοί are the compound nominative subjects of an implied form of εἰμί (Wallace 39–40; BDF §§127–28).
6. ἵνα τὸ αὐτὸ φρονῆτε: here the ἵνα clause functions epexegetically (rather than as a purpose clause), explaining πληρώσατέ (Wallace 476*; BDF §394*; GNTG §5.143; also, Lidija Novakovic, *Philippians: A Handbook on the Greek Text*, BHGNT [Waco, TX: Baylor University Press, 2020], 44; and Jerry Sumney, *Philippians: A Greek Student's Intermediate Reader* [Peabody, MA: Hendrickson, 2007], 41): "by thinking the same things"; or "by having the same mind."
7. ἔχοντες is likely an adverbial participle indicating means (Wallace 625–30; BDF §418; GNTG §5.192): "by having."
8. σύμψυχοι: this adjective might modify the participial clause that follows (τὸ ἓν φρονοῦντες), or it might stand independently, modifying the main clause (τὸ αὐτὸ φρονῆτε). Most translations read the adjective as a predicate adjective of an implied participial form of εἰμί (Wallace 39–40; BDF §§127–28; cf. ESV, NET, NIV, NRSV; see the discussion in Novakovic, *Philippians*, 44; Sumney, *Philippians*, 41).
9. τὸ ἓν φρονοῦντες: the article turns the numerical adjective into the direct object of φρονοῦντες (Wallace 233; BDF §263; GNTG §5.15). φρονοῦντες is likely an adverbial participle indicating means (Wallace 625–30; BDF §418; GNTG §5.192): "by being of one mind" (BDAG 292.2.a*).
10. μηδὲν is the direct object of a clause with an elided verb to be supplied from the context (see the discussion in BDF §§479–83); here, the context suggests a participial form (in continuity with the pattern Paul has been using both before and after) of πράσσω or ποιέω (see the discussion in Novakovic, *Philippians*, 45): "doing nothing."
11. κατ᾽ . . . κενοδοξίαν: κατά plus the accusative can indicate the nature, kind, peculiarity, or characteristics of a thing; it frequently serves as a periphrasis for the adverb (BDAG 513.5.b.ℶ*); ἐριθείαν ("selfishly"); κενοδοξίαν ("from conceit").

ἀλλὰ τῇ ταπεινοφροσύνῃ ἀλλήλους ἡγούμενοι¹² ὑπερέχοντας¹³ ἑαυτῶν,¹⁴
4 μὴ τὰ ἑαυτῶν¹⁵ ἑαυτῶν ἕκαστος¹⁶ σκοποῦντες¹⁷ ἀλλὰ καὶ τὰ ἑτέρων
ἕκαστοι.¹⁸

    5   Τοῦτο¹⁹ φρονεῖτε ἐν ὑμῖν ὃ²⁰ καὶ ἐν Χριστῷ Ἰησοῦ,
    6   ὃς²¹ ἐν μορφῇ θεοῦ ὑπάρχων²²
            οὐχ ἁρπαγμὸν²³ ἡγήσατο

12. ἡγούμενοι is likely an adverbial participle indicating manner (Wallace 627–28; BDF §418; *GNTG* §5.193): "considering"; "regarding."

13. ὑπερέχοντας: some verbs (ἡγέομαι) can take two accusatives. ὑπερέχοντας is a substantival participle (Wallace 619–21; BDF §413; *GNTG* §5.182) serving as the complement in an object-complement double accusative with ἀλλήλους as the object (Wallace 181–89 [183 n. 24]; BDF §157 [also §416.3*]; *GNTG* §5.77). Wallace suggests that this clause illustrates the use of an anarthrous participle in the accusative case along with a noun in the accusative case indicating indirect discourse after a verb of perception or communication (646*): "considering others better."

14. ἑαυτῶν is a genitive of comparison (Wallace 110–12; BDF §185; *GNTG* §5.51).

15. τὰ ἑαυτῶν: the neut.-acc.-pl. article serves as the substantive direct object of σκοποῦντες (Wallace 233; BDF §266; *GNTG* §5.15); in the context, "affairs" or "interests."

16. ἕκαστος: the singular form is regularly used with plural verbs; by the time of the New Testament the plural form of ἕκαστος was extremely rare (BDAG 298.b*).

17. σκοποῦντες: in this context, the participle has imperatival force (Wallace 650–52; BDF §468.2; *GNTG* §5.201): "Let each of you look after."

18. ἕκαστοι: the plural is peculiar given the use of the singular in 4a and the rarity of the plural in Greek writing at Paul's time. Novakovic reads ἕκαστοι as the nominative subject of a clause with an elided verb to be supplied from the context (see the discussion in BDF §§479–83); here, the context suggests repeating σκοποῦντες (*Philippians*, 47). Sumney reads ἕκαστοι as part of a compound subject with ἕκαστος of σκοποῦντες (*Philippians*, 43).

19. Τοῦτο: the neut.-acc.-sg. pronoun can either refer to what has come before (in this case summarizing what Paul has said about thinking in vv. 1–4) or to what follows (and so referring to Christ's thinking, which he is about to describe).

20. ὅ: the neut.-sg., relative pronoun requires the reader to supply a verb. It is either the nominative subject of an implied ἦν: "which was also in Christ Jesus" (cf. NET, NRSV); or the accusative object of an implied φρονεῖτε (ind. rather than impv.): "have this mindset among yourselves as the mindset you have in Christ Jesus" (BDAG 106.3*; ESV).

21. ὅς serves as the subject of all of the indicative and participial verbs in vv. 6–8.

22. ὑπάρχων is likely an adverbial participle indicating concession (Wallace 634–35; BDF §418.3; *GNTG* §5.191): "although."

23. ἁρπαγμὸν: some verbs (ἡγήσατο) can take two accusatives. ἁρπαγμὸν is the complement in an object-complement double accusative with τὸ εἶναι ἴσα as the object (see n. 13). The exact meaning of the term in this context has been debated. BDAG suggests "something to which one can claim or assert title by gripping or grasping, something

τὸ εἶναι ἴσα θεῷ,[24]

7   ἀλλ᾽ ἑαυτὸν ἐκένωσεν

        μορφὴν δούλου λαβών,[25]

        ἐν ὁμοιώματι ἀνθρώπων γενόμενος·[26]

        καὶ σχήματι[27] εὑρεθεὶς[28] ὡς ἄνθρωπος[29]

8   ἐταπείνωσεν ἑαυτὸν

        γενόμενος[30] ὑπήκοος μέχρι θανάτου,

        θανάτου δὲ[31] σταυροῦ.

9   διὸ καὶ ὁ θεὸς αὐτὸν ὑπερύψωσεν

    καὶ ἐχαρίσατο αὐτῷ τὸ ὄνομα

---

claimed" (133.2); alternatively, "a piece of good fortune, windfall, prize, gain" (133.2b). The interpreter must decide whether the object is something already obtained and so, to be hung onto, or something sought after. Consult the commentaries and secondary literature for a more precise understanding of the interpretive issues. BDAG offers the following suggestion: "a prize to be tenaciously grasped."

24. τὸ εἶναι ἴσα θεῷ: the articular infinitive is the object of ἡγήσατο in an object-complement double accusative (Wallace 181–89 [183 n. 24]; BDF §157; *GNTG* §5.77; for the substantive use of the infinitive, see Wallace 600; BDF §399; *GNTG* §5.164). ἴσα (neut.-pl.) is functioning like an adverb (BDAG 481*; BDF §434.1*) and so, in combination with τὸ εἶναι, can be translated: "being equal with God."

25. λαβών is likely an adverbial participle indicating means (Wallace 625–30*; BDF §418; *GNTG* §5.192). The aorist tense typically indicates time before that of the main verb but it does not necessarily do so. BDF emphasizes that in some instances, the action of the aorist participle is identical to that of the main verb (§339.2); which appears to be the case here: "by taking" (see Novakovic, *Philippians*, 51).

26. ἐν ὁμοιώματι ἀνθρώπων γενόμενος: γενόμενος is likely an adverbial participle indicating means (Wallace 625–30; BDF §418; *GNTG* §5.192): "by becoming like human beings" (BDAG 198.5.c*).

27. σχήματι is a dative of respect (Wallace 144–46*; BDF §197*; *GNTG* §5.68).

28. εὑρεθεὶς is an adverbial participle that might be indicating time; the aorist tense indicates time before that of the main verb (Wallace 623–27; BDF §418; *GNTG* §5.188; Novakovic, *Philippians*, 52): "when he was found"; or, it could be indicating means, like the previous two participles (Wallace 625–30; BDF §418; *GNTG* §5.192; Sumney, *Philippians*, 47): "by being found."

29. ὡς ἄνθρωπος: the comparative particle (ὡς) with the predicate nominative introduces the perspective from which a person, thing, or activity is viewed or understood with respect to character, function, or role (BDAG 1104.3.a.γ*): "as a human being."

30. γενόμενος is an adverbial participle, either indicating means or manner (Wallace 627–30; BDF §418; *GNTG* §§5.192–93): "[by] becoming."

31. δὲ indicates the explanation of the specific kind of death (BDAG 213.2*): "that is."

τὸ ὑπὲρ πᾶν ὄνομα,[32]

10 ἵνα ἐν τῷ ὀνόματι Ἰησοῦ[33]

πᾶν γόνυ κάμψῃ

ἐπουρανίων καὶ ἐπιγείων καὶ καταχθονίων[34]

11 καὶ πᾶσα γλῶσσα ἐξομολογήσηται ὅτι

κύριος Ἰησοῦς Χριστὸς[35]

εἰς δόξαν[36] θεοῦ πατρός.

12 Ὥστε, ἀγαπητοί μου, καθὼς πάντοτε ὑπηκούσατε, μὴ ὡς ἐν τῇ παρουσίᾳ μου μόνον[37] ἀλλὰ νῦν πολλῷ μᾶλλον ἐν τῇ ἀπουσίᾳ μου, μετὰ φόβου καὶ τρόμου τὴν ἑαυτῶν σωτηρίαν κατεργάζεσθε· 13 θεὸς γάρ ἐστιν ὁ ἐνεργῶν[38] ἐν ὑμῖν καὶ τὸ θέλειν καὶ τὸ ἐνεργεῖν[39] ὑπὲρ τῆς εὐδοκίας.[40] 14 Πάντα ποιεῖτε χωρὶς γογγυσμῶν καὶ διαλογισμῶν, 15 ἵνα γένησθε ἄμεμπτοι καὶ ἀκέραιοι,[41] τέκνα θεοῦ ἄμωμα[42] μέσον[43] γενεᾶς σκολιᾶς

32. τὸ ὑπὲρ πᾶν ὄνομα: the article turns the prepositional phrase into an attributive modifier of τὸ ὄνομα (Wallace 236; BDF §266; *GNTG* §5.16; Novakovic, *Philippians*, 54): "that is above every name."

33. ἐν τῷ ὀνόματι Ἰησοῦ: BDAG suggests that this phrase, in conjunction with κάμψῃ, means: "when the name of Jesus [is proclaimed]" (507.2*).

34. ἐπουρανίων καὶ ἐπιγείων καὶ καταχθονίων: these might be genitives of place (Wallace 124–25; BDF §186; *GNTG* §5.54): "in the heavenly and earthly and subterranean places"; or just possessive genitives "referring to those whose knees are bent" (Wallace 124 n. 142*; *GNTG* §5.35): "the knees of those in heaven."

35. κύριος Ἰησοῦς Χριστὸς: κύριος is the predicate nominative and Ἰησοῦς Χριστὸς the nominative subject of an implied ἐστίν (Wallace 39–40; BDF §§127–28).

36. εἰς δόξαν: εἰς plus the accusative indicating purpose (BDAG 290.4.f): "to the glory."

37. μὴ . . . μόνον: "not only" (BDAG 659.2.c.α*).

38. ὁ ἐνεργῶν is a substantival participle (Wallace 619–21; BDF §413; *GNTG* §5.182).

39. τὸ θέλειν . . . τὸ ἐνεργεῖν: these articular infinitives serve as the direct objects of ὁ ἐνεργῶν (Wallace 601–3 [235 n. 50*]); BDF §399.1*; *GNTG* §5.165.a*): "the desiring and the working."

40. ὑπὲρ τῆς εὐδοκίας: BDAG interpretes ὑπὲρ as indicating the moving cause or reason (1031.2*): "because of" or "for the sake of." BDF interprets the preposition to indicate that which one wants to attain (§231.2*), resulting in the same translation.

41. ἵνα γένησθε ἄμεμπτοι καὶ ἀκέραιοι: ἄμεμπτοι and ἀκέραιοι are predicate adjectives going with γένησθε: "in order that you might be blameless and innocent."

42. τέκνα θεοῦ ἄμωμα: ἄμωμα might be another predicate adjective like the previous ἄμεμπτοι and ἀκέραιοι. Or, it might modify τέκνα; one might, as Sumney suggests, translate it as "children who are spotless" (*Philippians*, 54).

43. μέσον is serving as an improper preposition with the genitive: "in the midst of" (BDAG 635.1.c*).

καὶ διεστραμμένης,⁴⁴ ἐν οἷς⁴⁵ φαίνεσθε ὡς φωστῆρες ἐν κόσμῳ, 16 λόγον ζωῆς ἐπέχοντες,⁴⁶ εἰς καύχημα ἐμοὶ⁴⁷ εἰς ἡμέραν Χριστοῦ, ὅτι⁴⁸ οὐκ εἰς κενὸν ἔδραμον⁴⁹ οὐδὲ εἰς κενὸν ἐκοπίασα. 17 Ἀλλ᾽ εἰ καὶ σπένδομαι ἐπὶ τῇ θυσίᾳ καὶ λειτουργίᾳ⁵⁰ τῆς πίστεως ὑμῶν, χαίρω καὶ συγχαίρω πᾶσιν ὑμῖν· 18 τὸ δὲ αὐτὸ⁵¹ καὶ ὑμεῖς χαίρετε καὶ συγχαίρετέ μοι.

19 Ἐλπίζω δὲ ἐν κυρίῳ Ἰησοῦ Τιμόθεον ταχέως πέμψαι⁵² ὑμῖν, ἵνα κἀγὼ εὐψυχῶ γνοὺς⁵³ τὰ περὶ ὑμῶν.⁵⁴ 20 οὐδένα γὰρ ἔχω ἰσόψυχον,⁵⁵

---

44. διεστραμμένης is an attributive participle (Wallace 617–18; BDF §413; *GNTG* §5.181), modifying γενεᾶς: "perverted."

45. ἐν οἷς: there is no plural noun to serve as antecedent to this plural, relative pronoun (γενεᾶς is grammatically singular but is collective) so this prepositional phrase is a *constructio ad sensum* (on the concept of *constructio ad sensum*, see the discussion in BDF §134): "among whom" (BDF §296*).

46. ἐπέχοντες is likely an adverbial participle indicating means (Wallace 625–30; BDF §418; *GNTG* §5.192): "by"; or cause (Wallace 631–32; BDF §418; *GNTG* §5.189): "because." ἐπέχω can mean "to holding on to" or "to hold out."

47. εἰς καύχημα ἐμοὶ: εἰς plus the accusative indicating purpose (BDAG 290.4.f *). ἐμοὶ is a dative of possession (Wallace 149–51; BDF §189; *GNTG* §5.61): "so that I might have a boast."

48. ὅτι is likely introducing the clausal complement of καύχημα: "that"; rather than indicating cause: "because" (see the observations in Novakovic, *Philippians*, 61).

49. ἔδραμον: aor.-ind.-act.-1-sg. < τρέχω.

50. τῇ θυσίᾳ καὶ λειτουργίᾳ: likely a hendiadys (the coordination of two ideas, one of which is dependent on the other; BDF §442.16; *GNTG* §5.260.a; see the notes in Novakovic, *Philippians*, 62; and Sumney, *Philippians*, 57): "sacrifice and service" or "sacrificial service."

51. τὸ δὲ αὐτὸ: "in the same way" (BDF §154*).

52. πέμψαι is a complementary infinitive going with Ἐλπίζω (Wallace 598–99; BDF §392; *GNTG* §5.163; BDAG 319.2*).

53. γνοὺς is an adverbial participle that might be indicating time; the aorist tense indicates time before that of the main verb (Wallace 623–27; BDF §418; *GNTG* §5.188): "when I come to know"; or, it could be indicating means (Wallace 625–30; BDF §418; *GNTG* §5.192): "by coming to know."

54. τὰ περὶ ὑμῶν: the article turns the prepositional phrase into the direct object of γνοὺς (Wallace 236; BDF §266; *GNTG* §5.16): "the things concerning you"; "about you"; "about your circumstances."

55. ἰσόψυχον: some verbs (ἔχω) can take two accusatives. ἰσόψυχον is the complement in an object-complement double accusative construction with οὐδένα as the object (see n. 13): "I have no one of like mind."

ὅστις γνησίως τὰ περὶ ὑμῶν⁵⁶ μεριμνήσει· 21 οἱ πάντες γὰρ τὰ ἑαυτῶν⁵⁷ ζητοῦσιν, οὐ τὰ Ἰησοῦ Χριστοῦ.⁵⁸ 22 τὴν δὲ δοκιμὴν αὐτοῦ γινώσκετε, ὅτι⁵⁹ ὡς πατρὶ τέκνον σὺν ἐμοὶ ἐδούλευσεν εἰς τὸ εὐαγγέλιον. 23 τοῦτον μὲν οὖν⁶⁰ ἐλπίζω πέμψαι⁶¹ ὡς ἂν ἀφίδω τὰ περὶ ἐμὲ ἐξαυτῆς·⁶² 24 πέποιθα δὲ ἐν κυρίῳ ὅτι καὶ αὐτὸς ταχέως ἐλεύσομαι.

25 Ἀναγκαῖον⁶³ δὲ ἡγησάμην Ἐπαφρόδιτον⁶⁴ τὸν ἀδελφὸν καὶ συνερ-γὸν καὶ συστρατιώτην μου,⁶⁵ ὑμῶν δὲ ἀπόστολον καὶ λειτουργὸν⁶⁶ τῆς χρείας μου, πέμψαι πρὸς ὑμᾶς, 26 ἐπειδὴ ἐπιποθῶν ἦν πάντας ὑμᾶς καὶ ἀδημονῶν,⁶⁷ διότι ἠκούσατε ὅτι ἠσθένησεν. 27 καὶ γὰρ⁶⁸ ἠσθένησεν

---

56. τὰ περὶ ὑμῶν: the article turns the prepositional phrase into the direct object of μεριμνήσει (Wallace 236; BDF §266; *GNTG* §5.16): "the things concerning you"; "about you"; "about your affairs."

57. τὰ ἑαυτῶν: the article turns the reflexive pronoun into the direct object of ζητοῦσιν (Wallace 233; BDF §266; *GNTG* §5.15): "their own affairs."

58. τὰ Ἰησοῦ Χριστοῦ: the article turns the genitive phrase into the direct object of ζητοῦσιν.

59. ὅτι might be epexegetical, explaining δοκιμὴν: "how"; it might introduce the clausal complement of γινώσκετε: "that"; or might be causal: "because" (see the discussions in Novakovic, *Philippians*, 66; and Sumney, *Philippians*, 61).

60. μὲν οὖν: "So, then" (BDAG 630.2.e).

61. πέμψαι is a complementary infinitive going with Ἐλπίζω (Wallace 598–99; BDF §392; *GNTG* §5.163; BDAG 319.2*).

62. ὡς ἂν ἀφίδω τὰ περὶ ἐμὲ ἐξαυτῆς: ὡς ἄν, when used with the subjunctive, indicates an event in the future (BDAG 1106.8.c.α*). ἀφίδω is aor.-subj.-act.-1-sg. < ἀφοράω. τὰ περὶ ἐμὲ: the article turns the prepositional phrase into the direct object of ἀφίδω (Wallace 236; BDF §266; *GNTG* §5.16): "how things go with me." ἐξαυτῆς means "soon." BDAG suggests translating the clause: "as soon as I see how things go with me" (158.2*).

63. Ἀναγκαῖον: Some verbs (ἡγησάμην) can take two accusatives. Ἀναγκαῖον is the complement in an object-complement double accusative with the infinitive phrase Ἐπαφρόδιτον . . . πέμψαι as the object (see n. 13): "I considered sending Epaphroditus . . . necessary" (Novakovic, *Philippians*, 68–69).

64. Ἐπαφρόδιτον is the accusative direct object of πέμψαι.

65. τὸν ἀδελφὸν καὶ συνεργὸν καὶ συστρατιώτην: all three nouns are in apposition to Ἐπαφρόδιτον.

66. ἀπόστολον καὶ λειτουργὸν is in apposition to Ἐπαφρόδιτον.

67. ἐπιποθῶν ἦν . . . ἀδημονῶν: the present participles combine with the imperfect verb of being to form the imperfect periphrastic construction (Wallace 647–49; BDF §§352–53; *GNTG* §§5.184–85): "he was longing . . . he was distressed."

68. καὶ γὰρ: "For even" or "yes, even" (BDF §496.2.i.α*).

παραπλήσιον θανάτῳ·⁶⁹ ἀλλ᾽ ὁ θεὸς ἠλέησεν αὐτόν, οὐκ αὐτὸν δὲ μόνον ἀλλὰ καὶ ἐμέ,⁷⁰ ἵνα μὴ λύπην ἐπὶ λύπην⁷¹ σχῶ. 28 σπουδαιοτέρως⁷² οὖν ἔπεμψα⁷³ αὐτόν, ἵνα ἰδόντες⁷⁴ αὐτὸν πάλιν χαρῆτε κἀγὼ ἀλυπότερος ὦ. 29 προσδέχεσθε οὖν αὐτὸν ἐν κυρίῳ μετὰ πάσης χαρᾶς καὶ τοὺς τοιούτους⁷⁵ ἐντίμους ἔχετε,⁷⁶ 30 ὅτι διὰ τὸ ἔργον Χριστοῦ μέχρι θανάτου ἤγγισεν⁷⁷ παραβολευσάμενος⁷⁸ τῇ ψυχῇ,⁷⁹ ἵνα ἀναπληρώσῃ τὸ ὑμῶν ὑστέρημα⁸⁰ τῆς πρός με λειτουργίας.⁸¹

Vocabulary

ἀδημονέω	to be very heavy
ἀκέραιος, ον	innocent, pure
ἄλυπος, ον	free from grief
ἄμεμπτος, ον	blameless, faultless

69. ἠσθένησεν παραπλήσιον θανάτῳ: παραπλήσιον in the neuter can serve as an adverb (BDAG 770*): "he became so ill he nearly died."

70. οὐκ αὐτὸν δὲ μόνον ἀλλὰ καὶ ἐμέ: "Not only him but also me."

71. ἐπὶ λύπην: "in addition to distress/grief" (BDF §235.3*).

72. σπουδαιοτέρως: "with special urgency" (BDAG 939.1*).

73. ἔπεμψα is frequently identified as an epistolary aorist (Wallace 562–63*; BDF §334*; GNTG §5.128). Paul has not yet sent Epaphroditus, but when the people in Philippi read the letter, he will have been sent, so the aorist tense is used. Translate this as a present tense: "I am sending."

74. ἰδόντες is an adverbial participle that might be indicating time; the aorist tense indicates time before that of the main verb (Wallace 623–27; BDF §418; GNTG §5.188): "when you see"; or, it could be indicating cause, providing the cause for the rejoicing (Wallace 631–32; BDF §418; GNTG §5.189): "because you see."

75. τοὺς τοιούτους: "such ones." Some verbs (ἔχετε) can take two accusatives. τοὺς τοιούτους is the object in an object-complement double accusative with ἐντίμους as the complement (Wallace 181–89 [183 n. 24]; BDF §157; GNTG §5.77): "hold such ones in honor" (BDAG 421.6*).

76. ἐντίμους ἔχετε: "hold in esteem" or "honor" (BDAG 340.1.b*).

77. μέχρι θανάτου ἤγγισεν: "came close to dying" (BDAG 270.2*). The similarity of wording to 2:8 is striking: γενόμενος ὑπήκοος μέχρι θανάτου.

78. παραβολευσάμενος is likely an adverbial participle indicating means (Wallace 625–30; BDF §418; GNTG §5.192): "by risking."

79. τῇ ψυχῇ is the dative complement of παραβολευσάμενος (BDAG 759*).

80. ἀναπληρώσῃ τὸ ὑμῶν ὑστέρημα: ἀναπληρόω τὸ ὑστέρημα can indicate making up for one's absence or lack; it can also mean to represent one who is absent (BDAG 70.3*).

81. τῆς πρός με λειτουργίας: τῆς . . . λειτουργίας is an objective genitive indicating what is lacking: "of service to me."

ἄμωμος, ον	spotless, unblemished, blameless
ἀναγκαῖος, α, ον	necessary
ἀναπληρόω	to fill up, supply, fulfill
ἀπουσία, ας, ἡ	absence
ἀσθενέω	to be weak
ἀφοράω	to look away, look up to
γενεά, ᾶς, ἡ	generation
γνησίως, adv.	genuinely, sincerely
γογγυσμός, οῦ, ὁ	murmuring, grumbling
γόνυ, ατος, τό	knee
διαλογισμός, οῦ, ὁ	thought, opinion, discussion; dispute, argument
διαστρέφω	to turn; to pervert
διότι	because, for, therefore
δοκιμή, ῆς, ἡ	character; proof, testing
δουλεύω	to serve as a slave
ἐγγίζω	to bring near, come near
ἐλεέω	to show mercy
ἐλπίζω	to hope
ἐνεργέω	to work
ἔντιμος, ον	precious
ἐξαυτῆς, adv.	immediately
ἐξομολογέω	to confess, admit
Ἐπαφρόδιτος, ου, ὁ	Epaphroditus
ἐπειδή	since, because, for
ἐπέχω	to hold, hold back; to notice, give close attention to
ἐπίγειος, ον	earthly, terrestrial
ἐπιποθέω	to greatly desire
ἐπουράνιος, ον	heavenly
ἐριθεία, ας, ἡ	strife
εὐδοκία, ας, ἡ	good pleasure, good will, approval; satisfaction
εὐψυχέω	to be encouraged
ἡγέομαι	to consider, regard
θυσία, ας, ἡ	sacrifice
ἴσος, η, ον	equal, fair, impartial, adequate; equally

ἰσόψυχος, ον	like-minded, equal, peer
κάμπτω	to bend
καταχθόνιος, ον	under the earth
κατεργάζομαι	to work, prepare, make, oppress, subdue
καύχημα, ατος, τό	object of boasting, pride
κενοδοξία, ας, ἡ	conceit
κενός, ή, όν	empty, foolish, worthless; vacuity
κενόω	to make of no effect, make empty
κοινωνία, ας, ἡ	fellowship, participation; society; sexual alliance
κοπιάω	to toil, grow tired, be weary
λειτουργία, ας, ἡ	service, ministry, worship
λειτουργός, οῦ, ὁ	servant, minister
λύπη, ης, ἡ	grief, pain
μεριμνάω	to be anxious for
μέχρι	(+ gen.) up to (prep.); until (conj.)
μορφή, ῆς, ἡ	form, appearance
οἰκτιρμός, οῦ, ὁ	compassion
ὁμοίωμα, ατος, τό	likeness
πάντοτε, adv.	always
παραβολεύομαι	to risk, expose to danger
παράκλησις, εως, ἡ	encouragement
παραμύθιον, ου, τό	comfort
παραπλήσιος, ία, ιον	coming near, nearly; resembling
παρουσία, ας, ἡ	coming, presence
προσδέχομαι	to receive; to wait for
σκολιός, ά, όν	crooked, bent
σκοπέω	to pay attention to; to watch closely
σπένδω	to pour out as a drink-offering
σπλάγχνον, ου, τό	entrails, heart, affection
σπουδαίως, adv.	earnestly
σταυρός, οῦ, ὁ	cross
συγχαίρω	to rejoice with
σύμψυχος, ον	united, as one
συνεργός, ον	helping, cooperative; fellow-worker
συστρατιώτης, ου, ὁ	fellow-soldier
σχῆμα, ατος, τό	form, outward form

σωτηρία, ας, ἡ	salvation
ταπεινοφροσύνη, ης, ἡ	humility
ταπεινόω	to humble, humiliate
ταχέως, adv.	quickly, soon
Τιμόθεος, ου, ὁ	Timothy
τρέχω	to run
τρόμος, ου, ὁ	trembling
ὑπακούω	to obey; to hear, listen
ὑπερέχω	to excel, exceed, be better than
ὑπερυψόω	to highly exalt
ὑπήκοος, ον	obedient
ὑστέρημα, ατος, τό	what is lacking
φαίνω	to appear, shine; to cause to shine
φόβος, ου, ὁ	fear, terror; reverence
φρονέω	to be wise, think
φωστήρ, ῆρος, ὁ	light, star
χαρίζομαι	to give; to favor; to forgive
χρεία, ας, ἡ	need, use, duty
χωρίς	(+ gen.) without (prep.); separately (adv.)

Teachings on How to Treat One Another

The author of this document has traditionally been associated with James the brother of Jesus. Many contemporary scholars doubt that identification, in part because of the quality of the Greek style. It is addressed to "the twelve tribes in the diaspora." This language is likely to be understood symbolically rather than literally. The date of the document is uncertain. Some of the language (such as we see in this selection) seems to indicate familiarity with Paul. This would require the text to have been written after the mid to late 50s CE. 1 Clement seems to show awareness of the document that would necessitate it being written before the mid-90s CE.

The document opens with an epistolary greeting but does not sustain this form. The contents of the document place it within the traditions of ancient wisdom literature. In chapter 2, the author attends to the problem of partiality toward the rich (vv. 1–13) and discusses the relationship between faith and works, including a discussion of how Abraham illustrates this relationship.

The discussion of faith and works can be compared with Paul's discussion in Romans 4 (§3.3). The discussion of Abraham connects to Paul, to Barnabas 9 (§2.9), and to Genesis 17 (§1.1).

1 Ἀδελφοί μου, μὴ ἐν προσωπολημψίαις ἔχετε¹ τὴν πίστιν τοῦ κυρίου ἡμῶν Ἰησοῦ Χριστοῦ τῆς δόξης.² 2 ἐὰν³ γὰρ εἰσέλθῃ εἰς συναγωγὴν⁴ ὑμῶν ἀνὴρ χρυσοδακτύλιος ἐν ἐσθῆτι λαμπρᾷ, εἰσέλθῃ δὲ καὶ πτωχὸς ἐν ῥυπαρᾷ ἐσθῆτι, 3 ἐπιβλέψητε δὲ ἐπὶ τὸν φοροῦντα⁵ τὴν ἐσθῆτα τὴν λαμπρὰν καὶ εἴπητε· σὺ κάθου ὧδε καλῶς,⁶ καὶ τῷ πτωχῷ εἴπητε· σὺ στῆθι ἢ κάθου ἐκεῖ ὑπὸ τὸ ὑποπόδιόν μου, 4 καὶ οὐ διεκρίθητε⁷ ἐν ἑαυτοῖς καὶ ἐγένεσθε κριταὶ διαλογισμῶν πονηρῶν;⁸ 5 ἀκούσατε, ἀδελφοί μου ἀγαπητοί· οὐχ⁹ ὁ θεὸς ἐξελέξατο τοὺς πτωχοὺς τῷ κόσμῳ πλουσίους ἐν

1. μὴ . . . ἔχετε: μὴ suggests the verb should be parsed as imperative rather than indicative.
2. τοῦ κυρίου ἡμῶν Ἰησοῦ Χριστοῦ τῆς δόξης: it is not precisely clear how to relate each of the genitives to each other and to τὴν πίστιν (see discussion in A. K. M. Adam, *James: A Handbook on the Greek Text*, BHGNT [Waco, TX: Baylor University Press, 2013], 34). τοῦ κυρίου is either a subjective genitive (Wallace 113–16; *GNTG* §5.38), referring to the Lord's own faith; or objective genitive (Wallace 117–18; BDF §163; *GNTG* §5.38), referring to faith in the Lord (both Wallace [116*] and Adam suggest it is objective). Ἰησοῦ Χριστοῦ is likely in apposition to τοῦ κυρίου: "our Lord Jesus Christ." τῆς δόξης might be an attributive genitive modifying τοῦ κυρίου (Wallace 86–88; BDF §167; *GNTG* §5.44): "glorious Lord Jesus Christ" (NET, NIV, NRSV all translate it this way); it might be an objective genitive (Wallace 117–18; BDF §163; *GNTG* §538): "Jesus Christ, the Lord of glory" (ESV reads it this way); it might be a genitive in apposition to Ἰησοῦ Χριστοῦ: "our Lord Jesus Christ, the Glory." This is the only place in the letter (apart from the opening verse) that reference is explicitly made to Jesus.
3. ἐὰν . . . εἰσέλθῃ . . . εἴπητε: ἐὰν with the subjunctive introduces the protasis of a third-class condition. The third-class condition can indicate something likely to occur in the future, something that might occur, or something that will not occur but hypothetically could (Wallace 469–71, 663, 696–99; BDF §§371, 373; *GNTG* §5.237). The protasis of this conditional statement continues into v. 3 and includes the verbs, εἰσέλθῃ (twice in v. 2), ἐπιβλέψητε (v. 3), and εἴπητε (twice in v. 3).
4. συναγωγὴν can refer to any place of assembly (whether primarily for religious assembly or primarily for other kinds of assembly); the author might have in mind a Jewish place of assembly—or even more specifically a Jewish place of assembly whose inhabits are followers of Jesus (BDAG 963*).
5. τὸν φοροῦντα is a substantival participle (Wallace 619–21; BDF §413; *GNTG* §5.182).
6. σὺ κάθου ὧδε καλῶς: σὺ is the nominative subject of κάθου. καλῶς probably means, in this context, something like: "in an excellent place" (BDAG 505.1*).
7. οὐ διεκρίθητε finally introduces the apodosis of the third-class condition begun in v. 2. The question expects "yes" in response: "have you made distinctions."
8. διαλογισμῶν πονηρῶν is likely an attributive genitive or a genitive of quality (Wallace 86–88*; BDF §165*; *GNTG* §5.52): "judges who make evil decisions."
9. οὐχ introduces a question expecting a positive response.

πίστει καὶ κληρονόμους[10] τῆς βασιλείας ἧς[11] ἐπηγγείλατο τοῖς ἀγαπῶσιν[12] αὐτόν; 6 ὑμεῖς δὲ ἠτιμάσατε τὸν πτωχόν.[13] οὐχ[14] οἱ πλούσιοι καταδυναστεύουσιν ὑμῶν[15] καὶ αὐτοὶ ἕλκουσιν ὑμᾶς εἰς κριτήρια; 7 οὐκ[16] αὐτοὶ βλασφημοῦσιν τὸ καλὸν ὄνομα τὸ ἐπικληθὲν ἐφ᾽ ὑμᾶς;[17]

8 Εἰ μέντοι νόμον τελεῖτε βασιλικὸν κατὰ τὴν γραφήν· ἀγαπήσεις τὸν πλησίον σου ὡς σεαυτόν,[18] καλῶς ποιεῖτε· 9 εἰ δὲ προσωπολημπτεῖτε, ἁμαρτίαν ἐργάζεσθε ἐλεγχόμενοι[19] ὑπὸ τοῦ νόμου ὡς παραβάται.[20] 10 ὅστις[21] γὰρ ὅλον τὸν νόμον τηρήσῃ, πταίσῃ δὲ ἐν ἑνί,[22] γέγονεν[23] πάντων ἔνοχος. 11 ὁ γὰρ εἰπών·[24] μὴ μοιχεύσῃς, εἶπεν καί· μὴ φονεύσῃς.[25] εἰ δὲ οὐ μοιχεύεις, φονεύεις δέ, γέγονας παραβάτης νόμου.

10. πλουσίους . . . κληρονόμους: some verbs (ἐξελέξατο) can take two accusatives. πλουσίους . . . κληρονόμους are the accusative complements in a double accusative object-complement construction with τοὺς πτωχοὺς as the object (Wallace 181–89 [183 n. 24]; BDF §157; *GNTG* §5.77): "[Did God not] choose the poor . . . [to be] rich . . . and heirs."

11. ἧς is in the genitive case because of attraction to its antecedent (τῆς βασιλείας). One expects it to be in the accusative case because it acts as the direct object of ἐπηγγείλατο. The attraction of the accusative case to the genitive is common (Wallace 338–39; BDF §294).

12. τοῖς ἀγαπῶσιν is a substantival participle (Wallace 619–21; BDF §413; *GNTG* §5.182).

13. τὸν πτωχόν: the singular is used for a collective (BDF §139*).

14. οὐχ introduces a question expecting a positive response.

15. ὑμῶν is the genitive object of καταδυναστεύουσιν (BDAG 516*).

16. οὐκ introduces a question expecting a positive response.

17. τὸ ἐπικληθὲν ἐφ᾽ ὑμᾶς: τὸ ἐπικληθὲν is an attributive participle (Wallace 617–18; BDF §412; *GNTG* §5.181), modifying τὸ καλὸν ὄνομα: "the good name that was invoked over you."

18. ἀγαπήσεις . . . σεαυτόν: the future has imperatival force (Wallace 569–70*; BDF §362; *GNTG* §5.108). The quotation is from LXX of Lev 19:18: ἀγαπήσεις τὸν πλησίον σου ὡς σεαυτόν·

19. ἐλεγχόμενοι is an adverbial participle, likely indicating result (Wallace 637–39*; *GNTG* §5.195).

20. ὡς παραβάται: here, ὡς identifies the role to which those who show favoritism are assigned by the law (BDAG 1104–5.3.a.γ*): "as transgressors."

21. ὅστις plus the subjunctive (τηρήσῃ . . . πταίσῃ) introduces an indefinite relative clause (Wallace 478–79*; BDF §380*; *GNTG* §5.216.c): "whoever"; "the one who."

22. ἐν ἑνί: ἑνί might be masc.-dat.-sg. modifying an implied νόμῳ: "one [law]"; or it might be neut.-dat.-sg. with the adjective acting as a substantive: "one thing."

23. γέγονεν is a proleptic or futuristic perfect. It refers to a state resulting from an action that takes place in the future from the time of the writing (Wallace 581*; BDF §344*): "has become."

24. ὁ . . . εἰπών is a substantival participle (Wallace 619–21; BDF §413; *GNTG* §5.182).

25. μὴ μοιχεύσῃς . . . μὴ φονεύσῃς: are prohibitive subjunctives (Wallace 469*; BDF §364; *GNTG* §5.141). The quotation comes either from Exod 20:13, 15 LXX; or Deut 5:17, 18 LXX (the Greek text is identical in both texts): οὐ μοιχεύσεις . . . οὐ φονεύσεις.

12 Οὕτως λαλεῖτε καὶ οὕτως ποιεῖτε ὡς διὰ νόμου ἐλευθερίας²⁶ μέλ-
λοντες²⁷ κρίνεσθαι.²⁸ 13 ἡ γὰρ κρίσις²⁹ ἀνέλεος τῷ μὴ ποιήσαντι³⁰ ἔλεος·
κατακαυχᾶται ἔλεος κρίσεως.³¹

14 Τί τὸ ὄφελος,³² ἀδελφοί μου, ἐὰν³³ πίστιν λέγῃ τις ἔχειν,³⁴ ἔργα δὲ
μὴ ἔχῃ; μὴ³⁵ δύναται ἡ πίστις σῶσαι³⁶ αὐτόν; 15 ἐὰν³⁷ ἀδελφὸς ἢ ἀδελφὴ³⁸
γυμνοὶ ὑπάρχωσιν καὶ λειπόμενοι ὦσιν³⁹ τῆς ἐφημέρου τροφῆς,⁴⁰ 16 εἴπῃ
δέ τις αὐτοῖς ἐξ ὑμῶν· ὑπάγετε ἐν εἰρήνῃ, θερμαίνεσθε καὶ χορτάζεσθε,

---

26. ἐλευθερίας might be a genitive of product (Wallace 106–7; *GNTG* §5.49): the law produces freedom; or it might be descriptive (Wallace 79–81; *GNTG* §5.34): the law characterized by freedom (see Adam, *James*, 47).

27. μέλλοντες is a substantival participle (Wallace 619–21; BDF §413; *GNTG* §5.182).

28. κρίνεσθαι is a complementary infinitive going with μέλλοντες (Wallace 598–99; BDF §392; *GNTG* §5.163).

29. ἡ . . . κρίσις is the nominative subject of an implied ἐστίν (Wallace 39–40; BDF §§127–28).

30. τῷ μὴ ποιήσαντι is a substantival participle (Wallace 619–21; BDF §413; *GNTG* §5.182).

31. κρίσεως is the genitive complement of κατακαυχᾶται: "mercy triumphs over judgment" (BDAG 517.2*).

32. Τί τὸ ὄφελος: Τί is the predicate nominative subject of an implied ἐστίν (Wallace 39–40; BDF §§127–28). The clause means something like, "What good does it do?" (BDAG 743*).

33. ἐὰν with the subjunctive (λέγῃ . . . ἔχῃ) introduces the protasis of a third-class condition (see n. 3). The protasis of this conditional statement continues into v. 16 and includes the verbs εἴπῃ and δῶτε.

34. ἔχειν: the infinitive indicates indirect discourse (Wallace 603–5*; BDF §§396–397.3; *GNTG* §5.166). πίστιν is the accusative direct object.

35. μὴ introduces a question expecting a negative answer.

36. σῶσαι is a complementary infinitive, going with δύναται (Wallace 598–99; BDF §392; *GNTG* §5.163).

37. ἐὰν with the subjunctive (ὑπάρχωσιν) introduces the protasis of a third-class condition (see n. 3).

38. ἀδελφὸς ἢ ἀδελφὴ: the compound subject typically will take a singular verb and adjective (Wallace 399–402; BDF §135; *GNTG* §5.26.b). Here they serve as the subject for a plural verb (ὑπάρχωσιν) and adjective (γυμνοὶ) resulting in *constructio ad sensum* (on the concept of *constructio ad sensum*, see the discussion in BDF §§134, 135.4*).

39. καὶ λειπόμενοι ὦσιν: λειπόμενοι is a predicate participle (Wallace 618–19*; BDF §414.1*). Neither Codex Sinaiticus (ℵ) nor Vaticanus (B) contain ὦσιν. If present, it continues the protasis of the third-class condition introduced by ἐὰν: "and [if] they are in need"; if not present, λειπόμενοι is part of a compound predicate joined with γυμνοὶ by καὶ: "[if a brother or sister are naked] and in need."

40. τῆς ἐφημέρου τροφῆς is the genitive complement of λειπόμενοι: "are in need of daily food" (BDAG 590.1.b*).

μὴ δῶτε δὲ αὐτοῖς τὰ ἐπιτήδεια⁴¹ τοῦ σώματος, τί τὸ ὄφελος;⁴² 17 οὕτως καὶ ἡ πίστις,⁴³ ἐὰν⁴⁴ μὴ ἔχῃ ἔργα, νεκρά ἐστιν καθ᾽ ἑαυτήν.⁴⁵

18 Ἀλλ᾽ ἐρεῖ τις· σὺ πίστιν ἔχεις, κἀγὼ ἔργα ἔχω. δεῖξόν μοι τὴν πίστιν σου χωρὶς τῶν ἔργων, κἀγώ σοι δείξω ἐκ τῶν ἔργων μου τὴν πίστιν.⁴⁶ 19 σὺ πιστεύεις ὅτι⁴⁷ εἷς ἐστιν ὁ θεός, καλῶς ποιεῖς· καὶ τὰ δαιμόνια πιστεύουσιν⁴⁸ καὶ φρίσσουσιν.

20 Θέλεις δὲ γνῶναι,⁴⁹ ὦ ἄνθρωπε κενέ,⁵⁰ ὅτι ἡ πίστις χωρὶς τῶν ἔργων ἀργή ἐστιν; 21 Ἀβραὰμ ὁ πατὴρ ἡμῶν οὐκ⁵¹ ἐξ ἔργων ἐδικαιώθη ἀνενέγκας⁵² Ἰσαὰκ τὸν υἱὸν αὐτοῦ ἐπὶ τὸ θυσιαστήριον; 22 βλέπεις ὅτι ἡ πίστις συνήργει τοῖς ἔργοις⁵³ αὐτοῦ καὶ ἐκ τῶν ἔργων⁵⁴ ἡ πίστις ἐτε-

41. τὰ ἐπιτήδεια τοῦ σώματος: τὰ ἐπιτήδεια is a substantival use of the adjective; τοῦ σώματος is a subjective genitive (Wallace 113–16; *GNTG* §5.38): "what the body needs."
42. τί τὸ ὄφελος: the apodosis following the lengthy protasis (introduced in v. 15) repeats the initial question raised in v. 14.
43. ἡ πίστις is the subject of ἐστιν (near the end of the verse) and the implied subject of ἔχῃ.
44. ἐὰν with the subjunctive (ἔχῃ) introduces the protasis of a third-class condition (see n. 3).
45. καθ᾽ ἑαυτήν likely is indicating isolation or separateness (BDAG 511.B.1.c*; Wallace 350–51*): "by itself."
46. ἐκ τῶν ἔργων μου: the preposition indicates the effective cause (BDAG 297.3.g.β*): "by my works."
47. ὅτι introduces indirect discourse (Wallace 456–58, 661; BDF §396; *GNTG* §5.218.c). It points to the content of what "you" believe.
48. τὰ δαιμόνια πιστεύουσιν: a neuter plural subject will typically take a singular verb (Wallace 399–400; BDF §133; *GNTG* §5.26.a). Wallace suggests that when a New Testament author wants to stress the individuality of each subject in the neuter plural subject, the author uses a plural verb rather than the singular verb normally expected (Wallace 400*). As Adams suggests, this might instead be an instance where the plural subject suggests a plural verb and so *constructio ad sensum* (*James*, 55; on the concept of *constructio ad sensum*, see the discussion in BDF §134).
49. γνῶναι is a complementary infinitive, going with Θέλεις (Wallace 598–99; BDF §392; *GNTG* §5.163).
50. ὦ ἄνθρωπε κενέ: ὦ is used to express emotion (Wallace 56–58*, 68–69*; BDF §146.1.b*): "O empty man."
51. οὐκ introduces a question expecting the answer "yes."
52. ἀνενέγκας is an adverbial participle that might be indicating time; the aorist tense indicates time before that of the main verb (Wallace 623–27; BDF §418; *GNTG* §5.188): "when he offered"; or it might be indicating cause (Wallace 631–32; BDF §418; *GNTG* §5.189): "because he offered."
53. τοῖς ἔργοις is the dative direct object of συνήργει: "was working together with his works" (BDAG 969*).
54. ἐκ τῶν ἔργων: the prepositional phrase indicates the impersonal means by which the verbal action was carried out (Wallace 434–35*): "by means of works."

λειώθη, 23 καὶ ἐπληρώθη ἡ γραφὴ ἡ λέγουσα·⁵⁵ ἐπίστευσεν δὲ Ἀβραὰμ
τῷ θεῷ, καὶ ἐλογίσθη αὐτῷ εἰς δικαιοσύνην⁵⁶ καὶ φίλος θεοῦ ἐκλήθη.
24 ὁρᾶτε ὅτι ἐξ ἔργων δικαιοῦται ἄνθρωπος καὶ οὐκ ἐκ πίστεως μόνον.
25 ὁμοίως δὲ καὶ Ῥαὰβ ἡ πόρνη οὐκ⁵⁷ ἐξ ἔργων ἐδικαιώθη ὑποδεξαμένη
τοὺς ἀγγέλους καὶ ἑτέρᾳ ὁδῷ ἐκβαλοῦσα;⁵⁸ 26 ὥσπερ γὰρ τὸ σῶμα χωρὶς
πνεύματος νεκρόν ἐστιν, οὕτως καὶ ἡ πίστις χωρὶς ἔργων νεκρά ἐστιν.

Vocabulary

ἀδελφή, ῆς, ἡ	sister
ἀναφέρω	to bring up, raise back up, bear, pay, add to, offer up
ἀνέλεος, ον	merciless
ἀργός, ή, όν	idle, lazy; useless
ἀτιμάζω	to dishonor
βασιλικός, ή, όν	royal; royal officer; palace
βλασφημέω	to slander, verbally abuse, blaspheme
γυμνός, ή, όν	naked
δείκνυμι	to show
διακρίνω	to evaluate, consider, doubt
διαλογισμός, οῦ, ὁ	thought, opinion, discussion
δικαιόω	to pronounce righteous, justify
ἐκλέγομαι	to choose, select
ἐλέγχω	to reprove, convict; to refute
ἔλεος, ους, τό	mercy
ἐλευθερία, ας, ἡ	freedom
ἕλκω	to attract, drag

55. ἡ λέγουσα is an attributive participle (Wallace 617–18; BDF §412; *GNTG* §5.181), modifying ἡ γραφὴ: "which says." The quotation is from Gen 15:6 LXX: καὶ ἐπίστευσεν Αβραμ τῷ θεῷ, καὶ ἐλογίσθη αὐτῷ εἰς δικαιοσύνην.
56. ἐλογίσθη αὐτῷ εἰς δικαιοσύνην: with ἐλογίσθη, εἰς plus the accusative can substitute for the predicate nominative (Wallace 47–48*; BDF §145): "it was credited to him as righteousness." BDAG suggests that λογίζομαι in the passive with the dative and εἰς plus the accusative means to credit something to someone as something (BDAG 597.1.a*): "it was credited to him as righteousness." See §3.3 in this volume.
57. οὐκ introduces a question expecting a positive response.
58. ὑποδεξαμένη . . . ἐκβαλοῦσα are adverbial participles that might be indicating time; the aorist tense indicates time before that of the main verb (Wallace 623–27; BDF §418; *GNTG* §5.188): "when she received . . . when she sent"; or that might be indicating cause (Wallace 631–32; BDF §418; *GNTG* §5.189): "because she received . . . because she sent."

ἔνοχος, ον	liable, guilty
ἐπαγγέλλομαι	to promise; to profess
ἐπιβλέπω	to pay special attention to, look on with care
ἐπικαλέω	to call on
ἐπιτήδειος, εία, ον	useful, necessary
ἐργάζομαι	to work
ἐσθής, ῆτος, ἡ	clothing
ἐφήμερος, ον	daily
θερμαίνω	to warm, warm oneself
θυσιαστήριον, ου, τό	altar
Ἰσαάκ, ὁ, indecl.	Isaac
καλῶς, adv.	well
καταδυναστεύω	to oppress
κατακαυχάομαι	to boast against
κενός, ή, όν	empty, foolish, worthless; vacuity
κληρονόμος, ου, ὁ	heir
κρίσις, εως, ἡ	judgment, decision, legal case
κριτήριον, ου, τό	court; judgment seat, tribunal
κριτής, οῦ, ὁ	judge
λαμπρός, ά, όν	splendid; bright; illustrious
λείπω	to leave, lack, forsake
λογίζομαι	to count, think, calculate
μέντοι	but, nevertheless
μοιχεύω	to commit adultery
ὁμοίως, adv.	likewise
ὄφελος, ους, τό	benefit, good
παραβάτης, ου, ὁ	one who disobeys; transgressor
πλησίον	(+ gen.) near; neighbor
πλούσιος, ία, ιον	rich
πόρνη, ης, ἡ	prostitute
προσωπολημπτέω	to show favoritism
προσωπολημψία, ας, ἡ	favoritism
πταίω	to cause to fall; to fall
πτωχός, ή, όν	poor
Ῥαάβ, ἡ, indecl.	Rahab
ῥυπαρός, ά, όν	shabby, impure, dirty
σεαυτοῦ	of yourself

συνεργέω	to work with, assist; to collaborate
τελειόω	to finish, make perfect
τελέω	to fulfill, finish, complete; to perform, carry out
τροφή, ῆς, ἡ	food, provisions, forage
ὑποδέχομαι	to receive
ὑποπόδιον, ου, τό	footstool
φίλος, η, ον	friend, beloved; friendly, agreeable, dear
φονεύω	to murder
φορέω	to wear; to bear
φρίσσω	to tremble, shudder
χορτάζω	to feed, to fill
χρυσοδακτύλιος, ον	with a gold ring
χωρίς	(+ gen.) without (prep.); separately (adv.)
ὦ	O (address), or Oh!; Alas!
ὥσπερ	as, just as

3.7. 1 PETER 4:1–19

Suffering Like Christ

This document presents itself as a letter from the apostle Peter to "resident aliens" (παρεπιδήμοις; 1:1) in the diaspora, identified as the five provinces of Asia Minor. The author sends greetings from "the chosen in Babylon" (5:13). The high level of Greek, in combination with the use of the term Babylon to refer to the city of Rome, suggests to most scholars that the letter is written pseudepigraphically sometime toward the end of the first century CE. The document makes use of an epistolary form similar to what we see in the letters of Paul.

The content of the letter seems to indicate that the recipients were gentiles. The author attempts to comfort persons suffering as a result of their faith. In chapter 4, the author is concerned with the moral lives of the recipients. Their lives must be distinguishable from outsiders; they must show care in how they treat one another; they should not be surprised when they suffer, but they must take care not to behave in ways that could warrant suffering.

1 Χριστοῦ οὖν παθόντος[1] σαρκὶ καὶ ὑμεῖς τὴν αὐτὴν ἔννοιαν[2] ὁπλίσα-σθε, ὅτι[3] ὁ παθὼν[4] σαρκὶ πέπαυται ἁμαρτίας[5] 2 εἰς τὸ μηκέτι ἀνθρώπων

1. Χριστοῦ . . . παθόντος: the participle is a genitive absolute (Wallace 654–55; BDF §423; GNTG §5.197). Here the meaning is likely causal, rather than temporal: "Since/Because Christ suffered."
2. τὴν αὐτὴν ἔννοιαν: "the same insight" or "the same way of thinking" (BDAG 337*).
3. ὅτι might be epexegetical, indicating the content of ἔννοια: "that"; it more likely is causal, indicating the reason for ὁπλίσασθε: "because" (see the discussion in Mark Dubis, *1 Peter: A Handbook on the Greek Text*, BHGNT [Waco, TX: Baylor University Press, 2010], 130).
4. ὁ παθὼν is a substantival participle (Wallace 619–21; BDF §413; GNTG §5.182).
5. ἁμαρτίας is the genitive complement of πέπαυται (BDAG 790.2*). Wallace identifies it as a genitive of separation (107–9*).

ἐπιθυμίαις ἀλλὰ θελήματι θεοῦ τὸν ἐπίλοιπον ἐν σαρκὶ βιῶσαι χρόνον.⁶ 3 ἀρκετὸς γὰρ ὁ παρεληλυθὼς χρόνος⁷ τὸ βούλημα⁸ τῶν ἐθνῶν κατειργάσθαι⁹ πεπορευμένους¹⁰ ἐν ἀσελγείαις, ἐπιθυμίαις, οἰνοφλυγίαις, κώμοις, πότοις καὶ ἀθεμίτοις εἰδωλολατρίαις. 4 ἐν ᾧ¹¹ ξενίζονται μὴ συντρεχόντων ὑμῶν¹² εἰς τὴν αὐτὴν τῆς ἀσωτίας ἀνάχυσιν¹³ βλασφημοῦντες,¹⁴

6. εἰς τὸ . . . χρόνον: this verse contains several challenges. εἰς plus the articular infinitive (τὸ . . . βιῶσαι) might indicate either the purpose or the result of "arming oneself" from 1b (Wallace 610; BDF §402.2; *GNTG* §§174–75); in this case, the subject of the infinitive would be "you" carried forward from ὁπλίσασθε. Alternatively, it might offer an explanation of what it means to have "finished with sin"; in this case, the subject of the infinitive would be an implied αὐτόν (with ὁ παθὼν as the antecedent). ἐπιθυμίαις and θελήματι might be datives of interest or advantage (Wallace 142–44; BDF §188; *GNTG* §5.60; cf. NIV and ESV): "for human desires . . . for God's will"; they might be datives of means (Wallace 162–63; BDF §195; *GNTG* §5.67; cf. NRSV): "by human desires . . . by God's will"; they are probably best understood as datives of rule (Wallace 157–58; Dubis, *1 Peter*, 131): "according to/in conformity with human desires . . . according to/in conformity with God's will." τὸν ἐπίλοιπον . . . χρόνον is an accusative of time (Wallace 201–2; BDF §161.2; *GNTG* §5.82), modifying βιῶσαι: "to [no longer] live the time remaining in the flesh" (see the discussion in Dubis, *1 Peter*, 132).

7. ἀρκετὸς . . . ὁ παρεληλυθὼς χρόνος: ὁ . . . χρόνος is the nominative subject of an implied ἐστίν (Wallace 39–40; BDF §§127–28). παρεληλυθὼς is an attributive participle (Wallace 617–18; BDF §412; *GNTG* §5.181), modifying χρόνος. ἀρκετὸς is a predicate nominative: "the time that has passed was sufficient."

8. τὸ βούλημα is the accusative object of κατειργάσθαι.

9. κατειργάσθαι is likely an epexegetical infinitive (Wallace 607; BDF §394; *GNTG* §5.167), explaining ἀρκετὸς: "to have done what the gentiles like to do" (BDAG 531.1*). The likely subject of the infinitive is an implied ὑμᾶς.

10. πεπορευμένους: Dubis identifies the participle as indicating cause (*1 Peter*, 134; cf. Wallace 631–32; BDF §418.1; *GNTG* §5.192): "because you engaged in"; it might be indicating means (Wallace 628–30; BDF §418; *GNTG* §5.181), explaining τὸ βούλημα τῶν ἐθνῶν κατειργάσθαι: "[by] living in" (BDAG 853.2*).

11. ἐν ᾧ marks the circumstance or condition under which something takes place (BDAG 329.7*): "in view of which."

12. μὴ συντρεχόντων ὑμῶν is a genitive absolute (Wallace 654–55; BDF §423; *GNTG* §197). The meaning might be temporal: "when you do not run together [with them]"; or causal: "because you do not run together [with them]."

13. τὴν αὐτὴν ἀσωτίας ἀνάχυσιν: "the same flood of debauchery."

14. βλασφημοῦντες is likely an adverbial participle indicating result (Wallace 637–39; *GNTG* §5.195; Dubis, *1 Peter*, 135–36), modifying ξενίζονται: "as a result, they slander [you]" (in context, the target is more likely the audience of the letter rather than God).

5 οἳ¹⁵ ἀποδώσουσιν λόγον¹⁶ τῷ ἑτοίμως ἔχοντι¹⁷ κρῖναι¹⁸ ζῶντας¹⁹ καὶ νεκρούς. 6 εἰς τοῦτο²⁰ γὰρ καὶ νεκροῖς εὐηγγελίσθη, ἵνα²¹ κριθῶσιν μὲν κατὰ ἀνθρώπους σαρκί,²² ζῶσιν δὲ κατὰ θεὸν²³ πνεύματι.²⁴

7 Πάντων δὲ τὸ τέλος ἤγγικεν. σωφρονήσατε οὖν καὶ νήψατε εἰς προσευχὰς²⁵ 8 πρὸ πάντων²⁶ τὴν εἰς ἑαυτοὺς ἀγάπην ἐκτενῆ ἔχοντες,²⁷ ὅτι²⁸ ἀγάπη καλύπτει πλῆθος ἁμαρτιῶν, 9 φιλόξενοι²⁹ εἰς ἀλλήλους ἄνευ

15. οἳ is the subject of ἀποδώσουσιν.

16. ἀποδώσουσιν λόγον: "To give an account to" (BDAG 109.2.c*).

17. τῷ ἑτοίμως ἔχοντι: ἔχοντι is a substantival participle (Wallace 619–21; BDF §413; *GNTG* §5.182). Here, ἔχοντι with ἑτοίμως has the meaning "to be ready" (BDAG 401*; 442.10.b*): "the one ready."

18. κρῖναι is either a complementary infinitive going with ἑτοίμως (Wallace 598–99; BDF §393.4*; *GNTG* §5.163); or epexegetical, explaining ἑτοίμως (Wallace 607; BDF §394; *GNTG* §5.167; Dubis, *1 Peter*, 1360): "ready to judge."

19. ζῶντας is a substantival participle (Wallace 619–21; BDF §413; *GNTG* §5.182).

20. εἰς τοῦτο: with reference to what follows: "for this reason" (BDAG 741.1.b.β).

21. ἵνα with the subjunctive (κριθῶσιν . . . ζῶσιν) normally introduces a purpose clause: "so that." Here, after the demonstrative (τοῦτο), it is perhaps explanatory: "for this purpose, namely, that" (BDAG 476.1.e*).

22. σαρκί is a dative of respect/reference (Wallace 144–46*; BDF §197; *GNTG* §5.68).

23. μὲν κατὰ ἀνθρώπους . . . δὲ κατὰ θεὸν: μὲν should probably be read concessively, here (BDAG 629.1.a): "although." κατὰ marks the norm or standard by which something is judged: "according to human standards . . . according to God's standard" (BDAG 512.5).

24. πνεύματι is likely a dative of agency but might be spacial (cf. ESV, NRSV; see the note in Dubis, *1 Peter*, 139).

25. εἰς προσευχὰς: εἰς marks the goal of the self-control and discipline (BDAG 290.4): "for the sake of [your] prayers."

26. πρὸ πάντων: πρὸ here marks precedence in importance (BDAG 864.3; BDF §213*): "above all."

27. τὴν εἰς ἑαυτοὺς ἀγάπην ἐκτενῆ ἔχοντες: ἐκτενῆ is in the predicate position. Because ἔχοντες is a verb that can take two accusatives, we should probably read ἐκτενῆ as the accusative complement in a double accusative object-complement construction with τὴν . . . ἀγάπην as the object (Wallace 181–89 [183 n. 24]; BDF §157; *GNTG* §5.77); translations vary on whether to gloss this word as "constant" (NRSV, BDAG 310*), or "earnest" (ESV, NET, NIV). ἔχοντες is an imperatival participle (Wallace 650–51*; BDF §468.2*; *GNTG* §201.b): "keep your love for one another constant."

28. The quotation is closer to the Hebrew text of Prov 10:12 than to the LXX text: πάντας δὲ τοὺς μὴ φιλονεικοῦντας καλύπτει φιλία.

29. φιλόξενοι is a predicate adjective in a clause with an implied imperatival form of εἰμί (Wallace 39–40; BDF §§127–28): "be hospitable."

γογγυσμοῦ, 10 ἕκαστος καθὼς ἔλαβεν χάρισμα³⁰ εἰς³¹ ἑαυτοὺς αὐτὸ διακονοῦντες ὡς καλοὶ οἰκονόμοι ποικίλης χάριτος θεοῦ. 11 εἴ³² τις λαλεῖ,
ὡς λόγια θεοῦ· εἴ τις διακονεῖ, ὡς ἐξ ἰσχύος³³ ἧς χορηγεῖ ὁ θεός,³⁴ ἵνα ἐν
πᾶσιν δοξάζηται ὁ θεὸς διὰ Ἰησοῦ Χριστοῦ ᾧ³⁵ ἐστιν ἡ δόξα καὶ τὸ κράτος
εἰς τοὺς αἰῶνας τῶν αἰώνων,³⁶ ἀμήν.

12 Ἀγαπητοί, μὴ ξενίζεσθε τῇ ἐν ὑμῖν πυρώσει³⁷ πρὸς πειρασμὸν³⁸
ὑμῖν γινομένῃ³⁹ ὡς ξένου ὑμῖν συμβαίνοντος,⁴⁰ 13 ἀλλὰ καθὸ κοινωνεῖτε
τοῖς τοῦ Χριστοῦ παθήμασιν, χαίρετε, ἵνα καὶ ἐν τῇ ἀποκαλύψει τῆς δόξης

---

30. ἕκαστος καθὼς ἔλαβεν χάρισμα: καθὼς might indicate the extent or degree to which
(BDAG 493.2*): "to the degree that one has received a gift"; in this context, it might be
better to read it as indicating cause (BDF §453.2; Dubis, *1 Peter*, 143): "because each one
has received a gift."

31. εἰς ἑαυτοὺς αὐτὸ διακονοῦντες: διακονοῦντες is an imperatival participle (Wallace
650–51; BDF §468.2; *GNTG* §201.b): "use it in service of one another."

32. εἴ τις λαλεῖ, ὡς λόγια θεοῦ: the apodosis in this first-class condition is elliptical (see
the discussion in BDF §§479–83). The reader must supply the verb before the ὡς clause;
here the context suggests the third-person singular imperative of λαλέω. In addition, ὡς
is used in elliptical constructions from which a participle has dropped (BDF §425.4*):
"[let him speak] as [someone speaking] the oracles."

33. εἴ τις διακονεῖ, ὡς ἐξ ἰσχύος: the apodosis in this first-class condition is elliptical (see
the discussion in BDF §§479–83). The reader must supply the verb before the ὡς clause;
here the context suggests the third-person singular imperative of διακονέω. In addition,
ὡς is used in elliptical constructions from which a participle has dropped (BDF §425.4*):
"[let him serve as someone serving] with strength."

34. ἧς χορηγεῖ ὁ θεός: ἧς is in the genitive case because of attraction to its antecedent
(ἰσχύος). One expects it to be in the accusative case because it acts as the direct object
of χορηγεῖ. The attraction of the accusative case to the genitive is common (Wallace
338–39; BDF §294).

35. ᾧ is a dative of possession (Wallace 149–50; BDF §189; *GNTG* §5.61).

36. εἰς τοὺς αἰῶνας τῶν αἰώνων: "forevermore" (BDAG 32.1.b*).

37. τῇ . . . πυρώσει is a dative of cause (Wallace 167–68*; BDF §196*; *GNTG* §5.71): "because
of the fiery ordeal."

38. πρὸς πειρασμὸν: πρὸς indicates the goal of the "fiery ordeal" (BDAG 793.1*; 874.3.c.β*):
"to test you."

39. γινομένῃ is an attributive participle (Wallace 617–18; BDF §412; *GNTG* §5.181), modifying τῇ . . . πυρώσει: "that is happening."

40. ὡς ξένου ὑμῖν συμβαίνοντος: ὡς with the participle is indicating comparison (BDF
425.3); in this case with a genitive absolute (Wallace 654–55; BDF §423; *GNTG* §5.197):
"as if something strange was happening to you" (BDAG 684.1.a.β*).

αὐτοῦ χαρῆτε ἀγαλλιώμενοι.⁴¹ 14 εἰ ὀνειδίζεσθε ἐν ὀνόματι Χριστοῦ,⁴² μακάριοι,⁴³ ὅτι τὸ τῆς δόξης καὶ τὸ τοῦ θεοῦ πνεῦμα⁴⁴ ἐφ᾽ ὑμᾶς ἀναπαύεται.⁴⁵ 15 μὴ γάρ τις ὑμῶν πασχέτω ὡς φονεὺς ἢ κλέπτης ἢ κακοποιὸς ἢ ὡς ἀλλοτριεπίσκοπος· 16 εἰ δὲ ὡς χριστιανός,⁴⁶ μὴ αἰσχυνέσθω, δοξαζέτω δὲ τὸν θεὸν ἐν τῷ μέρει τούτῳ.⁴⁷ 17 ὅτι ὁ καιρὸς⁴⁸ τοῦ ἄρξασθαι⁴⁹ τὸ κρίμα⁵⁰ ἀπὸ τοῦ οἴκου τοῦ θεοῦ·⁵¹ εἰ δὲ πρῶτον ἀφ᾽ ἡμῶν,⁵² τί τὸ τέλος⁵³ τῶν ἀπειθούντων⁵⁴ τῷ τοῦ θεοῦ εὐαγγελίῳ;⁵⁵ 18 καὶ εἰ ὁ δίκαιος

41. ἀγαλλιώμενοι is either an adverbial participle indicating manner (Wallace 627–28; BDF §418.5; *GNTG* §5.193), modifying χαρῆτε: "rejoice, shouting for joy"; or an attendant circumstance participle referring to an action that is parallel to the main verb (Wallace 640–45; *GNTG* §5.198): "rejoice and shout for joy."

42. ἐν ὀνόματι Χριστοῦ: ἐν likely identifies the reason for being reviled (BDAG 329.9): "because of the name of Christ."

43. μακάριοι is the predicate adjective of an implied ἐστε (Wallace 39–40; BDF §§127–28).

44. τὸ . . . τὸ τοῦ θεοῦ πνεῦμα: the repetition of the article before the substantive is unusual (BDF §269.6*): "the spirit of glory and of God."

45. τὸ τοῦ θεοῦ πνεῦμα . . . ἀναπαύεται appears to be a quotation of Isa 11:2: καὶ ἀναπαύσεται ἐπ᾽ αὐτὸν πνεῦμα τοῦ θεοῦ.

46. εἰ δὲ ὡς χριστιανός: the protasis in this first-class condition is elliptical (see the discussion in BDF §§479–83). The reader must supply the verb before the ὡς clause; here the context suggests τις πάσχει: "if [someone suffers] as a Christian."

47. ἐν τῷ μέρει τούτῳ: ἐν identifies the reason for being reviled (BDAG 329.9): "because of." τῷ μέρει is the reading in the NA28. The editors of the Editio Critica Maior presumably preferred τῷ μέρει because it is the more difficult reading: "because of this matter." The stronger manuscript evidence supports τῷ ὀνόματι (𝔓⁷², ℵ, A, B): "because of this name."

48. ὁ καιρὸς is the nominative subject of an implied verb; the reader must supply some form of εἰμί or, perhaps, γίνομαι (Wallace 39–40; BDF §128.4*): "It is time for" or "The time has come for."

49. τοῦ ἄρξασθαι: the articular infinitive in the genitive is either indicating purpose (Wallace 590–92; BDF §400; *GNTG* §5.161); or is epexegetical (Wallace 610), explaining ὁ καιρὸς.

50. τὸ κρίμα is the accusative subject of ἄρξασθαι.

51. ἀπὸ τοῦ οἴκου τοῦ θεοῦ: ἀπὸ marks the starting point for the beginning of judgment (BDAG 140.2.c): "with the household of God."

52. εἰ δὲ πρῶτον ἀφ᾽ ἡμῶν: the protasis in this first-class condition is elliptical (see the discussion in BDF §§479–83). The reader must supply the verb; the context suggests some form of ἄρχω introduced at the beginning of the sentence: "if it begins, first, with us."

53. τί τὸ τέλος: τὸ τέλος is the nominative subject of an implied ἐστίν (Wallace 39–40; BDF §§127–28): "what will the end be?"

54. τῶν ἀπειθούντων is a substantival participle (Wallace 619–21; BDF §413; *GNTG* §5.182).

55. τῷ τοῦ θεοῦ εὐαγγελίῳ: the dative complement of τῶν ἀπειθούντων (BDAG 99*).

μόλις σῴζεται,⁵⁶ ὁ ἀσεβὴς καὶ ἁμαρτωλὸς ποῦ φανεῖται; 19 ὥστε⁵⁷ καὶ οἱ πάσχοντες⁵⁸ κατὰ τὸ θέλημα τοῦ θεοῦ πιστῷ κτίστῃ⁵⁹ παρατιθέσθωσαν⁶⁰ τὰς ψυχὰς αὐτῶν ἐν ἀγαθοποιΐᾳ.⁶¹

Vocabulary

ἀγαθοποιΐα, ας, ἡ	doing good
ἀγαλλιάω	to exult, rejoice
ἀθέμιτος, ον	unlawful thing
αἰσχύνω	to be ashamed
ἀλλοτριεπίσκοπος, ου, ὁ	busybody
ἁμαρτωλός, ον	sinner, sinful
ἀναπαύω	to stop, rest, refresh; to die
ἀνάχυσις, εως, ἡ	pouring out; wide stream; excess
ἄνευ	(+ gen.) without
ἀπειθέω	to disbelieve, disobey
ἀποδίδωμι	to give back, pay
ἀποκάλυψις, εως, ἡ	revelation
ἀρκετός, ή, όν	sufficient
ἀσεβής, ές	impious, ungodly
ἀσέλγεια, ας, ἡ	licentiousness
ἀσωτία, ας, ἡ	reckless living; debauchery
βιόω	to live
βλασφημέω	to verbally abuse, blaspheme
βούλημα, ατος, τό	intention, purpose, will
γογγυσμός, οῦ, ὁ	murmuring, grumbling
διακονέω	to serve, wait on

56. The author appears to be quoting Prov 11:31 (LXX): εἰ ὁ μὲν δίκαιος μόλις σῴζεται / ὁ ἀσεβὴς καὶ ἁμαρτωλὸς ποῦ φανεῖται;
57. ὥστε here introduces an independent clause (BDAG 1107.1.a*): "so," "therefore."
58. οἱ πάσχοντες is a substantival participle (Wallace 619–21; BDF §413; *GNTG* §5.182).
59. πιστῷ κτίστῃ: the article is sometimes omitted in formulas such as this (BDF §257.3*): "to a faithful creator."
60. παρατιθέσθωσαν: pres.-impv.-mid.-3-pl. < παρατίθημι. In the middle voice with an accusative object and a dative indirect object (BDAG 772.3.b*): to entrust something to someone: "Let those who suffer according to the will of God entrust their lives to a faithful creator."
61. ἐν ἀγαθοποιΐᾳ: ἐν likely indicates the circumstance or condition (BDAG 329.10): "while doing good"; it could indicate means (BDAG 329.8): "by doing good."

ἐγγίζω	to bring near, come near
εἰδωλολατρία, ας, ἡ	image worship, idolatry
ἐκτενής, ές	constant, earnest
ἔννοια, ας, ἡ	thought, knowledge, insight, conception
ἐπιθυμία, ας, ἡ	desire, lust
ἐπίλοιπος, ον	left, remaining
ἑτοίμως, adv.	readily
ἰσχύς, ύος, ἡ	strength, power, might
καθό, adv.	insofar as, to the degree that; according to, as
κακοποιός, όν	mischievous; evil-doing
καλύπτω	to cover
κατεργάζομαι	to do [something]; to work, prepare, make, oppress, subdue
κλέπτης, ου, ὁ	thief
κοινωνέω	to share, take part
κράτος, ους, τό	power, might
κρίμα, ατος, τό	judgment, decree, decision
κτίστης, ου, ὁ	creator, founder
κῶμος, ου, ὁ	carousing, revelry
λόγιον, ου, τό	saying, oracle, revelation
μέρος, ους, τό	part
μηκέτι, adv.	no longer, no more
μόλις, adv.	scarcely, hardly
νήφω	to be sober, self-controlled
ξενίζω	to entertain as a guest; surprise (BDF §126.2*)
ξένος, η, ον	stranger, strange; guest, host
οἰκονόμος, ου, ὁ	manager, steward
οἰνοφλυγία, ας, ἡ	drunkenness
ὀνειδίζω	to reproach
ὁπλίζω	to equip; in the middle: to arm oneself with
πάθημα, ατος, τό	suffering, ailment
παρατίθημι	to set before; commend
παρέρχομαι	to pass by, pass away
πάσχω	to experience; to suffer, endure

παύω	to cease, stop
πειρασμός	temptation, test
πλῆθος, ους, τό	multitude
ποικίλος, η, ον	many-colored; diverse, various kinds
πότος, ου, ὁ	drinking party
ποῦ	where?
πρό	(+ gen.) before, above
προσευχή, ῆς, ἡ	prayer
πύρωσις, εως, ἡ	burning
συμβαίνω	to happen, befall
συντρέχω	to run together; to concur
σωφρονέω	to be in a right mind
τέλος, ους, τό	end, goal
φαίνω	to appear, shine; to cause to shine
φιλόξενος, ον	hospitable
φονεύς, έως, ὁ	murderer
χάρισμα, ατος, τό	gift
χορηγέω	to supply
χριστιανός, οῦ, ὁ	Christian

Bibliography

Adam, A. K. M. *James: A Handbook on the Greek Text*. BHGNT. Waco, TX: Baylor University Press, 2013.

The Apostolic Fathers, Volume 1: I Clement; II Clement; Ignatius; Polycarp; Didache. Edited and translated by Bart D. Ehrman. Loeb Classical Library. Cambridge: Harvard University Press, 2003.

Blenkinsopp, Joseph. *Isaiah 40–55: A New Translation with Introduction and Commentary*. Anchor Bible 19A. New York: Doubleday, 2002.

Brayford, Susan A. *Genesis*. Septuagint Commentary Series. Leiden: Brill, 2007.

Brookins, Timothy A., and Bruce W. Longenecker. *1 Corinthians 10–16: A Handbook on the Greek Text*. BHGNT. Waco, TX: Baylor University Press, 2016.

Carlson, Stephen C. "The Accommodations of Joseph and Mary in Bethlehem: Κατάλυμα in Luke 2.7." *New Testament Studies* 56 (2010): 326–42. DOI:10.1017/S0028688509990282.

Culy, Martin M., Mikeal C. Parsons, and Joshua J. Stigall. *Luke: A Handbook on the Greek Text*. BHGNT. Waco, TX: Baylor University Press, 2010.

Decker, Rodney J. *Mark 1–8: A Handbook on the Greek Text*. BHGNT. Waco, TX: Baylor University Press, 2014.

———. *Mark 9–16: A Handbook on the Greek Text*. BHGNT. Waco, TX: Baylor University Press, 2014.

Dubis, Mark. *1 Peter: A Handbook on the Greek Text*. BHGNT. Waco, TX: Baylor University Press, 2010.

Hays, Richard B. "'Have We Found Abraham to Be Our Forefather according to the Flesh?': A Reconsideration of Rom 4:1." *Novum Testamentum* 27 (1985): 76–98. DOI:10.2307/1560852.

Holmes, Michael, ed. and trans. *The Apostolic Fathers: Greek Texts and English Translations*. 3rd ed. Grand Rapids: Baker Academic, 2007.

Jobes, Karen H., and Moisés Silva. *Invitation to the Septuagint*. Grand Rapids: Baker Academic, 2000.

Matthewson, David L. *Revelation: A Handbook on the Greek Text*. BHGNT. Waco, TX: Baylor University Press, 2016.

Metzger, Bruce M. *A Textual Commentary on the Greek New Testament*. 2nd ed. Stuttgart: Deutsche Bibelgesellschaft, 1994.

Niederwimmer, Kurt. *The Didache: A Commentary*. Hermeneia. Minneapolis: Fortress, 1998.

Novakovic, Lidija. *Philippians: A Handbook on the Greek Text*. BHGNT. Waco, TX: Baylor University Press, 2020.

Novum Testamentum Graece. Edited by Barbara Aland, Kurt Aland, Johannes Karavido-poulos, Carlo M. Martini, and Bruce Metzger. Based on the work of Eberhard and Erwin Nestle. 28th ed. Stuttgart: Deutsche Bibelgesellschaft, 2012.

Olmstead, Wesley G. *Matthew 1–14: A Handbook on the Greek Text*. BHGNT. Waco, TX: Baylor University Press, 2019.

Ottley, Richard R. *The Book of Isaiah according to the Septuagint (Codex Alexandrinus)*. London: Cambridge University Press, 1904–1906.

Parsons, Mikeal C., and Martin M. Culy. *Acts: A Handbook on the Greek Text*. BHGNT. Waco, TX: Baylor University Press, 2003.

Plato. *Euthyphro, Apology, Crito, Phaedo*. Edited and translated by Chris Emlyn-Jones and William Preddy. Loeb Classical Library. Cambridge: Harvard University Press, 2017.

Septuaginta: Id est Vetus Testamentum Graece iuxta LXX interpretes. Edited by Alfred Rahlfs. Revised by Robert Hanhart. Stuttgart: Deutsche Bibelgesellschaft, 2006.

Sumney, Jerry. *Philippians: A Greek Student's Intermediate Reader*. Peabody, MA: Hendrickson, 2007.

Smyth, Herbert Weir. *Greek Grammar*. Revised by Gordon M. Messing. Cambridge: Harvard University Press, 1956.

Wevers, John William. *Notes on the Greek Text of Deuteronomy*. SCS 39. Atlanta: Scholars Press, 1995.

———. *Notes on the Greek Text of Genesis*. SCS 35. Atlanta: Scholars Press, 1993.

White, L. Michael, and G. Anthony Keddie. *Jewish Fictional Letters from Hellenistic Egypt: The Epistle of Aristeas and Related Literature*. WGRW 37. Atlanta: SBL Press, 2018.

Index of Syntactical Constructions

Included in this index are forms and constructions likely to be less familiar to a person with only one year of Greek. Not every form or construction mentioned in the notes is included in this index.

Index of Scripture
and Other Ancient Sources

This index includes the references to ancient literature mentioned in the introductions to the chapters and in the notes. It also includes references to the sections of literature included in this reader.